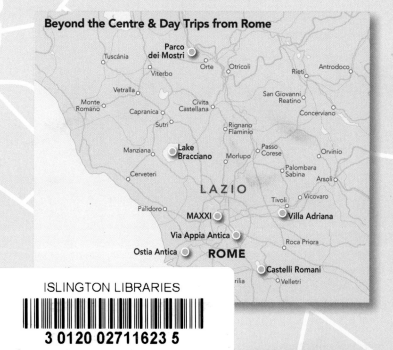

Beyond the Centre & Day Trips from Rome

Tuscánia
Parco
dei Mostri
Orte
Otricoli
Rieti
Antrodoco
Viterbo
Vetralla
San Giovanni
Reatino
Monte
Romano
Capranica
Civita
Castellana
Concerviano
Sutri
Rignano
Flaminio
Manziana
Lake
Bracciano
Morlupo
Passo
Corese
Orvinio
Cerveteri
Palombara
Sabina
Arsoli
LAZIO
Vicovaro
Palidoro
Tivoli
Villa Adriana
MAXXI
Via Appia Antica
Roca Priora
Ostia Antica
ROME
Castelli Romani
rilia
Velletri

EYEWITNESS TRAVEL
FAMILY GUIDE
ROME

EYEWITNESS TRAVEL

FAMILY GUIDE

ROME

DK

Penguin Random House

Contents

MANAGING EDITOR
MadhuMadhavi Singh

SENIOR EDITORIAL MANAGER
Savitha Kumar

SENIOR DESIGN MANAGER
Priyanka Thakur

PROJECT EDITORS Parvati M.
Krishnan, Karen Faye D'Souza

EDITOR Asad Ali

PROJECT DESIGNER
Stuti Tiwari Bhatia

DESIGNER Neha Dhingra

PICTURE RESEARCH MANAGER
Taiyaba Khatoon

PICTURE RESEARCH Lokesh Bisht,
Nikhil Verma

SENIOR DTP DESIGNER
Azeem Siddiqui

DTP DESIGNER Rakesh Pal

SENIOR CARTOGRAPHIC MANAGER
Uma Bhattacharya

SENIOR CARTOGRAPHER
Jasneet Arora

PHOTOGRAPHY
Anna Mockford and Nick Bonetti

CARTOONS Tom Morgan-Jones

OTHER ILLUSTRATORS Arun Pottirayil,
Studio Illibill, Kevin Jones
Associates, Martin Woodward,
Robbie Polley

DESIGN CONCEPT Keith Hagan at
www.greenwich-design.co.uk

Printed and bound in China

First published in Great Britain in 2013 by
Dorling Kindersley Limited, 80 Strand,
London WC2R 0RL. A Penguin Random
House Company

Reprinted with revisions 2015, 2017

16 17 18 19 10 9 8 7 6 5 4 3 2 1

Copyright 2013, 2017 © Dorling
Kindersley Limited, London

ISBN 978-0-2412-5697-8

*View of Rome from the terrace of
Il Vittoriano*

Visitors sitting in Piazza del Campidoglio, Capitoline Hill

How to Use this Guide

This guide is designed to help families get the most from a visit to Rome, providing expert recommendations for sightseeing with children along with detailed practical information. The opening section contains an introduction to Rome and its highlights, as well as all the essentials required to plan a family holiday (including how to get there, how to get around, health, insurance, money, restaurants, accommodation, shopping and communications), a guide to family-friendly festivals through the year and a brief historical overview.

The main sightseeing section is divided into areas. A "best of" feature is followed by the key sights and other attractions in the area, and options for where to eat, drink and play, and have a good time. At the back of the book are detailed maps of Rome, and a section listing essential words and phrases for family travel.

INTRODUCING THE AREA

Each area chapter is opened by a double-page spread setting it in context, with a short introduction, locator map and selection of highlights.

Locator map locates the area.

Brief highlights give a flavour of what to see in the area.

THE BEST OF...

A planner to show at a glance the best things for families to see and do in each area, with themed suggestions ranging from history, art and culture to gardens and games.

Sights have a page reference the first time they are mentioned here.

WHERE TO STAY

Our expert authors have compiled a wide range of recommendations for places to stay for families, from hotels and B&Bs that welcome children to self-catering apartments.

Easy-to-use symbols show the key family-friendly features of places to stay.

Price Guide box gives details of the price categories for a family of four.

SIGHTSEEING IN ROME

Each area features a number of "hub" sights (see below) that provide pragmatic and enjoyable plans for a morning, afternoon or day's visit. These give adults and children a real insight into the destination, focusing on the key sights and what makes them interesting to kids. The sights are balanced by places to let off steam, "take cover" options for rainy days, suggestions for where to eat, drink and shop with kids, ideas for where to go next and all the practicalities, including transport.

Introductory text focuses on the practical aspects of the area, from the best time of day to visit to how to get around it using public transport.

The hub map locates the sights featured in the chapter, as well as restaurants, shops, places to stay, transport, and the nearest playgrounds, supermarkets and pharmacies.

The Lowdown gives all the practical information you need to visit the area. The key to the symbols is on the back jacket flap.

The hub sights are the top places to visit in each area, and use lively and informative text to engage and entertain both adults and children.

Key Features uses artworks to show the most interesting features of each sight, highlighting elements likely to appeal to children.

Kids' Corner appears on all sightseeing pages (see below).

Find out more gives suggestions for downloads, games, apps or films to enthuse children about a place and help them to learn more about it.

Eat and drink lists recommendations for family-friendly places to eat and drink, from where to buy picnic supplies and snacks to proper meals and gourmet dining.

The Lowdown provides comprehensive practical information, including transport, opening times, costs, activities, suitable age range and how long to allow for a visit.

Letting off steam suggests a place to take children to run about following a cultural visit.

Next stop... suggests other places to visit, either near the hub sight, thematically linked to the sight or a complete change of pace for the rest of the day.

Further sights around each hub, selected to appeal to both adults and children, are featured on the following pages.

Kids' Corners are designed to involve children with the sight, with things to look out for, games to play, cartoons and fun facts. Answers to quizzes are given at the bottom of the panel.

Places of interest are described with an emphasis on the aspects most likely to attract children, and incorporating quirky stories and unusual facts. Each one includes a suggestion for letting off steam or taking cover.

The Lowdown provides the usual comprehensive practical and transport information for each sight.

Trevi Fountain, the largest Baroque fountain in
Rome, in Piazza di Trevi

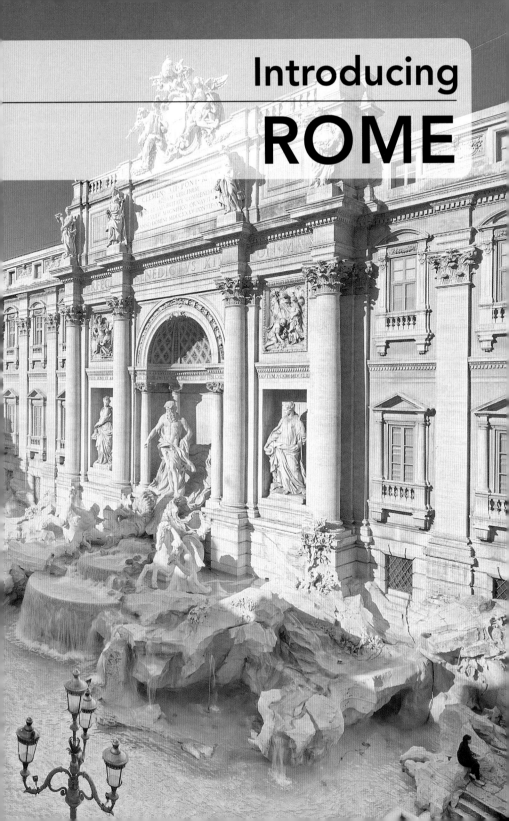

Introducing
ROME

The Best of Rome

Rome is a dynamic city that brings history to life like no other. Ancient Roman temples, Egyptian obelisks, Renaissance palaces, Baroque churches and world-famous works by Michelangelo, Raphael, Caravaggio and Bernini all jostle for space, while 2,800 years of ancient and urban myths, legends and anecdotes embroider every nook and cranny of the place with a colourful tapestry of politics and pleasure, entertainment and art.

Ancient Rome

Re-create a day in the life of an ancient Roman by starting off with a tour of the digitally re-created Roman *domus* (house) below **Palazzo Valentini** *(see p88)*, then go fantasy shopping at **Trajan's Markets** *(see pp86–7)* and make-believe bathing at the **Baths of Caracalla** *(see p230)*. Imagine watching a gladiator fight at the **Colosseum** *(see pp70–71)*, experience the splendour in which the Roman emperors lived by exploring the ruins of their palaces on the **Palatine Hill** *(see pp74–5)*, then admire the frescoes and mosaics from their luxurious homes in the **Palazzo Massimo** *(see pp98–9)*.

Explore the temples and basilicas of the **Roman Forum** *(see pp76–9)*, and see the Temple of Vesta, where girls had to keep a sacred flame alight on pain of death. Experience the virtual reality of a Roman villa at the **Baths of Diocletian** *(see p99)* or delve into the strange world of Roman funerary practices on the **Via Appia Antica** *(see pp228–9)* and at the Pyramid of Caius Cestius in **Testaccio** *(see p108)*. Find out about Roman drains and toilets at **Crypta Balbi** *(see p85)*. Make a couple of day trips: to **Ostia Antica** *(see pp236–7)* to explore the remains of a provincial town, and to Tivoli to see the ruins of **Villa Adriana** *(see pp238–9)*, the refined country retreat of Emperor Hadrian.

Rome in a weekend

To get the most out of a family weekend in Rome, stay at a hotel in the *centro storico*, so that you can see everything on foot. The areas around **Piazza Navona** *(see pp116–17)*, the **Pantheon** *(see pp122–3)*, **Campo de' Fiori** *(see pp130–31)*, the **Jewish Ghetto** *(see pp134–5)* and **Trastevere** *(see pp184–5)* are ideal bases. The digitally re-constructed Roman houses below **Palazzo Valentini**, a short walk from the main sights of the ancient centre, serve as a good starting point for many children. On a brief visit it might be better to see the **Colosseum** from the outside

Below left Actors dressed as gladiators at the Colosseum
Below Bernini's Fontana dei Quattro Fiumi, Piazza Navona

Above *The Colosseum, illuminated at night*
Right *At a Christmas fair in Piazza Navona*

only, or to book a child-friendly tour in advance. If there is no time to visit the **Roman Forum**, take a lift to the top of **Il Vittoriano** *(see p84)*, letting children see what buildings they can identify. If there is time, there are four frescoes of a garden, on the top floor of the **Palazzo Massimo**, almost guaranteed to impress kids. **Piazza Navona** with its Bernini fountains is the most extravagant of Rome's Baroque piazzas. Nearby, take in the ingenious Baroque church of **Sant'Ivo alla Sapienza** *(see p118)*, and paintings by Caravaggio in the churches of **San Luigi dei Francesi** *(see p118)* and **Sant'Agostino** *(see p119)*, before heading to the **Pantheon**. The morning market at **Campo de' Fiori** is a good place to buy lunch and watch Roman street life at its liveliest. Cross the Tiber, either at Ponte Sisto to see Trastevere, or at Ponte Sant'Angelo to see **Castel Sant'Angelo** *(see pp214–15)*. A weekend does not really leave time to see the **Vatican Museums** *(see pp206–13)* unless you book tickets in advance to see the **Sistine Chapel** *(see pp208–10)* first thing in the morning, but a walk around **St Peter's** *(see pp204–5)*, followed by a climb to the cupola atop the dome, will give great views over the whole of Rome, as well as into **Vatican City** *(see pp202–3)*.

Rome season by season

Spring and autumn are without doubt the best seasons to visit Rome. For the most part you can expect clear skies and sunshine, without it being too hot. Holy Week is a special, although extremely busy time to visit, culminating in the Pope's address on Easter Sunday. Summer can be very hot, but more and more Romans tend to stay in town during August rather than making the traditional escape to the seaside. There is a summer festival, Estate Romana, with a series of open-air concerts and films at **Villa Adriana** and other locations around the city. In the last two weeks of July, **Trastevere** holds the Festa de' Noantri, with processions of a statue of the Madonna, street parties with local food and wine, and fireworks. Keep sightseeing for early and late in the day in Tivoli. August is really only practical if you have a comfortable apartment or a spacious hotel room where children will have plenty of space to play. Air conditioning is not standard in Rome, but thick-walled old buildings do stay relatively cool.

From around mid-December until Epiphany (6 January) there is a lovely Christmas market in **Piazza Navona**.

Rome on a budget

Mercifully, much of what will appeal most to kids about Rome is free – pedestrianized piazzas, elaborate fountains, mazes of alleyways and the wide-open spaces of the city's parks. Entrance to most churches is free – some of them have world-famous paintings and frescoes, ranging from Caravaggio's *Madonna dei Pellegrini* with dirty toenails in **Sant'Agostino** *(see p119)* to the optical illusions of **Sant'Ignazio's** ceiling *(see p125)*. Children under the age of 6 and EU residents below 18 are allowed free entry to most museums; women enjoy free admission on International Women's Day *(see p14)* and the **Vatican Museums** are free on the last Sunday morning of the month. The Roma Pass *(see p23)* is valid for three days – it includes free public transport, free entry to the first two sights visited and discounts at most major museums and sights.

Families on a budget could consider staying in small apartments or in simple B&Bs – most of the apartments and some B&Bs have cooking facilities – saving the expenses of eating out at every meal. It is becoming increasingly common to find hotel rooms supplied with empty fridges rather than minibars – perfect for preserving picnic supplies. Simple *trattorie* where families could eat a plate of pasta apiece and come out with change from €40 still exist – although these days most of them are off the tourist track.

Contemporary Rome

Rome celebrated the beginning of the third millennium with a Holy Year, following a massive restoration drive in which scores of churches and palaces were cleaned and recovered. The city not only began the 21st century in the best shape it had been in for years, it took a step into the future by commissioning several key cultural buildings from cutting-edge architects of international repute. Renzo Piano's **Auditorium Parco**

della Musica *(see p224)* is a world away from the dusty concert halls of the past. Exuberant and non-elitist, it has a year-round season of concerts for children at weekends, and is as much a leisure venue as a concert hall, with restaurants, shops, a playground and even an ice rink in winter.

A couple of blocks from the auditorium, Zaha Hadid's **MAXXI** *(see pp222–3)* is a dramatic and compelling building on a human scale that does much to demystify contemporary art, the power of its architecture drawing visitors around and through its galleries, accompanied – in the case of children – by a Nintendo DS multimedia guide, which allows them to take photos. Spanning the Tiber, just beyond MAXXI, is the new Ponte della Musica, a cat's cradle of a foot-bridge of tubular steel; while in the Nomentana area is Odile Decq's radical conversion of an old Peroni factory into the **MACRO** *(see p179)* art space. This fun building even has illuminated, colour-changing bathrooms. Its glorious roof entrance terrace was created to acknowledge the numerous roof gardens created by Romans atop the neighbouring buildings.

Virtual reality technology has transformed the experience of understanding and imagining ancient Rome. Underneath **Palazzo Valentini**,

Below left Auditorium Parco della Musica at night
Below Frescoed ceiling in the church of Sant'Ignazio

Above *Rowing boats for rent on the lake in Villa Borghese park*

the ruins of two Imperial houses are restored to their former glory using computer-generated projections; **Time Elevator** *(see p156)* uses 3D film techniques to bring Rome's history to life; and at the **Baths of Diocletian**, the Museo Virtuale di Via Flaminia opened in 2012, which is essentially an interactive computer game in which kids can take on an avatar and, virtually, rewrite history.

Green Rome

Owing largely to the Renaissance popes and princes who left the city with a belt of country villas with vast, landscaped estates, Rome is one of the greenest cities in Europe. **Villa Borghese** *(see pp168–9)*, closest to the *centro storico*, is not only the largest green expanse in central Rome, but its villas hold some of the city's finest museums, making it an ideal destination for families who want to combine sightseeing with a day in the park. Perhaps the city's most evocative ruins are the ones surrounded by green and shaded by pines – such as the **Palatine Hill** and the **Baths of Caracalla** – while a walk along the lava slabs of the **Via Appia Antica**, or a picnic among the arcaded aqueducts of the **Parco degli Acquedotti** *(see p43)* is the perfect way of taking in a bit of culture and getting a good burst of country air at the same time. Rome's two largest parks, **Villa Ada** *(see p225)* and **Villa Doria Pamphilj** *(see p195)* – a little distance away from the centre, but quite easily accessible via public transport – are extensive enough to give visitors the calming sense of having arrived at a place that is far removed from the madding crowd of the city centre.

Gastronomic Rome

One of the great pleasures of Rome is its food, a feast that is as much a pleasure for the eyes as the mouth. At breakfast, café counters are laden with icing-sugar-dusted *cornetti* (croissants), sugared, deep-fried doughnuts and other pastries oozing custard, jam or chocolate; while for lunch, it is possible to have a filled *panino* in any of the city's numerous delicatessens. Also widely available are local snack specialities such as *supplì* (deep-fried rice balls) and *pizza bianca* (white pizza bread, usually stuffed with ham and cheese). Children may also enjoy picking and mixing their own hot lunch or dinner at a *tavola calda* – a distant descendant of the ancient Roman *thermopolium* – where ready-made hot dishes are laid out on a heated counter. Rome is, of course, famous for ice cream, and you and your children are likely to be tempted at every turn. At **Fassi** *(Via Principe Eugenio 65, 00185; 06 446 4740)*, in northeastern Rome, they have an old-fashioned ice-cream-making machine on display and you can enjoy gargantuan sundaes at the elegant parlour of **Café Giolitti** *(Via Uffici del Vicario 40, 00186; 06 699 1243)*. For an alternative, seek out one of the now rare *grattachecche* kiosks that sell shavings of ice grated from a block and served with fruit juice, fruit syrup and sometimes chopped fresh fruit. One of the most famous of these kiosks is **Sora Mirella** *(Lungotevere Anguillara, corner of Ponte Cestio)*, in Trastevere. Other traditional street foods include pots of fresh fruit salad and, in summer, slices of coconut or watermelon sold from little wagons; while the smell of roasted chestnuts fills the air in late autumn.

Rome through the Year

With its busy calendar of festivals and events, Rome is appealing in every season. However, the best times for families to visit the city are spring and autumn, when the weather is usually pleasant, and sometimes even warm enough to sunbathe and swim at the beaches and lakes outside the city. Easter and Christmas are obviously very special here, but there are other religious festivals worth seeing at other times of the year.

Spring

The Roman spring (*primavera*) begins around March. Temperatures can vary wildly, with rainfall and sunshine within the same hour, so come prepared.

MARCH

On the 8th – **International Women's Day** – men celebrate the women in their lives by giving them posies of mimosa; it is not unusual to receive one from a stranger on the street. On the 9th is the **Festa di Santa Francesca**, when motor vehicles are driven to the Roman Forum for their yearly blessing in the church of Santa Francesca Romana (*see p77*). On the third or fourth Sunday of the month, Rome's **Marathon** takes athletes from Piazza Venezia (*see p84*) all the way to the Basilica of San Paolo in EUR (*see p230*) and back. Less serious runners and lots of children

take part in the 4-km- (2-mile-) long **Fun Run**. Towards the end of the month, **Italy's Environmental Fund** (FAI) opens up churches, monuments and gardens usually closed to the public, for a weekend.

APRIL

Easter (*Pasqua*) is a big deal in Rome and the Vatican City. The **Holy Week** (*Settimana Santa*) events start with a big Mass on **Palm Sunday**, when olive tree branches are distributed in and outside churches. On **Good Friday**, the pope leads an outdoor Mass at the Colosseum (*see pp70–71*), with a Way of the Cross (*Via Crucis*) procession. These celebrations culminate on **Easter Sunday**, when the pope delivers his *Urbi et Orbi* (of city and world) address in Piazza San Pietro (*see p202*). On Easter Sunday, kids open gift-filled chocolate Easter eggs

(*uova di Pasqua*). On the following day (*Pasquetta*), it is customary to pack a rich picnic and head to a park or to the countryside to spend a day under the spring sun.

On the 21st, events are organized around the Piazza del Campidoglio (*see p80*) to commemorate the founding of the city by Romulus. On the 25th, various official celebrations take place in the city centre marking Italy's liberation from the Nazi-Fascist regimes. Many Romans spend time on the beach on this day off work. Around this time, the nationwide **Settimana della Cultura** (Culture Week) allows free access to state-run museums and historical sites.

MAY

On **Labour Day** (1 May), the workers' unions organize a free rock concert with popular Italian stars and some international guests in

Below left An opera performance during the Estate Romana festival
Below right Racehorses and jockeys at the Piazza di Siena International Horse Show

front of the church of San Giovanni in Laterano. In the first half of the month, the **International Open Tennis Championship** at the Foro Italico *(see p224)* sees the world's best players compete in an exclusive yet child-friendly setting.

May is the month of flowers. Rome's parks are dotted with daisies and the unkempt flowerbeds lining some of the streets are an explosion of red poppies. In the first week of the month, pots of azaleas line the Spanish Steps *(see p142)* for the annual **Azalea Show**, while on the second Sunday children traditionally give flowers to their mothers for **Mother's Day**. The seasonal rose garden, the Roseto Comunale *(see p106)*, in full bloom in May, opens at the start of the month. The gorgeous roses here provide an unmissable foreground to the imposing ruins of the Palatine Hill *(see pp74–5)* on the other side of the Circus Maximus *(see p106)*.

Kids and adults alike will enjoy the **Piazza di Siena International Horse Show**, which takes place in Villa Borghese *(see pp168–9)* around the end of the month and features competitions and races, as well as the re-enactment of the historic Battle of Pastrengo (1848); a hundred black and white horses simulate the battle. On **Pentecost**,

firemen scale the dome of the Pantheon *(see pp122–3)* to shower rose petals through its *oculus* upon the congregation attending Mass.

Summer

A hot summer means that Italian children have very long holidays, from mid-June to mid-September, and many families leave town for the beach or the mountains. Cultural festivals with plenty of child-friendly events include the **Estate Romana**, Rome's summer festival.

JUNE

On the 2nd, Italy celebrates the **Republic** with an Armed Forces parade down Via dei Fori Imperiali in front of the Italian President. Meanwhile, families queue up in front of the Quirinal for the yearly one-day opening of the Quirinal Gardens. The first week of June marks the start of beach season in the resorts in Lido di Ostia. On the feast of **Corpus Domini**, on the first or second Sunday of the month, the town of Genzano in the Castelli Romani *(see pp240–41)* celebrates with **Infiorata**, a flower-art festival in which the petals of half a million flowers are artfully arranged to create allegorical designs down the main street. The best part comes

after the show, when children are allowed to run through the petals and destroy the designs. On the 29th, Rome celebrates its patron saints, **Santi Pietro e Paolo**.

JULY

For the Estate Romana, the Isola Tiberina, or Tiber Island, turns into a summer village, with an outdoor cinema, small restaurants, shops, and bars where refreshing drinks can be enjoyed by the waterside. The **July Sounds Good** festival at the Auditorium Parco della Musica *(see p224)* brings to town the greats of the international pop, rock and jazz arena, while in July and August, **Opera Roma** continues out of doors at the Baths of Caracalla *(see p230)*. Rome's famous jazz villa, the **Casa del Jazz**, organizes nightly concerts in its lush gardens, and Villa Ada *(see p225)* hosts world music concerts every night in its **Rome Meets the World** event. Authentic Romanhood comes to life in Trastevere's **Festa de' Noantri** *(see p185)*, with two weeks of food, wine and dancing events to celebrate local and religious traditions. The festival includes a massive pillow fight in Piazza di Santa Maria in Trastevere *(see pp186–7)* and culminates in a brilliant fireworks display.

Below left Flower art during the Infiorata festival in Genzano, Castelli Romani
Below right International Open Tennis Championship at the Foro Italico

AUGUST

Visitors have the whole city more or less to themselves in August, which means less traffic and a more relaxed atmosphere. However, temperatures regularly top 30° C (85° F) and may even reach 35° C (95° F) and above, so it is best to stay out of the mid-day sun. Take a long siesta, then let the kids stay up until late to enjoy the balmy evenings. On the 5th, the basilica of Santa Maria Maggiore (see pp100–101) celebrates the **Festa della Madonna della Neve**, commemorating the miraculous snowfall of AD 352 with a special Mass dedicated to the Holy Virgin of the Snow, ending in a storm of white petals. On the night of the 10th, many families head to the Pincio Gardens (see p151) and gaze at the sky hoping to see meteor showers on **La Notte di San Lorenzo** (St Lawrence's Night). Everything shuts down on the 15th for **Ferragosto**, when the church celebrates the Assumption of the Blessed Virgin Mary, and, if Rome gets a bit boring, hop on to a train and join the crowds on Ostia's beaches.

Autumn

This is a lovely time to visit the city. The temperatures are cooler than in high summer and rain usually does

not set in until mid-November. October is the Romans' favourite month, with the *ottobrate romane*, which is what they call the warm, sunny October days. Autumn is also a celebration of nature, with seasonal produce such as persimmons, grapes, chestnuts, porcini mush-rooms and pumpkins on offer.

SEPTEMBER

Families start returning from their holidays in the first week of September. Schools reopen around the 14th and the football season starts (see p39).

OCTOBER

The Auditorium Parco della Musica hosts the **Rome Film Festival**, with two weeks of Italian and international cinema. Further afield, the small town of Marino in the Castelli Romani celebrates its **Sagra dell'Uva**, usually on the first weekend of the month. This is one of Italy's most famous wine festivals and is likely to be enjoyed by the whole family.

NOVEMBER

The **RomaEuropa** festival brings dance, music and video projections to the Teatro Palladium stage in the southern outskirts of Rome, with unexpected and often thought-provoking results.

Winter

Christmas lights make Rome all the more pretty and cosy, and the scent of roasted chestnuts pervades the streets around Piazza di Spagna (see pp142–3). Each church has its own Nativity scene, and some organize live re-enactments of the Nativity (presepi viventi), with real sheep and elaborate costumes.

DECEMBER

The **Festa dell'Immacolata**, or Feast of the Immaculate Conception, is celebrated on the 8th in Piazza di Spagna (see pp142–3), and marks the beginning of the Christmas season. On this day, a huge Christmas tree is erected in **Piazza Venezia** (see p84) and Nativity scenes are set up around the city.

The **Christmas Market** on **Piazza Navona** (see pp116–17), with stalls selling food, Christmas decorations and gifts, opens in the second week of December, as does the Auditorium Parco della Musica's **Christmas Village**, with an ice rink and indoor market. On **Christmas Eve** (Vigilia di Natale) families eat a meal of sea-food before attending Midnight Mass, and on **Christmas Day** (Natale) they celebrate with a large, meat-based lunch, which always ends with at least one slice of panettone, the traditional Christmas cake.

Below left A procession during the Sagra dell'Uva in Marino, Castelli Romani
Below right Nativity scene and Christmas tree in front of Il Vittoriano, Piazza Venezia

On **New Year's Eve**, the city lights up with fireworks, and Romans attend free rock and pop concerts in **Piazza del Popolo** *(see p150)* and other squares. Transport is usually free for the whole night but call 060608 to make sure as this can change from year to year.

JANUARY

The Christmas Market on Piazza Navona culminates on the 6th with the **Epiphany**, when good children receive presents and sweets and naughty ones get sweet charcoal from a friendly old witch called La Befana. Around the end of the month, Piazza Vittorio *(see p91)* in the multiethnic Esquiline neighbourhood become the setting for the **Chinese New Year** celebrations, with dragons, dances and sweets.

FEBRUARY

Rome's **Carnevale** is less spectacular than the ones in Venice or Viareggio, but the city has been making an effort to bring the old carnival celebrations back to life. The most important parades take place on *Martedì Grasso* (Shrove Tuesday) in Via del Corso *(see p138)* and Piazza del Popolo, where kids wearing costumes throw confetti at each other. The many Carnival events are listed every year on the official

website. February is also the dance month at the Auditorium Parco della Musica, with the **Equilibrio Festival** bringing in the best of the world's dancers and choreographers for two weeks of entertainment. Towards the end of the month, the **Six Nations Rugby Competition** brings two matches to the Olympic Stadium near the Foro Italico. Games are lively and fans are civilized, which makes this a fun event for the family.

The Lowdown

Spring
International Open Tennis Championship
www.internazionalibnlditalia.it
Italy's Environmental Fund (FAI)
www.fondoambiente.it
Marathon & Fun Run
www.maratonadiroma.it
Piazza di Siena International Horse Show
www.piazzadisiena.org
Settimana della Cultura
www.beniculturali.it

Summer
Casa del Jazz
www.casajazz.it
Estate Romana
www.estateromana.comune.roma.it
Festa de' Noantri
www.festadenoantri.it
July Sounds Good
www.auditorium.com
Opera Roma
www.operaroma.it
Rome Meets the World
www.villaada.org

Autumn
RomaEuropa
www.romaeuropa.net

Rome Film Festival
www.romacinemafest.it

Winter
Carnevale
www.carnevaleroma.com
Christmas Village
www.auditorium.com
Equilibrio Festival
www.auditorium.com
Six Nations Rugby Competition
www.rbs6nations.com

Italian School Holidays
Summer holidays last from mid-June to mid-Sep. Two weeks are given off for Christmas and five to ten days make up the Easter holidays.

Public Holidays
New Year's Day (1 Jan)
Epiphany (6 Jan)
Easter Monday (late Mar/Apr)
Liberation Day (25 Apr)
Labour Day (1 May)
Republic Day (2 Jun)
Santi Pietro e Paolo (29 Jun)
Ferragosto (15 Aug)
All Saints' Day (1 Nov)
Festa dell'Immacolata (8 Dec)
Christmas Day 25 Dec
Santo Stefano 26 Dec

Below left Dancers at the Chinese New Year celebrations, Piazza del Popolo
Below right La Befana handing sweets to a child during Epiphany

Getting to Rome

The easiest – and often the most economical – way of getting to Rome from most destinations is by air. Rome's two airports are served by national and low-cost airlines from all over the world, but families beginning their journey in Europe may want to consider the adventure of travelling by sleeper train. Civitavecchia, the closest port to Rome, has ferry connections with Sicily, Sardinia, Malta, Barcelona and Tunis.

Arriving by air

Rome has two major airports. **Fiumicino** (FCO), 30 km (19 miles) southwest of the city, is the main Italian hub for scheduled flights to and from most major European and global destinations – airlines include **KLM, Lufthansa, Qantas, Delta** and **American Airlines**. It is the hub for Italian national carrier **Alitalia** and is also used by low-cost companies such as **Aer Lingus, Air Berlin** and **easyJet**. Fiumicino, also known as Leonardo da Vinci, has four terminals. Nursery room facilities are available at the airport in areas D, G and H. There is a play area for young children in Terminal 3 Arrivals, and two toyshops, in Terminal 1 and area D. **Ciampino** (CIA), 15 km (9 miles) southeast of the city, is used mainly by low-cost and charter flights such as Aer Lingus, Air Berlin, **Blue Air, Eurowings, Ryanair** and

easyJet – usually the cheapest means of reaching Rome from within Europe. Also known as Giovan Battista Pastine, Ciampino has just one terminal. There are no toyshops or play areas here, but there are nursery rooms in Departures before and after security, and in the Arrivals hall. When searching for flights, note that many websites charge extra for the use of a credit card. It is often cheapest to look first at a comparison site such as *www.skyscanner.com* and then book directly through the website of the flight company.

Airport transfers

The fastest way into central Rome from Fiumicino is by the **Leonardo train**, which runs nonstop to Termini station. A one-way ticket costs €14 for adults, but children aged 12 and under travel free. There is also a

slower train to Ostiense, Trastevere and Tiburtina stations which takes 50 minutes but costs €8 one way. However, children pay full fare. The journey time from Fiumicino to Termini by bus is about an hour. **COTRAL** (€4.50 per person), **SIT** (€6 per person if booked online) and **Terravision** (€4 per person) buses all have frequent departures to Termini. Ciampino too is serviced by SIT (€4 per person), Terravision (€4 per person) and also **ATRAL** (€4 per person). The approximate journey time from Ciampino airport to Termini station is just 40 minutes.

White taxi cars have a 'TAXI' sign on top and charge a flat fare of €48 from Fiumicino and €30 from Ciampino to anywhere within the Aurelian Walls. It is worth considering that a metered taxi ride from Termini train station or bus terminus to destinations in the *centro storico*

Below *The interior of Fiumicino airport, one of Rome's two airports*

could cost €15 or more on a busy day. Several private companies run limo services to and from the airports for the same price as regular taxis, but these services need to be booked in advance.

Arriving by rail

Going to Rome by train is generally more expensive than flying. But it can be more of an adventure for a family. The Franco-Italian **Thello** runs every evening from Paris to Venice via Milan, Padua, Verona and Vicenza, with accommodation in sleeper carriages and couchettes. The facilities include a nice café-bar and restaurant.

Trenitalia operate high-speed trains between major cities. The superfast Frecciarossa helps connect Milan to Rome in 3 hours 25 minutes while the Frecciargento runs from Venice to Rome in just 3 hours 50 minutes. There are frequent departures from both these cities.

Italo also offers a stylish and fast train service between major cities, stopping at Rome. Tickets are sometimes cheaper than Trenitalia.

The Man in Seat 61 provides information on travelling by train, with details of most routes, timings and fares. Most international trains arrive at Termini station, Rome's main transport hub.

Arriving by coach

There is a network of coaches to the capital from major cities around Italy. Journey times can be quicker than by train, especially if a train journey involves changes. The best way of searching is on a website such as *www.orariautobus.it*. Rome's main coach station is Tiburtina, a little way out of the centre. It is on metro line B, with rapid connections to Termini and the *centro storico*.

By car

Families considering driving to Rome will find reliable route planners on *www.theAA.com* and *www.viamichelin.co.uk*. The Michelin site estimates petrol and toll costs, while the AA site is also useful when it comes to providing route options that avoid toll roads.

The streets of the city centre have been designated as ZTL (*zona a traffico limitato*), which means only residents can drive within it and park. The handiest car park for the *centro storico* is the underground one at Villa Borghese (entrance at Viale de Galoppatoio 33; *www.sabait.it*) and costs €2.20 per hour/€18 per day. It is linked by a passageway with the Spagna metro station.

There are several free car parks on the city periphery, usually located close to metro stations, and they are all listed under *parcheggio a raso* (level car park) on *www.060608.it*.

The Lowdown

Arriving by air
Aer Lingus www.aerlingus.com
Aeroporti di Roma www.adr.it
Air Berlin www.airberlin.com
Alitalia www.alitalia.com/GB_EN
American Airlines www.aa.com
Blue Air www.blueairweb.com
Delta www.delta.com
easyJet www.easyjet.com
Eurowings www.eurowings.com
KLM www.klm.com
Lufthansa www.lufthansa.com
Qantas www.qantas.com
Ryanair www.ryanair.com

Airport transfers
ATRAL www.atral-lazio.com
COTRAL www.cotralspa.it
Leonardo train www.trenitalia.it
SIT www.sitbusshuttle.com
Terravision www.terravision.eu

Arriving by rail
Italo www.italotreno.it
The Man in Seat 61 www.seat61.com
Thello www.italiarail.com/thello
Trenitalia www.trenitalia.it

Below left Taxis plying their trade in the city
Below right High-speed train connecting Rome with Milan, Venice and Naples

Getting around Rome

The best way to see Rome's *centro storico* is to walk. However, with children it may be judicious to use the extensive bus and tram network or the metro between areas of interest. Several key areas in the *centro storico* have been pedestrianized, including many streets around Piazza Navona, Piazza di Spagna, Campo de' Fiori, Trastevere and the Jewish Ghetto – but bear in mind that many Romans consider moped riding a pedestrian activity.

By bus and tram

Rome's bus and tram service, run by **ATAC** (Azienda Tramvie e Autobus del Comune di Roma), is cheap, reliable, frequent and quite comprehensive, although progress along the clogged streets can sometimes be slow. Routes are listed on stops, and electronic information panels that indicate the waiting time before the next bus are being installed at stops around the city centre. After 11:30pm a series of night buses take over, indicated by an "N" before the number. These are all listed on bus stops.

Buses get very crowded and have few seats, so families travelling with prams and young children will need to be fairly assertive about getting on and – especially – off the bus. There is a bell to press for request stops – and a sign saying *"fermata prenotata"* (stop booked) which will light up at the front of the bus. In addition to regular buses, several extremely useful electric minibuses also squeeze along the narrow streets of the *centro storico*.

There are numerous tram lines too – some of them served by historic green trams – of which routes 2, 3, 8 and 19 are the ones likely to be of most use to visitors. Trams have ticket vending machines on board.

By metro

Rome's underground system, the Metropolitana, has two metro lines – A and B – with Line C slowly burrowing its way across the city, its progress regularly halted by archaeological discoveries. Line A runs from Battistini in the west to Anagnina in the southeast. It connects key places of interest such as Piazza del Popolo (*see p150*), Via Vittorio Veneto (*see p161*), the Trevi Fountain (*see pp154–5*), Palazzo Barberini (*see p158*), the Museo Nazionale Romano (*see pp98–9*) and Nuovo Mercato Esquilino (*see p101*). Line B runs from Rebibbia in the northeast to Laurentina in the south, covering sites such as Testaccio (*see p108*), Aventine Hill, Colosseum (*see pp70–71*), and Cavour for Monti. Both lines cross at Stazione Centrale Roma Termini.

Stations closest to the places of interest include Colosseo, Spagna, San Giovanni, Ottaviano San Pietro and Piramide (for trains to Fiumicino). Both lines run from 5:30am until 11:30pm every day (till 1:30am on Friday and Saturday).

Line C, the third metro line, is still under construction. Some peripheral stations are already operational, and when entirely

Below left Tram in the streets of Rome
Centre Commuters boarding the train at a metro station in Rome

finished, the metro line will run from Clodio/Mazzini, beyond the Vatican City, out into the eastern suburbs, with central stations projected at Piazza del Risorgimento, Ottaviano San Pietro, Chiesa Nuova, Piazza Venezia and Fori Imperiali/Colosseo.

Tickets

The same tickets are valid within the city on buses, trams, metro, inter-city COTRAL buses and trains on the Roma-Lido, Roma-Viterbo and Roma-Giardinetti lines. Tickets are available at tobacconists and newsagents with an ATAC sticker in the window, from booths at major bus terminals and at ticket machines at several smaller bus hubs such as Largo Argentina. Regular tickets cost €1.50 and are valid for 100 minutes, day tickets (BIG) cost €7, 2-day tickets cost €12.50, 3-day tickets (BTI) cost €18 and weekly passes (CIS) cost €24.

There are two kinds of monthly passes: one at €35 that can be used only by the ticket holder, and the other at €53 that can be used by anyone. Children under 10 accompanied by an adult travel free. Tickets need to be validated the first time they are used, in the little machines on board.

By taxi

The easiest way to hail a taxi is to find the nearest *fermata dei taxi* (taxi stand). Central ones include Stazione Centrale Roma Termini, Piazza Venezia, Piazza delle Cinque Lune near Piazza Navona, Largo Argentina, Piazza San Silvestro, Piazza di Spagna, Piazza del Popolo and Piazza Barberini. Calling a taxi for pick-up costs more, as the meter is switched on as soon as the driver sets off. Going from one side of the city centre to the other can cost as little as €10 when traffic is light, but a lot more when traffic is heavy and at night or on Sundays and holidays, when a supplement is charged. There is a minimum charge of €3 (€4.50 on Sundays, and €6.50 between 10pm and 7am) up to and including five passengers. Additional passengers are charged an extra €1 per person. The first item of luggage is free; any other piece of luggage bigger than the standard cabin bag (35 x 25 x 50 cm, 13.8 x 9.8 x 19.7 in) is charged at €1 per item. Only take the official white cabs; call 060608 in case of any trouble. Make sure to mention the taxi's code, written on the side of the car.

There is a fixed price for rides from the airports to any destination within the Aurelian Walls (see p18). Check out the official taxi rates set by the Comune di Rome at www.tinyurl.com/nb4qq5t.

By train

There is a useful city line to Ostia Antica (see pp236–7) and Ostia Lido, leaving from Stazione Porta San Paolo, next to Piramide metro station. Regular bus, tram and metro tickets are valid for use.

Boat tours

Battelli di Roma runs trips up and down the Tiber between Isola Tiberina and the Ponte Nenni to the north throughout the year. There are just two embarkation points – at Isola Tiberina and Ponte Sant'Angelo (see p214) – making it more of a pleasure trip than a means of getting between sights. Tickets are, however, valid for 24 hours – passengers can hop on and off perhaps to see the Ponte Sant'Angelo, St Peter's (see pp204–5) and the Vatican, or to explore and have lunch around Piazza Navona (see pp116–17) and Campo de' Fiori (see pp130–31).

Following extensive damage caused by heavy rains over some years, regular service is currently suspended. Call 06 9774 5414 or check the website for further information on special tours.

Below right Taxis lining up in front of a taxi stand

By car

Driving is not recommended in Rome – roads are congested, street parking is difficult and parking in private garages is quite expensive, so public transport is a better option. Anyone bringing a car would be advised to consider staying in a B&B or hotel outside the centre where they can park safely for free. Breakdown services such as **ACI Breakdown** are available.

Firms such as **Avis**, **Hertz**, **Europcar** and **Thrifty** have rental offices at the airports, Stazione Centrale Roma Termini and in the city. However, you may get a better deal by booking a car in advance through a travel agent or online, or by using a local firm such as **Maggiore**.

Bus tours

Various companies offer different types of hop-on, hop-off bus tours of the city. The red double-decker open-topped buses of **City Sightseeing Rome** are one of the most popular hop-on, hop-off sightseeing buses in Rome. The 'Classic Tour' offered by City Sightseeing Rome runs daily from 9am to 5pm in winter, and to 7pm in summer. The tour begins and ends on Via Marsala and at

Largo di Villa Peretti at Stazione Centrale Roma Termini, with buses leaving every 15–20 minutes. The entire circuit takes around one hour and forty minutes and services all the main tourist attractions – Santa Maria Maggiore (see pp100–1), Colosseum, Circus Maximus (see p106), Piazza Venezia (see p84), Vatican, the Trevi Fountain, Spanish Steps (see p142), and Piazza Barberini. Tickets are available for one or two days and cost €25 and €28 respectively. For those staying close to one of the stops, they can be a good alternative to the ATAC Roma travel cards. The tour buses have a recorded audioguide, which is available in eight languages, and a free Wi-Fi connection. City Sightseeing Rome also offers variations of the classic tour, such as a Vatican ride, a combo ticket bundle which also includes tickets for the Battelli di Roma river cruises, and combo tickets which provide discounted access to the monuments.

Families who are interested in a tour with a Christian emphasis might prefer the **Roma Cristiana bus**, a yellow double-decker, with air conditioning, that runs from Piazza San Pietro (see p202) to Termini. It crosses Santa Maria Maggiore, the Trevi Fountain,

San Giovanni in Laterano, and other stops close to important religious sights of Catholic Rome. Buses operate from 9am to 5:30pm in winter, and to 6pm in summer. The hop-on, hop-off tickets cost €23 for a day and €27 for two days. The bus tour also includes the use of audioguides in all major languages. Visitors can book the tickets via Terravision (see p19).

Guided tours and activities

UK-based **Italian Connection** has an inspired portfolio of guided tours and activities for children and families, ranging from pizza-making and eating, to the chance to attend a school for gladiators. There are half-day walking tours taking in sights such as the Roman Forum, the Colosseum and the church of San Clemente (see pp92–3) – with an emphasis on the kind of horrible history that appeals to kids – and child-friendly tours of the Vatican, St Peter's and the Castle Sant'Angelo. Trips to sights further afield, such as the catacombs, can be made in a vintage Fiat Cinquecento or three-wheeler Api.

Below left Cyclists on the cycling path along the Tiber
Below right Open-topped City Sightseeing Rome tourist bus

MAXXI *(see pp222–3)*, a museum of modern art and architecture, organizes regular workshops and activities for children, mostly related to the ongoing exhibitions. Although mainly in Italian, all children are welcome, and the helpful staff almost always speaks English. Prices vary, depending on the activity.

Roma Pass

The three-day **Roma Pass** includes free use of the city's transport network, free entrance to two museums, reduced ticket prices to all other museums and archae-ological sites, and discounted tickets to exhibitions and events. It is priced at a reasonable €36. Check the website for a list of museums included in the Roma Pass scheme.

By bicycle or Segway

The city's unique bicycle-sharing scheme **Bikesharing Roma** is open to tourists, although only adult bikes are available. Registrations can be made at 10 metro stations, and cost €10. A rechargeable smartcard costs €5 and bicycles can also be rented at €1 per hour. Bicycles are available from 29 bicycle stations throughout

the city, and can be used for up to 24 hours at a time. They can be picked up at one station and returned at another.

Segways and bicycles can also be hired from **Rome by Segway**. It would probably be wise for families to stick to designated cycle routes and not venture on to the main roads and thoroughfares with heavy traffic. There are a few areas, such as the Villa Borghese and the banks of the Tiber, where bike lanes make for a relaxing way to see the city.

Horse-drawn carriages

Children might enjoy a gentle tour of the historic centre in *carrozzelle* or *botticelle* (horse-drawn carriages). These carry up to five people and can be rented from many points – Piazza di Spagna, the Colosseum, Trevi Fountain, St Peter's, Via Vittorio Veneto, Villa Borghese *(see pp168–9)*, Piazza Venezia and Piazza Navona. Trips can last anywhere from half an hour to an hour, half a day or a day. They tend to be expensive (prices start at €240/hr) but prices for longer rides are negotiable; fix the fare before you set off and make sure you understand whether the rate is per person or for the whole carriage.

The Lowdown

By bus & tram
ATAC *www.atac.roma.it*

Boat tours
Battelli di Roma
www.battellidiroma.it

By car
ACI Breakdown 803116
Avis *www.avisautonoleggio.it*
Europcar *www.europcar.it*
Hertz *www.hertz.it*
Maggiore *www.maggiore.it*
Thrifty *www.thrifty.com*

Bus tours
City Sightseeing Rome
www.city-sightseeing.com/tours/italy/rome.htm
Roma Cristiana Tours
www.terravision.eu/city_tour/roma-cristiana-open-bus

Guided tours & activities
Italian Connection 014 2472 8900;
www.tinyurl.com/84g57yo
MAXXI *www.fondazionemaxxi.it*

Roma Pass
www.romapass.it

By bicycle or Segway
Bikesharing Roma
www.bikesharing.roma.it
Rome by Segway
www.romebysegway.com/site

Below left *Horse-drawn carriage going past an ancient Roman temple*
Below right *Visitors on Segways outside the Colosseum*

Practical Information

Overall, Rome is a progressive European city with efficient infrastructure in place. Health hazards are minimal, pharmacies are well stocked, and children have a special place in Italian society and are welcome everywhere. However, a rather relaxed local attitude makes for variations in opening hours, and many places – including banks, offices and shops – close for 2 or 3 hours over lunch and open late in the afternoon, so a bit of forward planning might be in order.

Passports and visas

Italy is part of the European Union and EU citizens can enter Italy and stay indefinitely with a valid passport or identity card. Italy is part of the Schengen agreement, which means travellers moving from one Schengen country to another are not subject to border controls, although there are occasional spot checks. Citizens of the US, Canada, Australia and New Zealand can stay for up to three months on the pro- duction of a passport, which should be valid for three months beyond the end of the trip. For longer stays, however, they will need to make an advance application to their local Italian consulate for a visa.

All other nationals need a visa, and should consult the Italian **Ministero degli Esteri** website or local consulate for details of where and how to apply.

Travel safety advice

Visitors can get up-to-date travel safety information from the **Foreign and Commonwealth Office** in the UK, the **State Department** in the US and the **Department of Foreign Affairs and Trade** in Australia.

Customs information

For EU citizens there are no limits on goods taken into or out of Italy, provided they are for personal use only. Non-EU residents can claim back sales tax on purchases over €155 by filling in a tax-free form (*www.globalblue.com*).

Insurance

It is advisable to take out insurance against medical emergencies, travel cancellations or delays, emergency expatriation, theft and loss.

Health

Italy has a reciprocal health agreement with other EU member states. All EU nationals are entitled to free emergency treatment under Italy's public health-care system, on the production of a European Health Insurance Card (EHIC). The card is free and valid for five years. Forms are available in the UK at most post offices, or you can apply online. You will have to pay for any prescriptions upfront.

Australian Medicare also has a reciprocal agreement with Italy. All other nationalities should check the terms of their health insurance policies or buy travel insurance before they set out.

There are few health hazards in Rome. Tap water is drinkable. In summer, there is a slight risk of sunstroke and sunburn. Wear hats, high-protection sunscreen and light,

Below left A child drinking from one of the many fountains in Rome
Below right Via dei Fori Imperiali, crowded with pedestrians on a Sunday

sunproof clothing. Avoid too much time out in the sun, and drink plenty of water. When it is hot, it is best to avoid ice-cold water. Mosquitoes can be a problem, but are not malarial. Spray clothes, and exposed skin, with mosquito repellent if going out in the evenings. Calamine lotion – the most effective way to stop itching from mosquito bites – is not widely available, so bring your own supplies.

If you or your family are taking prescription medicines, try to bring enough supplies to last the duration of the stay. Many pharmacists can sell replacements for common drugs such as antibiotics and anti-inflammatories without a prescription and offer advice on minor ailments. Pharmacies are signalled by a green cross, and if a pharmacy is closed, there will be a notice on display with information of the nearest open pharmacy.

In Rome there are two 24-hour clinics called the **Guardia Medica Turistica** dedicated to taking care of tourists and foreigners. In Italy, resident children under 7 are legally required to be registered with a paediatrician rather than a general practitioner, while children aged 8–12 can be registered with either. While Guardia Medica Turistica doctors are prepared to treat minor ailments in children, for anything more serious, it is better to go to

the *pronto soccorso* (A&E/casualty) section of the excellent children's hospital, the **Ospedale Pediatrico Bambino Gesù.** If anyone is involved in an accident, call 118 for an ambulance or go to the *pronto soccorso* department of the nearest hospital. There is also a 24-hour English-language health helpline for tourists (06 4323 6291).

Personal safety

Italy is a relatively safe country, and, even in a big city like Rome, random street violence is rare. Drinking in excess is not a cultural norm – Italy suffers less from alcohol abuse than anywhere else in the Western world – although the vast influx of foreign students in recent years has made parts of the city centre – notably Campo de' Fiori and Trastevere – significantly rowdy. The *centro storico* is very well policed, but nevertheless pickpocketing is common, particularly at popular, crowded tourist sights and on buses – the Colosseum, the Trevi Fountain, Piazza Navona, Piazza di Spagna and bus 64 are all favoured by petty criminals. Wallets, passports, mobile phones, MP3 players and laptops should all be looked after with great care. Think twice before letting a child walk around Rome with a mobile phone

or MP3 player. The best strategy to avoid pickpockets and bag-snatchers is to try and blend in. Rome has a huge international community, so it is relatively easy to avoid looking like a tourist, even if you don't speak a word of Italian. Dress as you would normally in any city and avoid carrying rucksacks and waist belts, which will only act as a beacon to the nimble-fingered. Try to look like you know where you are going – if necessary, duck into a café to consult your map and guidebook.

Police

There are two crime-fighting forces in Italy: the **Carabinieri**, which is the military branch of the police; and **Polizia di Stato**, the civil branch. They fulfil more or less the same function, but can be distinguished by their uniforms.

If you are unfortunate enough to be a victim of crime, report the crime to the police as soon as you can. Unless you speak good Italian it is easier to report a crime in person than on the telephone. To make a claim for stolen goods on your insurance, you will need a crime report or *denuncia di furto o smarrimento* (claim of theft or loss) from either the Carabinieri or Polizia di Stato.

Below left *Police car at St Peter's Square*
Below right *Family admiring the Fontana delle Tartarughe, Piazza Mattei*

LOST AND FOUND

If you lose something around town, you may find that it has been handed in at the Oggetti Smarriti centre near Piramide metro station (06 6769 3214; open 8:30am–1pm Mon, Tue, Wed & Fri; 8:30am–5pm Thu). ID is required to claim the object, plus a crime report unless the object is clearly identifiable.

Money

Italy is one of the 17 European nations using the euro (€). There are 100 cents in a euro, eight coins (€2, €1, and 50, 20, 10, 5, 2 and 1 cents) and seven euro notes (€5, €10, €20, €50, €100, €200 and €500). While euro notes are identical within the eurozone, euro coins have a pan-European design on one face, and a country-specific design on the other. Italy's 5 cents coin features the Colosseum, and the €1 coin shows Da Vinci's Vitruvian Man.

ATMS AND BUREAUX DE CHANGE

The easiest way of getting cash in Rome is with a debit card from a *Bancomat* (ATM). Most cards will allow a maximum withdrawal of €250 per day. However, many banks charge for withdrawals and transactions abroad. Check the rates before you travel. Exchange rates in hotels and bureaux de change are rarely good. For more substantial withdrawals, the best exchange rate for currency will usually be at an Italian bank. Banks are open 8:30am to 1:30pm and usually 2:30pm to 4pm Monday to Friday.

TRAVELLER'S CHEQUES AND CASH PASSPORTS

Traveller's cheques have largely been replaced by prepaid currency cards or cash passports. These can be preloaded with euros, fixing the exchange rate before you leave your country, and used in shops and ATMs abroad. The maximum daily amount withdrawable from an ATM is usually €700, with a fee per withdrawal. The cards are available from **Thomas Cook**, **Travelex** and the **Cooperative Bank**.

DEBIT AND CREDIT CARDS

Debit or credit cards with a PIN can be used at many shops and restaurants, although check first in smaller places and B&Bs. Your card will be swiped and you will be asked whether you want the transaction processing as *Bancomat* (debit card) or *carta di credito* (credit card). You then have to key in your PIN. Credit cards with a PIN can also be used in Italian ATMs, but you will be charged interest from the date of withdrawal.

Communications

TELEPHONES

In Italy the regional phone code is an integral part of every number, and always has to be dialled. The area code for Rome is 06. European mobile phones will work on Italian networks, but Americans will need a tri-band phone. Check with your provider for roaming options – a cheaper alternative may be to purchase an Italian SIM card. The main phone operators are **TIM**, **Vodafone**, **Wind** and **3**. To use a payphone, buy a *scheda telefonica* (phone card) from a newsagent or tobacconist – there are virtually no coin-operated phones.

INTERNET

High-speed internet (ADSL) and Wi-Fi is available in cafés and hotels all over the city. The city council also provides free Wi-Fi in many of the piazzas. It is essential to have an Italian mobile number, as accounts are validated by asking potential users to dial a free number.

POSTAL SERVICES

The Italian postal system – Poste Italiane – although efficient, can be quite slow, and many Romans prefer the Vatican Post Office on Piazza San Pietro (see p202) instead. If speed is of utmost importance, you can use the postal system's

Below left A typical ATM centre in Rome
Below right Sign for a post office in the historic centre

courier service, Posta Celere, or, for international deliveries, Pacco Celere Internazionale.

Opening hours

Most major museums and sights, and many supermarkets and inter-national chain stores, stay open all day. Smaller shops may close for an hour or two at lunchtime, but an increasing number remain open. Many museums, art galleries and archaeological sites are closed on Mondays.

Public toilets

There are council-run public toilets all over the city. Some are free; some levy a small fee.

Time

Italy is 1 hour ahead of Greenwich Mean Time (GMT) in winter and 1 hour ahead of British Summer Time (BST) in summer.

Electricity

The voltage in Italy is 220 volts. Plugs have either two or three round pins. It is advisable to take a multi-plug adapter as the size of pins depends on the age of electrical installation.

Below left Cobbled streets in Trajan's Markets
Below right Dining at a family-friendly restaurant

Disabled facilities

Facilities for the disabled are few and far between in Italy. Toilets for disabled people in bars and restaurants are now more common and some hotels have adapted rooms, but access to sights is frequently stepped, with lifts often unattended or in disrepair.

Cobbled streets, randomly parked cars and scooters, and high kerbs can make it hard going for the visually and mobility impaired. Public transport is only slightly better, with many trams, trains, metro systems and buses still not wheelchair-accessible.

Etiquette

Children are feted in Italy, but that does not mean that they are not expected to respect others. Make sure that kids do not get under the feet of waiters in restaurants, and take crying babies outside to calm them. Italian children are always kept clean and tidy, so tomato-sauce faces or sticky ice-cream hands should be wiped.

A few basic words of Italian will always be appreciated – learn some functional phrases yourself and teach children to say *buon giorno* (good morning), *ciao* (hello/goodbye) and *grazie* (thank you).

The Lowdown

Passports and visas
Ministero degli Esteri
www.esteri.it
Australian Embassy
Via Bosio Antonio 5, 00161; 06 852 721; www.italy.embassy.gov.au
British Embassy
Via XX Settembre 80/a, 00187; 06 4220 0001; www.gov.uk/government/world/italy
Canadian Embassy
Via Zara 30, 00198; 06 8544 3937
Irish Embassy
Via Giacomo Medici, 00153; 06 585 2381; www.ambasciata-irlanda.it
New Zealand Embassy
Via Clitunno 44, 00198; 06 853 7501
US Embassy
Via Vittorio Veneto 119a, 00187; 06 46741; http://italy.usembassy.gov

Travel safety advice
Australia
Department of Foreign Affairs and Trade
www.dfat.gov.au
www.smartraveller.gov.au
UK
Foreign and Commonwealth Office
www.gov.uk/foreign-travel-advice
US
Department of State
www.travel.state.gov

Emergency numbers
Carabinieri 112
Fire Brigade 117
Medical Emergency 118
Polizia di Stato 113
Roadside Assistance 116

Health
Guardia Medica Turistica
Via Canova 19, 00186 (centro storico)
Via Morosini, 00153 (Trastevere)
Ospedale Pediatrico
Bambino Gesù
www.ospedalebambinogesu.it
UK Department of Health
www.dh.gov.uk

Visitor information
www.060608.it

Money
Cooperative Bank
www.co-operativebank.co.uk
Thomas Cook
www.thomascook.com
Travelex
www.travelex.com/GlobalWebsiteSelection

Communications
3 www.tre.it
TIM www.tim.it/home
Vodafone www.vodafone.it
Wind www.wind.it/it/privati

Lost cards (free calls)
800 819 014
800 870 866
800 874 333

Where to Stay

Rome offers memorable places to stay for all budgets – from opulent grand hotels and minimalist boutique hotels to friendly B&Bs and homely apartments in vibrant neighbourhoods. Self-catering apartments are another practical option for families. Many hotels have roof terraces or balconies where kids and adults can enjoy a reprieve from the crowded streets below. The listings (see pp242–51) are by area, following those in the guide's sightseeing section.

Where to look

Wonderful as it is to stay in the centro storico – especially around Campo de' Fiori (see pp130–31) and Piazza Navona (see pp116–17) – it is not only expensive, but also the most touristy part of the city. Families with young children may find it more relaxing – and, of course, economical – to stay in a more residential area of the city, where parks, playgrounds, everyday cafés and local markets give plenty of opportunities for downtime.

The charming, tangled streets of Trastevere (see pp184–5) are well worth considering, although the area does attract a noisy night-time crowd. Look for a hotel or B&B in a quiet alleyway, or in the more secluded area around Villa Sciarra (see p194). The Jewish Ghetto (see pp134–5) and Monti are both delightful places to stay – authentic neighbourhoods just off the beaten track – and located within walking distance of most sights. Those on a budget will find several B&B options around the Vatican (see pp202–3) and there are also several good-value places to stay around MAXXI (see pp222–3).

Hotels

Italian hotels are given an official rating from one to five stars based on an easily quantifiable checklist of facilities, such as the number of rooms with en-suite bathrooms. The stars are not a rating for standards of service or cleanliness, so they are no guide to the subtler attributes of a hotel, such as the style of decor or the friendliness of staff. When searching for a hotel, it is wise to ignore star ratings and to look instead at the style of a hotel, the level of its service and the prices of rooms. Rates that fluctuate according to demand, rather than season, are becoming increasingly common. The Italian flair for lifestyle, food, contemporary design and hospitality has resulted in some marvellous boutique hotels and B&Bs – several of which welcome families with children.

B&Bs

Ever since a law was passed a decade ago allowing ordinary people to offer bed and breakfast in their homes, literally hundreds of B&Bs have opened in Rome. The nicest offer excellent value for money as well as the opportunity to experience Italian hospitality at its best. Some of the more charming B&Bs serve fantastic breakfasts, with home-made jams and cakes, fresh

Below left Pleasant outdoor seating area at Buonanotte Garibaldi
Below right Charming poolside dining area, Radisson Blu

cornetti (croissants) and fruit. Other B&Bs do not have any staff on the premises – not necessarily a disadvantage, as families can end up with an entire two- or three-bed B&B to themselves.

If you are looking for a B&B on the Internet, be sure to ask how to contact the owner should the need arise, if breakfast is served in the B&B or at a local café, and if there is a kitchen for use – an excellent arrangement for those travelling with children.

Apartments

There are apartments of all kinds available for short stays in Rome, ranging from the simple and functional to the elaborate and stylish. When choosing an apartment, check whether electricity and gas are included, and whether there is free Wi-Fi.

Facilities and prices

Double rooms in Italian hotels usually have a *matrimoniale* (double bed), so if you prefer *due letti* (twin beds) ask when you book. Check in advance if a *culla* (cot) and *lettino* (extra bed) can be added. Bathrooms usually have showers, not baths. Many B&Bs have rooms without an en-suite bathroom, but usually there will be a bathroom across the corridor for your sole use. Rates in hotels are generally quoted per room; and in B&Bs, per person.

Discounts and hidden costs

Hotel and hotel-booking websites often offer huge discounts on standard rates and it is common for prices to be adjusted according to demand. Before booking, check prices at various kinds of accommodation. It is also well worth bargaining – families may be able to get extra beds in a room for free, an extra room at a discount or even free meals for kids. Some hotels still charge for Wi-Fi, and calling from the hotel room is expensive. Most B&Bs do not have phones for guest use, although some offer a rechargeable SIM card to their guests.

Most places include breakfast in the price, but check what the breakfast consists of before deciding whether to take the option or not. A breakfast of long-life croissants and packets of jam is best avoided. Instead head for the local café-bar for fresh *cornetti* (croissants) and a cappuccino or, for kids, a *latte caldo* (see p31).

The Lowdown

Hotel and B&B booking services
www.bbplanet.it
www.booking.com
www.enjoyrome.com
www.italybyitaly.it
www.tripadvisor.com
www.venere.it

Apartments
www.airbnb.it
www.at-home-italy.com
www.cross-pollinate.com
www.go2rome.com
www.niceflatinrome.com

Boutique hotels
www.i-escape.com

Travel and accommodation broker site
www.kayak.com

Booking

Book well in advance if you are travelling in peak season. Online reservations can often be made although not all websites belonging to individual hotels are secure, and it is unwise to email credit card details to a hotel. It is best to make bookings over the phone or by using a hotel- and B&B-broking organization with a secure site.

Below left *Attractive façade of Hotel Locarno*
Below right *Tastefully decorated room in Hotel Celio*

Where to Eat

Going out to eat with children is very much the norm in Italy, and Rome is no exception. The culture of eating with the family is just as important as exposing children to good food. Most city restaurants welcome kids. It is accepted practice for toddlers to share their parents' food and for older children to be given half-portions. There are no kids' menus. Prices given in this guide allow for a two-course lunch for a family of four (two adults and two children) without wine.

Practical information

Traditional Italian meals consist of an *antipasto* (starter), *primo* (pasta, risotto or soup), *secondo* (meat or fish), *contorno* (vegetable) and *dolce* (dessert) if you want something sweet to finish with.

Lunch is generally eaten between noon and 3pm. Restaurants are usually open for dinner between 7pm and midnight, but few Italians will eat before 8:30pm. Most eateries close one day a week, although in the *centro storico* many stay open seven days. In many restaurants a cover charge will be added to the bill and, in some, a service charge will be included too. Where it is not, it is common to leave a small tip, which is usually up to 10 per cent.

Set menus offer great value for families, and several are recommended in this book; some places have a series of formulas, allowing you to choose which and how many courses you want. Most menus will include water, and some will include wine, coffee and a cover charge – check carefully for hidden extras before ordering.

Types of restaurant

The once specific terms for different types of eateries have become blurred. A *ristorante* used to be a refined establishment of fine dining, but can equally apply to a joint round the back of Termini station dishing out indifferent pasta at inflated prices to unsuspecting tourists. *Trattorie* and *osterie* are pretty much interchangeable, and can either be old-fashioned places serving simple food that haven't changed in years, or terribly chic new establishments wanting to signal that they are re-visiting old culinary traditions. The original meaning of *enoteca* was simply "wine shop". However, these days it is not restricted to shops that only sell wine, but also wine shops that serve a few snacks or meals, and fully fledged restaurants that want people to know they have a serious wine cellar. Once upon a time pizzerias made only pizza, but these days they may well have pasta, meat and fish on the menu as well.

Cafés and bars

The average Italian visits simple café-bars at least twice a day – once for breakfast and again after lunch. These café-bars serve alcohol, soft drinks as well as coffee – most also sell pastries and sandwiches. In the *centro storico* – especially around Piazza Navona (*see pp116–17*), the Pantheon (*see pp122–3*) and Piazza di Spagna (*see pp142–3*) – ordinary

Below left *A variety of pasta dishes* **Below right** *Café on Piazza Navona*

café-bars are almost impossible to find, but there is one on virtually every street corner elsewhere in the city. Most Italians eat or drink standing up at the bar – there is an extra charge for sitting at a table. Find a bar you like close to where you are staying and visit the place regularly to get a feel of your part of the city.

BREAKFAST

A typical bar breakfast comprises a *cornetto* (croissant) filled with *crema* (custard), *cioccolato* (chocolate custard) or Nutella, ricotta or *marmellata* (jam), washed down with a cup of coffee, hot milk or hot chocolate. Look out as well for fried, sugared, doughnut-like pastries and *bignè* (huge, puffy clouds of light pastry filled to bursting with custard or chocolate), most commonly available around the Festa di San Giuseppe (19 March).

HOT CHOCOLATE

The Italian version of hot chocolate is known as *cioccolata calda*. It is dense and intense – more like a pudding than a drink – and most easily eaten with a spoon – a method that may or may not be messier than drinking it. Some children adore it, others find the texture too thick, the flavour too strong, and the fact that it forms a crust as it cools positively disgusting. For such kids, order a *latte caldo con cacao* (hot milk with chocolate powder sprinkled on top and sugar on the side) – which is more like British and North American hot chocolate.

Coffee world

Caffè
A short, strong shot of coffee, which is popularly known as an espresso abroad

Caffè lungo
Slightly longer and weaker than regular caffè – the water is allowed to run through the coffee for a bit longer

Cappuccino
Shot of coffee with hot and frothy milk

Caffè freddo
Cold, sweet coffee

Caffè macchiato
Caffè with a dash of hot milk

Caffè Americano
Caffè with hot water added to approximate American filter coffee

Latte macchiato
Hot milk with a dash of coffee

Caffè latte
Can either be like a cappuccino without foam, or a stronger version of a latte macchiato

Caffè corretto
Caffè with a shot of alcohol – grappa, sambuca and amaretto are common additions

Caffè con panna
Caffè with whipped cream

KIDS' CORNER

Offally rich

Dominated by offal, *cucina romana* is not for the faint-hearted, nor for those watching their waistline or cholesterol levels. Its origins are with the city's poor, who could only afford the bits of meat richer folk did not want. Liver on toast and braised oxtail with celery are some such dishes.

Offal-free Roman specialities

For those who cannot stomach offal, there are still several pretty much ubiquitous *cucina romana* dishes that are likely to appeal: *spaghetti cacio e pepe* – with grated pecorino cheese and freshly ground black pepper *bucatini all'amatriciana* – hollow spaghetti-like pasta with a sauce of bacon and tomato *scottadito* – tiny lamb chops eaten with the fingers.

Tasty phone cables!!
The best kind of suppli *is the* suppli al telefono – *a crumbed, deep-fried ball of risotto that turns into a telephone! When you bite into the ball of melted mozzarella in the middle you can stretch it out with your teeth like an old-fashioned phone cable.*

AMERICAN SPAGHETTI

According to legend, *spaghetti alla carbonara* was invented by American soldiers in Italy during World War II, who added their rations of bacon and dried egg to the local pasta. It has now become a Roman staple, but raw egg yolk replaces the egg powder.

Below *Menu in English outside a restaurant in Rome listing various dishes and drinks on offer*

Picnics

Choosing to have picnic lunches in Rome will not only save money, but also give your family the chance to savour some of the best food the city has to offer. The quality of ham, salami and cheese, even in the more modest corner shops, is acceptable, while the produce on sale in the speciality food shops scales gastronomic heights at prices that are too good to be true. Markets have a selection of fruit, vegetables and salads, and many of the city's bakeries make pizza, besides having a delicious range of breads.

Food to take away

Romans have been eating takeaway food for well over two millennia – ancient Roman apartment blocks did not have kitchens. Rome has numerous takeaway pizzerias that offer *pizze al taglio* (huge rectangular pizzas that are sold by the slice). Try to get them when they are fresh out of the oven. The best Roman pizza is light and crisp with a thin base.

Rosticcerie, which traditionally served spit-roast chicken, and the *tavola calda* ("hot table"), are direct descendants of the ancient Roman *thermopolium* (shops selling ready-to-eat food). Some dole out canteen-like food to tourists and workers; others offer delectable fare that should not be missed. *Friggitorie* devoted to making deep-fried street food such as dough balls; crumbed, deep-fried mozzarella or bechamel; *baccalà* (salt cod) and *supplì* (rice balls with a variety of fillings) are occasionally to be found, although such fried delicacies are often sold at cafés, *tavole calde* and pizzerias too.

Catering for children and special diets

All but the very smartest restaurants will be happy to welcome children, even late into the evening. Kids are often fussed over and special requests, such as heating up baby food and asking for food to share, will usually be catered for. However, highchairs and changing facilities are uncommon outside tourist spots. Although welcome, children will be expected to sit at the table and not to run around, so it is best to warn them in advance.

Pasta al pomodoro (pasta with tomato sauce) is the fail-safe Italian alternative to a children's menu, which rarely exists, but *carbonara* (bacon and egg), *amatriciana* (bacon and tomato) and pesto are just some of the other child-friendly sauces. Those with an aversion to tomato can choose rice or pasta *in bianco* (white), which comes plain with grated cheese, or *pizza bianca*.

Food allergies other than gluten intolerance *(celiachia)* are less readily understood, so be prepared with the right vocabulary to explain. Download a free translation card from *www.celiactravel.com/cards* or *www.tinyurl.com/pfnk4jz*.

Sandwiches and panini

Tramezzini (triangles of white bread with fillings) are rarely very tasty, but a simple *tost* (toasted white bread with ham and cheese) can be delicious. Many cafés have a good range of panini, in a variety of breads, that can be served as they are, or toasted on a grill. Good combinations are grilled aubergine and mozzarella, basil and tomato, and a chicken *cotoletta* (cutlet) with iceberg lettuce. A *pizza bianca*, split open and filled, is another tasty option.

Vegetarian

There are few strictly vegetarian restaurants, although Italian cuisine includes many meat-free dishes. The concept of vegetarian food is more widely understood now, although those of a nervous

Below left *Slices of pizzas to take away make for an easy lunch*
Below right *Sandwiches and focacce in a traditional bakery in Rome*

disposition may wish to check that there are no *brodo di carne* (broth), *pancetta* (bacon) or other meat products used in a dish before ordering. Vegan requirements may not be understood, so be ready to explain carefully what you cannot eat – check using an online translator.

Ethnic food

Rome is far from being a multi-ethnic city by American or Northern European standards, although it is becoming increasingly diverse racially. Ethiopian, Eritrean, North African, Brazilian and Indian restaurants and shops cater to the city's immigrant communities, while the presence of new Japanese and Southeast Asian restaurants reflects the contemporary trend.

Sweet treats and ice cream

Pasticcerie (pastry shops) are sometimes attached to cafés and they sell a mixture of cakes and biscuits. Bakeries (*panetterie*) are also a good source of ready-to-eat treats – many of them sell pizza and biscuits as well as freshly baked bread. There are *gelaterie* (ice-cream parlours) everywhere, but ice

cream is not excellent universally and sometimes is artificially flavoured and coloured. Even ice cream which is advertised as *produzione artigianale* (hand-crafted) and *produzione propria* (home-made) can often be found to be simply ice cream made in a machine on the premises using factory-made pastes and powders.

However, there are a host of fabulous ice-cream shops around town, from Giolitti, which started in 1900, to others such as San Crispino and Grom. These companies have revolutionized the world of ice cream. They only use natural and/or organic produce, which change according to the seasons.

The aperitivo

A fixed-price apéritif, served with abundant snacks – or with free access to a buffet – is becoming increasingly popular. It is often advertised as another Happy Hour option, and can be an excellent way to relax in the early evening, when children are peckish and parents, too, are in need of a drink. Some of the more chic bars are adults-only.

The most family-friendly places are those opening onto a pedestrianized piazza, so that children can run around and play while parents unwind.

Below left Buy picnic lunches from markets and delicatessens
Below right Various flavours of organic gelati on display

Shopping

In Rome, haute couture and chic boutiques rub shoulders with artisans' ateliers and small neighbourhood stores that appeal to both children and adults. The city's many toyshops and bookshops, clothing boutiques and large emporia are fun to explore, and crafts workshops add local colour. The centre also offers plenty of window-shopping, while the surrounding neighbourhoods are great for unusual bargains for those travelling on a budget.

Opening hours

Traditionally shops open from around 8:30am to 7pm but close for at least two hours at lunchtime as well as all day on Sundays and on Monday mornings. However, this no longer holds true in central Rome and other areas popular with visitors, where some shops now observe the so-called *orario continuato* (nonstop opening hours) – roughly 9:30am to 8pm with no lunch break – and are possibly open Sundays and Mondays too. However, some shops may close for a part, or all, of August.

What to buy

Rome has enough designer clothes shops to satisfy fashionistas, and shoe fetishists will not be disappointed either. **Artemide** lamps, funky **Alessi** kitchen utensils and **Bialetti** stove-top espresso machines make great souvenirs, but are not necessarily cheap in Rome. For more local flavour, look out for antique prints and books, hand-painted Italian ceramics or colourful cotton tablecloths and bedlinen. Kids may enjoy browsing wooden Pinocchio dolls, illustrated children's books, ballerina shoes and dresses. Romans love to dress their children elegantly and there are outfits to make any little princess swoon.

Since food in Italy is practically a religion, be sure to visit a delicatessen such as **Eataly**, to stock up on preserves, jams, olive oil, pesto, cheese and pasta.

Where to shop

Much of the *centro storico* is pedestrianized, making shopping a relatively relaxed activity, even with small children – a visit to a fashion shop can be followed by a *gelato* or a shoe-shopping spree can end with a run around a piazza. The city's main shopping street is Via del Corso, which has most of the national and international chains, and all kinds of gadgets and accessories. The backstreets such as Via Condotti (*see p142*) are far more boutiquey and pricey. Via di Campo Marzio, off Via del Corso, is lined with small boutiques selling pretty stationery, colourful shoes and fancy dresses.

Piazza Navona (*see pp116–17*) is good for antiques and vintage clothes, and also houses a few ateliers. Rome's younger crowd shops for clothing and accessories on the other side of Corso Vittorio and around Campo de' Fiori (*see pp130–31*).

Monti (*see p90*) and Trastevere (*see pp184–5*) offer a mix of young designers' boutiques, vintage and leather stores and artisans'

Below left Pinocchio dolls for sale in Trastevere
Below right Shoppers on Via del Corso, the city's main shopping street

Size Chart

Women's Clothes			Women's Shoes			Men's Shirts			Men's Shoes			Children's Clothes			Children's Shoes		
Italian	British	US	Italian	British	US	Italian (cm)	British (in)	US (in)	Italian	British	US	Italian (years)	British (years)	US (size)	Italian	British	US
38	8	6	36	3	5	36	14	14	39	6	7	2–3	2–3	2–3	24	7	7½
40	10	8	37	4	6	38	15	15	40	7	7½	4–5	4–5	4–5	25½	8	8½
42	12	10	38	5	7	39	15½	15½	41	7½	8	6–7	6–7	6–6x	27	9	9½
44	14	12	39	6	8	41	16	16	42	8	8½	8–9	8–9	7–8	28	10	10½
46	16	14	40	7	9	42	16½	16½	43	9	9½	10–11	10–11	10	29	11	11½
48	18	16	41	8	10	43	17	17	44	10	10½	12	12	12	30	12	12½
50	20	18				44	17½	17½	45	11	11	14	14	14	32	13	13½
						45	18	18	46	12	11½	14+	14+	16	33	1	1½
															34	2	2½

botteghe (workshops) in a relaxed atmosphere. Most of the shops here are small and unique but relatively expensive. Popular with teenagers for mainstream fashion is busy Via Cola di Rienzo, near the Vatican, which is lined with boutiques and retail chains.

Markets

Rome has around a hundred neighbourhood markets selling food, clothes and household goods. A trip to a local market can be a fun way to see and be a part of daily life in Rome, as well as to buy provisions for picnics. The most famous markets in Rome are Campo de' Fiori, with its spice and flower stalls; Piazza San Cosimato in Trastevere, rich with local colour; and the multi-ethnic Nuovo Mercato Esquilino (*see pp90–91*), near Termini station. The markets are open from Monday to Saturday in the mornings from around 7am to 1pm.

Head to Piazzale di Porta Portese in Trastevere on Sunday mornings for Rome's most famous flea market. On sale is everything from second-hand clothes, antiques, plants and ceramics to car parts. However, look out for pickpockets and keep the kids close to you at all times, as the market gets very crowded and it is easy to get lost. Around Christmas, visit the Piazza Navona Christmas market, packed with tree decorations, animals and figurines for Nativity scenes, and a myriad gift ideas.

Department stores

There are several department and chain stores in Rome. The most affordable and popular are **Upim** and **Oviesse**, which sell their own lines of children's and adults' clothes, as well as cosmetics and household goods. Upmarket department stores include **La Rinascente**, which sells designer brands, and **Coin**, which is less glitzy but strong on stylish wear. Or drop in at **Davide Cenci**, an upmarket store for men's clothes.

Below left *Davide Cenci, popular for men's clothes*
Below right *A flower stall in Campo de' Fiori*

Supermarkets

Rome has several supermarkets and finding one is never a problem. The biggest chains are **Conad**, **Sigma** and **Carrefour**, while popular discount supermarkets are **Lidl**, **Todis** and **Tuodì**. Most supermarkets stay open all day until 8:30pm, and many open on Sundays.

For a more personal experience, enter an *alimentari*, which may have a better selection of cheese, ham and salami, but at higher prices. A shopkeeper will serve you, so you may need to be able to explain what you want in Italian, with hand gestures.

Kids may enjoy spotting the differences between foodstuffs in Rome and back home. See how many varieties of pasta you can spot together. When picking up snacks, look out for the favourites of Italian children – *pizza bianca* (pizza without the tomato topping), mild cheeses such as mozzarella or parmesan, *frollini* (biscuits) or *merendine* (individually wrapped mini cakes).

Kids' clothes and shoes

The best-known chain stores for kids are the all-Italian baby gear brand **Prenatal**, and **Chicco**, and the French **Du Pareil Au Même** (DPAM) and **Z**, with their affordable collections for 0- to 14-year-olds. The streets around Via Condotti and the Pantheon offer quite a few options for more stylish kids' clothes.

Natinudi imports the most colourful and creative clothes from the world over; **Tipimini** sells original and alternative garments for little girls; and the French chain **Petit Bateau** sells high-quality clothes, often with stripes or navy themes.

Children's shoe shops are just about everywhere, but, if looking for bargains, head to outlets such as **A Piccoli Passi** that sell the previous season's stock for less. For something a bit more down-to-earth, drop by the international chains on Via del Corso.

Toys

The most famous toyshop in town is **Al Sogno** in Piazza Navona, which sells everything from Barbie dolls to teddy bears the size of real bears. For educational, natural toys, visit Città del Sole *(see p123)*, which has several branches around town and stocks a good range of imported toys. Spanish chain **Imaginarium** specializes in original toys for kids of all ages, including kids' cameras, dolls' houses, puppets and baby gear. **La Giraffa** and **Toys Center** have branches within and beyond the city walls.

Books and DVDs

Little bookworms will not face any problems finding a new picture or book to devour – **Feltrinelli**, a multi-language bookshop, has a large children's section. The English-language **Almost Corner Bookshop** in Trastevere is cosy and intimate, while **Giunti Kids** is a gorgeous children's bookshop, with mainly Italian books, but there is a small selection of books in English and lots of picture books. The shop occasionally even stages small performances.

DVDs can be bought at most bookstores and newsstands – just make sure that English is among the language choices. For music CDs, head to **Discoteca Laziale** on Via Mamiani, right by Termini Station.

Arts and crafts

Get the kids to capture Rome's beauty. Stock up on pencils and sketchbooks at **SEC Cartolerie Internazionali**, a well-stocked stationery shop near Torre Argentina. If looking for more professional art equipment, visit Poggi *(see p123)* and Vertecchi *(see p143)*. For inspiration visit the small *botteghe* in Trastevere and watch craftsmen make leather goods, globes and wooden toys.

Below left Traditional souvenirs on display outside a shop
Centre Toys on display in a shop in Rome

Souvenirs

Whether or not you are religious, window-shopping for religious souvenirs can be a fun activity for the whole family. Church candles and religious icons can be found at one of the many Christian goods stores in the Borgo Pio area in the Vatican City, or on Via di Santa Chiara near the Pantheon. For a world of potions, syrups and soaps made by monks around Italy, visit I Monasteri, near Piazza Navona.

Classic souvenirs, such as plaster reproductions of the Colosseum, miniature churches or icons of the pope, can be found around most tourist sites, either from street vendors or shops. Stop by Too Much for fun T-shirts, action figures of the pope, and other quirky souvenirs.

Returns and tax refunds

Roman shop assistants are not always eager to help, so be prepared to be assertive. Some of the smaller shops may not let you try on clothes or return them, either. Kids are welcome in most shops, as long as they are well behaved. As a general rule, it is not possible to get a refund on purchases even if they are faulty, although it may be possible to exchange them – be sure to keep the receipt as proof of purchase.

The Lowdown

What to buy
Alessi www.alessi.it
Artemide www.artemide.com
Bialetti www.bialetti.com
Eataly www.roma.eataly.it

Department stores
Coin www.coin.it
Davide Cenci www.davidecenci.com
Oviesse www.ovs.it
La Rinascente www.rinascente.it
Upim www.upim.it

Supermarkets
Carrefour www.carrefour.it
Conad www.conad.it
Lidl www.lidl.it
Sigma www.supersigma.it
Todis www.todis.it
Tuodì www.tuodi.it

Kids' clothes and shoes
Chicco www.chicco.com
Natinudi www.natinudi.it
Du Pareil Au Même www.dpam.it
Petit Bateau www.petit-bateau.it
A Piccoli Passi Piazza di San Cosimato 14, 00153; 06 6456 2264

Prenatal www.prenatal.it
Tipimini Via del Pellegrino 89, 00186
Z www.generation.z-enfant.com/it

Toys
La Giraffa www.lagiraffagiocattoli.it
Imaginarium www.imaginarium.it
Al Sogno www.alsogno.com
Toys Center www.toyscenter.it

Books and DVDs
Almost Corner Bookshop Via del Moro 45, 00153; 06 583 6942
Discoteca Laziale www.discotecalaziale.com
Feltrinelli www.lafeltrinelli.it
Giunti Kids www.giunti.it

Arts and crafts
SEC Cartolerie Internazionali Via Arenula 85, 00186

Souvenirs
I Monasteri www.aimonasteri.it
Too Much www.toomuch.it

Returns and tax refunds
Mediaworld www.mediaworld.it
Trony www.trony.it

Electronic goods sold by large chains such as **Trony** or **Mediaworld** are an exception.

Debit cards and credit cards are accepted in all major stores, but are not always welcome in small shops.

Non-EU residents can get a rebate on sales tax (IVA) paid on items over €155. Ask for a receipt at the time of purchase, and allow goods to be checked at the airport and have the receipt stamped when you depart.

Below right Books for sale in the Feltrinelli bookshop

Entertainment

Public entertainment was essential to everyday life in ancient Rome, and the Colosseum was at the heart of all public events. Today, gorgeous ruins, lush parks, Baroque cloisters and ultra-modern concert halls across the city provide a stunning backdrop for performances. Football is an obsession as well, with the two home teams playing every week at the Olympic Stadium. Summer is the best time to enjoy the Roman night, with events for all ages and tastes.

Practical information

The official Visitor Information (see p27) service of Rome provides up-to-date information on what is on, as well as a ticket-booking service. Daily newspapers *Il Messaggero* and *La Repubblica* list the evening's entertainment, and *La Repubblica's* Thursday supplement *TrovaRoma* provides a day-by-day rundown on events. *Where Rome*, a monthly magazine, includes in-depth listings. English-language online magazine *Wanted in Rome* is another source of information. Tickets to major events can be bought online and by phone from **TicketOne** or **Listicket**.

Music, opera and dance

The Auditorium Parco della Musica (see p224) is home to both the Accademia di Santa Cecilia, the city's top classical music foundation, and the Musica per Roma foundation, which hosts rock and pop concerts most nights. The auditorium also organizes regular children's and family concerts, a circus festival, a dance festival, electronic music nights and art exhibitions. Churches in Rome frequently play host to classical concerts, while the **Teatro Olimpico** is the main venue for contemporary and modern dance.

Opera lovers should try to catch a summer performance at the **Teatro dell'Opera**, when the theatre moves outdoors to the magnificent Baths of Caracalla (see p230). Rome also enjoys an active jazz scene and, in summer, the city's parks transform into buoyant venues where it is easy to bring kids. Villa Ada presents **Rome Meets the World** – a renowned world music festival. The **Casa del Jazz** (see p15), a gorgeous villa with a garden overlooking the city walls, also offers a lively jazz and blues programme. Major rock concerts take place in July as part of the **Rock in Roma** festival, in the large arena of the Capannelle Hippodrome on Via Appia Nuova.

Theatre, puppets, the circus and movies

Rome's many theatres mainly stage performances in Italian and rarely put on shows for children. An exception is the **Teatro Vascello**, which has a dedicated programme for primary-school-age kids, but shows are mainly in Italian. Another venue is the **Teatro Palladium**, which puts on a range of contemporary shows and is home to the RomaEuropa festival (see p16).

Below Ice-skating rink at the Auditorium Parco della Musica

Puppetry comes alive in the Teatro di San Carlino (see p168) in Villa Borghese and in the Teatrino di Pulcinella on the Janiculum Hill (see pp190–91), with daily shows.

Look for "V.O." next to film names in listings to avoid getting a dubbed version. Kids can enjoy cartoon screenings at the Cinema dei Piccoli (see p168), Rome's only children's cinema. Nearby is the Globe Theatre (see p168), built in 2003, which stages plays by Shakespeare and other Elizabethan dramatists, in Italian.

Spectator sports

Football (calcio) is Rome's most popular spectator sport, and the **Stadio Olimpico** is home to both the local clubs, **AS Roma** and **SS Lazio**. Matches take place between September and May, normally on Sundays, and tickets can be bought at one of the AS Roma or SS Lazio shops. The local derby is probably best avoided due to potential trouble between fans. The **Italian Tennis Open** is held in late April– May at the Foro Italico (see p224), and tickets can be bought online.

The **International Horse Show** attracts crowds at the end of May and ends with a re-enactment of the 1848 Pastrengo charge (see p15).

The Lowdown

Practical information
Listicket
www.listicket.it
Il Messaggero
www.ilmessaggero.eu
La Repubblica
www.repubblica.it
TicketOne
www.ticketone.it
Wanted in Rome
www.wantedinrome.com
Where Rome
www.whererome.it

Music, opera and dance
Casa del Jazz
www.casajazz.it
Rock in Roma
www.rockinroma.com
Rome Meets the World
www.villaada.org
Teatro dell'Opera
www.operaroma.it
Teatro Olimpico
www.teatroolimpico.it

Theatre, puppets, the circus and movies
Teatro Palladium
www.teatropalladium.uniroma3.it
Teatro Vascello
www.teatrovascello.it

Spectator sports
AS Roma
www.asroma.it
International Horse Show
www.piazzadisiena.org
Italian Tennis Open
www.internazionalibnlditalia.it
SS Lazio
www.sslazio.it
Stadio Olimpico
www.stadiumguide.com/olimpico

Amusement parks
Rainbow Magicland
www.magicland.it
Zoomarine
www.zoomarine.it

Amusement parks

The city boasts three good theme parks for families. **Zoomarine** features live dolphin shows, a shark tank and other sea-inspired attractions. **Rainbow Magicland** is an enchanted kingdom populated by fairies, Vikings and warlocks who wander from castle to castle as visitors enjoy rollercoaster rides. On a hot day, head to Hydromania (see p47) for its pools and water slides.

Outdoor activities

Ice-skating is a favourite winter activity in Rome. The most popular temporary ice rink is set up in the amphitheatre of the Auditorium Parco della Musica. Rollerbladers meet every Wednesday night year-round in the Pincio Gardens (see p151) and tour the city in big groups. Viale delle Terme di Caracalla in southern Rome is a popular jogging destination.

Below left Stadio dei Marmi, Foro Italico
Below right Play in progress at Teatro di San Carlino, Villa Borghese

Spot the Architectural Styles

Let children become architectural detectives. It won't be long before they are able to tell the difference between an Ionic and a Corinthian column, spot a bit of Roman brickwork or identify the varieties of precious Roman marbles recycled in the floors of medieval churches. A camera with a zoom is useful for looking at details high up on buildings, while a magnifying glass and torch will make examining Cosmati and mosaic floors in churches more fun.

Roman improvements

The architects and engineers of Imperial Rome combined the Classical styles of Ancient Greece with new forms such as the arch, the dome and the vault – stronger, sturdier and longer-lasting features than the traditional Greek row of columns with a horizontal architrave.

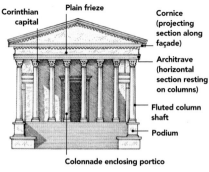

Corinthian capital

Plain frieze

Cornice (projecting section along façade)

Architrave (horizontal section resting on columns)

Fluted column shaft

Podium

Colonnade enclosing portico

Classical Greek Architecture

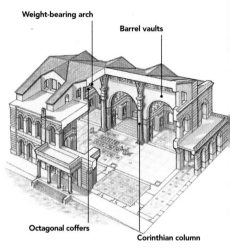

Weight-bearing arch

Barrel vaults

Octagonal coffers

Corinthian column

Reconstruction of the Basilica of Maxentius and Constantine

Roman retro

There were three styles of Classical columns, borrowed from Ancient Greece: Doric, with plain capitals; Ionic, with scrolly capitals, and Corinthian, whose capitals were inspired by the foliage of the acanthus plant.

Acanthus leaves

Doric column

Ionic column

Corinthian column

Roman to Romanesque

The first Christian churches were based on the Roman basilica: oblong, with three naves, each usually ending in an apse. From the 10th to the 13th centuries, most churches were built in the Romanesque style, which used the rounded arches of Ancient Rome. The nave of San Giovanni in Laterano retains its 4th-century floorplan.

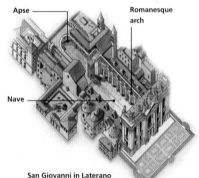

Apse

Romanesque arch

Nave

San Giovanni in Laterano

Renaissance recycling

The architects of the Renaissance (15th–16th centuries) designed buildings using ancient Roman architectural elements.

Classical Roman architecture dictated the use of strict geometrical proportions, which were adopted and further developed during the Renaissance. Columns, pilasters, lintels, semicircular arches and hemispherical domes replaced irregular medieval styles.

Bramante's Tempietto (see p194) is considered one of the best examples of Renaissance architecture.

Classical proportions and Doric columns in Bramante's Tempietto

The bombastic Baroque baldacchino in St Peter's with its twisted columns

Let's do the twist

Baroque archichects enjoyed breaking rules and developing new forms, twisting columns, exaggerating and embellishing elements of Classical architecture and covering everything they could with gold and a sprinkling of cherubs.

Apart from extravagant churches (see pp48–9) and palace interiors, architects revelled in designing fountains, such as Trevi Fountain (see pp154–5), full of sea monsters, ancient gods and exotic animals.

Rock and roll

The area around Rome was created by volcanoes, which last erupted about 40,000 years ago, and much of the stone used to build the city is of volcanic origin. Volcanoes produce many different kinds of rock – some of it light, and full of air bubbles like pumice and tufa, others slick, dense and hard-wearing, such as lava and basalt. Pumice was used in the concrete for the Pantheon (see pp122–3) roof.

Another type of stone, marble was used to build prestigious buildings such as the Colosseum (see pp70–71) and the colonnades of Piazza San Pietro (see p202).

TRAVERTINE
The most typical Roman stone, Travertine is a cream-coloured, pitted limestone, which is still being quarried near Tivoli. It is lighter – and was more plentiful – than marble or granite.

BRICK
The most common building material was clay bricks. Look out for *opus reticulatum* (bricks stacked in a diamond-shaped grid), the most frequently used brick-building style.

CARRARA MARBLE
Italy's finest marble comes from Tuscany and was used in Trajan's Column (see p88).

PENTELIC MARBLE
The Temple of Hercules Victor in Piazza della Bocca della Verità (see pp104–105) was built using this white marble.

COLOURED MARBLE
Elaborate inlaid floors and geometrical designs for church interiors were often made from coloured marble taken from ancient buildings.

Granite A hard pink or grey volcanic rock used for the columns of the Pantheon.

Giallo antico This ancient yellow marble was recovered from older buildings.

Verde antico A green marble that was recycled from ancient buildings and often incorporated into the mosaic-style floors created by the Cosmati family.

Rosso antico This ancient red marble was also used in Cosmatesque floors. It can be seen in the basilica of Santa Maria Maggiore (see pp100–101).

Parks and Playgrounds

Rather than small leafy squares in the centre, Rome has a wealth of spacious parks on its fringes, most of which are descendants of the ribbon of private gardens and estates that circumscribed the city in ancient times. Today these parks offer much-needed respite for families after long days of sightseeing. Kids can enjoy a variety of activities ranging from boating and playing games to watching puppet shows and even skating, while parents watch from under shady trees. As a bonus, many also contain, or are next to, some of Rome's top sights.

Historic green spaces

Extravagant affairs, the gardens belonging to the elite of Imperial Rome were intricately landscaped around statues, fountains and other water features, and had pavilions for elegant alfresco dining and private performances of poetry and plays. Hundreds of years later, the leading aristocratic families of Renaissance Rome followed in the footsteps of the ancient Romans, and created sophisticated gardens and refined villas which they could repair to with their friends on summer evenings to escape the heat of the city centre. Many of these remained in the families until they were bought by the city council and opened to the public in the 20th century. It is still possible to see traces of aristocracy in the landscaping, villas, follies and statues of many of the parks below.

Above Families watching a performance in progress, Bioparco Below Children playing in Villa Borghese

Villa Borghese

Overlooking Piazza del Popolo, Villa Borghese (see pp168–9), with its extension, the Pincio Gardens (see p151), forms central Rome's prime park. Its origins as an aristocratic estate are still evident in its majestic villas, museum collections, ornamental lake and numerous statues.

Today, there are excellent cafés, a replica of the Globe Theatre, an outdoor cinema, a children's activity centre and a zoo, while in summer the park hosts many cultural events. As well as running, walking and playing here, families can rent bikes, including kids' bikes and toddler seats, go-carts, self-drive rickshaws

and roller-skates. It is also possible to go boating on the lake. There is a small funfair with a carousel, a large area of wilderness near Villa Giulia (see pp170–71) and great opportunities for walks and biking at GNAM (see p172).

The Arca della Conservazione, one of the best playgrounds in Rome, is located in the grounds of the Bioparco (see pp176–7). This child-sized wooden ship offers swings, ropes, ladders and climbing frames, tailor-made for imaginative play. Preschool children may enjoy the wooden play equipment at the Casina di Raffaello (see p168), which has an indoor area with books and cushions, and offers activities, workshops and storytelling sessions. The playgrounds of Villa Borghese are used by both visitors and locals, so you might meet kids who speak the same language as yours.

Above *Visitors in a wooded garden, Villa Ada* **Below** *Child sitting on a water-spouting lion, Piazza del Popolo*

Villa Celimontana

Closest to the ancient sites of the centre is the lovely Villa Celimontana *(see p72)*. Located on the Celian Hill, it is an intimate, tree-shaded world away from the busy roads at the foot of the hill. There is a small playground, and plenty of space for games and picnics. Kids can also go for short pony rides as well as enjoy skating on the roller-skating rink.

Gardens of the Aventine

The little public gardens of the Aventine Hill *(see p106)*, Parco Savello, with its lemon and orange trees, and Parco Sant'Alessio, are handy retreats. The parks are good for a picnic or an interlude from sightseeing, although they have no playgrounds, and ball games are not permitted. The Aventine Hill is also home to the city's lovely Roseto Comunale, open only when the roses are in bloom (May–June).

Parco Adriano

At the foot of the Castel Sant'Angelo *(see pp214–15)* is the Parco Adriano. The park has a playground with swings and slides, and offers ice-skating in winter and is the perfect place to let off steam after a visit to St Peter's *(see pp204–5)* and the Vatican Museums *(see pp206–13)*.

Further afield

The best parks for more free-ranging games are all on the outskirts of Rome. In the western suburbs of the city is the enormous Villa Doria Pamphilj *(see p195)*. The playground here is lovely, and the park has a sophisticated bistro to retreat to when adults tire of pushing swings.

To the north is Villa Ada *(see p225)*, which has a cycling path and a mini roller-skating rink as well, although children need to carry their own skates. Near Villa Ada is the **Parco Nemorense** – also known as the Parco Virgiliano – with a play-

house, miniature lake and café. Within the Auditorium Parco della Musica *(see p224)* is a tiny but inventive play area with balancing beams, swinging rings and a series of interconnected slides. It is also possible to ice-skate on a rink here in winter.

There are several country parks on the southern periphery of the city. These include the Parco della Caffarella along the Via Appia Antica *(see pp228–9)*, and the **Parco degli Acquedotti**, which has cycle paths and walking trails.

Piazzas

The small playgrounds in some of Rome's piazzas offer not only a chance for children to let off steam, but also let children and adults alike take part in the everyday life of a typical Roman neighbourhood. Even those without a playground are good for a quick run around between sights. In the Trastevere area, the playground on Piazza San Cosimato is good for taking breaks from sightseeing.

The Lowdown

Parco degli Acquedotti
Via Lemonia, 00174; 24 hrs; www.parcoacquedotti.it; www.tinyurl.com/7rast54 (for brochures)

Parco Nemorense
Via Nemorense (corner with Via Panaro), 00199; sunrise–sunset daily

Underground Rome

Over the past 3,000 years, layers of rubble from buildings destroyed by floods, fires, earthquakes and enemy troops, interspersed with everyday household waste, have buried much of ancient Rome. Excavations – as well as tunnelling for the metro – have helped rediscover many sights that were long lost. Delve into catacombs, find a temple buried under San Clemente, and look out for occasional tours and special openings of Rome's secret underground sites.

Going underground

In 2005, builders working in the basement of Palazzo Valentini (see p88) on Piazza Venezia discovered the remains of two villas that had belonged to wealthy patrician families in ancient times. The villas were not only excavated, but have been reconstructed using 3D projections and digital technology, so that visitors can see virtual re-creations of life in a Roman domus (house). Archaeologists also discovered a rubbish dump on the site, full of broken pots, oyster shells and chicken bones chucked out by a Renaissance kitchen.

Two houses belonging to middle-class Roman families were discovered under the church of SS Giovanni e Paolo (see p72) near the Colosseum. Several frescoes have survived, along with everyday items such as a sewing needle made of bone.

Santa Cecilia was martyred in the baths of her house in Trastevere, and Santa Cecilia in Trastevere (see pp188–9) was built over the site. Santa Cecilia's house, baths and the remains of the medieval tannery that succeeded them can still be visited below the church.

When archaeologists and engineers dug down under Piazza Venezia (see p84) to build a metro station in 2001, they found the ruins of a glass factory and an ancient university. There are plans to construct a station-cum-museum below the piazza.

Drains, water cisterns and toilets

The excavations beneath the Crypta Balbi (see p85) reveal how Rome has used and abused its land over the centuries. It is possible to see a series of ancient Roman drains and water cisterns which were used as cesspits during the Middle Ages; an ancient Roman theatre converted into a public toilet; and a ritual bath from a Mithraeum (Temple of Mithras) that was later used as a trough for animals.

In 2001, a stretch of the Aqua Vergine aqueduct and the ruins of an ancient Roman apartment block were discovered beneath a cinema near the Trevi Fountain. It is now known as La Città dell'Acqua (see p155) and is open to the public.

To see part of ancient Rome's main drain, the Cloaca Maxima (see p79) – a large section of which runs under the Roman Forum – take a guided tour below San Pietro in Carcere at the foot of the Capitoline Hill. In summer it is possible to visit the Cisterna delle Sette Sale (see

Below left A passageway between St Peter's and Castel Sant'Angelo **Centre** Altar of Mithras below San Clemente church
Below right Ruins of the Cisterna delle Sette Sale

p95), which once held 8 million litres (2 million gallons) of water to supply the Baths of Trajan (see pp94–5).

Churches and catacombs

Of Rome's churches, San Clemente (see pp92–3) is one of the most fascinating. The 12th-century church was built over a 4th-century church, which in turn was built over a 1st-century apartment block with a temple to the pagan god Mithras in one of its underground rooms.

Another church known for its subterranean treasures is Santa Maria della Concezione (see p161). The catacombs below the church contain the bones of thousands of dismantled skeletons wired together into various elaborate forms. It is possibly the spookiest sight in Rome!

Spend a day exploring the Via Appia Antica (see pp228–9), along which are several catacombs and tombs. These vast catacombs were hollowed out of the soft tufa beyond the confines of the ancient city to hold the remains of thousands of Christians.

Take a guided tour of the Catacombs of Priscilla (see p225), near Villa Ada. The catacombs here contain the tombs of over 40,000 Christians and the earliest-known image of the Madonna and Child.

Secret passages

Rome has its fair share of secret passageways, which were put to an array of uses. Emperor Nero had a cryptoporticus (secret passage) built to link his palace on the Palatine Hill (see pp74–5) with the Domus Aurea (see p94). Emperor Hadrian also had a cryptoporticus constructed at the Villa Adriana (see pp238–9), so that the noisy delivery carts could go by without disturbing the peace.

Guided tours take visitors underneath the Colosseum to see the ingenious system of lifts, pulleys and trapdoors that were used to raise wild animals to the surface of the arena during the bloody games. In summer, it is possible to visit the secret passageway from the Vatican to the Castel Sant'Angelo (see pp214–15), used by popes to escape in times of political unrest.

Exploring underground Rome

Walking-tour specialist **Context** runs an Underground Rome for Families walk (€330 for up to six people; book in advance), which brings Roman history to life by exploring it layer by layer. The interactive tours visit multi-layered San Clemente and the Case Romane under SS Giovanni e Paolo. **Rome Tour for Families** offers an Underground Rome tour (€320 for a 4-hour tour for four people; excluding entrance fees), with an emphasis on investigating Rome's transition from a pagan to a Christian city.

Roma Sotterranea specializes in tours of underground places that cannot normally be visited, including the aqueducts, the Cloaca Maxima and the underground tunnels of Villa Ada. The **Comune di Roma** has published a leaflet available online, Roma Segreta, listing underground sights that can be visited, while the organization **Sotterranei di Roma** has an app downloadable from its website with a guide to underground chambers, and sometimes runs tours.

The Lowdown

Exploring underground Rome

Comune di Roma
Roma Segreta www.tinyurl.com/27rh8jz

Context
www.contexttravel.com

Roma Sotterranea
www.romasotterranea.it

Rome Tour for Families
www.rometourforfamilies.com

Sotterranei di Roma
www.sotterraneidiroma.it

Below left Stuccowork on an underground gallery, Palatine Hill
Below right A macabre shrine in Santa Maria della Concezione church

Aquatic Rome

By the 4th century BC, the waters of the Tiber were too polluted to drink, and aqueducts were built to bring supplies of fresh water to feed the city's fountains, from where citizens would get their daily supply of water. Fountain building was revived in the Renaissance and reached its height in the 17th century, when architects such as Bernini created exuberant centrepieces for the city's piazzas. Until fairly recently fountains were used for cooling off in summer, but these days full immersion is only permitted in the nearby sea and lakes.

Aqueducts

In 312 BC, Rome's first aqueduct, the Aqua Appia, was built to bring in water daily from a spring around 16 km (10 miles) away from the city. The Aqua Appia, like most aqueducts, was built underground to protect it from attack, but later aqueducts, such as the Aqua Claudia, were magnificent structures with the water being carried along dramatic multiple-arched bridges that sliced across the Roman countryside. The points where the aqueducts entered the city were marked with monumental fountain . or *mostre*.

The most impressive surviving Roman aqueduct in the city centre is the Aqua Claudia. A series of tall brick arcades survives on the Celian Hill (*see p72*), behind the church of Santo Stefano Rotondo. But to see the best of Rome's aqueducts, head to the Parco degli Acquedotti (*see p43*), where visitors can cycle, walk, picnic or take a guided tour among the dramatic remains of several ancient Roman aqueducts.

Above *The ruins of an aqueduct in the Parco degli Acquedotti*

Baths and toilets

With nine aqueducts bringing in a regular supply of water, the Romans built elaborate bath complexes and several public toilets. The best preserved among these is the Baths of Caracalla (*see p230*), while the most impressive ancient Roman public toilet is accessible via the Crypta Balbi (*see p85*). Some bath complexes, such as the Baths of Diocletian (*see p99*), have been converted into museums.

Fountains

One of the first actions of the Goths when they attacked Rome in AD 410 was to destroy the aqueducts. Rome floundered without a supply of fresh water, and life in the medieval city had none of the sophistication that had become the norm during the years of the Roman Empire. Finally, in the 15th century, Pope Nicholas V decided that something had to be done to make Rome a suitable capital for the Christian world. One of his first actions was to rebuild the ruined Aqua Vergine. He also decided to mark the arrival point of the aqueduct in the city with a *mostra*, just as the Romans had done. Other *mostre* include the Trevi Fountain (*see pp154–5*), the Fontana dell'Acqua Paola (*see p194*) on the Janiculum Hill and Acqua Felice on Via XX Settembre. However, people needed fresh

water closer to their homes, and over the centuries virtually every piazza in Rome was given a fountain. While some were magnificent creations by the most talented artists and architects of the era, others were basic fountains used by the people of Rome for their daily needs.

Unlike olden times, today, chemicals are added to the water in monumental fountains to help keep them clean and preserve the stone. But the city still has 2,500 drinking fountains or *nasoni* and several that were designed for animals – such as the drinking troughs for horses on Campo de' Fiori (*see pp130–31*) and Largo di Torre Argentina.

Fun in the water

These days, those who want to splash around in water need to head to the sea, to a lake or to a

Above Tritons and sea horses at the magnificent Trevi Fountain **Left** Fontana della Barcaccia, Piazza di Spagna **Bottom left** Fontana del Tritone, Piazza Barberini

swimming pool. Most swimming pools in Rome are operated as private clubs, but one can also take a dip in the Piscina delle Rose at EUR *(see p230)*.

Around 30 km (18 miles) north of Rome is Lake Bracciano *(see p241)*. It has good beaches for swimming and paddling at the Lungolago Argenti below Bracciano town and between the villages of Trevignano and Anguillara. It is also possible to swim in the lakes of the Castelli Romani *(see pp240–41)*.

There are plenty of places near Rome for a day at the beach – the Roman coast suits all budgets and preferences. Catch a train from Stazione Centrale Roma Termini to Santa Marinella, where there is a crescent of lovely, clean sand 10 minutes' walk from the train station. Alternatively, drive down to one of the Blue Flag beaches in Lazio such as Anzio, Sperlonga, Sabaudia and San Felice Circeo. For a fun-filled day, head to the **Hydromania** theme park, connected by free shuttle buses from near Stazione Centrale Roma Termini and Cinecittà.

It is also normally possible to go for boat rides on the Tiber, but heavy rains in recent years have caused serious damage and the service has been temporarily discontinued. Thanks to the several sections of rapids in the river as it flows through

Rome, the kayaking races organized every year tend to be dramatic and exciting. Dragon boat racing is popular as well, with events being held on the Tiber, at the Laghetto in EUR and on Lake Bracciano.

The Lowdown

Rome's best fountains
Fontana Barberini
Piazza Barberini, 00197
Fontana della Barcaccia
(see p142)
Fontana Farnese
Piazza Farnese, 00186
Fontana dei Quattro Fiumi
(see p116)
Fontana delle Tartarughe
(see p135)
Fontana del Tritone
(see p160)
Trevi Fountain
(see pp154–5)
Visit *www.colosseo.org/nasoni/ inasonidiroma.asp* to see a map of Rome's *nasoni* and, to find out more about fountains and how they work, visit *www.fountainsinthecity.com/ learn/history.html*

Fun in the water
Boat trips
www.battellidiroma.com
Dragon Boat events
www.dragonboat.it
Hydromania
open mid-May–mid-Sep;
www.hydromania.it
Kayak events
www.ficlazio.it

Rome's Churches

Although the idea of going to church may elicit groans from most kids, Rome's churches are treasure troves of art and sculpture. Hunting for a painting or statue by a famous artist, switching the lights on in a gloomy niche to reveal a brilliantly hued mosaic, or searching for skeletons and other symbols on elaborate tombs can be a lot of fun – and a far more intimate experience than visiting a large museum.

Ancient temples

One pagan temple survives virtually unaltered since it was erected in the 2nd century AD. The Pantheon (see pp122–3), "Temple of all the Gods", has a domed interior based on a perfect sphere said to have been designed by Emperor Hadrian after contemplating a pumpkin. It was reconsecrated as a Christian church in the 7th century. Other Roman temples have been incorporated into Christian churches at various times. The most interesting of these is Santi Cosma e Damiano, which was created inside the Temple of Romulus in AD 526, although children may find its huge 18th-century Nativity scene of most interest. The Baroque façade, built in 1602, looms behind the columns of the temple. Another church that clearly shows its ancient Roman origins is Santa Costanza, built as a mausoleum for Constantine's daughter. It is a round church with some splendid 4th-century mosaics.

Early Christian and medieval churches

Many of Rome's churches date back to the days when Christianity was a minority sect and Christian worship banned. Several began life as private houses where Christians would worship in secret, and which became places of pilgrimage after a member of the community was killed for their beliefs.

Below Santa Cecilia in Trastevere (see pp188–9) are the baths that belong to the house in which the saint was martyred, while the Case Romane, below the church of SS Giovani e Paolo (see p72), contains frescoed rooms and a small museum containing everyday objects discovered on the site. St Peter's (see pp204–5) grew up on the site where the saint was buried – the ancient cemetery can still be visited below the present basilica.

Renaissance

By the Renaissance, the papacy had become one of the key players in European politics, and churches were created to be elaborate temples to power and wealth.

The greatest undertaking of the Renaissance popes was the rebuilding of St Peter's. Disagreements on the form it should take meant that, although work started in 1506, it was not completed until well into the 17th century. Fortunately, this did not prevent the building of the great dome designed by Michelangelo. As well as working

Below left Impressive interior of the Pantheon, which became a church in AD 609
Below right Elegant façade of Santa Cecilia in Trastevere

on St Peter's, Michelangelo also provided the Sistine Chapel with its magnificent frescoes. On a completely different scale, another key work of Renaissance architecture is Bramante's tiny Tempietto (*see p194*), on the Janiculum Hill.

The church of Santa Maria della Pace (*see pp120–21*), on the other hand, was treated as a place to see and be seen, where the wealthy of Rome would gather in their finery and where beautiful women would come to Mass in search of a rich husband or boyfriend. Santa Maria della Pace has a cloister by Bramante, some frescoes by Raphael and a charming portico by Pietro da Cortona. Also of interest is Michelangelo's imaginative use of the great vaults of the Roman Baths of Diocletian in the church of Santa Maria degli Angeli.

There are other churches worth visiting for the sake of their impressive paintings and sculptures. Santa Maria del Popolo (*see pp148–9*), for example, has two great paintings by Caravaggio, the esoteric Chigi Chapel designed by Raphael, and a series of 15th-century frescoes by Pinturicchio. San Pietro in Vincoli (*see p96*), besides having the chains with which St Peter was bound in prison, also has Michelangelo's statue of Moses, while Sant'Agostino (*see p119*) and San Luigi dei Francesi (*see p118*) have canvases by Caravaggio, controversially realistic works that were considered shocking in their time.

Baroque

The Counter-Reformation inspired the lavish style of churches such as Il Gesù (*see p127*) and Sant' Ignazio (*see p125*). The best-loved examples of Roman Baroque are the later works associated with Bernini, such as the great colonnade and *baldacchino* he built for St Peter's. Of the smaller churches he designed, perhaps the finest is Sant' Andrea al Quirinale (*see p159*), while Santa Maria della Vittoria (*see p160*) houses his Cornaro Chapel, a theatre of sculpture starring the *Ecstasy of St Teresa*.

You should also see many churches by Bernini's rival, Borromini. Sant'Agnese in Agone and San Carlo alle Quattro Fontane (*see p159*) are famed for the dramatic concave surfaces of their façades, while the sharp, complex structure of Sant'Ivo alla Sapienza (*see p118*) makes it one of the miniature Baroque masterpieces and may have your kids itching to create a similar geometric marvel with protractors and set squares.

Below left Creation of the World *mosaic in Santa Maria del Popolo*
Below right The Baroque baldacchino *in St Peter's*

The Good, the Bad and the Ugly

The Roman Empire lasted for almost 500 years, during which time it saw 140 emperors. Over 30 were assassinated, executed, murdered or poisoned, and several went mad. The Empire was eventually divided into two parts – the Western Roman Empire, which ended when the Germanic warlord Odoacer defeated Romulus Augustus, in AD 476, and the Eastern Roman Empire, which continued until the Ottoman Turks captured Constantinople in 1453.

Augustus

Rome's first emperor, Augustus (r.27 BC–AD 14), only found out that he had been adopted by Julius Caesar after Caesar's assassination in 44 BC. Then known as Octavian, he joined forces with Caesar's supporters – Mark Antony and Marcus Aemilius Lepidus – and defeated the assassins. However, disagreements developed and Octavian became sole leader after Lepidus was driven into exile and Mark Antony committed suicide in 31 BC.

He is generally considered the best of Rome's emperors, an intelligent man who brought stability to the Roman Empire. He and his wife, Livia, lived a frugal life in a modest house on the Palatine Hill. He insisted that Livia and his daughter, Julia, spun and wove cloth, and lived mostly on bread, dates and grapes.

Above The Maritime Theatre in the Villa Adriana, created by Emperor Hadrian

Tiberius

Augustus prepared his stepson Tiberius (r.14–37) to rule the Roman Empire by sending him to lead armies abroad, and he is remembered as a great general. However, when Augustus forced him to divorce his wife and marry another woman, Tiberius fled to the island of Rhodes in Greece, saying that he wanted nothing more to do with the Empire.

When Augustus died he returned to rule as emperor, but he had a half-hearted approach to his job, and eventually ran off to the island of Capri and spent his days swimming, reading and listening to music, often with his nephew Caligula.

Caligula

According to an astrologer, Caligula (r.37–41) had as much chance of becoming emperor as he had of crossing the bay of Baiae on horseback. So, as soon as he became emperor, he had a pontoon bridge strung across the bay and spent the next two days riding his horse across it. As time went on, he became more insane and cruel. He was eventually assassinated.

Nero

Nero (r.54–68) was another mad emperor, who once tried to race around the Circus Maximus (see p106) in a chariot pulled by camels. He was blamed for starting a great fire in Rome in AD 64, so that he could build a new capital. He began with the Domus Aurea and erected a giant statue of himself, the Colossus of Nero. Nero killed his wife and mother, ordered the Senate to commit suicide and then killed himself.

Vespasian

Emperor Vespasian (r.69–79) built the Colosseum over what had been a lake in the grounds of the Domus Aurea, to show Romans that a new era had begun and that their lives were going to improve. He was famous for levying a tax on the urine that was collected for the cloth trade in public toilets.

Domitian

Domitian (r.81–96) was a vindictive, paranoid man who was terrified of being assassinated. He certainly had a talent for making enemies – he stole his wife from another man, and then had him killed for complaining! Consequently, when Domitian built the Domus Flavia, he had the walls of the courtyard lined with selenite, so that he could see if anyone was creeping up behind him. In the end he was assassinated in his bedroom. His wife was a suspect!

Above left Marble relief of Emperor Vespasian *Above* Tiberius on the terrace of his villa in Capri *Left* Trajan's Column among other ruins *Bottom* Sculpture of Emperor Constantine in Palazzo dei Conservatori

Trajan

Spanish by birth, Trajan (r.98–117) was one of the greatest Roman emperors and under him the Roman Empire became bigger than ever. He commissioned many important new buildings in Rome – Trajan's Column, Trajan's Markets and the Baths of Trajan. He was also the first emperor to think about the welfare of the people, and founded the *alimenta*, a corn dole for the urban poor.

Hadrian

Trajan's successor was another excellent emperor, an intellectual as well as a great soldier. Hadrian (r.117–138) had huge passion for Greek culture and architecture and is credited with the design of the Pantheon (see pp122–3). He also created the Villa Adriana, to which he would escape to read and think.

Diocletian

By the time Diocletian (r.284–305) came to the throne, the Empire was in a sorry state. One of the first things he did was to introduce price controls. Eventually Diocletian decided that the only way to manage the Empire would be to split it into two halves: the Western Empire, with its capital in Rome, and the Eastern Empire, with its capital in Byzantium. He also believed that the rise in Christianity was to blame for the instability of the Empire. He was responsible for martyring more Christians than any other emperor.

Constantine

The Empire was re-united under Constantine (r.306–337) and he moved the capitol to Byzantium, which was renamed Constantinople. Rome's days as the most important city in the world were clearly over. He was the first emperor to convert to Christianity and issued the Edict of Milan in AD 313, officially tolerating Christianity in the Empire.

Imperial Buildings

Augustus Ara Pacis (see p147); Forum of Augustus, Fori Imperiali (see p89); Houses of Livia and Augustus; Palatine Hill (see pp74–5)

Nero Domus Aurea (see p94)

Vespasian Colosseum (see pp70–71)

Domitian Domus Flavia (see p74)

Trajan Trajan's Markets (see pp86–7); Trajan's Column (see p88); Baths of Trajan (see pp94–5)

Hadrian Villa Adriana (see pp238–9)

Diocletian Baths of Diocletian (see p99)

Constantine Statue of Emperor Constantine, St Peter's (see p204)

Everyday Life in Ancient Rome

The quality of life of an ancient Roman depended on the amount of money he or she had. There was a great divide between the rich and poor. The rich lived in palatial houses in the top locations with the best of everything – from exotic food to expensive clothing and sophisticated plumbing and heating. The poor, on the other hand, lived in basic apartment blocks that did not even have stoves, and worked menial jobs for little or no money.

Housing

The villas of the wealthy were usually built around a central court-yard garden, or peristyle. Underfloor heating, fuelled by burning wood, kept the houses warm in winter. Walls were frescoed and floors were inlaid with marble, but there was very little furniture.

The poor lived in crowded apartment blocks or *insulae*. The poorest – and roughest – quarter in ancient Rome was Subura, now known as Monti. Walking the streets of Subura was hazardous, since residents were accustomed to throwing the slops from their chamber pots straight into the street.

Food

The houses of the wealthy and middle classes had kitchens, but ovens were banned in most *insulae*

and the poor would get their food from *thermopolia* (cafés). Many Roman families were given a weekly ration of grain. The better off would take it to be milled and then baked into bread, but the poor, who could not afford this, would eat the grain boiled in water. The staple foods were beans, bread and lentils, and most people ate little meat.

The wealthy enjoyed elaborate meals of sow's udders stuffed with giant African snails, stuffed dormice, pregnant lamprey, salted tuna garnished with egg and, for dessert, *dulce domestica* (stuffed and marinated dates).

Clothing

Only men were permitted to wear togas – semicircles of woollen cloth that were three times the wearer's height. Wrapping a toga was a

tricky business, and it could take over an hour to get dressed! Women wore a *stola* – a long tube of cloth held together at the top by two brooches, thereby creating neck and arm holes. A wide belt called a *zona* made the dress more shapely. Dyes, of course, were all natural. The most expensive was purple, or murex, extracted from a special kind of snail. For daily wear, a simpler knee-length tunic belted at the waist was preferred by men, women and children. The most comfortable underpants – the *subligaculum* – were tied like bikini pants and made of silk, as was the *mamillare*, a kind of brassiere.

Toilets

Although private houses – and even some *insulae* – had their own toilets, many Roman men preferred to go

Below left Frieze depicting Roman citizens wearing togas, Ara Pacis **Centre** *Ancient Roman gold and silver coins*

to the public toilets or *forica* – a long bench with holes in it above a channel of running water, where people would sit and chat. Sponges on sticks were used instead of toilet paper.

Bathing

Only the wealthiest Romans had baths in their houses. Most people went to public baths to socialize and exercise, as well as get clean. The baths had a *palestra* (gym) and an *apodyterium* (changing room) where people would undress before going into the baths area. Here they would pass through a series of progressively hotter rooms before plunging into an ice-cold pool. There was no soap – Romans used olive oil and scraped the dirt off their skin with an instrument known as a *strigil*.

Children

School started at the crack of dawn. Children learned to write on a wax tablet and to do maths with an abacus. Girls rarely received much education, as it was considered more important for them to learn domestic skills, and poor children were expected to work from a young age. Only the children of the rich had toys – rag dolls, miniature animals, toy chariots, marbles and board games have been found.

Health

Falling ill or having an accident in ancient Rome was a dangerous business. The causes of diseases were not understood, and were often believed to be punishments sent by the gods. Many Roman doctors were quacks who charged a fortune. One attempted to cure a hunchback by placing several large rocks along his spine. The hunchback was crushed to death – his back, apparently, was as straight as a rod.

Holidays

Rich families had houses in the countryside around Rome. Country villas were surrounded by gardens, where vegetables and fruit were cultivated. Very rich families had seaside villas – the most popular holiday area was the Bay of Naples.

Money

Coins were created in a mint on the **Capitoline Hill** *(see pp80–81)*. *Denarii* were made of silver, *aureii* of gold, *dupondii* and *sestertii* of brass, and *as* of bronze. In around AD 200, a Roman could buy a little fruit with 1 *as* and a pint of wine with 1 *sestertius*. A soldier would earn 450 *denarii*, and a house in a posh area would cost about half a million *denarii*.

Below Baths of Neptune at Ostia Antica

Life of a Gladiator

Blood sports, organized in arenas such as the Colosseum and Circus Maximus, were the most popular form of entertainment in ancient Rome. The spectacles would often begin with "comic" fights between obese women, dwarfs, clowns and cripples. Then, with a blast of trumpets, the true gladiators would appear, and sword fights would begin, with the crowd screaming for the gladiator on whom they had placed their bets.

Who were gladiators?

Gladiators were usually slaves, war captives or condemned criminals. They were sentenced to *damnati ad gladium* – condemned to die either by execution or by fighting to the death as gladiators. New recruits were heavily guarded and had no freedom. Successful gladiators became celebrities and several women fell in love with them, and patrons showered them with gifts. Occasionally men volunteered to be gladiators – Emperor Commodus (r.180–192) shocked Rome by fighting in the Colosseum (see pp70–71).

Could women be gladiators?

Some upper-class women thought the life of a gladiator was glamorous and trained as gladiators.

According to the historian Tacitus, these women usually made fools of themselves. Emperor Domitian (r.81–96), however, loved watching women fight. His contemporary, the satirical poet Martial, reported that a woman overcame and killed a lion.

How did they train?

Gladiators lived and trained in gladiator schools. Rome's biggest was the Ludus Magnus, close to the Colosseum and connected to it by an underground tunnel.

Ugly recruits were rejected – and presumably sent for execution – because the crowds liked gladiators to be good-looking. Doctors and trainers would evaluate a recruit and decide what he would specialize in. Recruits trained using wooden swords, and were taught to die

without showing any fear. Each gladiator had a personal trainer called a *lanista*, or bladesman, and trained for months – even years – before fighting in the arena.

Recruits considered ready to fight in the arena were called *Tiri*. Their faces, legs and hands were tattooed to identify them and stop them from escaping.

How many types of gladiators were there?

Big beefy gladiators were selected to be heavily armed, while lighter, nimbler men were lightly armed and trained to rely on quick reactions and speed. Gladiators known as *Dimachaeri* were armed with two swords, *Thracians* had curved swords, *Essedari* fought from chariots, *Equites* fought on

Below left *Actors dressed as gladiators and a Roman senator, Colosseum*
Below right *The ruins at Ludus Magnus, an ancient gladiator training school*

horseback and *Laquearii* were armed with a lasso, while *Retiarii* had a weighted net and a trident.

There were also several kinds of novelty gladiators. *Andabatae* wore helmets without any eyeholes and were forced to fight blind and bare-chested; *Bestiarii* fought wild animals; *Paegniarii* fought wild animals armed only with a bullwhip; and *Pregenarii* were comic gladiators who fought with wooden swords.

Volunteers

Sometimes freemen decided to become gladiators. Free gladiators were given more freedom than regular gladiators – they were not shackled, and were even allowed to leave the barracks.

Diet

Gladiators slept shackled in cells, which were unlocked at dawn, in time for the first meal of the day. They were fed a high-protein diet, with plenty of meat, fish, cheese and eggs, but were not allowed to drink wine – only goats' milk and water. Gladiators were not allowed to speak at meals, and were kept in shackles. Health and hygiene were of utmost importance – gladiators were given regular massages and took frequent baths. They were expected to fight between three and five times every year.

The night before a fight

The night before a fight, a public dinner, called a *coena libera*, was held, to allow the public to get a close view of the gladiators and decide which one they wanted to bet on. Gladiators were allowed to choose what they wanted to eat for what could turn out to be their last meal.

After a fight

As soon as a gladiator had been killed, a man dressed as Charon, the ferryman of the Underworld, entered, checked to see that he was dead, ordered attendants to carry the corpse away, and to rake over the bloodstained sand so that a new combat could begin.

Victorious gladiators became heroes and received gifts from admirers. They were also paid every time they fought, which meant successful ones could amass a fortune. But it was only when the emperor decided they had earned their freedom that they no longer had to fight.

Below left 19th-century lithograph showing gladiators in combat
Below right Gladiators fighting on horseback

Badly Behaved Popes

The pope is believed to be Christ's representative on earth, following in the footsteps of St Peter, the first bishop of Rome. Although there have been some great spiritual leaders, for much of its two millennia of history power seems to have been far more important to the papacy than religion. Many popes behaved as badly as the Roman emperors, others as extravagantly as princes, using their power to amass great fortunes and promote the interests of their families.

Stephen VI

Furious with his predecessor, Formosus, Pope Stephen (r.896–897) had his rotting corpse exhumed and put on trial. The corpse was found guilty of all charges, and had three fingers removed before being chucked into the Tiber. Stephen himself was eventually thrown into prison and strangled to death.

Benedict IX

Benedict IX (r.1032–44, 1045 and 1047–48) was pope no fewer than three times. The first time he step-ped down after selling the papacy, but he returned the following year, and then sold the papacy again. Two years later – during which he seems to have got married – he was back again, but only lasted a year before being dethroned by his successor, Pope Damascus II.

Alexander VI Borgia

One of the most badly behaved of all popes, Alexander (r.1492–1503) had already met the displeasure of the then pope when he was a cardinal, but managed to become pope himself by buying a majority of the votes. He didn't give up either girlfriends or wild parties after he took office. He had 12 children, including Cesare Borgia, whom he made a bishop at the age of 7, and a cardinal at the age of 18, despite that fact that a few years earlier Cesare had killed and decapitated his own grandfather and stuck his head on a pole.

Julius II Della Rovere

An irascible, impatient man who looked like a grumpy Santa Claus, Julius (r.1503–13) was more a soldier than a pope. He drank too much,

swore as heavily as his troops and would ride his horse up the stairs of the papal palace to his bedroom. He had several children and advised his secretary to have three girlfriends at a time in memory of the Holy Trinity. When he first looked at the statue of himself in the role of Moses, created by Michelangelo (see p96), he asked the sculptor what he had carved under his arm. "A bible," replied Michelangelo. "A bible?" roared the pope. "What do I know of bibles? I am a warlord; give me a sword instead."

Leo X De' Medici

After the death of Julius II, the cardinals gathered in Rome to elect a new pope. They slept in cells divided by thin walls, and one night awoke to a terrible smell. It turned

Below left The vengeful Stephen VI
Below right Alexander VI Borgia and Cesare Borgia

out that Leo (r.1513–21) had an illness that left him covered with suppurating boils, and that one of these had burst. Leo bribed his doctors to tell the cardinals that he was so ill he would only last a few weeks. Thinking that putting Leo on the throne would give them more time to choose, the cardinals elected him. But Leo made a miraculous recovery and remained on the throne for eight years, during which time his sale of indulgences to those who gave money for St Peter's almost destroyed the Catholic Church by precipitating the Reformation.

Urban VIII Barberini

Urban VIII (r.1623–44) was an elegant man, and an intellectual who was fascinated by the ideas of Galileo. He met Galileo several times, and even allowed him to publish his book on the heliocentric universe, before changing his mind and subjecting him to interrogation, the threat of torture and house arrest by the Inquisition. He was also a friend of Bernini's, and commissioned many of his finest works. Among these were the *baldacchino* in St Peter's (see pp204–5). However, his patronage of the arts, coupled with the constant expense of war, resulted in huge debts.

Below left Portrait of Julius II Della Rovere
Below right The coat of arms of Pope Innocent X Pamphilj

Innocent X Pamphilj

To Innocent X (r.1644–55), being pope offered the perfect opportunity to boost the wealth of his family. He ordered the redesign of Piazza Navona largely in order to increase the value of land owned by his family – his palazzo was in the piazza – and financed the project by levying a tax on basic foods.

When he was dying, Innocent's sister-in-law, Olimpia, visited him to steal two coffers of coins from his bedroom. After his death she pleaded poverty so that she would not have to pay for his funeral. His body was dumped in a rat-infested cellar until a monsignor agreed to pay for the burial.

Alexander VII Chigi

Chigi (r.1655–57) was elected largely because the cardinals thought he was not the kind of person to give all the most important jobs in Rome to his family. However, Chigi soon began to behave like his predecessors, giving plum jobs to his kin. He was also a patron of Bernini – although he had less time for Borromini, whom he thought difficult. Despite this, Borromini incorporated Chigi's symbol into the decoration of Sant'Ivo alla Sapienza (see p118).

The History of Rome

Rome has played a leading role in the history, not only of Europe, but of the world. At its peak the Roman Empire stretched from England to Africa, but through trade and commerce its impact was felt as far away as India and China. Many countries have adopted political and legal systems based on those of Rome, while buildings across the world imitate styles that originated here and were developed in the cultural ferment of the Renaissance and Baroque eras.

How it all began

According to legend, the wicked Amulius usurped the throne of his brother, Numilius, King of Alba Longa. Amulius thought he had no further rivals, but Numilius's daughter, Rhea Silvia, had a visit by the god Mars and afterwards gave birth to twins, Romulus and Remus. They were abducted by Amulius, packed into a basket and left to drift – or drown – in the Tiber. But the gods steered them into a marsh at the foot of the Capitoline Hill, where a she-wolf looked after the boys until a shepherd decided to adopt them. Years later, the god Mars appeared to them and explained who they were. After killing Amulius

Romulus and Remus, Rome's legendary founders, suckled by the she-wolf

they returned to the hills of their childhood to found a new city. However, they soon began to argue over who should be in charge. Romulus and his followers occupied the Palatine; Remus and his men, the Aventine. A battle ensued and Romulus won. If it had been the other way around, Rome might have ended up being called Reme.

Etruscan tyrants

At the time when Rome was founded, the Etruscans dominated the Italian peninsula. While other tribes were content with simply pottering around as farmers and shepherds, the Etruscans created 12 city states in what is now Lazio and Tuscany, and in 616 BC they seized power in Rome.

Power of the people

Romans soon grew tired of tyrannical leaders and in 509 BC rose up against King Tarquinius Superbus and founded a Republic. Instead of being controlled by an

absolute monarch, Rome was now ruled by two consuls, elected by the senate, and two tribunes, elected by the people.

Tarquinius Superbus, the seventh and final King of Rome, and a tyrannical ruler

The world becomes Roman

Rome prospered and grew. Local tribes were subdued, and over the centuries Rome fought its way south into Sicily and Carthage, North Africa. By 146 BC Rome was the biggest power in the world, controlling most of the Mediterranean coastline, and it continued to expand (reaching its greatest extent in AD 117). Conquered people became Roman

Timeline

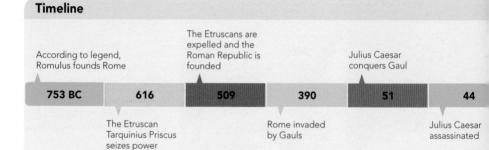

According to legend, Romulus founds Rome		The Etruscans are expelled and the Roman Republic is founded		Julius Caesar conquers Gaul	
753 BC	**616**	**509**	**390**	**51**	**44**
	The Etruscan Tarquinius Priscus seizes power		Rome invaded by Gauls		Julius Caesar assassinated

Brutus, one of Caesar's assassins, after his defeat by Mark Antony and Octavian

citizens; conquered settlements became cities; and Roman ideas, politics, laws and technology became part of everyday life for people from the wilds of northern England to the shores of Africa.

The assassination of Julius Caesar

In 87 BC, a power struggle between the two consuls – Lucius Cornelius Sulla and Gaius Marius – led to civil war. Sulla won and took control of Rome. But, in the meantime, Gaius Marius's nephew, Julius Caesar, emerged as a formidable military leader, conquering Gaul and Britain, before returning to Rome to fight a war against Pompey. Caesar won, and was declared "dictator of Rome for life". Appalled to see power concentrated in the hands of a single individual, a group of Republicans led by Brutus and Cassius assassinated Caesar in the Theatre of Pompey on 15 March in 44 BC.

The age of Augustus

The murder of Caesar threw Rome into turmoil. Caesar's deputy, Mark Antony, joined forces with Caesar's adopted son, Octavian, and fought and defeated an army led by Brutus and Cassius at the battle of Philippi in 42 BC. The civil war raged on until 27 BC, when Octavian, now known as Augustus, became Rome's first emperor. Augustus ruled for 40 years, transforming Rome from "a city of brick to a city of marble", creating the first Imperial Forum, and filling the Campus Martius – the area of Rome now covered by the *centro storico* – with new temples, basilicas, theatres and monuments.

The fall of Rome

After years of prosperity, the increasing decadence of the wealthy, as well as the sheer logistics of keeping such a large empire running, was taking its toll. By the 3rd century AD, Rome was falling apart and Christianity was on the rise. Emperor Diocletian had hundreds of Christians killed as he attempted to extinguish the cult. But Christianity flourished, and in AD 313 Emperor Constantine became a Christian himself. Rome's glory days were over even as Constantine shifted the capital of the Empire to Byzantium. The rich and powerful moved east, and the city was attacked by Goths and Vandals invading from the north. Rome's population shrank, the city decayed and disease was rife.

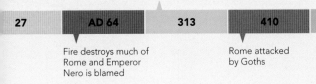

ctavian becomes
mperor Augustus

Emperor Constantine becomes a Christian

| 27 | AD 64 | 313 | 410 |

Fire destroys much of Rome and Emperor Nero is blamed

Rome attacked by Goths

The rise of the papacy

In the 7th century Pope Gregory the Great turned Rome's fortunes around, sending missionaries to Europe to spread the word of the Church, and drawing hordes of pilgrims to the city. New churches were built, and the pope and his city became the power centre of the Christian world. When Frankish ruler Charlemagne invaded Italy in AD 800, he was crowned Holy Roman Emperor in St Peter's, but over the centuries the conflicts and rivalry between the Empire and the papacy would divide Europe.

Renaissance revival

Power in Rome gradually became concentrated in the hands of a few exceptionally rich families. Virtually all popes came from one of these families, who commissioned the

Fontana del Moro, a Baroque fountain in Piazza Navona

greatest artists and architects of the time to fill the city with magnificent new palaces, grand piazzas and amazing churches – influenced by the styles of recently rediscovered ancient Roman buildings, statues and frescoes. Bramante, Michelangelo and Raphael all worked in the city, transforming it from a neglected medieval backwater into the most splendid metropolis of the Western world. In 1527, however, the power struggle between the Holy Roman Empire and the papacy resulted in the Sack of Rome, when the unruly troops of Charles V rampaged throughout the city, burning and looting palaces and churches, thus leaving just a fraction of its former glory.

Counter-Reformation and the Baroque

Meanwhile, in northern Europe, opposition to the fabulously rich – and famously corrupt – papacy was growing, in particular because of the selling of "indulgences" that guaranteed entry to heaven, and people began to embrace the Protestant movement.

In a response, the Catholic Church introduced massive changes – controversial books were burned, radical thinkers tortured, and artists were told exactly what they were and were not allowed to paint. As the Church regained confidence – although not political power – popes such as Sixtus V, Urban VIII and

Statue of King Vittorio Emanuele II at Il Vittoriano

Innocent X commissioned the extravagant Baroque piazzas, fountains, palaces and churches that define the city of Rome today.

Unification

Magnificent as it may have looked, Rome was still a minor player on the world stage. The centre of action on the Italian peninsula was in the north, with politicians, thinkers and revolutionaries such as Giuseppe Mazzini, Count Camillo Cavour and Garibaldi spearheading the Risorgimento movement to unify Italy – until then a diverse collection of city-states and principalities under foreign rule.

Giuseppe Garibaldi made several failed attempts to capture Rome – which was under the protection of the French army – but on 20 September 1870, Italian troops managed to enter the city and Rome was declared capital of the new Italy, under the Piedmontese King Vittorio Emanuele II. New streets – Via Nazionale, Via del

Timeline

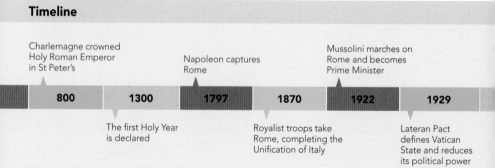

Charlemagne crowned Holy Roman Emperor in St Peter's

800

1300

The first Holy Year is declared

Napoleon captures Rome

1797

1870

Royalist troops take Rome, completing the Unification of Italy

Mussolini marches on Rome and becomes Prime Minister

1922

1929

Lateran Pact defines Vatican State and reduces its political power

Tritone and Via Veneto – were cut through the city centre and a vast area was demolished to make room for Il Vittoriano monument.

The Mussolini years

After World War I, disillusionment, national debt and social unrest culminated in massive support for the rising ex-Socialist politician Benito Mussolini. In October 1922, Mussolini marched on Rome with his Blackshirts and, within three years, he was running a Fascist dictatorship, with the dream of re-creating the power and glory of the ancient Roman Empire. A huge construction programme began – 15 churches and many medieval houses were torn down to make way for broad new roads such as Via dei Fori Imperiali and Via della Conciliazione, and an imposing new suburb, EUR, was built to the south of the city. In the Lateran Pact of 1929, the Vatican City became a recognized state within the kingdom of Italy. Mussolini passed anti-Semitic laws in 1938 and in 1940 Italy joined World War II on the side of Nazi Germany. In September 1943, two months

Mussolini marching into Rome followed by his Blackshirts

after the Allies had landed in Sicily, the king took power away from Mussolini and Italy officially swapped sides in the war. Rome was bombed by both sides before being liberated by the Allies on 4 June 1944.

Modern-day Rome

In the chaos after the war, a new art form emerged with Neo-Realist cinema, including Rossellini's *Rome, Open City* (1945) and De Sica's *Bicycle Thieves* (1948), both filmed on the war-torn streets of the city. As a political centre, however, Rome was riven by divisions between left- and right-wing parties, and by the 1970s international terrorism held the country to ransom.

After more than 50 changes of government, the 1990s saw the rise of Italy's modern antihero, Silvio Berlusconi, who, despite many scandals, managed to become Italy's longest serving postwar prime minister, until he was made to resign on corruption charges in 2012.

Famous for its past, Rome is embracing the future with sensitivity: much of the historic centre is now closed to traffic, and the first stretch of the city's much-needed third metro line was inaugurated in November 2014. Radical new buildings, such as MACRO and MAXXI, have been designed to incorporate pre-existing architecture. The economic crisis, however, means hard times ahead for the Eternal City.

HEROES & VILLAINS

Street names

The heroes of the Italian Unification have had streets named after them in almost every Italian town and village – and Rome is no exception. Look at a map and see if you can find streets or piazzas named after them, and after some of the key dates in modern Italian history:

Risorgimento
Garibaldi
Mazzini
Cavour
King Vittorio Emanuele II
XX Settembre

Nero

Roman Emperor Nero (AD 37–68) is famous for fiddling while Rome burned. In fact, he couldn't have, as fiddles hadn't been invented then, but he was callous. He is said to have ordered the death of his father, his half-brother and two wives (probably) and his mother (definitely) – although it is hard to know how much contemporary historians exaggerated, as they didn't like him much.

Giuseppe Garibaldi

In 1860, Giuseppe Garibaldi (1807–82) led an army of a thousand red-shirted volunteers (*I Mille*) to Sicily, beginning the Unification of Italy. Known as the Risorgimento, the movement led to the creation of a united country, rather than separate states ruled by foreign powers and local kings.

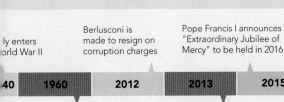

...ly enters ...orld War II	Berlusconi is made to resign on corruption charges	Pope Francis I announces "Extraordinary Jubilee of Mercy" to be held in 2016	
...40	1960	2012	2013	2015
	Olympic Games held in Rome		Pope Francis I is elected as the new pope after Benedict XVI abdicates	

Bernini's colonnade surrounding
Piazza San Pietro, Vatican City

Exploring
ROME

Ancient Rome

Nowhere does history come alive as vividly as it does in the ancient centre of Rome. Not only is there lots to see, but thanks to ancient Roman writers there are plenty of stories of Roman life to entertain kids, while the city's museums are beginning to use virtual reality technology to re-create history for the visitor. This is also the greenest part of the city and its seven hills afford great views of its numerous piazzas and parks.

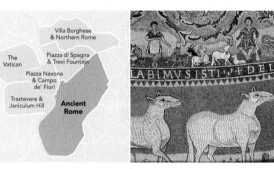

Villa Borghese
& Northern Rome

The
Vatican

Piazza di Spagna
& Trevi Fountain

Piazza Navona
& Campo
de' Fiori

Trastevere &
Janiculum Hill

**Ancient
Rome**

Highlights

Colosseum
Take a seat in the Colosseum and imagine gory combats between gladiators, lions and tigers (see pp70–71).

The Palatine Hill and Roman Forum
Walk to the Palatine Hill to see ruins of monuments. Then try to find Rome's belly button and an ancient drain in the Roman Forum (see pp74–5 & 76–9).

Il Vittoriano
Get whisked to the top of this white marble monument by glass elevator for fabulous views of the ancient centre of Rome (see p84).

Palazzo Valentini
Explore the ruins of Imperial Roman houses and see the reliefs on Trajan's Column come to life like a cartoon strip, on a dazzling multimedia tour under Palazzo Valentini (see p88).

San Clemente
Travel back in time at San Clemente, a multi-layered church spanning 2,000 years of history (see pp92–3).

Museo Nazionale Romano
Step into the painted paradise of an ancient Roman garden at Museo Nazionale Romano's Palazzo Massimo (see pp98–9).

Above right Shepherds and sheep in the Tree of Life mosaic, San Clemente church
Left Visitors walking among the impressive ruins of the Roman Forum

The Best of
Ancient Rome

The most concentrated cluster of ancient Roman ruins lies in the area bounded by the Capitoline, Palatine, Esquiline and Quirinal hills. This was where the fates of nations were decided, triumphs were celebrated and citizens were entertained by gladiatorial combats. The most desirable residential area was the Palatine Hill, where emperors, poets and politicians lived in luxury, even as they plotted against and murdered one another.

In the footsteps of the Caesars

Begin with the ancient buildings that children might already have heard about. Imagine what it would have been like to attend a gladiatorial combat or wild animal fights at the **Colosseum** (see pp70–71). Picture visitors in the **Roman Forum** (see pp76–9) as toga-wearing ancient Romans busy visiting its temples, law courts and triumphal arches and, at the **Palatine Hill** (see pp74–5), as members of the Imperial family relaxing in their sumptuous palaces.

A rendezvous with legends

Visit sights that have lent themselves to legends. Stop by the **Palatine Hill**, where the she-wolf is said to have suckled Romulus and Remus. Look up at the **Torre delle Milizie** (see p86), from which Nero supposedly watched Rome burn. Walk by the **Altar of Julius Caesar** (see p76), where his ashes were placed, or the **Rostrum** (see p78), from which Shakespeare had Mark Antony make his speech, "Friends, Romans, countrymen..."

Left A family taking in the impressive Arch of Septimius Severus in the Roman Forum Below Trajan's Markets, with the Torre delle Milizie behind

Above *Visitors enjoying superb views of the city from the terrace of Il Vittoriano* **Left** *Stained-glass painting on display in the Palazzo Massimo, Museo Nazionale Romano*

Roam with the Romans

There is plenty of evidence around of the daily life of ancient Romans. Imagine how the poor lived in *insulae* (apartment blocks), the best preserved of which is on **Piazza Venezia** *(see p84)*. Relive a life of luxury in the residence of an ancient Roman aristocratic family as it is digi-tally re-created in the ruins below **Palazzo Valentini** *(see p88)*. Walk into the **Palazzo Massimo** *(see pp98–9)* to see frescoes and mosaics from the ancient city's wealthiest homes. Stroll through **Trajan's Markets** *(see pp86–7)*, an ancient Roman shopping mall and dole office. Check out displays such as the bone needles and bronze buckles at the **Case Romane del Celio** on the **Celian Hill** *(see p72)*, and finds

from a Roman rubbish dump, which include fragments of glass from a glassworks, at **Crypta Balbi** *(see p85)*; all these help to capture the texture of everyday life in ancient Rome.

Bella Vista

Walk up one of the seven hills of Rome. The **Capitoline** *(see pp80–81)*, **Palatine**, **Celian** and **Aventine** *(see pp102–103)* hills are all very green and offer the best perspectives. In the afternoon in autumn and winter, there is the added spectacle of millions of starlings forming swirling vortices across the sky.

For a bird's-eye view of the **Roman Forum**, saunter up the **Capitoline** and **Palatine** hills and challenge children to identify all the monuments they have seen from up close. Take a ride in a glass elevator to the top storey of **Il Vittoriano** *(see p84)* for fantastic vistas of Rome. For more views, climb up to the terraces of **Trajan's Markets** and the **Capitoline Museums** *(see pp82–3)*. Save the best for the end – the **Piazza dei Cavalieri di Malta** *(see p107)* offers the most famous view in the city.

Hi-tech history

In recent years 3D animation techniques and computer technology have revolutionized some of the city's sites, and installations re-creating ancient buildings and sculptures are becoming popular in its museums. Marvel at the virtual reconstruction of the ruins of a patrician villa beneath **Palazzo Valentini**, or visit the fascinating and fun **Time Elevator** *(see p156)*, a multimedia, multisensory cinema.

Colosseum and around

The ancient centre is Rome's most visited area, so crowds and long queues are virtually unavoidable. Arriving at the Colosseum and the Roman Forum as soon as they open, pre-booking tickets or using the Roma Pass (see p23) mean shorter queues. Although surrounded by roads choked with traffic, and flanked by chaotic Piazza Venezia, many of the sights here are interconnected and can be accessed from one another without using main roads. The area is well served by buses.

Ancient Rome

The ruins of the Colosseum, ancient Rome's famous arena

Places of Interest

SIGHTS
1. Colosseum
2. Arch of Constantine
3. Celian Hill
4. Ludus Magnus
5. Palatine Hill
6. Roman Forum
7. Capitoline Hill
8. Capitoline Museums
9. Piazza Venezia
10. Il Vittoriano
11. Crypta Balbi
12. Trajan's Markets
13. Palazzo Valentini
14. Trajan's Column
15. Fori Imperiali

EAT AND DRINK
1. Panificio Disa
2. Caffetteria Faiola
3. Bibenda Wine Concept
4. Caffè Propaganda
5. SISA
6. Hostaria i Clementini
7. Made in Sud
8. Naumachia
9. Papagiò
10. Santeo
11. Zerosettantacinque
12. Anima Mundi
13. Il Bocconcino
14. Pizza e Mortadella
15. Daruma Sushi
16. La Bottega del Caffè
17. Cavour 313
18. Pizzicheria
19. Antico Caffè del Teatro Marcello
20. Trattoria Ara Coeli
21. La Taverna degli Amici
22. Kosher Delight
23. Cin Cin Bar
24. Pane Vino e San Daniele
25. Da Giggetto
26. Beppe e i Suoi Formaggi
27. Caffè Ducatti
28. Carlo Polica
29. Bar Tavola Calda La Licata
30. Taverna Romana
31. Osteria Corte del Grillo
32. Caffè Costantino
33. La Carbonara
34. Ciuri Ciuri
35. Super Elite
36. La Vecchia Roma

See also Capitoline Museums (p83) and Il Vittoriano (p84)

SHOPPING
1. Little Big Town

WHERE TO STAY
1. Hotel Forum
2. Hotel de Monti
3. Paba
4. Hotel Celio
5. BB Colosseum 2
6. Lancelot
7. I Fotografi
8. Kolbe Hotel Rome

🚗 **Metro** Colosseo (Line B) & Cavour (Line B). **Bus** C3, H, X60, X80, 30, 40, 44, 46, 53, 60, 62, 63, 64, 70, 71, 75, 80, 81, 84, 85, 87, 95, 117, 119, 130, 160, 170, 175, 186, 190, 204, 271, 492, 571, 628, 630, 640, 715, 716, 780, 781, 810, 850 & 916. **Tram** 3 & 8

ℹ️ **Visitor information** Tourist Information Point: Via Nazionale (near Palazzo delle Esposizioni), 00184; 060608; open 9:30am–7pm daily; www.060608.it. Visitor Centre: Via dei Fori Imperiali, 00186; 06 6994 0488 or 060608; open 9:30am–7pm daily; www.turismoroma.it

🛒 **Supermarkets** Conad City: Via del Boschetto 52, 00184. Tuodì: Via Annia 18, 00184. **Markets** Circo Massimo farmers' market: 74 Via San Teodoro, 00186; Sun

🎪 **Festivals** Epiphany (6 Jan): procession of the Santo Bambino from Santa Maria in Aracoeli. Ash Wednesday (Feb/Mar): pope processes from the Basilica of Santa Sabina to the Circo Massimo. Festival of Santa Francesca (9 Mar): cars, buses and trams are blessed at Santa Francesca Romana. Good Friday (Mar): pope leads a procession to the Colosseum. Estate Romana (Jul–Aug): opera, dance, concerts, cinema and theatre in venues all over the city.

➕ **Pharmacies** Farmacia Savignone: Via dei Serpenti 125, 00184; 06 488 2973; open 8:30am–10:30pm Mon–Fri, 8:30am–7:30pm Sat. Farmacia Piram: Via Nazionale 228, 00184; 06 488 0754; open daily. Farmacia Arenula: Via Arenula 73, 00186; 06 6880 3278; open 7:30am–10pm Mon–Sat, 6–10pm Sun; www.tinyurl.com/n869dej

🛝 **Nearest play areas** Parco del Colle Oppio (entrance on Via Labicana), 00184. Villa Celimontana (entrance on Piazza della Navicella), 00184. Largo della Sanità Militare (between Colosseum and Celian Hill). Ludus Magnus Via San Giovanni in Laterano, 00184. Monte Caprino park, Via Tempio di Giove, 00186. Villa Aldobrandini, Via IV Novembre, 00187.

① Colosseum
Gladiatorial combat and wild beasts

In AD 72, Emperor Vespasian commissioned the Colosseum, Rome's first purpose-built blood-sports arena, on the marshy site of a lake in the grounds of the Domus Aurea (see p94). Spectacles often began with wild animals performing circus tricks, and the gladiatorial combat would commence with comic battles, after which the real gladiators, in ceremonial helmets and armour, would fight each other to the death. At the opening games in AD 80, 9,000 beasts and scores of gladiators were killed.

Bust of Vespasian

Key Features

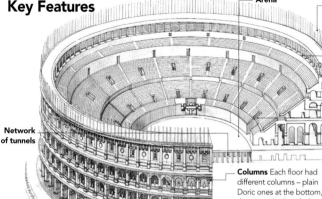

Arena

The velarium A vast awning fixed to the upper storey, the *velarium* could be hoisted to shade spectators from the sun.

Colonnade To stop flirting, women were segregated from men behind a colonnade.

Internal corridors

Vomitoria These were the exits from each numbered section of the seating tiers.

Entry routes The Colosseum could seat up to 55,000 people. The entry routes to the seats were reached by the staircases that ran through the building.

Network of tunnels

Columns Each floor had different columns – plain Doric ones at the bottom, then Ionic (with curled tops) and above that Corinthian, the most ornate, with acanthus-leaf decoration.

Arched entrances

Network of tunnels Waiting animals were kept in cages under the arena floor before being winched up in lifts.

Internal corridors The broad design made it easier for the large, unruly crowds to enter and get seated quickly.

Arched entrances The crowds entered the Colosseum via 76 numbered, arched entrances.

The Lowdown

🌐 **Map reference** 9 B2
Address Piazza del Colosseo 1, 00184; 06 3996 7700; *www. the-colosseum.net*

🚗 **Metro** Colosseo (Line B). **Bus** C3, 53, 60, 75, 85, 87, 117, 175, 186, 271, 571 & 810. **Tram** 3

🕐 **Open** mid-Feb–end Mar: 8:30am–4:30pm daily; end Mar–end Aug: 8:30am–7:15pm daily; Sep: 8:30am–7pm daily; Oct & Nov: 9am–6:30pm daily; Nov–mid-Feb: 8:30am–4:30pm daily

💲 **Price** €24–39 (includes the Roman Forum and Palatine Hill); under 18s free; underground

and third tier €8. A 7-day Archeologia Card (€25 per person) includes entry to the Baths of Caracalla and Museo Nazionale Romano.

👫 **Skipping the queue** Instead of buying tickets at the Colosseum, Forum or Palatine, save time by booking at *www.ticketclic.it* or by phone (€2 booking fee). Roma Pass holders (see p23) gain direct entry via a special turnstile.

🍴 **Guided tours** Compulsory for the third tier (€8). Tour guide for the Colosseum: €5; audioguide: €5.50

👫 **Age range** 5 plus

🏃 **Activities** Get a children's audio-guide from *www.coopculture.it*

⏱ **Allow** 45 mins–1 hr

♿ **Wheelchair access** Yes, to the arena; lifts to some upper levels

☕ **Café** Refreshment booths outside

🛍 **Shop** The shop at the entrance sells souvenirs and books.

🚻 **Toilets** Near the entrance

Good family value?
The Colosseum's combination of gory history and space for exploring makes it one of the city's most child-friendly sights.

Letting off steam

Head away from busy roads up Via Claudia to the **Celian Hill** *(see p72)*, where animals destined for the Colosseum were kept in a zoo. The quietest of the city's seven hills, it has a park with a playground in the **Villa Celimontana**.

Peaceful Villa Celimontana on the Celian Hill, ideal for ball games and picnics

Eat and drink

Picnic: under €25; Snacks: €25–40; Real meal: €40–80; Family treat: over €80 (based on a family of four)

PICNIC Panificio Disa *(Via San Giovanni in Laterano 64, 00184; closed Sun)* sells excellent focaccia bread, pizza and sandwiches. Pick up a picnic lunch and eat it in the park at Villa Celimontana or at the small playground on Largo della Sanità Militare.
SNACKS Caffetteria Faiola *(Via Celimontana 6–8, 00184; 06 7049 2953; open daily)* is a charming café, with a lovely outdoor seating area, serving excellent pizzas and sandwiches. The staff is friendly and attentive.
REAL MEAL Bibenda Wine Concept *(Via Capo d'Africa 21, 00184; 06 7720 6673; closed Sun)*, a contemporary wine bar, offers toasted sandwiches for kids while adults can try carpaccio of Chianina steak or plates of hot melted cheese with grilled vegetables.
FAMILY TREAT Caffè Propaganda *(Via Claudia 15, 00184; 06 9453 4255; closed Mon)* is an expensive restaurant-café-bar with a great buzz. Try

Bar with macaroons on display, Caffè Propaganda

the broccoli soufflé with pecorino cheese and organic tomato sauce, frittata with seasonal vegetables, gourmet hamburgers, sandwiches and home-made hot chocolate.

Find out more

DIGITAL For more on the Colosseum visit *www.howstuffworks.com/search. php?terms=ancient+rome&gallery= 1&media=video*, which has several excellent short videos for children. Visit *www.bbc.co.uk/cbbc/games/ terrible-treasures-game* for a game developed by the Horrible Histories team based around the Colosseum.
FILM Watch Audrey Hepburn and Gregory Peck ride past the Colosseum – and many other famous city sights – on a Vespa in *Roman Holiday* (1953).

Take cover

Walk along Via Labicano to **San Clemente** *(see p92)*, where you can travel back in time from a 12th-century church to the remains of a Roman temple built within the ruins of a 1st-century house.

The Palatine Hill, home to some of Rome's most ancient ruins

Next stop...

UP AND DOWN The Colosseum gives a strong impression of what life was like for the masses in ancient Rome. Walk up to the **Palatine Hill** *(see pp74–5)* to get an impression of how the wealthy lived. Alternatively, walk over to Via Labicana, behind the Colosseum, to peer down at the barracks where the gladiators lived and trained. Continue to the **Ludus Magnus** *(see p73)*, where the red-brick ruins of the largest gladitorial school and barracks in Rome are sunk below street level.

② Arch of Constantine

The triumph of stolen goods

A triumphal arch, the Arch of Constantine was one of the last Imperial monuments to be erected in Rome. Shortly after its construction, Emperor Constantine shifted the capital of the Roman Empire to Constantinople (now Istanbul). Dedicated in AD 315, the arch commemorates Constantine's victory over his co-emperor, Maxentius, at the Battle of the Milvian Bridge in 312. He credited this victory to a dream in which he had a vision of the Cross and heard the words "in this sign you shall conquer". There is nothing particularly Christian about the arch, which was designed to demonstrate Roman supremacy and incorporates reliefs and statues taken from buildings all over the city. The eight figures on top, for example, are Dacians (Romanians), taken from Trajan's Forum (see p88), and the man shown giving bread to the poor is actually Marcus Aurelius.

Letting off steam

Walk accross the road to the lovely park of **Villa Celimontana** where children can run around and play games.

The magnificent Arch of Constantine near the Colosseum

The Lowdown

- 🌐 **Map reference** 9 B2
  Address Between Via di San Gregorio & the Colosseum
- 🚗 **Metro** Colosseo (Line B). **Bus** C3, 53, 60, 75, 85, 87, 117, 175, 186, 271, 571 & 810. **Tram** 3
- 🚶 **Age range** 6 plus
- ⏱ **Allow** 15 mins
- ♿ **Wheelchair access** Yes
- 🍴 **Eat and drink** PICNIC SISA (Via dei SS Quattro 67, 00184; 06 709 6347; 8am–8pm Mon–Sat, 8am–1:30pm Sun) is the ideal place to pick up a delicious picnic lunch to eat at Villa Celimontana. FAMILY TREAT Hostaria i Clementini (Via San Giovanni in Laterano 106, 00184; 06 4542 6395; www.iclementini.it; open daily) offers Roman specialities such as spaghetti alla carbonara (with bacon and egg) or spaghetti cacio e pepe (with ewes' cheese and black pepper)
- 🚻 **Toilets** No

③ Celian Hill

Peacocks, punishments and a playground

Largely undeveloped save for a vast military hospital and a handful of churches, the Celian Hill rises, green and tranquil, across the road from the Palatine Hill (see pp74–5). Although it was heavily populated in the latter years of the Empire, the hill was almost abandoned after the Goths sabotaged the aqueducts in AD 530, thereby cutting off its water supply. Jagged fragments of the aqueducts can be seen today.

In the late 19th century, the remains of shops and two Roman houses were discovered under the Church of SS Giovanni e Paolo. The **Case Romane del Celio**, as they are known, with their beautifully restored frescoes including one showing girls feeding peacocks, ducks and geese, and walls painted to resemble precious marble, are well worth a visit. A small collection of everyday household objects is displayed here: a teaspoon, sewing needles made of bone and a bronze buckle.

Above the church of SS Giovanni e Paolo is the pine-shaded park of **Villa Celimontana**, the loveliest in central Rome, and a perfect destination for a picnic and games after seeing sights such as the Palatine Hill, Colosseum or San Clemente (see pp92–3). The park has a playground with swings, rope-climbing frames, climbing arcs and seesaws, pony rides and a small roller-skating and cycling rink. It also hosts a jazz festival in summer.

Children prone to nightmares should probably not be taken to **Santo Stefano Rotondo**, whose walls are decorated with gruesome scenes of ghoulish martyrdoms. Opt instead for **Santa Maria in Domnica**, which has a gorgeous mosaic in the apse. It shows the Madonna surrounded by the Apostles, with Christ depicted as a miniature boy, rather than a baby, sitting on her lap.

Take cover

If it rains during a trip to the park of **Villa Celimontana**, duck into the **Case Romane del Celio** and check out their colourful frescoes.

Byzantine mosaic in the apse, Santa Maria in Domnica church

The Lowdown

🌐 **Map reference** 9 B3
Address Celian Hill, 00184. Case Romane del Celio: Clivo di Scauro; 06 7720 1975; www.caseromane. it. Villa Celimontana: Piazza della Navicella. Santo Stefano Rotondo: Via di Santo Stefano Rotondo 7; 06 4211 9130; www.santo-stefano-rotondo.it. Santa Maria in Domnica: Piazza della Navicella; www.santamariaindomnica.it

🚗 **Bus** 117

🕐 **Open** Case Romane del Celio: 10am–1pm & 3–6pm Thu–Mon. Villa Celimontana: 7am–sunset daily. Santo Stefano Rotondo: 9:30am–12:30pm & 3–6pm daily in summer, 2–5pm in winter. Santa Maria in Domnica: 9am–noon & 3:30–7pm daily in summer, till 6pm in winter

💶 **Price** Case Romane del Celio: €16–28; under 12s free

🎫 **Guided tours** Case Romane del Celio: night tours; check website

👫 **Age range** Case Romane del Celio & Santo Stefano Rotondo: 8 plus

⏱ **Allow** Case Romane del Celio: 30 mins. Villa Celimontana: 1–2 hrs. Santo Stefano Rotondo: 10 mins. Santa Maria in Domnica: 20 mins

♿ **Wheelchair access** Yes

🍴 **Eat and drink** SNACKS Made in Sud (Via San Giovanni in Laterano 46, 00184; 06 7045 4900) offers tasty fried goodies to take away. REAL MEAL Naumachia (Via Celimontana 7, 00184; 06 700 2764; www.naumachiaroma.com) serves traditional Italian cuisine, including a delicious cacio e pepe (cheese and pepper) pasta

🚻 **Toilets** Yes, in Villa Celimontana

quality of their life could be far better and they were permitted to marry, and some even had children.

The Ludus Magnus was built by emperor Domitian (AD 81–96) in the valley between the Esquiline and the Celian hills, right on the doorstep of the Colosseum. The brickwork was originally covered with marble, though this has long since disappeared. At the centre of the Ludus Magnus there was a miniature arena in which the gladiators practised, with space for a limited number of spectators. There were two entrances – that on Via Labicana was reserved for important visitors.

Letting off steam

Either visit **Villa Celimontana** or walk down to the playground on **Largo della Sanità Militare**.

One of the many stone statues that populate the peaceful Villa Celimontana

④ Ludus Magnus
A fight to the death

Sunk below street level on the corner of Via Labicana are the red-brick ruins of a gladiators' barracks and training school. The largest of its kind in ancient Rome, it was connected to the Colosseum by an underground tunnel (which unfortunately cannot be visited).

Once a man or boy had been condemned – or occasionally volunteered – to be a gladiator, they were confined to these heavily guarded barracks for training. Most gladiators were slaves, criminals or prisoners taken in one of Rome's wars. Life was tough – gladiators were shackled unless training – but if they managed to survive, the

The Lowdown

🌐 **Map reference** 9 C2
Address Via Labicana, 00184

🚗 **Metro** Colosseo (Line B). **Bus** C3, 53, 60, 75, 85, 87, 117, 175, 186, 271, 571 & 810. **Tram** 3

🕐 **Open** There is no public access to the site, but it can be seen clearly from the street above

👫 **Age range** 9 plus

⏱ **Allow** 15 mins

🍴 **Eat and drink** PICNIC Panificio Disa (see Colosseum p71). FAMILY TREAT Papagiò (Via Capo d'Africa 26, 00184; 06 700 9800; closed Sun) serves excellent spaghetti papagiò with seafood; oven-baked in a paper parcel) and sea bass baked with potatoes and artichokes

KIDS' CORNER

For the steely nerved...

In Santo Stefano Rotondo, look at the wall paintings and their labels and see if you can find...
1 The saint who was buried alive
2 The saint who was tied to a wheel
3 The saint who was tied to two wild bulls
4 The emperors who seem to have been the most to blame for the martyrdoms

....
Answers at the bottom of the page.

Glorious moments
Constantine's arch celebrates what he thought were the most glorious moments in the history of the Roman Empire. Design an arch that celebrates the best moments in your life. What would you put on it?

DISARMED!

The obelisk in the park of Villa Celimontana comes from the Temple of the Sun in Heliopolis, Egypt. It was moved to the park in the 19th century. While moving it, however, the supports broke and one of the workers had his arm trapped under the obelisk. The arm was amputated, and remains buried under the obelisk even today.

Line drawing

Look carefully at the face of the Madonna in Santa Maria in Domnica and notice how the eyebrows and nose are created with a single black line. Can you draw some people you know in the same style?

....

⑤ Palatine Hill
Mirrored walls and rainbow floors

With pine trees covering its slopes and wild flowers surrounding its ruins in spring, the Palatine Hill is one of Rome's loveliest ancient sites. According to legend, this was the spot where Romulus and Remus founded their first camp. Later, it became home to the glitterati of the late Republic and to the Imperial family. Today, the remains of elaborate fountains, colourful marble floors, fine stone carvings, columns, stuccoes and frescoes can be seen within the magnificent walls of the Imperial palaces.

Detail on an ancient column

Key Features

Cryptoporticus Neroniano A secret passageway, this was built by Nero to link his new palace, the Domus Aurea (see p94), with the Palatine.

House of Augustus

Domus Flavia

Museo Palatino Highlights here include a double-faced statue of Dionysus and a model of the Palatine during the Bronze Age.

Domus Augustana

Entrance from the Roman Forum

House of Livia

Stadium

The Houses of Livia and Augustus Rome's first emperor, Caesar Augustus (r. 27 BC– AD 14), and his wife Livia lived in two small houses, which have beautifully preserved frescoes and mosaic floors.

Domus Augustana This two-storey palace was where the emperors lived. Look out for the pink-and-yellow marble floors, and the elaborate fountains.

Domus Flavia Built by Emperor Domitian, the walls of the peristyle in this palace are lined with shiny selenite to act as a mirror.

Stadium The curved recess of this sunken oval garden probably held a box from which emperors could watch the wealthy strolling by or riding in sedans and carriages.

The Lowdown

🌐 **Map reference** 9 A3
Address Entrances from Via di San Gregorio 30 & the Roman Forum, 00184; 06 3996 7700; www.archeoroma.beniculturali.it

🚗 **Metro** Colosseo (Line B). **Bus** 60, 75, 84, 85, 87, 117, 175, 186, 271, 571, 810 & 850

🕐 **Open** end Oct–15 Feb: 8:30am–4:30pm, closing times vary rest of the year; check website for details (last adm: 1 hr before closing). House of Augustus: summer: 2:30–6:30pm Mon, Wed & Thu, 8:30am–1:30pm Sat & Sun; winter: 11am–sunset. House of Livia: currently closed.

💶 **Price** €24–39 (includes the Forum and Colosseum); under 18s free. Tickets are valid for two days.

👫 **Skipping the queue** At the Palatine, queues are shorter than those at the Forum. Buy tickets and the Roma Pass (see p23) in advance at www.ticketclic.it or by phone (€2 booking fee).

🚩 **Guided tours** Audioguides are available at the Palatine Hill (€5) and on www.coopculture.it (free). Call to book tours.

👫 **Age range** 5 plus

⏱ **Allow** 2–3 hrs
♿ **Wheelchair access** Yes, limited
☕ **Café** Refreshment vans outside
🛍 **Shop** The bookshop at the main Forum entrance has a few children's books on ancient Rome as well as posters, souvenirs and photo books.

🚻 **Toilets** In the museum

Good family value?
The Palatine Hill has a lot of green space to explore and trees to rest under, making it the ideal place for families to visit.

Ruins of the Palatine Hill from the Circus Maximus

Letting off steam

Across the road from the Via San Gregorio entrance is the **Circus Maximus** *(see p106)*, where children can tear down the slopes, kick a ball or fly a kite. Or take the **Piazza del Campidoglio** *(see p80)* exit at the other end of the Roman Forum *(see pp76–9)* to avoid exiting into heavy traffic, where kids can run around the piazza or along the wooded paths of **Monte Caprino park** *(Via Tempio di Giove, 00184)*.

Eat and drink

Picnic: under €25; Snacks: €25–40; Real meal: €40–80; Family treat: over €80 (based on a family of four)

PICNIC Santeo *(Via di San Teodoro 88, 00186; 06 6992 0945; open daily)* is famous for its profiteroles, *mont blanc* (chestnut and whipped cream dessert), mousses, jewel-coloured macaroons and quiches. Enjoy a picnic on the slopes of the Circus Maximus.

SNACKS Zerosettantacinque *(Via dei Cerchi 65, 00186; 06 687 5706; open daily)* is a friendly bar great for a light lunch of salad, pizza, stuffed focaccia or *piadine* (Italian flatbread).

REAL MEAL Anima Mundi *(Via del Velabro 1, 00186; 06 9603 0061; open daily)* offers simple lunches of lasagne, *melanzane parmigiana* (baked aubergine with parmesan cheese), salads and delicious desserts such as tiramisù.

FAMILY TREAT Il Bocconcino *(Via Ostilia 23, 00184; 06 7707 9175; www.ilbocconcino.com; closed Wed)* is a popular and relaxed little restaurant where the emphasis is on local dishes made from carefully sourced seasonal ingredients.

Find out more

DIGITAL Check out the digital reconstruction of Nero's vast palace on *www.tinyurl.com/7p7qpoa*.

Take cover

To shelter from the ferocious summer sun, stretch out beneath an umbrella pine. In winter rain, escape the elements in the Houses of Livia and Augustus if they are open. The only other option is the museum.

Next stop...

REVISIT ROYALTY Experience luxury on the top floor of the **Palazzo Massimo** *(see pp98–9)*, with its collection of frescoes and mosaics from the homes of ancient Rome's elite. See portraits of Imperial families in the **Capitoline Museums** *(see pp82–3)*. Walk on to the **Parco del Colle Oppio** *(Via Labicana, 00184)* and try to imagine the extent of Nero's shortlived palace, Domus Transitoria.

Mosaics in the Palazzo Massimo, part of the Museo Nazionale Romano

⑥ Roman Forum
Sacred flames and game boards

In the early days of the Republic, the Forum was much like a piazza – an open space where people would shop, eat, pray and exchange news. But by the 2nd century BC, Rome controlled not only Italy, but also Greece, Spain and North Africa, and the need for a more dignified centre arose. Food stalls and street hawkers were replaced with courts of law, business centres and monuments. As the population expanded, the Forum became too small. However, emperors continued to build monuments here and celebrated military victories with parades of war booty and prisoners.

Temple of Vesta,
Roman Forum

Key Features of the Roman Forum: East

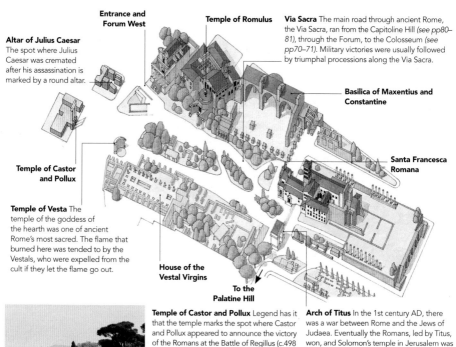

Entrance and Forum West

Temple of Romulus

Via Sacra The main road through ancient Rome, the Via Sacra, ran from the Capitoline Hill (see pp80–81), through the Forum, to the Colosseum (see pp70–71). Military victories were usually followed by triumphal processions along the Via Sacra.

Altar of Julius Caesar The spot where Julius Caesar was cremated after his assassination is marked by a round altar.

Basilica of Maxentius and Constantine

Temple of Castor and Pollux

Santa Francesca Romana

Temple of Vesta The temple of the goddess of the hearth was one of ancient Rome's most sacred. The flame that burned here was tended to by the Vestals, who were expelled from the cult if they let the flame go out.

House of the Vestal Virgins

To the Palatine Hill

Temple of Castor and Pollux Legend has it that the temple marks the spot where Castor and Pollux appeared to announce the victory of the Romans at the Battle of Regillus (c.498 BC). The three columns supporting a broken slice of entablature – all that is left of the temple – are one of the Forum's prettiest ruins.

Arch of Titus In the 1st century AD, there was a war between Rome and the Jews of Judaea. Eventually the Romans, led by Titus, won, and Solomon's temple in Jerusalem was sacked. Carved on this arch, which was erected to celebrate the victory, are soldiers carrying the spoils of war.

Basilica of Maxentius and Constantine A vast, barrel-vaulted basilica, this once held a colossal marble statue of Emperor Constantine, parts of which, including the great hand, are now on display in the Capitoline Museums (see pp82–3). In the 7th century AD, the shiny golden tiles that covered the arched vaults of the basilica were stripped off and used to decorate St Peter's Basilica (see pp204–5).

Temple of Romulus This circular Roman temple was converted into the vestibule of the church of Santi Cosma e Damiano in the 6th century AD. Inside the church is a beautifully carved Neapolitan *presepio* (Nativity scene). The main entrance is on Via dei Fori Imperiali.

Santa Francesca Romana Every year on 9 March, devout Roman drivers queue up outside this church to get their vehicles blessed by Santa Francesca Romana, the patron saint of drivers.

House of the Vestal Virgins Girls between the ages of 6 and 10 were selected to become Vestals and sent to live in the House of the Vestal Virgins. They were taken from their families and their hair was cut off and hung on a lotus tree as an offering to the gods. Their main job was to tend to the sacred flame in the Temple of Vesta. They also baked sacrificial cakes with the flour that they milled in the grinding room and bakery. The house has a beautiful courtyard with lily ponds and now headless statues of the Vestals.

The Lowdown

🌐 **Map reference** 12 H6
Address Largo Salara Vecchia, 00186; 06 3996 7700; *www. archeoroma.beniculturali.it*

🚗 **Metro** Colosseo (Line B). **Bus** 60, 75, 84, 85, 87, 117, 175, 186, 271, 571, 810 & 850

🕐 **Open** end Oct–15 Feb: 8:30am–4:30pm, closing times vary during the rest of the year; check website for details (last adm: 1 hr before closing)

💶 **Price** €24–39 (includes the Palatine Hill and Colosseum); under 18s free. Tickets are valid for two days.

🎫 **Skipping the queue** Tickets can be bought at *www. ticketclic.it* or by phone (€2 booking fee). Buy a Roma Pass (see p23) and enter via a special, faster queue.

🚩 **Guided tours** Audioguides (€5) are available at the Palatine Hill or on *www.coopculture.it* (free). Call to book tours.

👫 **Age range** 5 plus

⏱ **Allow** 2–3 hrs

♿ **Wheelchair access** Yes, limited

☕ **Café** Refreshment vans outside the entrance to the Palatine Hill.

🏷 **Shop** The bookshop at the main entrance offers several books for children.

🚻 **Toilets** In the Museo Palatino (see p74)

Good family value?
To get the most out of the site, children need to be able to run around and find things for themselves, so come early in the morning before the crowds start to arrive.

⑥ The Roman Forum continued ▶

Roman Forum continued
Key Features of the Roman Forum: West

Santa Maria Antiqua This church was converted from a 2nd-century-AD Roman building in the 6th century. Archaeologists have created digital models of the building in various stages of its life, and have revealed six layers of Byzantine frescoes, one on top of the other.

To Piazza del Campidoglio

Arch of Septimius Severus

Temple of Saturn

The Umbilicus A stone mound, this was believed to be the centre, or belly button, of ancient Rome.

Rostrum

Basilica Julia A law court, Basilica Julia had room for four cases to be tried at a time in "courts" divided by curtains. Carved into its steps are game boards – people passed the time between cases by playing games here.

Temple of Saturn Dedicated to Saturn, god of justice, strength and time, this temple was rebuilt several times. The current ruins date from AD 283, when Emperor Diocletian rebuilt it after a fire.

Entrance and Forum East

Comitium According to legend, the Comitium was founded by Romulus. It comprised a market, several temples and the Curia – now reconstructed – where the Senate met, and the Lapis Niger, a sacred stone of mysterious significance.

Basilica Aemilia A rectangular meeting hall founded in 179 BC, the basilica was where bankers, moneylenders and tax officials traded. The hall was still in use half a century later, when the Goths invaded Rome and set the Forum on fire – the pavement is spotted with tiny splashes of rust and verdigris, the remains of coins that melted in the heat.

Letting off steam
Leave by the main exit for a run around the **Parco del Colle Oppio** (Via Labicana, 00184).

View of the Colosseum from the Parco del Colle Oppio

Eat and drink
Picnic: under €25; Snacks: €25–40; Real meal: €40–80; Family treat: over €80 (based on a family of four)

PICNIC Pizza e Mortadella (Via Cavour 279, 00184; open daily) offers all the ingredients for a gourmet picnic, including crisp pizza slices, stuffed focaccia, roast chicken, lasagne, grilled vegetables, cheeses, hams and salamis and mouthwatering cakes and tarts. Put together a picnic lunch and head to the Parco del Colle Oppio or to the Monte Caprino park.
SNACKS Daruma Sushi (Via dei Serpenti 1, 00184; 06 4893 1003; www.darumasushi.com; closed Sun lunch) serves a variety of sushi, sashimi, miso soup and noodles. The restaurant also offers free delivery services to many hotels.
REAL MEAL La Bottega del Caffè (Piazza Madonna dei Monti 5, 00184; 06 474 1578; open daily) is a bustling bistro and café located at

The pretty outdoor seating area of La Bottega del Caffè

the heart of Monti, the area behind the Fori Imperiali (see p89), and has plenty of outdoor tables and space on the piazza for children to play.
FAMILY TREAT Cavour 313 (Via Cavour 313, 00184; 06 678 5496; summer: closed Sun) began as a wine bar and developed into a restaurant. Its modern European dishes such as cannelloni with wild chicory, anchovies, ricotta and chilli, and couscous with beef, prunes and almonds, reflect what is fresh in the

Arch of Septimius Severus This triumphal arch, one of the best preserved and most striking monuments in the Forum, is dedicated to Septimius Severus (r.193–211), who led a number of battles, and his sons, Caracalla and Geta. The arch was erected by the Roman senate to celebrate their victory over the Parthians.

Rostrum The stage from which politicians made speeches in ancient Rome was called a rostrum, a word that is still used to refer to platforms used by teachers and public speakers. In Roman times, rostrums were decorated with the prows of captured ships.

Cloaca Maxima The main drain or sewer of ancient Rome, this was where the bodies of executed criminals and martyred saints – among them St Peter – were thrown.

KIDS' CORNER

Challenge an adult
Below the Lapis Niger is a column inscribed "etis eht selpmart ohw enoyna no sesruc erid." The inscription is written in "boustrophedon". Ask an adult if they know what this is.
(Clues: It is a kind of writing. In Greek "bou" means "ox", and "strophe" means "the act of turning". One line is written from right to left, and the next from left to right, in the same direction that an ox or a tractor would plough a field!)

MERRY SATURNALIA
The Temple of Saturn was the focus of the annual Saturnalia winter festival, which had much in common with Christmas: schools were closed, a fair and market were held, presents, including woolly socks and slippers, were exchanged, and special dinners were held.

market. The restaurant also offers a selection of carpaccios, cheeses, hams and salamis, salads and wines.

Find out more
DIGITAL Visit *www.historyforkids. org/learn/romans/architecture/forum. htm* for a clear explanation of the Forum's history. Younger children can check out *www.bbc.co.uk/cbbc/ games* for a Terrible Treasures game set in a Roman sewer.

Next stop...
VIRTUAL ROME To learn more about how people lived, visit the actual remains and digital reconstructions of Roman houses under **Palazzo Valentini** (see p88). For an aerial view of the Forum, take the glass elevator up **Il Vittoriano** (see p84). Or discover the secrets revealed by an ancient Roman rubbish dump – and walk through an ancient drain – at the **Crypta Balbi** (see p85).

Humbled magician
In the 1st century AD, Simon Magus, a magician, decided to prove that his powers were superior to those of saints Peter and Paul by levitating above the Forum. The SS dropped to their knees and prayed to God to humble him. Simon immediately plummeted to his death.

The Roman Forum and Colosseum from Il Vittoriano

⑦ Capitoline Hill
Geometry, symmetry and other trees

One of the seven hills of Rome, the Capitoline Hill was first the fortified centre of ancient Rome and later home to its most important temples. The broad flight of steps leading up the hill was designed by Michelangelo, as was the Piazza del Campidoglio at its head. At the centre of the piazza is a gilded bronze statue of Marcus Aurelius, the original of which is in the Capitoline Museums. Legend has it that when the last gold leaf flakes off the statue, the world will end.

Gilded bronze statue of Marcus Aurelius

Key Sights

Il Vittoriano (see p84)

Santa Maria in Aracoeli

Statue of Marcus Aurelius

Palazzo Nuovo (see p83)

Piazza del Campidoglio

Roman *insula* Dwarfed by the huge Vittoriano are the ruins of an ancient Roman apartment block where some of the city's poorer families lived. Visible are the fourth, fifth and part of the sixth storeys; the rest is underground.

Palazzo dei Conservatori (see p82)

Aracoeli staircase Literally meaning "stairway to heaven", the Aracoeli staircase leads to the church of Santa Maria in Aracoeli. Popular belief is that anyone who climbs the staircase on their knees will win the lottery.

Tarpeian Rock In ancient Rome, traitors were thrown to their deaths from this cliff, named after Tarpeia, the daughter of a Roman general, who, according to mythology, betrayed Rome to the Sabines.

Cordonata

Monte Caprino park

Santa Maria in Aracoeli The church has a replica of a miraculous figure of baby Jesus, the original of which was stolen in 1994 and was said to have the power to revive the dead.

Cordonata Statues of the Dioscuri – Castor and Pollux – stand at the head of the ramp whose treads were designed to resemble the ropes put across steep paths to help people climb them.

The Lowdown

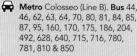

🌐 **Map reference** 12 G5
Address Capitoline Museums: see pp82–3. Santa Maria in Aracoeli: Piazza del Campidoglio 55, 00186; 06 6976 3839

🚗 **Metro** Colosseo (Line B). **Bus** 44, 46, 62, 63, 64, 70, 80, 81, 84, 85, 87, 95, 160, 170, 175, 186, 204, 492, 628, 640, 715, 716, 780, 781, 810 & 850

🕐 **Open** Santa Maria in Aracoeli: summer: 9am–6:30pm daily; closes at 5:30pm in winter

💲 **Price** Santa Maria in Aracoeli: free

👫 **Age range** 4 plus

⏱ **Allow** 1 hr (excluding the Capitoline Museums)

♿ **Wheelchair access** Yes, in the piazza & the Capitoline Museums

🚻 **Toilets** In the Capitoline Museums and Il Vittoriano

Good family value?
The lack of traffic and plenty of activities for children makes this a good and inexpensive place to keep children entertained.

Prices given are for a family of four

Letting off steam

Run races up and down the many flights of stairs near the Piazza del Campidoglio.

Staircase leading to the church of Santa Maria in Aracoeli

Eat and drink

Picnic: under €25; Snacks: €25–40; Real meal: €40–80; Family treat: over €80 (based on a family of four)

PICNIC Pizzicheria *(Via de' Delfini 25, 00186; 06 679 3001; closed Sat pm)* is an old-fashioned *alimentari* (grocery store) that offers a deli counter and fresh bread. Buy a picnic lunch and eat it on the Aracoeli staircase.
SNACKS Antico Caffè del Teatro Marcello *(Via del Teatro di Marcello 42, 00186; 06 678 5451; open daily),* located across the road from the Monte Caprino park, has a tempting range of sandwiches and pastries.
REAL MEAL Trattoria Ara Coeli *(Piazza dell'Ara Coeli 5, 00186; 06 679 2491)* is a simple trattoria serving hearty Roman dishes prepared with ingredients of the highest quality. Try the delicious *pasta alla carbonara* and *cacio e pepe* (cheese and pepper).
FAMILY TREAT La Taverna degli Amici *(Piazza Margana 36–7, 00186; 06 6992 0637; closed Sun pm & Mon am)* is located on a pretty little

Sumptuous food on display in Antico Caffè del Teatro

square. Specialities include courgette flowers stuffed with ricotta, *ossobuco* (braised veal shanks) and *tagliata* (thinly sliced rare steaks).

Shopping

Little Big Town *(Via C. Battisti 130, 00187; 06 6992 4226; open daily),* a toy shop housed in a three-storey building, has a wide selection of toys and games.

Find out more

DIGITAL For fun facts about the Piazza del Campidoglio, visit *www.tinyurl.com/8x34zsv.*
FILM Watch an entertaining film about Michelangelo on *www.tinyurl.com/mqdxyjh.* Woody Allen's romantic comedy *To Rome with Love* (2012), starring Jesse Eisenberg, features the Piazza del Campidoglio and 69 other sights in Rome.

People on the terrace of the wedding-cake-like Vittoriano

Take cover

If the children are not in the mood to visit the **Capitoline Museums** *(see pp82–3),* take cover in **Il Vittoriano** *(see p84)* or go to the church of Santa Maria in Aracoeli on the Piazza del Campidoglio to see the replica of the miraculous Bambino Gesù (baby Jesus).

Next stop...

ON MICHELANGELO'S TRAIL
After visiting the Piazza del Campidoglio and the Cordonata, carry on to see the other works by Michelangelo, in the **Sistine Chapel** *(see pp208–209),* **St Peter's** *(see pp204–205),* **Santa Maria sopra Minerva** *(see p124)* and **San Pietro in Vincoli** *(see p96).*

(see pp82–3), (see p84), (see pp208–209), (see pp204–205), (see p124), (see p96).

KIDS' CORNER

Piazza del Campidoglio Q & A
Look carefully at the geometric design on the Piazza del Campidoglio.
1 Is it a circle or an oval?
2 How many points does the star at the centre have?
3 How many points does the geometric flower at the centre have?
4 How many steps can you climb up or down from the piazza?

Answers at the bottom of the page.

FULL HOUSE
It is believed that up to 380 people may have lived in the *insula* by the Aracoeli staircase, which may have had more than six storeys. The poet Horace complained about having to climb 200 steps to get to his top-floor flat.

Dear Santa
Many Roman children write their Christmas letters to Santo Bambino – the statue of the baby Jesus in the chuch of Santa Maria in Aracoeli – instead of Santa Claus. At Christmas time, the statue is placed in a beautiful crib, and on 6 January every year he is carried down the Aracoeli staircase in a procession attended by thousands of people.

Answers: 1 It is an oval. **2** 12. **3** 12. **4** 124.

⑧ Capitoline Museums

Giant body parts and a granite crocodile

Housed within two majestic Renaissance palaces flanking Michelangelo's trapezoid Piazza del Campidoglio, the Capitoline Museums contain Rome's finest and most famous collection of Classical sculpture as well as a gallery of Renaissance art.

The collection began back in the mid-15th century, when Pope Sixtus IV donated several bronze statues to the people of Rome, making the Capitoline Museums the oldest public museum in the world.

Palazzo dei Conservatori

The most stunning piece in this museum is the gilded bronze equestrian statue of Marcus Aurelius, now in a grand glass hall. It is quite unlike any other Roman sculpture: there is a tenderness about the emperor that is a world away from the idealized statues of Constantine and others – it is easy to become convinced that it is breathing. A copy of the statue is in the middle of Piazza del Campidoglio.

While much of the palazzo is given over to ancient sculpture, the art galleries on the second floor hold works by artists such as Caravaggio, Van Dyck and Titian, among others.

The museum also has a section devoted to the piazza in the Iron Age, with interactive computer programmes that may appeal to older children. Several rooms are dedicated to finds from some of the Roman gardens that once graced the Esquiline Hill, including a gory statue of *Marsyas*, who was flayed alive. The statue was carved from purple-red marble to make it look like raw flesh.

Palazzo dei Conservatori

Caffè Capitolino

④ ⑤ **Piazza Caffarelli entrance**

① ② ③

Museum entrance from Piazza del Campidoglio

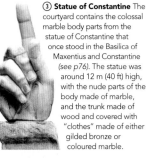
③ **Statue of Constantine** The courtyard contains the colossal marble body parts from the statue of Constantine that once stood in the Basilica of Maxentius and Constantine (see p76). The statue was around 12 m (40 ft) high, with the nude parts of the body made of marble, and the trunk made of wood and covered with "clothes" made of either gilded bronze or coloured marble.

④ **Statue of Marcus Aurelius** An entire light-flooded room is dedicated to the marvelous equestrian statue of Marcus Aurelius. Standing 11 ft (4 m) high, it is unlike any other Roman sculpture.

⑤ **Temple of the Jupiter Capitolinus** On display off the Marcus Aurelius Exedra are the foundations of an Etruscan Temple of Jupiter, Juno and Minerva.

① **Spinario** The 1st-century-AD bronze statue of a boy trying to remove a thorn from his foot stands in the Hall of Triumphs.

② **She-wolf** The Etruscan bronze statue of Lupa, the she-wolf who nursed the legendary twins Romulus and Remus, dates from the early 5th century BC. The twins were added in the 15th century.

Prices given are for a family of four

The Lowdown

🌐 **Map reference** 9 A1
Address Piazza del Campidoglio 1, 00187; 060608; www.museicapitolini.org

🚗 **Metro** Colosseo (Line B). **Bus** 44, 46, 62, 63, 64, 70, 80, 81, 84, 85, 87, 95, 160, 170, 175, 186, 204, 492, 628, 640, 715, 716, 780, 781, 810 & 850

🕐 **Open** 9am–8pm Tue–Sun (last adm: 1 hr before closing)

💲 **Price** €23–42; reduced fee for 6- to 26-year-olds; under 6s free

🚻 **Skipping the queue** Queues tend to form only when large tour groups arrive. The quietest times to visit the museums are early morning and lunchtime. Buy tickets in advance from 060608. Alternatively, buy a Roma Pass (see p23).

Guided tours Audioguides (€5) in all major European languages are available at the museums.

👫 **Age range** 5 plus

⏱ **Allow** 2–3 hrs

♿ **Wheelchair access** Yes

🍴 **Eat and drink** PICNIC Kosher Delight (Via del Portico d'Ottavia 12, 00186; closed Fri pm & Sat) is a kosher deli. Buy cold cuts (bresaola or carne secca), hummus, and challah bread and eat by the ruins of the Teatro Marcello. REAL MEAL Caffè Capitolino (Piazza Caffarelli 4, 00187; 06 6919 0564; Tue–Sun), located on the top floor of the Palazzo dei Conservatori and accessed via the museum or, for non-ticket holders, from the Piazza Caffarelli entrance, opens onto a roof terrace with lovely views. The café serves panini, salads, simple pasta dishes and mains.

🛍 **Shop** The shop at the museum entrance offers an appealing selection of children's books in Italian and English.

🚻 **Toilets** Near the museum entrance and by the café

Palazzo Nuovo

A gallery below Piazza del Campidoglio links the Palazzo dei Conservatori to the Palazzo Nuovo. Begin by following signs to the Tabularium, which take visitors past the ruins of the Temple of Veiovis to the foundation of the ancient Roman Public Records Office, from where there are good views out over the Roman Forum (see pp76–9).

Once upstairs, start with the Egyptian room just off the main courtyard, which has an interesting array of Egyptian statues found in the streets around the church of Santa Maria sopra Minerva, where there was an important temple to the Egyptian goddess Isis. Look out for the two monkeys, a granite crocodile and two sphinxes. The main galleries are located on the first floor. Stop by the Hall of the Emperors, which has marble portraits of the Imperial family, and the Hall of the Philosophers, which has portraits of Greek politicians, scientists and literary figures.

Letting off steam

Head across to Il Vittoriano (see p84), where kids will enjoy taking the glass elevator to the terrace.

KIDS' CORNER

Can you spot...

In the Palazzo Nuovo's Hall of the Emperors see if you can spot:

1 An empress with a striped shawl and black hair
2 A lady with her hair twisted into pasta-like spirals
3 A lady with hair like curls of butter
4 A lady with hair like snails
5 A lady with ringlets like sausages
6 A boy with ears that stick out

Answers at the bottom of the page.

SNAKE OR DOG?

The marble statue of the girl with the dove has a snake curling at the hem of the girl's skirts. However, the restorers had made a mistake. The "snake" was originally the tail of a dog.

Thorny message

The Spinario is said to be a shepherd boy named Gnaeus Martius, who had to deliver an important message to the Roman Senate. He ran without stopping and, even when he had been pricked by a thorn in his foot, he only stopped to remove it after the message had been delivered. The boy became a symbol of loyalty, and was often known as Fedelino, meaning "little loyal one".

Answers: 1 Lucilla. 2 A Flavian Woman. 3, 4 & 5 Ritratto femminile. 6 Valente or Onorio.

Palazzo Nuovo

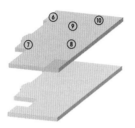

⑥ Room of Doves On one of the walls of this room is a mosaic of doves that once decorated the floors of Villa Adriana (see pp238–9), and in the centre is a marble statue of a little girl playing with a pet dove.

⑦ Capitoline Venus One of the finest works on display in the museum, this statue dates from around AD 100–150 and is a Roman copy of the original carved in the 4th century BC by the Greek sculptor Praxiteles. The statue depicts Venus with an urn of water and a towel: according to legend, the advent of spring was marked by the goddess taking her annual bath.

⑧ Alexander Severus as Hunter In this 3rd-century-AD statue, the emperor's pose is a pastiche of Perseus holding up the head of Medusa the Gorgon after he had killed her.

⑨ Discobolus The twisted torso was part of a Greek statue of a discus thrower. An 18th-century French sculptor, Monnot, made the additions that turned him into a wounded warrior.

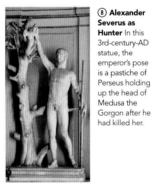

⑩ Dying Gaul This Roman copy of a 3rd-century-BC Greek work depicting a Gaul with a wound and unruly hair is one of the most famous statues on display in the museum.

⑨ Piazza Venezia
A secret university

Dominated by Il Vittoriano, Piazza Venezia is the busiest square in central Rome. As the main hub of the city, it was the obvious choice for a metro station and ever since 2001, when the construction work began, the piazza has been buzzing with activity. As engineers and archaeologists dug down, they came across an ancient Roman glass factory and then two flights of staircases that probably belonged to Hadrian's Athenaeum, an ancient university where intellectuals would meet for debates and readings. Today, the plan is to build a station-cum-museum under the piazza.

On one side of the piazza is **Palazzo Venezia**, built in the 15th century for Pope Paul II.

The magnificent white marble building of Il Vittoriano

View of Piazza Venezia from the terrace of Il Vittoriano

The palazzo is most famous as the headquarters of the Fascist dictator Mussolini, who had his apartment and offices here and would address the people of Rome from the balcony overlooking the piazza. Today it houses a museum, which has a rich collection ranging from early Renaissance paintings and painted wedding chests to Neapolitan ceramic figurines, although it is most visited when hosting a major exhibition.

Around the back of the palazzo is **San Marco**, the church of the Venetians, which has some fine 9th-century mosaics on its apse.

Letting off steam
Carefully cross the busy Piazza Venezia to **Il Vittoriano** and take the glass elevator to the terrace for views of ancient Roman ruins.

⑩ Il Vittoriano
A typewriter with a point of view

Officially known as the Altar of the Nation, and unofficially as the typewriter or wedding cake, Il Vittoriano is an enormous white marble building, which opened in 1911 in honour of Vittorio Emanuele II and the unified Italy, of which he was king. It is so immense – the equestrian statue of the king in the centre measures 12 m (40 ft) from the horse's nose to its tail, which makes it as huge as the statue of Constantine (see p82) – that it makes the soldiers guarding it and the people visiting it look like ants.

For most of its life the monument has been closed to the public, but it is now open and definitely worth a visit. The views from it are spectacular, whether from the lower levels, the glass elevator or the terrace. The small museums inside are of limited interest, but the building often hosts interesting exhibitions. There is a café with a terrace, and exits and entrances from the monument give direct access onto the Aracoeli staircase (see p80) and, from the café, via the rooms of Santa Maria in Aracoeli, to the Piazza del Campidoglio (see p80).

Letting off steam
Walk to the **Piazza del Campidoglio**, behind Il Vittoriano, where children can run up and down the many staircases. Then head to the garden of **Villa Aldobrandini** (Via IV Novembre, 00197), which offers ample space for kids to run around and also to enjoy a picnic lunch.

The Lowdown

🌐 **Map reference** 12 G4
Address Palazzo Venezia: Via del Plebiscito 118, 00187; 06 6999 4388; www.tinyurl.com/7y2owm4

🚌 **Bus** H, 30, 40, X60, 62, 63, 64, 70, X80, 81, 85, 87, 95, 119, 160, 170, 175, 186, 271, 492, 571, 628, 630, 716, 810 & 850

🕐 **Open** Palazzo Venezia: 8:30am–7:30pm Tue–Sun. Ticket offices close at 6:30pm.

💶 **Price** Palazzo Venezia: €10–15, expect to pay more during exhibitions; under 18s free

🎫 **Skipping the queue** Palazzo Venezia: book well in advance for major exhibitions either by calling 060608 or on www.060608.it or www.ticketone.it

👥 **Guided tours** Audioguides (free) can be downloaded from the museum's website.

🚹 **Age range** Palazzo Venezia museum: 9 plus

⏱ **Allow** 1–2 hrs

♿ **Wheelchair access** Yes

🍴 **Eat and drink** PICNIC Cin Cin Bar (Via C. Battisti 129, 00187; open daily) is a great place to munch on sausage-and-potato-pie or a plate of baked pasta. REAL MEAL Pane Vino e San Daniele (Piazza Mattei 16, 00186; 06 687 7147; open daily) specializes in polenta with pheasant ragù (ragout) and potatoes baked with mushrooms and cheese.

🛍 **Shop** The museum's first-floor shop sells guidebooks, art books, catalogues and posters.

🚻 **Toilets** On the first floor

The Lowdown

- **Map reference** 12 G5
- **Address** Via San Pietro in Carcere, 00187; 06 678 0664; www.tinyurl.com/88jg9n9
- **Bus** H, 30, 40, X60, 62, 63, 64, 70, X80, 81, 85, 87, 95, 119, 160, 170, 175, 186, 271, 492, 571, 628, 630, 716, 810 & 850
- **Open** 9:30am–5:45pm Mon–Thu, 9:30am–6:45pm Fri & Sun. Lift: 9:30am–6:30pm Mon–Thu, 9:30am–7:30pm Fri–Sun
- **Price** Free. Lift: €14–21; under 10s free
- **Skipping the queue** Lift: there are often queues at sunset. Visit at other times to avoid crowds
- **Age range** All ages
- **Allow** 1 hr
- **Wheelchair access** Yes
- **Eat and drink** SNACKS The café on the terrace (Via San Pietro in Carcere & Piazza Aracoeli, 00187; 06 678 0905; open daily) serves milkshakes and sandwiches, and is a nice place for breakfast or a snack. FAMILY TREAT Da Giggetto (Via del Portico di Ottavia 21–22, 00186; 06 686 1105; closed Mon) serves Jewish-Roman specialities such as deep-fried artichokes and coda di vaccinara (oxtail stew)
- **Toilets** In the café

⑪ Crypta Balbi
The story of a rubbish dump

The newest branch of the Museo Nazionale Romano, the Crypta Balbi tells the story of how the piece of land and buildings directly behind it were used, abused and reused over the centuries. In the 1980s, archaeologists discovered a private theatre built in 13 BC on an abandoned plot of land between two convents. On excavating the esedra (curved part of the theatre), archaeologists found fragments of a marble semicircle of seats set above a drain – an ancient latrine, which dates back to the 1st century AD and seems to have been designed for the wealthy. By the 3rd century, the area had fallen from grace and blocks of flats for the poor had been built, one of them with a Mithraeum in the basement. It is possible to walk along a series of Roman drains and water cisterns below the museum itself.

Exhibits at the Crypta Balbi, Museo Nazionale Romano

Displays in the museum show finds from the site, including fragments of glass from the glassworks and the graves of two children and an adult discovered in the esedra.

Letting off steam
Walk along the Tiber footpath, or explore the mainly traffic-free Jewish Ghetto (see pp134–5).

The Lowdown

- **Map reference** 12 E5
- **Address** Via delle Botteghe Oscure 31, 00186; 06 3996 7700; www.archeoroma.beniculturali.it
- **Bus** H, 30, 40, 46, 62, 63, 64, 70, 87, 119, 130, 186, 190, 271, 492, 571, 630, 780, 810 & 916. Tram 8
- **Open** 9am–7:45pm Tue–Sun (last adm: 1 hr before closing)
- **Price** €14–21 (includes all four sites of the Museo Nazionale Romano); under 18s free; the ticket is valid for 3 days.
- **Skipping the queue** Queues are unlikely
- **Guided tours** Free. 7pm Tue, 3pm Sun. Call to book
- **Age range** 8 plus
- **Allow** 1 hr
- **Wheelchair access** Yes, in the museum
- **Eat and drink** PICNIC Beppe e i Suoi Formaggi (Via Santa Maria del Pianto 11, 00186; Tue–Sun) is known for its home-made cheese and its Italian salami and hams. SNACKS Caffè Ducati (Via delle Botteghe Oscure 35, 00186; 06 6889 1718; open daily) serves pastries for breakfast, light lunches and cocktails in the evening
- **Shop** The museum bookshop on the ground floor sells books on ancient Rome
- **Toilets** On the ground floor

Picnic under €25; Snacks €25–40; Real meal €40–80; Family treat over €80 (based on a family of four)

⑫ Trajan's Markets
Retail therapy, Roman-style

Trajan's Markets were the world's first shopping mall, a complex of 150 shops laid out on five levels. Built in the 2nd century AD, the markets had shops that sold everything from fish – kept alive in fresh- and saltwater tanks – to spices, fruit, flowers, wine, oil and fabrics. The dour, red-brick complex is well preserved, with a main hall, a paved street with shops opening off it, and a three-storey crescent containing yet more shops. When it opened, it had the same impact on the city as hypermarkets do today – small specialist markets such as the Forum Boarium, selling meat, and Forum Holitarium, selling fruit and vegetables, lost a lot of trade.

Key Features

Main Hall The main hall had two storeys, with shops on either side. On the upper floor were the offices from where the *annona* (the free corn ration given to Roman men and boys) was shared out.

Via Biberatica The main street that runs through the market, Via Biberatica (literally "drinking street") is named after the drinking inns and taverns that once lined it, and is paved with huge basalt cobbles.

Market Shop

Concert Halls

Upper Corridor The shops here were thought to have sold wine and oil, as a number of *amphorae* (storage jars) were found here.

The Terrace There are great views over Trajan's Forum and Column *(see pp88–9)* from the terrace.

Upper Corridor

Torre delle Milizie For centuries it was believed that this was the tower from which Emperor Nero watched Rome burn. However, investigations proved that this structure, which stands above the markets, was built in the Middle Ages.

Market Shop Shops like this had a partially bricked-up arched entrance with smaller rectangular doors and windows, and a wooden storage loft above.

Concert Halls The two large halls on the lowest level were used for concerts.

The Lowdown

🌐 **Map reference** 12 H4
Address Via IV Novembre 94, 00187; 060608; www.060608.it; www.mercatiditraiano.it

🚗 **Metro** Cavour (Line B). **Bus** H, 40, 60, 64, 70, 71, 117 & 170

🕐 **Open** 9:30am–7:30pm daily

💲 **Price** €23–32.50 (on non-exhibition days); prices vary on exhibition days

👪 **Skipping the queue** There are queues only on exhibition days.

🎧 **Guided tours** Audioguides (€4) are available in all major European languages and make the visit more enjoyable.

👫 **Age range** 8 plus

⏱ **Allow** 1 hr

♿ **Wheelchair access** Yes, on the upper floors of the complex

☕ **Café** No café on site, but the Caffè Costantino, located just across the road, is a friendly little café *(see p88).*

🛍 **Shop** The bookshop in the ticket office on the ground floor has some excellent books for children in English and Italian.

🚻 **Toilets** On the ground floor

Good family value?
This is a rather academic site – the videos re-create the buildings, but not the atmosphere of the ancient markets – so it is likely to appeal mostly to older children.

Diners waiting for a table outside Taverna Romana

Letting off steam

The palms and orange trees in the walled garden of **Villa Aldobrandini**, across the street from Trajan's Markets, soar high above Via IV Novembre. The garden offers space for children to run around, and there are benches for picnics too.

Eat and drink

Picnic: under €25; Snacks: €25–40; Real meal: €40–80; Family treat: over €80 (based on a family of four)

PICNIC Carlo Polica *(Via dei Serpenti 150–151, 00184; closed Thu pm & Sun)* is one of Rome's oldest delis and offers salami, cured meats and cheeses from all over Italy. Pick up gourmet sandwiches and head to Villa Aldobrandini for a picnic lunch.
SNACKS Bar Tavola Calda La Licata *(Via dei Serpenti 165, 00184; 06 488 4746)* is a popular bar-café which serves great sandwiches, including vegetarian, vegan and gluten-free options.

REAL MEAL Taverna Romana
(Via Madonna dei Monti 78, 00184; 06 4745 3253; closed Sun pm) is an authentic place for a traditional lunch of *pasta e ceci* (with chick-peas), *pasta e fagioli* (with beans) or *maltagliati con ricotta fresca* ("badly cut" pasta with fresh ricotta). Meat dishes include slow-cooked guinea fowl.
FAMILY TREAT Osteria Corte del Grillo *(Salita del Grillo 6B, 00184; 06 6992 2183; www.cortedelgrillo. com; open daily lunch & dinner)* is a fine restaurant where they demonstrate the freshness of their fish by serving it raw; cooked fish is served as well. Select a fish and the chef will bake it in a crust of salt, poach it in broth, roast or grill it.

Find out more

DIGITAL Watch videos reconstructing the markets and Fori Imperiali on *www.mercatiditraiano.it*. For something less academic, the PlayStation game Tomb Raider Chronicles 5, level 2, is set in Trajan's Markets. If not a game-player, watch Lara Croft breaking into the markets at *www.tinyurl. com/88dwcyo*. Also check out the Horrible Histories Roman Kitchen Nightmares at *www.youtube.com/ watch?v=wyNRpTNYADQ*.

Next stop...

TRAILING TRAJAN Walk down to see **Trajan's Column** *(see p88)* and the remains of the **Fori Imperiali** *(see p89)*, and then make a visit to the fabulous museum underneath **Palazzo Valentini** *(see p88)*.

Spacious dining area at Bar Tavola Calda La Licata

KIDS' CORNER

Roman shopping list
Imagine that you are the cook's slave at the elegant house down the road from Trajan's Markets. The cook asks you to go to the market to buy the following ingredients. Can you guess what might be cooking?
Chopped meat
Pepper
Cumin
Savory
Rue
Parsley
Juniper berries
Garum (fermented fish sauce)
Intestines of pig

Answers at the bottom of the page.

BUT THAT'S NOT FAIR...
Free corn was originally distributed only to grown men, but Trajan, anxious to have a supply of strong, well-fed men to join the army, allowed 5,000 boys to receive it as well. Elsewhere in Italy, Trajan introduced a cash allowance for children, but girls got less than boys, and in one town 300 boys and just 36 girls received money!

A cupboard staple
Romans could not live without *garum* – just as some people today cannot live without tomato ketchup or mayonnaise. Here is a recipe from a Roman cookery book by Apicius:
"Take the entrails, gills, blood and juice of a tuna, and add salt. Place in a sealed vessel and leave for two months." Yum...

Answers: Sausages! And your job will probably be to clean the intestines and then stuff them with the meat, herbs and spices.

⑬ Palazzo Valentini

A virtual house makeover

In 2005, builders at work beneath Palazzo Valentini, the seat of the Province of Rome, discovered what turned out to be the remains of two grand houses that belonged to wealthy patrician families of Imperial Rome. Elegant living rooms, courtyards, baths and kitchens were unearthed, with traces of mosaics, frescoes and coloured marbles.

Computer technology, light and sound effects, films and projections have been used to reconstruct the houses, resulting in a museum that brings ancient Rome to life better than anywhere else in the city. Tours take visitors to a *caldarium* with a Jacuzzi-like hot tub, a *tepidarium* (lukewarm-water bath) where bathers could relax over a game of chequers, and a *frigidarium* (cold-water bath) that opened onto a garden, with a swimming pool and a pool for children. As visitors watch, mosaic floors, marble pavements and walls are "restored" to their former glory, while sound effects re-create an earthquake that buckled the floors in AD 38. During the Renaissance, the area was used as a *butto* (rubbish dump). This too has been reconstructed in the museum. A sheep's horn, oyster shells, chicken bones, clam and tortoise shells found here give useful clues about the diet of Renaissance Romans.

A second, shorter itinerary, takes visitors to a newly excavated section of Trajan's Forum. Here, the museum screens a film that reconstructs the interior of the Emperor's libraries, as well as an intelligent animation of scenes from Trajan's Column, which is well worth watching.

Letting off steam

Visit the walled gardens of **Villa Aldobrandini** *(see p87)*, where there is enough space for children to run around, plenty of trees for adults to sit under and several benches where picnic lunches can be consumed.

Elaborate bas relief of figures on Trajan's Column

⑭ Trajan's Column

The world's first cartoon strip?

Created in AD 113 to celebrate two victorious Roman campaigns in Dacia (present-day Romania), Trajan's Column, together with its base and pedestal, is 40 m (131 ft) high, precisely the height of the spur of the Quirinal Hill that was cut away to make room for Trajan's Forum. Spiralling around the column, like one of the scrolls that would have been kept in Trajan's libraries, are carvings that tell the stories of the campaigns, so full of detail that some archaeologists think they may

have been based on Trajan's own war diary. It is not just battles that are depicted, but the realities of life at war for both Romans and Dacians.

The Romans are shown arriving in Dacia with their supplies in boats, building a camp, cutting down trees, sinking wells and constructing huts. Battle scenes show the Dacians being attacked, as well as Dacian attacks on the Romans, and even the aftermath of a battle. After the first campaign, the Dacians continued to resist, before the Romans attacked a walled town and set fire to it. The carvings also show a Dacian priest distributing poison to those who prefered to die than be conquered. It is extremely difficult to see these scenes from the ground, which makes one wonder how the Romans would have been able to see it. Standing on the upper floor of the two libraries that flanked the column would have made some of the scenes visible, but there would still have been sections that were out of sight. Today, the best way to see the column in detail is to watch animated films in Palazzo Valentini or take the metro out to EUR *(see p230)* in southern Rome to see casts at eye level.

Letting off steam

Walk up to the gardens of **Villa Aldobrandini** or to the playground at **Parco del Colle Oppio** *(Via Labicana, 00184).*

Visitors reading an information board outside the Fori Imperiali

⑮ Fori Imperiali
Ego alley

As Rome became an international power and the city expanded, the original Forum became too small, and emperors began to build new *fora* – the Fori Imperiali. Building a new forum was also a very good way for an emperor to demonstrate his importance to the populace and the world. All had temples, were surrounded by walls, were symmetrical, and all but one were built to celebrate a victory.

Caesar built his Forum, complete with heated public toilet, to celebrate his conquest over Gaul. He spent a fortune buying up and demolishing houses on the site he had selected, and dedicated a temple to Venus, with statues of himself and Cleopatra inside. Augustus's Forum celebrated his victory over Caesar's assassins, Brutus and Cassius, and the temple at its centre was dedicated to Mars the Avenger, whose statue looked suspiciously like Augustus. Domitian's Forum, of which little remains, celebrated his capture of Jerusalem, while Nerva's was the smallest – little more than a corridor leading to a temple dedicated to the goddess Minerva.

Forum of Caesar, with remains of the Temple of Venus

The Forum of Trajan – built after the emperor's victory over the Dacians – was probably the most ambitious. An entire slice of the Quirinal Hill was dug away to make room for it. Dominated by Trajan's Column, it included two libraries and was overlooked by Trajan's Markets. Recent excavations reveal more and more of this forum. All are closed to the public, though visitors can view them from Via dei Fori Imperiali.

Letting off steam
Go for a walk around Monti and let the children run around and play on traffic-free **Piazza Madonna dei Monti**.

The Lowdown
- 🌐 **Map reference** 12 H5
  Address Via dei Fori Imperiali, 00186; *www.mercatiditraiano.it*
- 🚗 **Metro** Colosseo (Line B)
- 🕐 **Open** Closed to the public
- 🚩 **Guided tours** Enquire at Trajan's Markets.
- 👫 **Age range** 9 plus
- ⏱ **Allow** 30 mins
- ♿ **Wheelchair access** Yes, to perimeter roads
- 🍴 **Eat and drink** PICNIC Super Elite *(Via Cavour, 232, 00184)* is a good supermarket that sells all the essentials for a sumptuous picnic by the Forum. *FAMILY TREAT* La Vecchia Roma *(Via Leonina 10, 00184; 06 474 5887; closed Sun)* is a lovely traditional place with daily specials written on a board outside. Let the children try the *scottadito* (literally finger-burning) lamb chops.
- 🚻 **Toilets** At the visitor centre opposite the Roman Forum

KIDS' CORNER
Answer these...
In Palazzo Valentini, see if you can find the answers to these questions:
1 Where can you find an ancient Roman Jacuzzi and a children's paddling pool?
2 What made the floors of ancient Rome buckle in AD 38?
3 When might roast mutton, tortoise soup and oysters have been on the menu?

Answers at the bottom of the page.

INVISIBLE WEAPONS
The sculptors of Trajan's Column had carved weapons for some soldiers, but drilled holes into the hands of others so that metal weapons could be bolted on later. None of these metal weapons have survived, of course. Some soldiers have neither a carved weapon nor a hole in their hands – a sign, perhaps, that the column was created in a bit of a rush.

A perfect script
The carved script on the base of Trajan's Column is one of the most elegant examples of the Roman alphabet. There is even a modern font based on the script, called Trajan. The Trajan Typeface Animation on *www.tinyurl.com/7k922tt* is a short cartoon based on the battle scenes on the column, with all the figures made out of letters and symbols from the Trajan font.
Can you draw a picture of a Roman emperor using only capital letters, numbers and symbols? (Hint – you can use the letters backwards or upside down or any way you like.)

Answers: 1 In the ancient Roman *domus* (house) underneath. **2** An earthquake. **3** In Renaissance Rome.

San Clemente and around

The largest and highest of Rome's seven hills, the Esquiline Hill stretches from the Colosseum and Forum up to Termini station and the busy grid of 19th- and 20th-century streets around Piazza Vittorio Emanuele II. The area is heavily congested with traffic, apart from Colle Oppio, whose ancient sights are far less visited than those in the centre. The area is well connected by metro and bus services. The fashionable Monti area just above Via dei Fori Imperiali, with its appealing restaurants, shops, and hotels can be easily explored on foot.

Ancient Rome

Palazzo Massimo p98

San Clemente p92

The Lowdown

🚗 **Metro** Colosseo (Line B), Cavour (Line B), Termini (Lines A & B) & Vittorio Emanuele (Line A). **Bus** C2, C3, H, 16, 36, 38, 40, 53, 64, 85, 86, 87, 90, 92, 105, 117, 170, 175, 186, 217, 310, 360, 571, 649, 714, 810 & 910. **Tram** 3

ℹ️ **Visitor information** Visitor Centre, Via dei Fori Imperiali, 00186; open 9:30am–7pm daily; Oct–Mar: 8:30am–4:30pm daily. Tourist Information Point, Termini, Via Giovanni Giolitti 34, 00185; open 8am–6:45pm daily. Tourist Information Point, Via Nazionale (near Palazzo delle Esposizioni), 00184; 060608; open 9:30am–7pm daily; www.turismoroma.it

🛒 **Supermarkets** Conad City, Via del Boschetto 52, 00184. **Markets** Nuovo Mercato Esquilino covered market, Via Principe Amedeo, 00185; 7am–1pm Mon–Sat

🎉 **Festival** Festa della Madonna della Neve (5 Aug): the celebration of the Feast of Our Lady of the Snow in Santa Maria Maggiore

➕ **Pharmacies** Farmacia Savignoni di Maria Bartoleschi: Via dei Serpenti 125, 00184; 06 488 2973; open 8:30am–10:30pm Mon–Fri, 8:30am–7:30pm Sat. Farmacia Piram: Via Nazionale 228, 00184; 06 488 0754; open daily

🎏 **Nearest play areas** Parco del Colle Oppio, Via IV Novembre, 00187. Piazza Vittorio Emanuele II, 00185

People on the steps of San Pietro in Vincoli church

Figurines at the Museo Nazionale d'Arte Orientale

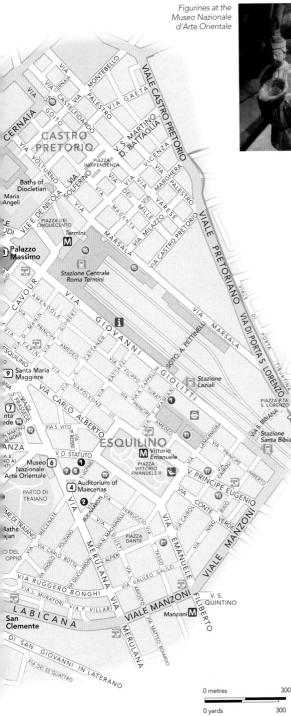

Places of Interest

SIGHTS
1. San Clemente
2. Domus Aurea
3. The Baths of Trajan
4. Auditorium of Maecenas
5. San Pietro in Vincoli
6. Museo Nazionale d'Arte Orientale
7. Santa Prassede & Santa Pudenziana
8. Palazzo Massimo
9. Santa Maria Maggiore

EAT AND DRINK
1. Panificio Disa
2. Caffetteria Faiola
3. Trattoria Luzzi
4. Li Rioni
5. Made in Sud
6. Os Club
7. Panella
8. Tempio di Mecenate
9. Pizza e Mortadella
10. Cuoco e Camicia
11. Nuovo Mercato Esquilino
12. Hang Zhou
13. Palazzo del Freddo
14. Il Pane
15. Coop
16. W.O.K.
17. Himalaya's Kashmir
18. Trimani Il Wine Bar
19. Pietro Roscioli
20. Antica Osteria Angelino dal 1899
21. Trattoria Da Danilo

SHOPPING
1. Selli International Food Store
2. Città del Sole

WHERE TO STAY
1. Radisson Blu
2. Relais Fori Imperiali
3. Retrome
4. Duca d'Alba
5. Hotel Grifo
6. BB Il Covo
7. Hotel Artorius

① San Clemente
Time to time-travel

The church of San Clemente gives visitors a chance to travel back in time and also provides an insight into how buildings were modified over the years. At street level is a 12th-century church with decorative elements, some of which, such as the apse mosaic, reflect medieval taste, while others, notably the frescoes of St Catherine of Alexandria, reflect Renaissance style. Below is a 4th-century church built to honour San Clemente, who was martyred by being tied to an anchor and drowned. This was built over a temple dedicated to the cult of Mithras, which in turn was built in a 1st-century AD aristocratic house.

Courtyard of San Clemente church

Key Features

Apse mosaic The mosaic on the apse in the upper church represents the crucified Christ as a Tree of Life. Leafy tendrils, with birds flying between them, spiral over the apse. The sheep represent the 12 Apostles.

Cappella di Santa Caterina

Lower church This church was filled with rubble so that the new church could be built on top. It took 40 years of shovelling to clear it out.

The cloister

Upper church

Apse mosaic

Schola Cantorum Salvaged from the lower church, the 8th-century *schola cantorum* was an enclosure where the choir sat.

Steps to the lower church

Temple of Mithras

Triclinium

Madonna and Divine Child This fresco was originally that of the Byzantine Empress Theodora. It was converted into a Madonna by adding a baby and a halo.

Stairs to the Roman house

Cappella di Santa Caterina In the 15th century, scenes from the life of St Catherine of Alexandria were painted by the Renaissance artists Masolino and Masaccio. The artists' sketches for these frescoes – one of which shows St Catherine on the ground as a man raises his arm to strike her – are also on display here.

Triclinium A room inside the Temple of Mithras, the *triclinium* has stone benches and a stone altar showing Mithras killing a bull.

Letting off steam

The cloister of San Clemente is a nice place to sit and unwind after touring the church. The nearest green area is the little playground at **Largo della Sanità Militare**, and just a little further away is the pine-shaded park and playground of **Villa Celimontana** (see p72).

Prices given are for a family of four

Villa Celimontana, one of the loveliest parks in Rome, perfect for a family picnic

Eat and drink

Picnic: under €25; Snacks: €25–40; Real meal: €40–80; Family treat: over €80 (based on a family of four)

PICNIC Panificio Disa (Via San Giovanni in Laterano 64, 00184; closed Sun) offers focaccia and pizza. Pick up a picnic lunch and eat it at the park of Villa Celimontana.

The Lowdown

- 🌐 **Map reference** 9 C2
- **Address** Via di San Giovanni in Laterano, 00184; 06 7740 021; www.basilicasanclemente.com
- 🚗 **Metro** Colosseo (Line B). **Bus** C3, 53, 85, 87, 117, 186, 571 & 810. **Tram** 3
- 🕐 **Open** Upper church, Lower church & Mithraeum: 9am–12:30pm & 3–6pm Mon–Sat, noon–6pm Sun
- 💲 **Price** Lower church: €20–30; under 6s free
- 👪 **Skipping the queue** Queues are unlikely

- ⏱ **Allow** 1 hr
- 👫 **Age range** 7 plus. The numerous flights of stairs and uneven surfaces make it difficult for families with toddlers in or out of pushchairs
- ♿ **Wheelchair access** No
- 🚻 **Toilets** Next to the ticket desk

Good family value?
San Clemente is entertaining for kids, though some might be spooked out by the cold and damp cellars housing the Mithraeum.

Homely interiors of Li Rioni, popular for pizzas

SNACKS Caffetteria Faiola *(Via Celimontana 6–8, 00184; 06 7049 2953; open daily)* serves excellent pizzas and sandwiches. The staff is friendly and attentive.
REAL MEAL Trattoria Luzzi *(Via Celimontana 1, 00184; 06 709 6332; closed Wed)* is an extremely popular, relatively low-priced trattoria which serves thin-crust pizzas and traditional Roman dishes such as *rigatoni amatriciana, pasta e fagioli* and *coda di vaccinara*.
FAMILY TREAT Li Rioni *(Via dei SS Quattro 24, 00184; 06 7045 0605; open pm only; closed Tue)* specializes in thin-crust pizzas made in a wood-fired oven. It also offers fried food such as *crochette di pollo* (chicken croquettes) or *crochette di patate* (potato croquettes) and *olive ascolane* (deep-fried, breaded stuffed olives).

Find out more
DIGITAL Learn about the Mithras cult, its Asian origins and how it became popular with Roman soldiers at www.tinyurl.com/6s6engv.

Next stop...
EARLY CHRISTIAN CHURCHES
See more evidence of early Christianity at **Santa Sabina** *(see p107)*, **Santa Cecilia in Trastevere** *(see pp188–9)* or **Santa Pudenziana** *(see p97)*. Also stop by the **Catacombs of Priscilla** *(see p225)*, which contain the world's earliest known image of the Madonna and Child.

Interior of Santa Sabina, a 5th-century AD Roman basilica-style church

KIDS' CORNER

I spy San Clemente!
1 On the apse mosaic of the upper church, can you find: (a) a peacock? (b) a magpie?
2 In the lower church, can you find the *piscina* or pool where Christians were baptized?
3 Rome was flooded in the year 1912. Find the plaque that marks the water level as you walk down the stairs of the Mithraeum.

Answers at the bottom of the page.

RITES OF INITIATION
The all-male Mithras cult was very popular and rivalled Christianity. Followers, who believed that Mithras had brought life to the world by spilling the blood of a bull, had to undergo scary initiation ceremonies such as trials by ice, fire, starvation and thirst.

Catherine wheel
St Catherine of Alexandria was tortured by being tied to a wheel. According to legend, the wheel collapsed, injuring spectators, so she was untied and beheaded instead. Look carefully at the fresco and you will see the wheel. The saint gave her name to the Catherine Wheel firework.

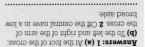

Answers: 1 (a) At the foot of the cross. **(b)** To the left and right of the arm of the cross. **2** Off the central nave in a low broad aisle.

Interior of the Domus Aurea, the massive palace built by Roman Emperor Nero

② Domus Aurea
Nero in Wonderland?

Some of the most exciting discoveries in recent times have been made in the Parco del Colle Oppio, the extensive hilly park scattered with red-brick ruins across the road from the Colosseum *(see pp70–71)*. The site of splendid gardens in the early days of the Empire, it was here that Nero built his palatial Domus Aurea (Golden House). Built in AD 64, after a fire wiped out much of the ancient city, it stretched over the Esquiline, Palatine *(see pp74–5)* and Celian *(see p72)* hills.

According to ancient Roman literature, the Domus Aurea's landscaped grounds had a huge artificial lake, complete with real ships and fake seaside villages, bath complexes, gardens, zoos,

woods, parks, grottoes, nymphaeums and elegant porticoes. There was also a long secret passage connecting it with the palaces of the Palatine Hill. The palace walls were caked with fine coloured marbles, frescoes, gold and precious stones. One of the rooms had a ceiling painted with stars and planets that revolved to imitate astronomical movements. Nero enjoyed the palace only briefly, for in AD 68 he committed suicide.

Subsequent emperors did everything to erase all trace of Nero's excesses. Vespasian drained the lake and built the Colosseum on its site, while the luxurious palace rooms were stripped of their decorations, filled with earth and buried beneath the new bath complexes of Titus and Trajan.

In the late 15th century, a Roman boy fell through a cleft on the Colle Oppio and found himself in a cave decorated with exquisite, detailed and weird frescoes. As word spread, several young artists, including Raphael, got themselves lowered into the cave by ropes. What they discovered was one of the original rooms of the Domus Aurea, but it was the word "grotto" that stuck, and the painting style the frescoes inspired became known as "grotesque".

Letting off steam
Unwind at the playground in the **Parco del Colle Oppio** *(Via Labicana, 00184)*. Children can also run around and play in the park and playground at **Villa Celimontana** *(see p72)*, which is a 10-minute walk away.

The Lowdown
- 🌐 **Map reference** 9 C1
  Address Via della Domus Aurea 1, 00184; 06 3996 7700; *www. tinyurl.com/nm3o9uj*
- 🚗 **Metro** Colosseo (Line B) & Cavour (Line B). **Bus** C3, 53, 85, 87, 117, 186, 571 & 810. **Tram** 3
- 🕐 **Open** Sat & Sun; visits by guided tours only; call to book
- 🏛 **Guided tours** Occasional tours may be possible; call to check
- 🍴 **Eat and drink** PICNIC Panificio Disa *(see San Clemente, p92)*. SNACKS Made in Sud *(Via San Giovanni in Laterano 46, 00184; 06 7045 4900; closed Mon pm)* serves delicious fried delicacies
- 🚻 **Toilets** No

③ The Baths of Trajan
Rub a dub dub

Between AD 104 and 109, Emperor Trajan built a complex of baths over the ruins of the Domus Aurea. There were sections for women as well as men, and the baths included a theatre, gym and reading rooms as well as warm, cold and hot pools. Besides these structures, an intricate system of subterranean passageways was also in place to service and maintain the facilities. In 2011, a huge mosaic showing Apollo with the Muses was found beneath the Baths of Trajan, and below that, a huge fresco known as the "painted city". It was painted high up on the exterior wall of a house, and would have been easily visible to passers-by. It probably dates from the time of Vespasian.

The baths can only be viewed from the Parco del Colle Oppio. Walk along the perimeter to see the high curved walls of the *esedra*,

The Lowdown
- 🌐 **Map Reference** 9 C1
  Address Baths of Trajan: Parco di Colle Oppio, Via Labicana, 00184. Cisterna delle Sette Sale: Via delle Terme di Traiano 5b
- 🚗 **Metro** Colosseo (Line B) & Cavour (Line B). **Bus** C3, 53, 85, 87, 117, 186, 571 & 810. **Tram** 3
- 🕐 **Open** Baths of Trajan: open daily. Cisterna delle Sette Sale: occasional events and guided tours only; call 060608 for details
- 💶 **Price** Baths of Trajan: free. Cisterna delle Sette Sale: depends on the event
- 🏛 **Guided tours** Occasional, limited tours of the baths; call 060608; *www.060608.it*
- 👫 **Age range** Baths of Trajan: 9 plus. Cisterna delle Sette Sale: 5 plus
- 🏃 **Activities** Cisterna delle Sette Sale: occasionally in summer
- 🕐 **Allow** 30 mins
- ♿ **Wheelchair access** No
- 🍴 **Eat and drink** PICNIC Panificio Disa *(see San Clemente, p92)*. FAMILY TREAT Os Club *(Via delle Terme di Traiano 4/a, 00184; 06 4893 0379; closed Mon)* is a smart, contemporary oasis in a garden, ideal for a special tea, dinner or a relaxed Sunday brunch
- 🚻 **Toilets** No

which probably held a garden with statues, and read the interesting information boards, which will help to make sense of the place.

The water for the baths came from a vast cistern, the **Cisterne delle Sette Sale**, which could store up to 8 million litres (2 million gallons) of water. Visit by appointment, and go down into the large cistern. It is an evocative experience, especially when it has water in it and the sun's rays cover the walls with eerie reflections.

Take cover

Walk to the church of **San Pietro in Vincoli** (see p96) to see the chains with which St Peter was manacled in the Mamertine prison. A thunderous-looking statue of Moses and a pair of dying slaves by Michelangelo are the highlights.

④ Auditorium of Maecenas

King-size entertainment!

A flamboyant patron of the arts, Maecenas was an advisor to Emperor Augustus. His gardens were elaborate and full of statues, which can now be seen in the Capitoline Museums (see pp82–3). On the edge of the Parco del Colle Oppio, on Via Merulana, is the Auditorium of Maecenas, which may have been a cool summer dining room. Some archaeologists think water may have cascaded down the flight of steps at the back.

The walls retain traces of beautiful frescoes – fake windows with views of gardens, flowers, birds, ornamental urns and a procession of Dionysus, the god of wine.

Letting off steam

The nearest park is the **Parco del Colle Oppio**, which is peaceful and ideal for children to enjoy some ball games and have fun.

The Lowdown

- 🌐 **Map Reference** 9 D1
- **Address** Largo Leopardi 2, 00185; 060608; www.060608.it
- 🚗 **Metro** Vittorio Emanuele (Line A)
- 🕐 **Open** Guided tours only; by appointment only
- Ⓟ **Price** €12–22; under 6s free
- 🎫 **Guided tours** Call 060608 to book
- 🚻 **Age range** 9 plus
- ⏱ **Allow** 30 mins
- ♿ **Wheelchair access** Yes
- 🍽 **Eat and drink** SNACKS Panella (Largo Leopardi 2, 00185; 06 487 2651; open daily) is a chic delicatessen-café that serves fabulous breads, grissini, pizzas, pastries, savoury strudels, Greek cheese pies, salads and vegetables to eat in or take away. REAL MEAL Tempio di Mecenate (Largo Leopardi 14, 00185; 06 487 2653; open daily) is the place for a simple pasta dish, or a main course of hearty sausages or chicken with peppers
- 🚻 **Toilets** No

A tree-lined walkway at Parco del Colle Oppio

Picnic under €25; **Snacks** €25–40; **Real meal** €40–80; **Family treat** over €80 (based on a family of four)

⑤ San Pietro in Vincoli

Moses and the miraculous chains

According to legend, St Peter was imprisoned twice – first in Jerusalem and then in the Mamertine Prison where he eventually died. The two *vincoli* (chains) used to shackle him while he was in prison were subsequently taken to Constantinople. In the 5th century, Empress Eudoxia deposited one in a church in Constantinople and sent the other to her daughter (also called Eudoxia) in Rome. She in turn gave hers to Pope Leo I, who had San Pietro in Vincoli built to house it. Some years later, the second chain was brought to Rome, where it linked miraculously with its partner. The chains are now kept in an illuminated gold and glass box below the main altar.

The church is better known for a statue of Moses by Michelangelo, commissioned by Pope Julius II as part of a grand tomb for himself. Michelangelo spent months choosing the marble and produced

The statue of Moses by Michelangelo in the church of San Pietro in Vincoli

several designs before the pope settled on a colossal wall-tomb adorned with over 40 statues. But he soon lost interest and forced Michelangelo to abandon the tomb and paint the Sistine Chapel ceiling. Michelangelo completed just a pair of dying slaves and the central statue of Moses in which he looks angry, aggressive and powerful. The marble from which he is chiselled is warm-toned and gleaming, almost as if he might rise to his feet at any moment and remonstrate with the world in a thunderous voice. The other statues, by followers of Michelangelo, seem dull, lifeless and static by comparison.

Letting off steam

The church is a short walk away from the **Parco del Colle Oppio** *(see p94)*, where there is a playground for kids.

⑥ Museo Nazionale d'Arte Orientale

East meets West

Rome's Oriental museum offers a contrast to all the Western Classical art in the city – and a chance to compare styles. There is pre-Islamic, Islamic, Hindu, Buddhist and Taoist art from a wide range of countries. While some parts of the museum have been reorganized in contemporary style, in other rooms the presentation is more traditional.

The first section of the museum is devoted to Hinduism and Buddhism, with displays that include a Cambodian linga complete with offerings of paper garlands and incense. Also present are several bronzes from Chhattisgarh, India, including numerous Mother and Child statues. Children may like the miniature Han Dynasty models in the Chinese section. Made for tombs, they include a pig in a sty, a granary with a mill and several dancing figures. Also look out for the green- and mustard-glazed figures of a Ming Dynasty funeral procession.

In the Gandharan section are carved friezes with the same sense of drama and narrative as those of Trajan's Column *(see p88)* and statues of the Buddha that have the same fluidity and life about them as the Classical Greek statues in the collections of the Museo Nazionale Romano, the Capitoline Museums *(see pp82–3)* and the Vatican Museums *(see pp206–13)*.

Letting off steam

Go to **Piazza Vittorio Emanuele II**, which has a central garden and play area for kids – in the heart of Rome's most vibrant multiethnic area.

The Lowdown

- 🌐 **Map reference** 9 C1
  Address Piazza di San Pietro in Vincoli 4/a, 00184; 06 9784 4950
- 🚗 **Metro** Colosseo (Line B) & Cavour (Line B)
- 🕐 **Open** 8:30am–12:30pm & 3–6pm daily (till 7pm in summer)
- 💲 **Price** Free; €0.50 to illuminate the statue of Moses
- 👫 **Skipping the queue** Tour groups might obstruct the statue of Moses from view. Visit early morning or late evening to avoid crowds
- 🚻 **Age range** 7 plus
- ⏱ **Allow** 20 mins
- ♿ **Wheelchair access** Yes
- 🍽 **Eat and drink** SNACKS Pizza e Mortadella *(Via Cavour 279, 00184; open daily)* sells pizza, roast chicken, salamis, cakes and tarts. Picnic at Parco del Colle Oppio. FAMILY TREAT Cuoco e Camicia *(Via M Polacco 2/4, 00184; 06 8892 2987; www. cuocoecamicia.it; closed Sat lunch and Sun)* offers a lunch of *tagliolini* (Italian egg noodles) with prawns and courgettes or a hearty soup of chickpeas and sausage
- 👫 **Toilets** No

The Lowdown

- 🌐 **Map reference** 9 D1
  Address Via Merulana 248, 00185; 06 4697 4831; *www. museorientale.beniculturali.it*
- 🚗 **Metro** Vittorio Emanuele (Line A). Bus 16, 360, 649 & 714
- 🕐 **Open** 9am–2pm Tue, Wed & Fri; 9am–7:30pm Thu, Sat & Sun
- 💲 **Price** €12–18; EU under 18s free; under 6s free
- 👫 **Skipping the queue** There are rarely any queues
- 🚶 **Guided tours** Call to book
- 🚻 **Age range** 10 plus
- ⏱ **Allow** 1–2 hrs
- ♿ **Wheelchair access** Yes
- 🍽 **Eat and drink** PICNIC Nuovo Mercato Esquilino *(Via Principe Amedeo, 00185; closed Sun)* stocks picnic supplies. Enjoy a picnic lunch in the garden of Piazza Vittorio. REAL MEAL Hang Zhou *(Via Principe Eugenio 82, 00185; 06 487 2732; open daily)* serves Chinese food, noodles and spring rolls
- 🛍 **Shop** Small bookshop near the entrance selling art books
- 👫 **Toilets** Near the ticket office

7 Santa Prassede & Santa Pudenziana

Cardboard box or jewel box?

Entering the scruffy-looking **Santa Prassede** is a bit like walking into a cardboard box. To make an impact one family member should go in first with a supply of €1 coins. The rest of the family can then walk in to the gloom before the first one drops a coin into a slot to turn the lights on – turning it into a jewel box.

The church's apse is covered with sparkling Byzantine mosaics showing haloed figures looking down from heaven, which is depicted as a gold- and-blue-walled city with an angel at each gate and a queue of people waiting to be admitted. Giving the scene the feel of an earthly paradise are spindly-legged lambs, feather-duster-like palm trees and vivid red poppies. In the centre of the apse, saints Prassede and Pudenziana stand with Christ in between them, and SS Peter and Paul beside them. The Cappella di San Zeno is encrusted with dazzling

Top Byzantine mosaics in the Cappella di San Zeno, Santa Prassede
Above Santa Pudenziana church

mosaics whose colours shine. The mosaics in the church of **Santa Pudenziana** are less striking but they are one of the city's few surviving examples of early Christian mosaics.

Letting off steam

Head to the **Parco del Colle Oppio** or the playground on **Piazza Vittorio Emanuele II** to unwind.

The Lowdown

🌐 **Map reference** 5 D6 & 5 C6
Address Santa Prassede: Via Santa Prassede 9/a, 00184; 06 488 2456. Santa Pudenziana: Via Urbana 160, 00184; 06 481 4622

🚇 **Metro** Vittorio Emanuele (Line A). **Bus** 16, 360, 649 & 714

🕐 **Open** Santa Prassede: 7:30am–noon & 4–6:30pm daily. Santa Pudenziana: 8:30am–noon & 3–6pm daily

💶 **Price** Free

👫 **Age range** 4 plus

⏱ **Allow** Santa Prassede: 30 mins; Santa Pudenziana: 10 mins

♿ **Wheelchair access** Partial

☕ **Eat and drink** PICNIC Palazzo del Freddo (Via Principe Eugenio 65, 00185; 06 446 4740; closed Mon) offers great ice creams and desserts. Eat in the gardens of Piazza Vittorio Emanuele II. SNACKS Il Pane (Via di San Martino ai Monti 26, 00184; closed Sun) offers bread, pizza bianca and groceries

🛍 **Shop** Postcards are available at the shop near the entrance

🚻 **Toilets** No

⑧ Palazzo Massimo
The painted garden

One of the four branches of the Museo Nazionale Romano, the luminous 19th-century Palazzo Massimo has an exceptional and beautifully displayed collection of exhibits dating from the 2nd century BC to the end of the 4th century AD. The courtyard, with its portico of marble statues dappled with light and shade, is a marvellous place to begin a tour. The highlights of the museum are too many to name; however, the exquisite frescoes from the Villa of Livia are a must-see.

Statue on display in the museum

Key Features

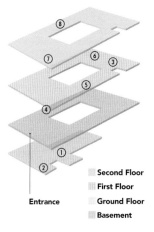

② Ivory Mask of Apollo The mask was discovered in 1995 in northern Rome by illegal excavators. It was part of what is known as a chyselephantine statue. These are extremely rare and were built around wooden frames on which ivory was used to depict the skin, and gold leaf or precious textiles represented the clothing.

④ Bronzes of the Boxer and Prince These bronze statues were made in several parts and then fused together. Different mixtures of metals were used for different effects – a high percentage of copper gives a red hue to the boxer's lips, nipples and wound.

⑥ The Boats of Nemi These elaborate bronzes – including a head of Medusa, lions and wolves – decorated two luxury boats that Emperor Caligula used for parties on the Lake of Nemi *(see p240)*.

⑦ Livia's Garden Four delightful floor-to-ceiling frescoes of a garden, with fruit trees, birds and flowers from the country villa of Emperor Augustus' wife Livia, adorn the second floor. The lighting is designed to simulate the change of light from dawn till dusk.

⑧ Mosaics These mosaics belonged to the baths of a private villa. Search for the boy riding a dolphin, and the fragments of a mosaic showing an octopus, moray eel and lobster fighting.

- Second Floor
- First Floor
- Ground Floor
- Basement

Entrance

① Everyday Life Display On show here are ivory dice and needles, tiny spoons for mixing make-up, a set of compasses and a tiny abacus. A computer nearby shows how much items cost in ancient Rome.

② The Grottarossa Mummy The mummy of an eight-year-old girl and objects that were buried with her – including her doll – are on display here.

⑤ The Discus Throwers Stunningly displayed together are two Roman copies of the *Discobolus*, a 5th-century BC sculpture by the Greek sculptor Myron.

The Lowdown

🌐 **Map reference** 5 C5
Address Largo di Villa Peretti 1, 00185; 06 3996 7700; www. archeoroma.beniculturali.it

🚇 **Metro** Termini (Lines A & B).
Bus C2, H, 36, 38, 40, 64, 86, 90, 92, 105, 170, 175, 217, 310, 360, 714 & 910

🕐 **Open** 9am–7:45pm Tue–Sun

⊖ **Price** €14–28 (includes all four branches of the Museo Nazionale Romano); EU under 18s free; under 6s free. Tickets are valid for 3 days. A 7-day Archeologia Card (€25 per

person, €15 reduced) includes entry to the Baths of Caracalla and the Colosseum

🏃 **Skipping the queue** Book in advance at www.coopculture.it

🚻 **Guided tours** Free tours of Palazzo Massimo every Sunday at 10am, in Italian; Audioguides (€5.50 for 70 mins) are available in English, Spanish, French, Italian and German

👫 **Age range** 5 plus

⏱ **Allow** 1–2 hrs

♿ **Wheelchair access** Yes

☕ **Café** There are refreshment booths outside the museum

🛍 **Shop** The bookshop on the ground floor sells some children's books

🚻 **Toilets** On every floor

Good family value?
Palazzo Massimo is a great museum for families not only because the exhibits are interesting and likely to appeal to children, but also because the museum is airy, rarely crowded and inexpensive.

Letting off steam

This is a busy and traffic-congested part of Rome, but the gardens around the **Baths of Diocletian** (Viale Enrico De Nicola, 79, 00185) – another branch of the Museo Nazionale Romano – are accessible without a ticket and a good place for children to run around. There are benches for picnics or weary parents.

Above Entrance to the Baths of Diocletian gardens **Below** Wine bottles on display, Trimani Il Wine Bar

Eat and drink

Picnic: under €25; Snacks: €25–40; Real meal: €40–80; Family treat: over €80 (based on a family of four)

PICNIC Coop (Via Marsala 60, 00185; open daily) sells all that is needed for a picnic lunch at the gardens of the Baths of Diocletian.
SNACKS W.O.K. (Stazione Centrale Roma Termini, Via Marsala, 00185; open daily) is good for a quick meal of Oriental noodles, rice dishes, Thai curry or samosas.
REAL MEAL Himalaya's Kashmir (Via Principe Amedeo 325–327, 00185; 06 446 1072; open daily for lunch and dinner) serves Indian snacks and dishes such as samosas, tandoori chicken and a generous thali with meat and vegetable dishes, rice, naan and raita.
FAMILY TREAT Trimani Il Wine Bar (Via Cernaia 37/b, 00185; 06 446 9630; Mon–Sat) is an elegant but relaxed wine bar, great for a light lunch or full meal. Try the quiche with escarole spiked with flecks of prune, or a tartare of Piedmontese beef with shards of pungent Castelmagno cheese. Crispy polenta with warm salami might be a hit with the kids.

Find out more

DIGITAL The Cambridge Latin Course on www.tinyurl.com/7hhjbyq is a lively resource in English, with links to photos, information, videos, articles and reconstructions of all aspects of Roman life, and is likely to be of interest to children.

Next stop...

SPRAWLING BATHS Built in AD 298–306 under Emperior Diocletian, the **Baths of Diocletian** were the most extensive in Rome, with room for up to 3,000 bathers at a time and a swimming pool that measured 3,500 sq m (37,674 sq ft). Its collection is currently undergoing major reorganization but exhibitions are often held in the surviving halls of the baths.

⑨ Santa Maria Maggiore
Mary's giant church

The biggest among the 26 churches in Rome dedicated to the Virgin Mary, Santa Maria Maggiore was originally built by Pope Liberius in the 4th century. It was renovated and improved upon by many popes over the centuries, which gave it an unusual mix of different architectural styles, although it still retains its early medieval structure. One of the four papal basilicas – the most important churches in Rome – it has a beautiful interior lined with sparkling mosaics telling stories of the Old Testament.

Sculpture of Pope Sixtus V, Cappella Sistina

Key Features

Cappella Paolina Designed by Flaminio Ponzio for Pope Paul V Borghese, this chapel is packed with spectacular works of art by masters such as Guido Reni and Cavalier d'Arpino.

Coffered Ceiling This gilded and intricately coffered ceiling was encrusted with gold, said to be the first brought back from America by Columbus.

Baldacchino

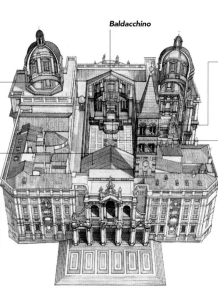

Cappella Sistina This chapel was built for Pope Sixtus V by Domenico Fontana and houses the pope's tomb.

Reliquary of the Holy Crib This fancy crystal container designed by Giuseppe Valadier in the mid-1800s is said to contain a few pieces of ancient wood that were part of baby Jesus's manger.

Obelisk The Egyptian obelisk located behind the basilica is 15 m (49 ft) tall. It was erected by Pope Sixtus V in 1587 as a landmark for pilgrims.

Baldacchino Four purple-red porphyry columns support the towering *baldacchino* – altar canopy – designed by Ferdinando Fuga in the 1740s.

Mosaics Some dating back to the 5th century, the mosaics here are among the most ancient in Rome. Follow stories of the Old Testament along the nave and the triumphal arch – from the Parting of the Red Sea to the Fall of Jericho.

Prices given are for a family of four

The Lowdown

🌐 **Map reference** 5 D6
Address Piazza Santa Maria Maggiore, 00185; 06 6988 6800; www.vatican.va/various/basiliche/sm_maggiore/index_en.html

🚗 **Metro** Cavour (Line B). **Bus** 16, 70, 71, 75, 360, 649 & 714. **Tram** 14

🕐 **Open** 7am–6:45pm daily

💲 **Price** Free

🎫 **Guided tours** Audioguides (€5) available in English, Italian, Spanish, French and German

👫 **Age range** 7 plus

⏱ **Allow** 45–60 mins

♿ **Wheelchair access** Yes

🛍 **Shop** Small shop to the right of the main entrance selling religious articles

🚻 **Toilets** Through the gift shop on the right side of the main entrance

Good family value?
Enjoy free entry to one of the most important churches of Rome and see the most famous mosaics in town.

Façade of Santa Maria Maggiore, completed for the Holy Year of 1750

Letting off steam

Head towards the grassy **Parco del Colle Oppio** (*see p94*), which has plenty of space for children to kick a ball around or play a game of tag.

Eat and drink

Picnic: under €25; Snacks: €25–40; Real meal: €40–80; Family treat: over €80 (based on a family of four)

PICNIC Nuovo Mercato Esquilino (*Via Principe Amedeo 184, 00185; closed Sun*) offers yummy treats from fruits and vegetables to cured meats and cheese. Grab a bite to eat and head for one of the piazza's many benches.
SNACKS Pietro Roscioli (*Via Buonarroti 46, 00185; 06 446 7146; closed Sun*) sells fresh bread, pizza by the slice and other tasty fare.
REAL MEAL Antica Osteria Angelino dal 1899 (*Via Capo d'Africa 6, 00185; 06 6476 4663*) serves traditional Roman dishes such as *cacio e pepe* and *saltimbocca alla Romana* (sautéed rolls of veal, prosciutto and sage).

FAMILY TREAT Trattoria da Danilo (*Via Petrarca 13, 00185; 06 7720 0111; www.trattoriadadanilo.it; closed Sun, Mon dinner only*) dishes out pasta treats such as gnocchetti with pistachio nuts and bacon, as well as a marvellous antipasto spread. Try the fried cod and fried anchovies.

Shopping

Selli International Food Store (*Via dello Statuto 28/30, 00185; 06 474 5777; open Mon–Sat, 9am–7:30pm*) sells exotic ingredients and also goods such as Marmite and peanut butter for the homesick. **Città del Sole** (*Via Buonarroti 6, 00185; 06 487 1328; closed Sun; www.cittadelsole.it*) stocks colourful toys for kids, as well as gadgets and games for young adults.

Find out more

DIGITAL Download the smartphone app iView Santa Maria Maggiore by D'Uva Workshop from *www.duvaws.com* and carry it along to explore the basilica with a unique multimedia guide. After a real-life visit, take a virtual tour at *www.vatican.va* under the Basilicas and Papal Chapels section to learn more about this big, glittering church and see fantastic photographs.

Next stop...

MEDIEVAL MOSAICS AND ALCHEMY Visit **Santa Prassede** and **Santa Pudenziana** (*see p97*) to see more brilliant mosaics. Then head to Piazza Vittorio Emanuele II and search for the Magic Door inside the piazza's gardens. Once the entrance to an alchemy studio, this ancient door is believed to have mystical powers.

Apse mosaic detail in the Church of Santa Pudenziana

Piazza della Bocca della Verità and around

A fascinating area with a plethora of sights, the Aventine Hill is an unexpected haven in central Rome. At the foot of this verdant hill is the vast Circus Maximus, now a massive multi-laned road with a green space known as Circo Massimo. On the far side of the Aventine Hill is Testaccio, a vibrant and family-friendly neighbourhood. The area is easy to get around and well connected to the centre by bus.

Ancient Rome

Piazza Bocca della Verità
p104

0 metres   300
0 yards   300

The Pyramid of Caius Cestius and the Porta di San Paolo

Places of Interest

SIGHTS
1. Piazza della Bocca della Verità
2. Circus Maximus
3. Gardens of the Aventine
4. Santa Sabina
5. Piazza dei Cavalieri di Malta
6. Testaccio
7. Pyramid of Caius Cestius
8. Centrale Montemartini

● EAT AND DRINK
1. Pizzicheria
2. Antico Caffè del Teatro Marcello
3. Sora Margherita
4. Ba' Ghetto
5. Alimentari Giacomini
6. Bar dei Cerchi
7. Gusto Massimo
8. Court Delicati
9. Volpetti
10. Eataly
11. Volpetti Più
12. Pasticceria Andreotti
13. Felice
14. Cornetteria Due
15. Al Biondo Tevere

● SHOPPING
See Piazza dei Cavalieri di Malta (p107) and Testaccio (p108)

● WHERE TO STAY
1. Villa San Pio
2. Sant'Anselmo
3. Hotel Aventino
4. Domus Aventina

Colourful flowers on display at a stall in Testaccio market

The Lowdown

🚗 **Metro** Circo Massimo & Piramide (Line B). **Bus** C3, 23, 25, 30, 44, 75, 81, 95, 130, 160, 175, 271, 280, 628, 715 & 716. **Tram** 3

ℹ️ **Visitor information** Visitor Centre, Via dei Fori Imperiali, 00186; open 9:30am–7pm daily; Oct–Mar: 8:30am–4:30pm daily

🛒 **Supermarkets** Emmepiù, Viale Aventino 88, 00153; open 8am–8pm Mon–Sat. Conad, Piazza Vittorio Bottego 47, 00154; open 8am–8pm daily. Coop, Piazzale dei Partigiani 33A, 00154; open 8am–8pm daily.
Markets Testaccio market, Via Volta; Mon–Sat am

➕ **Pharmacies** Farmacia S Sabina: Viale Aventino 78/c, 00153; open 8am–1pm & 4–8pm Mon–Sat. Farmacia Arenula: Via Arenula 73, 00186; 06 6880 3278; open 7:30am–10pm Mon–Sat, 6–10pm Sun

🐾 **Nearest play areas** Piazza Santa Maria Liberatrice, Testaccio, 00153. Roseto Comunale, Via di Valle Murcia, 00153. Parco Savello, Piazza Pietro d'Illiria, 00153. Villa Celimontana (entrance on Piazza della Navicella), 00184. Monte Caprino park, Via Tempio di Giove, 00184

Elaborate ceiling fresco in the Santa Sabina church

① Piazza della Bocca della Verità
A medieval lie detector

The wedge-shaped piazza occupies the site of ancient Rome's first port and its oldest market, the Forum Boarium. It is named after the Bocca della Verità, or "mouth of truth", a marble medallion at Santa Maria in Cosmedin once thought to be a drain cover. In the Middle Ages, suspected liars had to put their hand in. If they were lying, it would, supposedly, snap shut. If it really did work, the medieval Romans must have been the most honest on earth!

Bocca della Verità, Santa Maria in Cosmedin

Key Sights

Casa dei Crescenzi An 11th-century fortified tower, the Casa dei Crescenzi was built by the powerful Crescenzi family to keep watch over the bridge where they collected a toll. The tower is studded with fragments scavenged from ancient Roman buildings.

Ponte Rotto The "Broken Bridge" is the one remaining arch of an ancient Roman bridge across the Tiber. Originally known as the Pons Aemilius, it dates back to 142 BC and was the first stone bridge in Rome.

Temple of Portunus This remarkably well-preserved Republican temple was dedicated to Portunus, the god of rivers and ports.

Temple of Hercules Victor A beautiful Republican-era temple dedicated to Hercules, this is often, mistakenly, called the Temple of Vesta because it is circular like the Temple of Vesta (see p76) in the Roman Forum.

Santa Maria in Cosmedin & Bocca della Verità

Mithraeum of Santa Prisca Dedicated to the pagan god Mithras, this temple features many Mithraic symbols, including frescoes depicting the initiation of members. Call 060608 before a visit (reservation required).

Arch of Janus Merchants and cattle dealers would meet to do business in the shade of this arch. The only four-sided arch in Rome, it is named after the two-faced god Janus, the protector of arches, gates and doors. The niches on the arch held statues that have long disappeared.

Arco degli Argentieri

Arch of Janus

The Lowdown

- 🌐 **Map reference** 8 H2
  Address Santa Maria in Cosmedin: Piazza della Bocca della Verità 18, 00186; 06 678 7759
- 🚗 **Bus** 23, 44, 81, 85, 87, 95, 122, 160, 175 & 628
- 🕐 **Open** Santa Maria in Cosmedin: summer: 9:30am–6pm daily, till 5pm in winter
- 👪 **Skipping the queue** Santa Maria in Cosmedin: lunchtime is when queues are the shortest
- 👫 **Age range** 7 plus
- ⏱ **Allow** 1 hr
- ♿ **Wheelchair access** Yes
- 🚻 **Toilets** No

Good family value?
There is a lot to see and nothing that is too demanding or takes up too much time. There is space to rest with a lawn, benches and a fountain by the two temples. It is all free, so excellent family value.

Arco degli Argentieri This arch was created in AD 204 in honour of Emperor Septimius Severus and his family by the moneychangers who worked at the market.

Prices given are for a family of four

Santa Maria in Cosmedin A medieval church, Santa Maria in Cosmedin has fantastic Cosmati work (geometric mosaics) on its floor, choir, bishop's throne and on the canopy over the main altar. Set into the wall of its portico is the Bocca della Verità, with its queue of nervous visitors.

Open spaces of Parco Savello with Santa Sabina in the background

Letting off steam

The nearest park is the **Monte Caprino park** (Via Tempio di Giove; 00186) and the quickest way to get there is along Via del Teatro di Marcello. Alternatively, take a walk up the Aventine Hill, where children can run around in the **Parco Savello** (see p106).

Diners sitting at outdoor tables at Ba' Ghetto, a popular restaurant

Eat and drink

Picnic: under €25; Snacks: €25–40; Real meal: €40–80; Family treat: over €80 (based on a family of four)

PICNIC Pizzicheria (Via dei Delfini 25, 00186; 06 679 3001; closed Sat pm) has a deli counter and fresh bread. Pick up a picnic lunch and head to the Monte Caprino park.

SNACKS Antico Caffè del Teatro Marcello (Via del Teatro di Marcello 42, 00186; 06 678 5451; open daily) is perfect for a quick breakfast or a superior sandwich lunch.

REAL MEAL Sora Margherita (Piazza delle Cinque Scole 30, 00186; 06 687 4216; closed Sun, Tue dinner & alternate Thu) is a lively, old-fashioned trattoria with no written menu.

FAMILY TREAT Ba' Ghetto (Via del Portico d'Ottavia 57, 00186; 06 6889 2868; closed Fri pm & Sat am) is a refined place serving what many

judge to be the best Jewish food in Rome. Try the deep-fried artichokes, the deftly spiced shish kebabs or the salt cod Roman-Jewish style.

Find out more

DIGITAL Inspired by the swirly Cosmati mosaics in Santa Maria in Cosmedin? If so, make a geometrical mosaic on *www.tinyurl.com/672a4u*, or download free photomosaic-making software such as Shape Collage or Mosaic Maker to create one with photographs taken of Rome.

Next stop...

GEOMETRY AND CRIMINOLOGY Visit **San Clemente** (see pp92–3) for more mosaics. Then visit the **Museo Criminologico** (see pp134) to see the methods used by the authorities – ancient, medieval and modern – to force people to tell the truth.

Vivid frescoes in the Cappella di Santa Caterina, San Clemente church

Circus Maximus, now a grassy esplanade in front of the Palatine Hill

② Circus Maximus

What a circus!

The oldest and most popular mass entertainment arena in ancient Rome and the size of six football pitches, the oval-shaped Circus Maximus could seat 380,000 people – over seven times as many as the Colosseum. It dates back to the 4th century BC, and was in use for over 900 years – the last races were held in AD 549. The stadium was most famous for its chariot races, but other events – wild beast fights, athletic contests and even mock sea battles – were also held here. It was used for public crucifixions, with the crosses set up along a low wall that ran along the centre. The arena was surrounded with arcades where vendors sold snacks and wine, and astrologers read horoscopes and told fortunes.

Today, the Circus Maximus is surrounded by multi-laned highways, but it is a good place to play ball or roll down the slopes.

Letting off steam

The lovely pine-shaded park of **Villa Celimontana** (*see p72*) in central Rome is ideal for a picnic after seeing ancient sites. There is a playground with pony rides and a small roller-skating and cycling ring. It also hosts a jazz festival in summer.

③ Gardens of the Aventine

Ancient roses and aromatic orange trees

The Aventine Hill is one of the seven hills of Rome – lush, leafy and residential, and with three public gardens. One of the few locations in central Rome where the birdsong is louder than the traffic, it is a good place for a quiet picnic after sightseeing in the ancient centre.

In May and June, make a beeline for the **Roseto Comunale**, the public Rose Garden, where over 1,200 varieties of roses from all over the world are cultivated. Among them are even primordial species that existed 40 million years ago, and roses that were famous in antiquity,

such as the Damascene rose. Every year in May, the gardens host an international Rose Competition, Il Concorso Internazionale Premio Roma.

The Aventine's other garden, **Parco Savello**, better known as the Giardino degli Aranci, is planted with orange trees and offers fantastic views over the Tiber to the Vatican City (*see pp202–3*).

Take cover

Cool down in the church of **Santa Sabina**, known for its fascinating moonstone windows and its carving of the Crucifixion.

The Lowdown

- 🌐 **Map reference** 8 H3
  Address Roseto Comunale: Via di Valle Murcia, 00153. Parco Savello: Piazza Pietro d'Illiria, 00153
- 🚗 **Metro** Circo Massimo (Line B). **Bus** 81, 175, 628 & 715
- 🕐 **Open** Roseto Comunale: late Apr–late Jun 8:30am–7:30pm daily. Parco Savello: 7am–sunset daily
- 💶 **Price** Free
- 📞 **Guided tours** Call 06 574 6810 to book a tour of the rose garden
- 👫 **Age range** All ages
- 🏃 **Activities** Roseto Comunale: children's events are sometimes organized. Call to check
- ⏱ **Allow** Roseto Comunale: 1 hr
- ♿ **Wheelchair access** Yes
- 🍴 **Eat and drink** PICNIC Alimentari Giacomini (*see Circus Maximus*). REAL MEAL Gusto Massimo (*Via del Circo Massimo 5a, 00153; 06 574 5762; open daily*) serves pasta and is perfect for a family meal
- 🚻 **Toilets** Next to the shop at Sant'Anselmo (*see p107*)

The Lowdown

- 🌐 **Map reference** 9 A3
  Address Via del Circo Massimo, 00153
- 🚗 **Metro** Circo Massimo (Line B). **Bus** C3, 81, 160, 175, 628 & 715
- 👫 **Age range** All ages
- 🕐 **Allow** 30 mins
- 🍴 **Eat and drink** PICNIC Alimentari Giacomini (*Viale Aventino 106, 00153; closed Sun*) has a deli counter. Pick up sandwiches and head back to the Circus Maximus for a picnic. SNACKS Bar dei Cerchi (*Via dei Cerchi 49, 00153*) is a friendly, simple espresso bar that also serves pastries and hearty sandwiches
- 🚻 **Toilets** No

Umbrella-pine-lined avenue, Parco Savello

④ Santa Sabina

Moonstone windows

Founded in the 5th century AD, Santa Sabina is a perfect example of a Roman basilica-style church. Its windows are made of thin slices of selenite, a milky white mirror-like stone, which the Greeks named after Selene, goddess of the moon. The church still retains its original wood-panelled doors carved with scenes from the Bible, including one of the earliest surviving images of the Crucifixion. These are visible from the narthex, the porch-like structure in front of the church. In the nave is the magnificent mosaic tombstone of one of the first leaders of the Dominican Order, Muñoz de Zamora (d.1300).

Letting off steam

Visit the **Parco Savello**, where children can run around in the shade of the orange trees while adults take in the fantastic views of Rome.

The Lowdown

🌐 **Map reference** 8 H3
 Address Piazza San Pietro d'Illiria 1, 00153

🚗 **Metro** Circo Massimo (Line B). **Bus** 23, 280 & 716

🕐 **Open** 8:15am–12:30pm & 3:30–6pm daily

🎫 **Price** Free

🚻 **Age range** 6 plus

⏱ **Allow** 20 mins

♿ **Wheelchair access** Yes

🍴 **Eat and drink** PICNIC Alimentari Giacomini (see Circus Maximus). REAL MEAL Court Delicati (Viale Aventino 41, 00153; 06 574 6108; closed Mon) is one of Rome's best Chinese restaurants

🚻 **Toilets** Next to the shop at Sant'Anselmo

A child looking through the famous keyhole at the Priorato di Malta

⑤ Piazza dei Cavalieri di Malta

Through the keyhole

Decorated with obelisks and military trophies, this ornate walled piazza was designed by the 18th-century artist Piranesi. It is named after the Order of the Knights of Malta (Cavalieri di Malta), a mysterious military religious order that dates back to the Crusades. Located off the piazza is the **Priorato di Malta**, the residence of the Grand Master of the Knights of Malta. It is famous for its bronze keyhole, through which visitors can see a miniature view of St Peter's, which seems to be an arm's length away at the end of a tunnel of trees.

Take cover

The church of **Sant'Anselmo**, just behind the piazza, has a shop (Tue–Sun) that sells soaps, honey, conserves, sweets, liqueurs and various other things made by the church's Benedictine monks.

The Lowdown

🌐 **Map reference** 8 H4
 Address Priorato di Malta: Piazza del Cavalieri di Malta, 00153

🚗 **Metro** Circo Massimo (Line B). **Bus** 23, 280 & 716

🕐 **Open** Daily

 Skipping the queue Priorato di Malta: queues for the keyhole are shortest in the early morning and at lunchtime

🚻 **Age range** 5 plus

⏱ **Allow** 20 mins

♿ **Wheelchair access** Yes

🍴 **Eat and drink** SNACKS Volpetti (Via Marmorata 47/a, 00153; 06 574 2352; closed Sun) offers goodies such as goat's cheese with crystallized papaya and hams that melt on the tongue. FAMILY TREAT Eataly (Piazzale XII Ottobre 1492, 00153; 06 9027 9201; open daily) is a four-storey food market with a dozen restaurants serving great Italian food

🚻 **Toilets** Next to the shop at Sant'Anselmo

Shoppers at a vegetable stall in Testaccio market

⑥ Testaccio

An offaly interesting neighbourhood

Dominated by two bizarre structures – a pyramid and a gasometer – Testaccio is a gutsy working-class neighbourhood that has become a fashionable place to live, especially for families. For decades, most of the residents of the area worked at the slaughter-house, and Testaccio remains famous throughout Rome for its butchers and *trattorie*, which specialize in offal and dishes made from offal. The daily food market, which used to be located on Piazza di Santa Maria Liberatrice, is now housed in a building at the end of the Via Volta, and it continues to sell superb delicacies.

The slaughterhouse has been converted into a venue for concerts. It also houses the Testaccio branch of the contemporary art gallery **MACRO** (Museo d'Arte Contemporanea Roma) *(see also p179)*. The nearby **Monte Testaccio**, made up of shards of terracotta, owes its existence to the butter-fingered dockers of ancient Rome, who broke so many amphorae while unloading wine at the nearby docks, that there were enough pottery shards to build a mountain. It was soon discovered that the shard-mountain remained cool all year and caves were hollowed into its sides for storing wine. Today, the caves are occupied by nightclubs and car repair shops.

The area also has good play-grounds, including the one on leafy Piazza Santa Maria Liberatrice.

Take cover

If there is nothing going on at **MACRO**, stop by the several ecologically minded children's clothes boutiques and toyshops.

⑦ Pyramid of Caius Cestius

Egypt in Rome?

Testaccio's most extraordinary sight is the Pyramid of Caius Cestius, a marble pyramid built in the late 1st century BC by Caius Cestius, whose main job was to organize parties for the emperor. At the time – spurred

The Lowdown

- 🌐 **Map reference** 8 H5
  Address Pyramid of Caius Cestius: Piazzale Ostiense, 00154. Protestant Cemetery: Via Caio Cestio, 00153; 06 574 1900. Museo della Via Ostiense: Via Raffaele Persichetti 3, 00153; 06 574 3193

- 🚇 **Metro** Piramide (Line B). **Bus** 23, 30, 75, 130, 280 & 716. **Tram** 3

- 🕐 **Open** Pyramid of Caius Cestius: open only for guided tours. Protestant Cemetery: 9am–5pm Mon–Sat, 9am–1pm Sun. Museo della Via Ostiense: 9am–1:30pm Tue–Sat

- 💰 **Price** Pyramid of Caius Cestius: varies. Protestant Cemetery: donation of €3 requested. Museo della Via Ostiense: free

- 🏳 **Guided tours** Pyramid of Caius Cestius: book at the Museo della Via Ostiense

- 👫 **Age range** 6 plus

- 🕐 **Allow** Pyramid of Caius Cestius: 30 mins. Protestant Cemetery: 30 mins. Museo della Via Ostiense: 15 mins

- 🍴 **Eat and drink** PICNIC Pasticceria Andreotti *(Via Ostiense 54, 00154; 06 575 0773; open daily; www.andreottiroma.it)* sells cornetti and snacks. FAMILY TREAT Felice *(Via Mastro Giorgio 29, 00153; 06 574 6800; open daily)* serves hearty *testarelle d'abbacchio* (lamb sweetbreads) and sausage with pork rind and peas

- 🚻 **Toilets** No

The Lowdown

- 🌐 **Map reference** 8 H5
  Address MACRO: Piazza Orazio Giustiniani 4, 00153; 06 6710 70400; www.museomacro.org

- 🚇 **Metro** Piramide (Line B). **Bus** 23, 30, 75, 130, 280 & 716. **Tram** 3

- 🕐 **Open** MACRO: 4pm–10pm Tue–Sun (only during exhibitions)

- 💰 **Price** MACRO: €17–33, under 6s free; €3 reduced admission for EU 6–25s

- 🏳 **Skipping the queue** MACRO: buy tickets online to skip queues at the ticket counter

- 🏳 **Guided tours** Call for information

- 👫 **Age range** All ages

- 🕐 **Allow** 4–5 days

- ♿ **Wheelchair access** MACRO: yes

- 🍴 **Eat and drink** SNACKS Volpetti *(see p107)* offers uncommon delights such as gorgonzola steeped in sweet wine, delicious hams and golden crusted pies of ricotta and spinach. REAL MEAL Volpetti Più *(Via Alessandro Volta 8, 00153; closed Sun; www.volpetti.com)* is one of the finest self-service joints in town. Sample the delicious food, which includes dishes such as *tonno alla cacciatora* (tuna with rosemary, garlic and chilli), roast chicken, rare roast beef, black rice with grilled vegetables and red rice with chickpeas and rosemary, and finish with the pears in red wine or the baked apples

- 🛍 **Shops** MACRO Bookshop *(Via Orazio Giustiniani 4, 00153; 06 5713 7514)* has a wide selection of architecture and art books, as well as many design objects and toys. Mini Me *(Via Mastrogiorgio 37/b, 00153)* has stylish Scandinavian clothes for kids. Check out the gorilla socks and the jumpers in which the arms form the trunk of an elephant

- 🚻 **Toilets** In bars and at the MACRO

on by the fame of Cleopatra – all things Egyptian were highly fashionable and Caius decided to build himself a pyramid as a tomb.

Behind the pyramid is the **Protestant Cemetery**, where Rome's non-Catholics, mainly English and German, are buried. The most famous grave is that of the English poet John Keats (d.1821), whose epitaph reads: "Here lies One Whose Name was writ in Water".

Across the road is the Porta di San Paolo, whose turreted towers are home to the **Museo della Via Ostiense**. The museum has displays on the history of Via Ostiense, a road that has connected Rome to the coast since ancient times.

Take cover

Visit the **Centrale Montemartini**, a museum of classical sculptures housed in an old electricity plant.

⑧ Centrale Montemartini

The power of art

In 1997, this enormous early 20th-century thermo-electric power plant was restored and reopened to house part of the collections of the Capitoline Museums (see pp82–3). The combination of Classical statues and monumental industrial turbines is stunning, and the displays and information boards are full of fascinating facts and are far more up-to-date than those in the original museums.

The finds from Largo Argentina, including five toes, a finger, an arm and a head from an 8-m- (26-ft-) high statue of the goddess Fortuna, are on display here. Other highlights include finds from the horti (gardens) of Imperial Rome – the basin of a huge fountain from the Horti Maecenas on Parco del Colle Oppio and mosaics of two hunting scenes from the Horti Liciniani.

Letting off steam

Relax under a tree, while children prance around in the **Parco della Resistenza dell'Otto Settembre** (Viale Manlio Gelsomini, 00153).

Roses in full bloom, Parco della Resistenza dell'Otto Settembre

Top Statues lining a hall at the Centrale Montemartini **Above** Carved urns on display in the Centrale Montemartini

The Lowdown

🌐 **Map reference** 8 H6
Address Via Ostiense 106, 00153; 06 574 8042; www.centralemontemartini.org

🚌 **Bus** 25 & 271

🕐 **Open** 9am–7pm Tue–Sun

💰 **Price** €15–28; under 6s free

🚶 **Skipping the queue** There are rarely any queues

🎫 **Guided tours** Call 060608 to book

👫 **Age range** 6 plus

⏱ **Allow** 45 mins

♿ **Wheelchair access** Yes

🍴 **Eat and drink** PICNIC Cornetteria Due (Via Ostiense 94, 00154; 06 574 3913; 24 hrs daily) is perfectly placed for a sandwich, pastry and coffee. REAL MEAL Al Biondo Tevere (Via Ostiense 174, 00154; closed Tue) serves simple Roman cuisine such as amatriciana as well as other meat and fish specialities. There is a lovely terrace which affords scenic views of the Tiber

🚻 **Toilets** Yes, on the ground floor

Piazza Navona
& Campo de' Fiori

The heart of Rome is a maze of cobbled streets and piazzas studded with fountains, palaces and churches. All around, layers of history are haphazardly superimposed – medieval streets and piazzas echo the ancient Roman street plan; churches are built over pagan temples; and fashionable bars, *gelaterie* and boutiques do business alongside old-fashioned *trattorie* and markets that have existed for centuries.

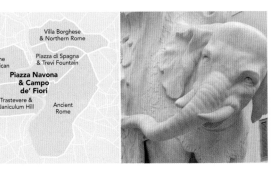

Highlights

Piazza Navona
Marvel at the theatrical fountains while children enjoy performances by buskers and mime artists in lively Piazza Navona (*see pp116–17*).

San Luigi dei Francesi and Sant'Agostino
Step into San Luigi dei Francesi and Sant'Agostino to discover the dirty-toenailed realism of Caravaggio (*see pp118–19*).

Pantheon
Visit the Pantheon, an astonishing feat of Roman engineering, whose porticoes once housed a fish market (*see pp122–3*).

La Maddalena
Decide which of the several *gelaterie* near the La Maddalena church serves the tastiest ice cream (*see pp126–7*).

Campo de' Fiori
Wander around and shop at the bustling food market in Campo de' Fiori and see where Brutus assassinated Caesar (*see pp130–31*).

Jewish Ghetto
Walk down the pedestrianized streets of the Jewish Ghetto, where all of Rome's Jews were confined in 1555 by Pope Paul IV (*see pp134–5*).

Above right Elephant sculpture on Bernini's obelisk outside Santa Maria sopra Minerva church *Left* People enjoying dinner in Piazza della Rotonda at sunset, against the backdrop of the Pantheon

The Best of
Piazza Navona & Campo de' Fiori

Rome's *centro storico* (historic centre) will appeal to adults and children alike. Two millennia of high art and architecture intermingle seamlessly with the more contemporary pleasures of people-watching and ogling splendid window displays of food, clothes and toys galore. Great monuments, fountains, palazzos and piazzas may dominate, but the eagle-eyed will spot relics of the ancient city at almost every turn.

Splendid set pieces

Over the last two thousand years, the vision of artists and architects, backed by the eternal desire of emperors, popes and princes to leave an indelible mark on the city, has punctuated the centre's web of twisting, narrow streets with exuberant set pieces. Stop at the Egyptian obelisk on **Piazza di Montecitorio** *(see p126)*, part of a sundial created by Emperor Augustus; the Column of Marcus Aurelius *(see p126)*, the centrepiece of Piazza Colonna; and the **Pantheon** *(see pp122–3)*, which still has the world's largest unreinforced concrete dome.

Centuries later, Renaissance and Baroque popes and princes commissioned great artists to beautify the area's churches, palazzos and piazzas. Marvel at sensational fountains, such as the Fontana dei Quattro Fiumi on **Piazza Navona** *(see pp116–17)*, and magnificent works of art, including famous pieces by Italian greats such as Caravaggio at **San Luigi dei Francesi** *(see p118)* and **Sant'Agostino** *(see p119)*,

Raphael in **Santa Maria della Pace** *(see pp120–21)*, and Michelangelo in **Santa Maria sopra Minerva** *(see p124)*.

Fashion, shops and street life

Leave plenty of time to browse the shops and enjoy the bustle of the city centre: the colourful food market of **Campo de' Fiori** *(see pp130–31)* and the boutiques around **Piazza Navona** and **Campo de' Fiori** are all testimony to the dedication that Romans have to making themselves, and their city, look great. Younger children will doubtless prefer the living statues (spot one of Tutankhamun if you can) and vendors of laser-whizzers who congregate on **Piazza Navona**, **Campo de' Fiori** and outside the **Pantheon**. If window-shopping and street entertainment do not appeal, people-watching may – try the Piazza San Lorenzo in Lucina, northeast of the Pantheon, for fashionista-spotting and **Piazza Navona** for watching the world (and his wife) walk by.

Below The magnificent Fontana dei Quattro Fiumi on Piazza Navona

Above Candle-lit altar and frescoes at the grand Sant'Ignazio church **Middle** Colourful displays of fresh fruit at the Campo de' Fiori market **Bottom** Fountain in front of the Pantheon, Piazza della Rotonda

Renaissance and Baroque secrets

Children may groan if parents suggest going to church, but they will soon discover that churches here are exciting treasure troves of art and architecture. What is more, admission is free, and popping inside for 10 minutes to look at a painting – with the added bonus of dropping coins in a slot to illuminate it – can make far more of an impact on a child than a long visit to a museum. Discover the dirty feet and toenails of figures by Caravaggio at **San Luigi dei Francesi** and **Sant'Agostino**, wonder why there are pagan *Sibyls* in the church of **Santa Maria della Pace**, take in the 3D optical illusions on the ceilings of **Sant'Ignazio** *(see p125)* and **Sant'Andrea della Valle** *(see pp118–19)* and be amazed by the architectural trickery of Borromini at **Sant'Ivo alla Sapienza** *(see p118)* and **Palazzo Spada** *(see p132)*.

An ancient Roman treasure hunt

Visitors can discern several ancient buildings by looking at the street plan of the present – mostly medieval – *centro storico*. Walk to **Piazza Navona**, which occupies the site of what was once a stadium, and the Via di Grottapinta off **Campo de' Fiori**, which follows the curve of the ancient **Teatro di Pompeo** *(see p130)*. Look out for bathtubs from the Baths of Caracalla, which form fountain basins in **Piazza Farnese** *(see p132)*, and fragments from Roman buildings that have been incorporated into several modern structures – the most famous is the **Temple of Hadrian** *(see p126)*. In the **Jewish Ghetto** *(see pp134–5)*, see a row of gnawed Corinthian columns that form a porch for the church of Sant'Andrea in Pescheria. Finally, wander around the streets near the **Pantheon**, full of relics from the city's temple to the Egyptian goddess Isis.

Piazza Navona and around

Sights are densely concentrated along the tangle of narrow streets around the open spaces of Piazza Navona and the Pantheon, making it a joy to explore the area on foot. Children can see a lot without having to walk very far and there are many appealing shop windows and ice-cream parlours to keep spirits up, although the cobbled streets make for a bumpy ride for toddlers in pushchairs. There are no metro stations here but buses skirt the district on the main roads. This busy area throngs with visitors in the evenings and at weekends.

Piazza Navona &
Campo de' Fiori

Carving of angels on a receptacle for holy water, La Maddalena

Places of Interest

SIGHTS	EAT AND DRINK		SHOPPING
① Piazza Navona	1 Carrefour Express	19 Green T	1 Berté
② San Luigi dei Francesi	2 Casa e Bottega Café	20 Sapore di Mare	2 Libreria Fanucci
	3 Da Tonino	21 Enoteca Spiriti	3 Poggi
③ Sant'Ivo alla Sapienza	4 La Rosetta	22 Da Armando al Pantheon	4 Città del Sole
④ Sant'Andrea della Valle	5 Caffè Sant'Eustachio	23 Carrefour Express	See also Via dei Coronari (p121) & Piazza di Montecitorio (p126)
	6 Ciuri Ciuri	24 Cambi	
⑤ Sant'Agostino	7 Caffé Argentina	25 Matricianella	WHERE TO STAY
⑥ Palazzo Altemps	8 RosticceRì	26 Gran Caffè la Caffetiera	1 Hotel Fontanella Borghese
⑦ Santa Maria della Pace	9 Casa Bleve	27 Osteria dell'Ingegno	
⑧ Via dei Coronari	10 Blue Ice	28 Vitti	2 Hotel Parlamento
⑨ Pantheon	11 Casa Coppelle	29 Trattoria dal Cavalier Gino	3 Hotel Due Torri
⑩ Piazza della Minerva	12 C.A.C.S Antica Norcineria		4 Hotel Portoghesi
⑪ Palazzo Doria Pamphilj		30 Gelateria della Palma	5 Hotel Raphael
	13 La Campana	31 Enoteca al Parlamento	6 Navona Palace Residence
⑫ Sant'Ignazio	14 Lo Zozzone	32 Gelateria Origini	
⑬ Temple of Hadrian	15 Etabli	33 Enoteca Corsi	7 Teatro Pace 33
⑭ Piazza di Montecitorio	16 Ristorante Il Fico	See also Palazzo Doria Pamphilj (p124) & Santa Maria della Pace (p120)	8 Hotel Navona
⑮ La Maddalena	17 L'Antica Salumeria		9 Hotel Santa Chiara
⑯ Il Gesù	18 Il Panino Ingegnoso		

Assumption of the Virgin, a fresco by Filippo Lippi in Santa Maria sopra Minerva church

The Lowdown

🚌 **Bus** C3, 30, 40, 46, 62, 64, 70, 81, 87, 98, 116, 119, 130, 186, 190, 492, 571, 628, 810, 870, 881 & 916

ℹ️ **Visitor information** Tourist Information Point, Piazza delle Cinque Lune (near Piazza Navona), 00186; 060608; open 9:30am–7pm daily. Visitor information centre, Via Marco Minghetti (off Via del Corso), 00187; 060608; open 9:30am–7pm daily; www.turismoroma.it

🛒 **Supermarket** Carrefour Express, Via del Governo Vecchio 119, 00186.
Market Campo de' Fiori market; 8am–1pm Mon–Sat

🎭 **Festivals** Festa della Befana (Nov–early Jan), a Christmas market. Carnival (on the 5 days before Shrove Tue). Mostra dell'Antiquariato (May & Oct), antiques festival on Via dei Coronari

➕ **Pharmacy** Farmacia Senato: Corso del Rinascimento 50, 00186; 06 6880 3760; open 7:30am–midnight Mon–Fri, 8:30am–midnight Sat, noon–11pm Sun

🎯 **Nearest play areas** Parco Adriano (near Castel Sant'Angelo), 00193. Monte Caprino park, Via Tempio di Giove, 00186. Or play in the piazzas as Roman kids do

Visitors looking at paintings on the artists' stalls, Piazza Navona

① Piazza Navona
Tooth-pullers and fortune-tellers

Rome's most famous and dramatic piazza, Piazza Navona is surrounded by cafés and dominated by the Egyptian obelisk, cascading waters and gleaming marble statues of Bernini's Fontana dei Quattro Fiumi. Located on the site of an ancient Roman stadium, the oval piazza has long been the social centre of Rome, where astrologers told fortunes; barbers and tooth-pullers set up stalls; buskers and acrobats provided entertainment and during the Renaissance the Carnival was celebrated with jousting, races and fancy-dress parties. Today it is equally bustling.

Fontana di Nettuno

Key Sights

Fontana dei Quattro Fiumi Bernini's fountain (1651) symbolizes how Pope Innocent X (the dove) triumphed over paganism (the obelisk) and brought peace (an olive branch) to the world (the four rivers).

Sant'Agnese in Agone

Fontana di Nettuno This fountain is a 19th-century work showing the sea god Neptune struggling with a sea monster.

Fontana del Moro Bernini sculpted a Moor wrestling with a dolphin at the centre of this fountain.

Pasquino For over 500 years Romans have been attaching political or social comments to the "talking" statue in Piazza di Pasquino.

Obelisk

Obelisk In the centre of the Baroque Fontana dei Quattro Fiumi, this Egyptian obelisk came from the ancient temple of Isis nearby.

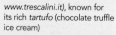

Sant'Agnese in Agone The church was built over the rooms in which St Agnes was imprisoned. Borromini's startling concave façade (1657) was part of a revamp of the piazza by Pope Innocent X.

River gods, Fontana dei Quattro Fiumi
The great rivers are represented as gods. The Nile has his face covered, Plate sits on silver, Ganges holds an oar and Danube is touching the papal coat of arms.

Prices given are for a family of four

The Lowdown

🌐 **Map reference** 11 D3
Address Piazza Navona, 00186

🚗 **Bus** C3, 30, 40, 46, 62, 64, 70, 81, 87, 116, 119, 130, 186, 190, 492, 571, 628, 810 & 916

🚶 **Skipping the queue** Visit early in the day to beat the crowds and go in the early evening to people-watch

👫 **Age range** All ages

⏱ **Allow** 1–2 hrs

♿ **Wheelchair access** Yes

☕ **Café** Many cafés line the piazza. One of the best is Bar Tre Scalini (Piazza Navona 28–9, 00186;

www.trescalini.it), known for its rich *tartufo* (chocolate truffle ice cream)

🚻 **Toilets** In the cafés around the piazza, although these are open only to customers; buy an espresso or water at the bar

Good family value?
The piazza is great fun and has plenty of space for kids to run around. Buskers, caricature artists, vendors of laser whirlies, "performing" fluffy animals and myriad toys provide great entertainment for kids.

Visitors on the cobbled streets of Via dei Coronari

Letting off steam

There is plenty of space on Piazza Navona, but it can get extremely crowded. Escape the throngs by walking down Via dei Coronari (see p121) and Via del Panico to the Ponte Sant'Angelo. Cross the Tiber and join the river path on the other side of the bridge, or play in the **Parco Adriano** near the Castel Sant'Angelo (see pp214–15).

Eat and drink

Picnic: under €25; Snacks: €25–40; Real meal: €40–80; Family treat: over €80 (based on a family of four)

PICNIC Carrefour Express (Piazza Nicosia 35, 00186; open daily) offers basic provisions. Pick up a picnic lunch and eat it at the piazza.

SNACKS Casa e Bottega Café (Via dei Coronari 183, 00186; 06 686 4358; open daily) is a welcoming café, perfect for breakfast, a light lunch or an afternoon tea of dainty sandwiches and biscuits. Kids will enjoy a typical Italian *merenda* (snack) – hot chocolate with cream, biscuits and fruit, or fresh fruit juice with yogurt.

REAL MEAL Da Tonino (Via del Governo Vecchio 18–19, 00186; 06 908 6508; closed Sun) is a cheerful trattoria offering gargantuan portions of pasta, crisp roast potatoes, simple grilled steaks and veal stew with mushrooms and peas.

FAMILY TREAT La Rosetta (Via Della Rosetta 8/9, 00186; 06 686 1002) is one of the finest seafood restaurants in Rome. Located in the heart of the historical centre, it serves an excellent variety of raw fish dishes, prepared with the freshest seasonal ingredients, and a fabulous lobster linguine.

Shopping

Berté (Piazza Navona 108, 00186; 06 687 5011) is one of the best toy-shops in Rome, selling dolls, dolls' houses and enough furry animals to open a fluffy zoo. **Libreria Fanucci** (Piazza Madama 8, 00186; 06 686 1141) has a delightful selection of illustrated books for children in several languages.

Find out more

DIGITAL Learn how gravity fountains work and how to make one at www.tinyurl.com/767snte, www.tinyurl.com/y9tqbjh and www.howstuffworks.com.
FILM Several scenes of *Angels and Demons*, based on Dan Brown's thriller of the same name, were filmed on the piazza.

Take cover

The Museo Nazionale Romano's **Palazzo Altemps** (see p120) is a great place to spend a rainy day. Alternatively, spend hours browsing the toys at **Berté**.

Next stop...

FONTANA DELLE TARTARUGHE Visit the Fontana delle Tartarughe in the Jewish Ghetto (see pp134–5), which shows Bernini working on a less monumental scale… designing tortoises!

Statue in the inner courtyard of the Palazzo Altemps

Gilded ceiling of the San Luigi dei Francesi church

② San Luigi dei Francesi

The life of a saintly tax officer

Dedicated to their patron St Louis, San Luigi dei Francesi is the church of Rome's French community. It is famous for its chapel, which was decorated by the ground-breaking 17th-century artist Caravaggio, who was commissioned to paint three scenes from the life of St Matthew. The first, *The Calling of St Matthew*, shows the saint being called by Jesus and St Peter from the tax office. Light glints on the rims of coins, shimmers on velvets, brocades and an ostrich plume, and spotlights

the faces of the main characters. The second, *The Martyrdom of St Matthew*, is bathed in a sickly, greenish light and depicts the saint's martyrdom. The third, *The Inspiration of St Matthew*, is Caravaggio's second attempt at the scene and shows St Matthew talking to an airborne angel. Caravaggio's first attempt at the third scene was rejected by the priests of San Luigi, who objected to Matthew appearing as a dishevelled and apparently illiterate peasant – the angel appears to be teaching him to read. The rejected painting ended up in Berlin, where it was destroyed during World War II.

Letting off steam

Walk to **Piazza Navona** (*see pp116–17*) or cross the Tiber to the **Parco Adriano** by the Castel Sant'Angelo (*see pp214–15*).

③ Sant'Ivo alla Sapienza

Bees, jelly moulds and dragons

A hexagonal church with a scalloped cupola and spiralling gold pinnacle, this is one of the most ingenious of the churches built by the 17th-century architect Francesco Borromini. The interior is shaped like an exotic geometric flower, with alternating scooped and sharply angled bays forming the "petals". In the courtyard, Borromini incorporated elements from the coats of arms of six popes. Look for bees (Pope Urban VIII Barberini), doves with olive branches in their beaks (Pope Innocent X Pamphilj), a star and jelly mould (Pope Alexander VII Chigi), dragon (Pope Gregory VIII Buoncampagni), dragon and eagle

(Pope Paul VI Borghese) and a lion holding some pears (Pope V Montalto).

Letting off steam

Head back to the **Piazza Navona** or cross the Tiber to the **Parco Adriano**.

The Lowdown

- 🌐 **Map reference** 11 D3
  Address Corso del Rinascimento 40, 00186
- 🚌 **Bus** C3, 30, 70, 81, 87, 116, 130, 186, 492 & 628
- 🕐 **Open** 9am–noon Sun
- 💲 **Price** Free
- 👫 **Age range** 5 plus
- ⏱ **Allow** 20 mins
- ♿ **Wheelchair access** Yes
- 🍴 **Eat and drink** PICNIC Caffè Argentina (*Largo Di Torre Argentina 51, 00186; 06 679 2371*) serves good cappuccinos and delicious sandwiches. SNACKS RosticceRi (*Corso del Rinascimento 83–85, 00186; 06 6880 8345; open daily; closed Sun pm; www.rosticceri.com*) offers a delicious array of takeaway food. A separate vegetarian counter offers a wide range of dishes such as vegetable couscous and rice salad
- 👫 **Toilets** No

The Lowdown

- 🌐 **Map reference** 11 D3
  Address Piazza di San Luigi dei Francesi 5, 00186; 06 68 8271
- 🚌 **Bus** C3, 30, 70, 81, 87, 116, 130, 186, 492 & 628
- 🕐 **Open** 10am–12:30pm & 3–7pm daily; closed Thu pm
- 💲 **Price** Free. €1 for the lights
- 👫 **Age range** 7 plus
- ⏱ **Allow** 20 mins
- ♿ **Wheelchair access** Yes
- 🍴 **Eat and drink** PICNIC Caffè Sant'Eustachio (*Piazza Sant'Eustachio 82, 00186; 06 6880 2048; open daily*) has excellent pastries and an inviting display of hot and cold lunch dishes, ideal to tempt kids with. Enjoy a picnic lunch on the stairs to the church. SNACKS Ciuri Ciuri (*Largo del Teatro Valle 1–2, 00186; 06 9826 2284; open daily*) serves Sicilian street food
- 🛍 **Shop** The bookshop next door has children's books in French
- 👫 **Toilets** No

④ Sant'Andrea della Valle

Magical skies

The most interesting feature of Sant'Andrea della Valle is its dome. Stand underneath and stare up at the ceiling frescoes. Suddenly, all the clouds will start to seem real, and the figures above them will seem to float out from the walls and hang suspended in three-dimensional space. This optical illusion was created by the 17th-century artist Lanfranco, one of the two artists commissioned by the church. His rival, Domenichino, was so angry when he lost most of the commission that he tampered with the scaffolding erected in the dome, hoping that Lanfranco would fall and break his neck.

Letting off steam

Head to **Piazza Navona** or **Campo de' Fiori** (*see pp130–31*), where children can run around and have

The Lowdown

- 🌐 **Map reference** 11 D4
  Address Piazza Sant'Andrea della Valle, 00186; 06 686 1339
- 🚗 **Bus** C3, 30 40, 46, 62, 64, 70, 81, 87, 116, 130, 186, 190, 492, 571, 628 & 916
- 🕐 **Open** 7:30am–12:30pm & 4:30–7:30pm daily
- 🅿 **Price** Free
- 👪 **Age range** 5 plus
- ⏱ **Allow** 20 mins
- ♿ **Wheelchair access** Yes
- 🍴 **Eat and drink** PICNIC Caffé Argentina (see Sant'Ivo alla Sapienza). FAMILY TREAT Casa Bleve (Via del Teatro Valle 48, 00186; 06 686 5970; closed Sun) is famous for its Sfizi di Bleve, a feast of innovative antipasti. Also savour their involtini (stuffed rolls), beef tartare and swordfish
- 🚻 **Toilets** No

fun. At the end of the day's sightseeing, cross the Tiber to the **Parco Adriano**.

⑤ Sant'Agostino
The Madonna with dirty toenails

Inside Sant'Agostino is one of the most popular Madonnas in Rome – an elegant marble statue by the 15th-century Italian artist Jacopo Sansovino that looks like a Roman goddess and may indeed have been inspired by a statue of Juno. Known as the *Madonna del Parto* (Madonna of Childbirth), the statue is surrounded by photographs of babies, children's drawings, embroidered hearts and blue bunnies – gifts from those whose prayers to the Madonna for a child were answered. To one side is a book in which people from

all over the world have written their prayers. The church also has Caravaggio's *Madonna dei Pellegrini* (Madonna of the Pilgrims) on display. The sculpture shows two pilgrims, with the filthy soles of their feet in full view, kneeling before the Madonna, who stands barefoot in the doorway of a house with a flaking wall, holding baby Jesus. The painting caused a shock on its unveiling in 1603 – people were accustomed to seeing the Madonna on an altar, not standing barefoot in a doorway and, what is more, with dirty toenails.

Letting off steam

Stroll along the Tiber on the pedestrian pathway and stop at one of the *grattachecca* kiosks to pick up a fruit-syrup-flavoured ice.

The Lowdown

- 🌐 **Map reference** 11 D2
  Address Piazza di Sant'Agostino 80, 00186; 06 6880 1962
- 🚗 **Bus** C3, 30, 70, 81, 87, 116, 130, 186, 492 & 628
- 🕐 **Open** 7:30am–noon & 4–7:30pm daily
- 🅿 **Price** Free
- 👪 **Age range** 7 plus
- ⏱ **Allow** 20 mins
- ♿ **Wheelchair access** Yes
- 🍴 **Eat and drink** PICNIC Blue Ice (Via dei Baullari 141, 00186; open daily) serves vividly coloured ice cream. Eat it in Piazza Navona. FAMILY TREAT Casa Coppelle (Piazza delle Coppelle 49, 00186; 06 6889 1707; open daily) is a Franco-Roman restaurant with a tempting range of dishes such as tarte Tatin (upside-down tart) of caramelized artichokes and scallions, risotto with pear and gorgonzola and rack of lamb with vermouth and apple
- 🚻 **Toilets** No

Fresco of angels on the ceiling of Sant'Agostino church

Ancient Roman sculptures and frescoed walls in Palazzo Altemps, Museo Nazionale Romano

⑥ Palazzo Altemps

Life and death in marble

A branch of the Museo Nazionale Romano *(see pp98–9)*, the Palazzo Altemps houses mainly Greek and Roman sculptures from the private collections of noble Roman families in the 16th and 17th centuries and is most famous for its Ludovisi collection, which includes around 100 sculptures. There is plenty of space, and information boards in both Italian and English are full of intriguing background and fascinating detail.

Families interested in Egyptian statues should head to the first floor, which has finds from the gardens of Maecenas and the Temple of Isis that once stood close to the Pantheon *(see pp122–3)*. Look for the fragment of a slab carved with scenes from the *navigium isidis* (literally, "vessel of Isis"), an ancient Roman festival that marked the advent of the seafaring season and honoured the goddess Isis. It features sacred baboons, the bull-god Bes and women dancing.

Beyond this is a room dominated by two colossal statues – the marble head, hands and feet from a statue of either Aphrodite or Persephone, with holes in the forehead, earlobes, hair and neck into which jewellery would have been inserted. Opposite this room is the huge Juno Ludovisi, now thought to be a portrait of Augustus's wife Livia or of Claudius's mother Agrippina.

Also on the first floor is the museum's prize exhibit, the Ludovisi Throne, which was long assumed to show the birth of Aphrodite from sea foam; some now think it shows Persephone, the goddess of spring, returning from the Underworld. Look out for the 2nd-century red marble statue of a maenad, which was once part of a fountain and has holes in its eyes and mouth through which water gushed out. Finally, do not miss the *Suicidal Galatian*, which was found in a garden near the residence of Julius Caesar. It shows a man holding a dying woman with one hand, about to stab himself with the other. He probably killed his wife, before killing himself, preferring to die rather than submit to the Romans. The statue may have formed part of the same sculpture group as the *Dying Galatian* in the Capitoline Museums *(see pp82–3)*.

Letting off steam

Cross the Tiber and head to the **Parco Adriano** near the Castel Sant'Angelo *(see pp214–15)* for ice-skating and games.

⑦ Santa Maria della Pace

Catwalk to church

One of the most fashionable churches in Renaissance Rome, Santa Maria della Pace was frequented by artists, aristocrats and bankers as well as by women who considered going to Mass a great opportuntity to show off their best clothes and find wealthy husbands and admirers. The interior of the church, a short nave ending in an octagonal cupola, houses Raphael's famous frescoes of four *Sibyls* – mythological women said

The Lowdown

🌐 **Map reference** 11 C3
Address Piazza Santa Maria della Pace, 00186; 06 686 1156

🚌 **Bus** C3, 30, 70, 81, 87, 116, 130, 186, 492 & 628

🕐 **Open** 9–11:45am Mon, Wed & Sat

👫 **Age range** 9 plus

⏱ **Allow** 20 mins

♿ **Wheelchair access** Yes

🍴 **Eat and drink** PICNIC Lo Zozzone *(Via Teatro della Pace 32, 00186; 06 6880 8575; open daily)* offers irresistible squares of crisp pizza bianca, filled with everything from ricotta and tuna, tomatoes and rocket to ricotta and cherry or chocolate. REAL MEAL The Chiostro Bramante Bistrot serves scrambled eggs and bacon; omelettes; pear, gorgonzola and walnut salad; artichoke pasta, and baguettes with goat's cheese, honey and baby spinach. Choose whether to sit in the exquisite cloister or in the lounge, which has a window perfectly positioned for looking at the *Sibyls*

🛍 **Shop** There is a gift shop selling art books and gadgets in the Chiostro del Bramante

🚻 **Toilets** No

to have a direct communication with the gods, and hence able to prophesize the future. The *Sibyls* range from a beautiful young blonde woman to a very old lady, each receiving a revelation from an angel. They are best seen from the **Chiostro del Bramante**, the cloister, located behind the church.

Letting off steam

Walk either to **Piazza Navona** *(see pp116–17)* or **Campo de' Fiori** *(see pp130–31)*, where children can run around.

8 Via dei Coronari

The road to God

Medieval pilgrims on their way to St Peter's Basilica *(see pp204–5)* walked along this street before crossing the Tiber. Of the many shops that sprang up to part the pilgrims from their money, the most enduring were those of the rosary makers – or *coronari* – who gave the street its name. The street is now famous for its antique shops,

although there are other kinds of shops here, too. It is at its most magical in May and October during the Mostra dell'Antiquariato, when a red carpet is thrown down, torches are lit outside the shops, and lemon and kumquat trees in pots line the street.

Take cover

Visit the **Palazzo Altemps** and enjoy some quiet moments in a place steeped in history.

Interior of an antiques shop on Via dei Coronari

The Lowdown

🌐 **Map reference** 11 B2
Address Via dei Coronari, 00186

🚌 **Bus** C3, 30, 46, 70, 81, 87, 98, 116, 130, 186, 492, 628, 870 & 881

👫 **Age range** 7 plus

⏱ **Allow** 1 hr

♿ **Wheelchair access** Yes

🍴 **Eat and drink** SNACKS Etabli *(Vicolo delle Vacche 9/A, 00186; 06 9761 6694)* is a trendy café that also serves salads and simple dishes. REAL MEAL Ristorante Il Fico *(Via di Monte Giordano 49, 00186; 06 687 5568)* has hearty meat and seafood dishes and a pleasant outdoor patio

🛍 **Shops** Le Tele di Carlotta *(Via dei Coronari 228, 00186)* sells tiny hand-embroidered cushions. Kouki at No. 26 has a wide variety of beads that visitors can choose to have strung. At No. 225 is a jaw-dropping collection of locks and keys in a nameless shop

🚻 **Toilets** No

⑨ Pantheon
Pondering pumpkins

The world's best-preserved Roman building, the Pantheon, according to one version, was designed by the goddess Cybele. In fact, the designer was probably Emperor Hadrian (r.117–138), who is said to have been inspired by contemplating a pumpkin. Whatever the truth, stepping inside the Pantheon is an incredible experience, especially on sunny days, with the sunlight streaming in through the hole, or *oculus*, at the top of the dome, and on rainy days too, when water pours in.

Sculpture on the Tomb of Raphael

Key Features

The *oculus*

Portico Marcus Agrippa, Emperor Augustus's general, constructed a temple on this site between 27 BC and 25 BC. It was destroyed in a fire in AD 90. The present portico is built on its foundations and shows the inscription "Marcus Agrippa built this" in Latin.

Coffering The hollow coffers in the dome help to reduce its weight. Many Renaissance and Baroque architects copied this technique.

Dome exterior The exterior of the dome is a shallow shell covering the interior like a lid. It was originally covered in gilded bronze tiles, but the metal was stripped off by the Byzantine Emperor Constantine the Bearded in AD 663 and melted down to be made into coins.

The drum The walls of the cylindrical drum supporting the dome are 6 m (20 ft) thick.

Tomb of Raphael

Tomb of Raphael The artist is buried in the Pantheon along with many Italian kings and queens. His body rests below a Madonna by Lorenzetto (1520).

Piazza della Rotonda The lively piazza in front of the Pantheon is dominated by a fountain with an obelisk taken from a temple to Isis that once stood where the Collegio Romano stands today.

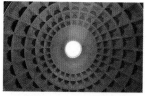

Dome interior The Pantheon's dome was the largest in the world for 1,300 years and is still the largest unreinforced concrete dome in the world. It was cast by pouring 4,550 tonnes (5,000 tons) of concrete over a wooden frame.

The Lowdown

🌐 **Map reference** 12 E3
Address Piazza della Rotonda, 00186; www.pantheonroma.com

🚌 **Bus** C3, 30, 40, 46, 62, 64, 70, 81, 87, 116, 130, 186, 492 & 628

🕐 **Open** 9am–7:30pm Mon–Sat, 9am–6pm Sun

€ **Price** Free

🧍 **Skipping the queue** Arrive early to avoid the crowds. One of the busiest times is sunset

🎫 **Guided tours** Tours (€20–40; under 7s free) can be booked on the website. Download audioguides (€1.99) and videoguides (€3.99) from the website

👫 **Age range** 5 plus

🕐 **Allow** 30 mins
♿ **Wheelchair access** Yes
🚻 **Toilets** No

Good family value?
The Pantheon is officially a church, and entrance is free. It will appeal to children who like science, technology and building things.

A child playing with an actor dressed as a gladiator, Piazza della Rotonda

Letting off steam

Have fun on **Piazza della Rotonda** in front of the Pantheon, where kids can dance to the buskers or run after a laser whizzy toy.

Eat and drink

Picnic: under €25; Snacks: €25–40; Real meal: €40–80; Family treat: over €80 (based on a family of four)

PICNIC L'Antica Salumeria *(Piazza della Rotonda, 00186; 06 687 5989)* offers bread and basic provisions. If Piazza della Rotonda is too crowded for a picnic, try the nearby Piazza della Minerva.

SNACKS Il Panino Ingegnoso *(Piazza di Pletra 35, 00186)* is a sandwich bar that offers a wide range of delicious sandwiches, named after famous inventors.

REAL MEAL Green T *(Via Pie' di Marmo 28, 00186; 06 679 8628; closed Sun)* is Rome's best Asian restaurant. Both food and decor are stylish, and the menu ranges from spring rolls and five-spiced duck to unusual regional Chinese dishes.

FAMILY TREAT Sapore di Mare *(Via Pie' di Marmo 36, 00186; 06 678 0968; closed Mon lunch)*, with its stacks of polystyrene fish boxes

and displays of fresh fish looks like a fishmonger, but it is one of Rome's finest seafood restaurants.

Shopping

Poggi *(Via Pie' di Marmo 38–9, 00186; www.poggi1825.it)* is a great art shop, a 2-minute walk away from the Pantheon. **Città del Sole** *(Via della Scrofa 65, 00186; www.cittadelsole.it)* is a stimulating toyshop with an emphasis on creative and educational toys.

Find out more

DIGITAL Download the official Pantheon app for an iPhone or iPad from *www.pantheonroma.com* before visiting. Alternatively, *www.tinyurl.com/d3rmwe2* has facts on the history of cement and concrete – frothy volcanic pumice was used in the Pantheon's dome, because it was so light. Kids can get more information on *www.cement.org/cement-concrete-basics* or make cement from sand, water and cornflour following instructions on *www.tinyurl.com/726jopv*.

Next stop...
EGYPTIAN TREASURE HUNT

The obelisk on Piazza della Rotonda comes from the Temple of Isis that once stood on the site of the nearby Collegio Romano. There is another obelisk on **Piazza della Minerva** *(see p124)*; a marble foot of Isis on Via di Pie' di Marmo and a stone cat from the temple on Via della Gatta. The eroded head of Isis is outside the church of San Marco off **Piazza Venezia** *(see p84)*. For more Egyptian finds, head to the **Capitoline Museums** *(see pp82–3)*.

Piazza della Rotonda in front of the Pantheon

⑩ Piazza della Minerva

Elephants, God and science

Located just behind the Pantheon, Piazza della Minerva is home to one of Rome's most bizarre monuments: a cheeky marble elephant sculpture with a miniature obelisk on its back, designed by Bernini in 1667. Elephants represented intelligence and obelisks denoted wisdom. The inscription on the base makes the meaning clear: "A robust intelligence is required to support solid wisdom." The words were chosen by papal patron Alexander VII. The sculpture is a tribute to his wisdom.

Overlooking the sculpture is the church of **Santa Maria sopra Minerva**, built in the 13th century on the site of a Roman temple to Minerva, goddess of wisdom. With its blue starry vaults, pointed arches and stained-glass windows, it is the only Gothic church in Rome. Inside, the *Madonna dell'Annunziata* by Renaissance artist Antoniazzo Romano shows the Madonna giving money to three little blonde girls kneeling next to Cardinal Juan Torquemada, who founded a charity in 1460 to provide dowries for poor girls who would otherwise have been unable to marry. In the 16th and 17th centuries, the church became the

The enormous nave in the church of Santa Maria sopra Minerva

Inquisition's headquarters – Galileo was put on trial here in 1632 for saying that the earth moved around the sun. Look for the tomb of the head Inquisitor, Pope Paul IV, who excommunicated Elizabeth I of England, confined Rome's Jews to the Ghetto (see pp134–5), and called Michelangelo's *The Last Judgment* "stew of nudes," although the artist's *Cristo della Minerva* (1521) stands by the altar.

Letting off steam

The **Piazza della Minerva** is traffic-free and great for a run around. Picnic on the flight of steps up to the church, or perch on the cannon-balls that surround the square.

⑪ Palazzo Doria Pamphilj

The palace of paintings

The stunning Palazzo Doria Pamphilj is one of the few privately owned Roman palaces that is open to the public. Its oldest parts date from 1453. On display is the Doria Pamphilj family's vast art collection as well as their sumptuous private apartments. These include: the Smoking Room created for the Princess Emily Doria, daughter of the Duke of Newcastle who married a Doria prince in 1882; the Ballroom, with walls of rose-printed silk; the Yellow Room, decorated with zodiac signs; and the Green Room, lit by a multi-hued Murano glass chandelier.

The art collection is on display in the Galleria Doria Pamphilj. Exhibits include: Caravaggio's *Rest During the Flight to Egypt*, in which the Virgin affectionately nuzzles baby Jesus while Joseph holds up a sheet of music to an angel playing the

The Lowdown

- **Map reference** 12 F4
  Address Via del Corso 305, 00186; 06 679 7323; www.doriapamphilj.it
- **Bus** 62, 64, 85, 95, 175, 492, 630 & 850
- **Open** 9am–7pm daily
- **Price** €24–40 (inclusive of audioguides); under 11s free
- **Skipping the queue** There are rarely any queues
- **Age range** 8 plus
- **Allow** 1 hr
- **Wheelchair access** Yes
- **Eat and drink** PICNIC Carrefour Express (Via del Governo Vecchio 119, 00186; open daily) offers provisions for a picnic lunch that can be eaten at the Villa Aldobrandini. SNACKS The Caffè Doria inside Palazzo Doria Pamphilj (entrance from Via della Gatta; open daily) serves pastries, dishes for lunch and delicious nibbles
- **Shop** The bookshop near the ticket counter has an interesting collection of books and souvenirs
- **Toilets** On the second floor

violin; a portrait of the family's ancestor Pope Innocent X by the Spanish artist Velázquez; and Titian's *Salome with the Head of John the Baptist*. Salome was a dancer who so enraptured King Herod that he agreed to grant her anything she wished. She asked for, and was given, the head of St John the Baptist. The contrast between the beautiful Salome and the severed head of the saint was very popular with artists.

Letting off steam

Return to **Piazza della Minerva** or cross busy Piazza Venezia (see p84) to run around the **Piazza del Campidoglio** (see p80).

The Lowdown

- **Map reference** 12 E3
  Address Piazza della Minerva 42, 00186; 06 679 3926
- **Bus** C3, 30, 70, 81, 87, 116, 130, 186, 492 & 628
- **Open** Santa Maria sopra Minerva: 7:10am–7pm Mon–Sat, 8am–noon & 2–7pm Sun
- **Age range** 7 plus
- **Allow** 20 mins
- **Wheelchair access** Yes
- **Eat and drink** SNACKS Enoteca Spiriti (Via Sant'Eustachio 5, 00186; 06 6889 2199; closed Sun) is a great place for a light lunch of varied bruschetta, Parma ham and figs and smoked meats. FAMILY TREAT Da Armando al Pantheon (Salita de'Crescenzi 31, 00186; 06 6880 3034; closed Sat eve & Sun) serves delicious spaghetti cacio e pepe, alla carbonara and amatriciana as well as tagliolini with asparagus
- **Toilets** No

⑫ Sant'Ignazio

Virtual reality

Stepping inside the church of Sant'Ignazio is like walking into a heavenly ballroom. Walk to the nave and look for a star set into the pavement. Stand here, look up and get someone to put a coin into the slot. The church will flood with light, and the roof will seem to burst open to reveal a blue sky full of glamorous angels sucked up to heaven – as if by a vacuum cleaner – to where St Ignatius, the founder of the Jesuit Order, floats on a fluffy cloud. Believe it or not, the dome does not exist at all – it is just a painted disc! The frescoes in the nave celebrate the missionary work done by the Jesuits all over the world, with four women representing Europe, Asia, America and Africa. The church is at its loveliest in the evening, when its marble columns and pavements gleam, and its polished brass glints in the lamplight.

Letting off steam

A 5-minute walk away, **Piazza San Lorenzo in Lucina** is a great place to have coffee while children play. Alternatively, explore the *gelaterie* of Via della Maddalena and Via Uffici del Vicario (*see p127*).

The Lowdown

- 🌐 **Map reference** 12 F3
  Address Piazza di Sant'Ignazio, 00186; 06 679 4406
- 🚌 **Bus** 81, 116, 117 & 492
- 🕐 **Open** 7:30am–12:20pm & 3–7:20pm daily
- 🎟 **Price** Free
- 👪 **Age range** 5 plus
- ⏱ **Allow** 20–30 mins
- ♿ **Wheelchair access** Yes
- 🍴 **Eat and drink** PICNIC Cambi (*Via del Leoncino 30, 00186; 06 687 8081; closed Sun*) has a deli counter, wine, fresh bread and pizza slices, all perfect for a picnic lunch that can be eaten in Piazza di Sant'Ignazio or Piazza della Minerva. FAMILY TREAT Matricianella (*Via del Leone 3, 00186; 06 683 2100; closed Sun*) is a trattoria offering a great meal of crisp mixed fried vegetables followed by a pasta dish. It is also well known for its lamb
- 🚻 **Toilets** No

Above Cafés on Piazza San Lorenzo in Lucina Below Frescoes on the fake dome of Sant'Ignazio church

Ancient stone columns of the Temple of Hadrian

⑬ Temple of Hadrian

From temple to stock exchange

Embedded in the wall of what was once Italy's stock exchange are 11 chewed Corinthian columns and a frieze embedded with lions. These belong to a temple erected in AD 145 by Emperor Antoninus Pius (r.138–161) in honour of his adoptive father, Hadrian. The opening scenes of Antonioni's film *L'Eclisse* (1962) show a young Alain Delon working at the exchange.

Letting off steam

The **Piazza di Pietra** behind the temple is a pedestrianized square, perfect for a quick rest or bite to eat.

The Lowdown

- 🌐 **Map reference** 12 F3
  Address Piazza di Pietra, 00186
- 🚌 **Bus** 116
- 👫 **Age range** 8 plus
- ⏱ **Allow** 10 mins
- ♿ **Wheelchair access** Yes
- ☕ **Eat and drink** PICNIC Gran Caffè la Caffettiera *(Piazza di Pietra 65, 00186; 06 6798147; closed Sun)* serves coffee, milkshakes, sandwiches and pastries. *FAMILY TREAT* Osteria dell'Ingegno *(Piazza di Pietra 45, 00186; 06 678 0662; closed Sun)* has an unusual selection of lunch dishes such as potato soup or lasagne with broccoli and pecorino
- 🚻 **Toilets** No

⑭ Piazza di Montecitorio

A Roman sundial

The first thing that visitors see on approaching Piazza di Montecitorio from Via della Guglia is jagged lumps of rock sticking out from the façade of the Palazzo di Montecitorio. The palace was designed by Bernini and now houses the Chamber of Deputies, one of Italy's two houses of parliament; the other is the Chamber of the Senate in the Palazzo Madama next to Sant'Ivo alla Sapienza *(see p118)*. At the centre of the piazza is a giant Egyptian obelisk that was once part of a huge sundial laid out by Emperor Augustus in 10 BC. The centre of this sundial was near the

Façade of the Palazzo di Montecitorio, Piazza di Montecitorio

present-day Piazza San Lorenzo in Lucina, and the shadow was cast by the obelisk. It was moved to its present location in 1792.

The adjoining Piazza Colonna is named after the Column of Marcus Aurelius rising from its centre, an imitation of Trajan's Column *(see p88)*. The piazza is home to the heavily guarded Palazzo Chigi, residence of the prime minister.

Take cover

Shelter from rain in the **Galleria Alberto Sordi** *(Piazza Colonna, 00186; www.galleriaalbertosordi.it)*, which has a toyshop, clothes shops and a bookshop.

⑮ La Maddalena

The icing-sugar church on ice-cream street

Dedicated to Mary Magdalene, this pretty church, with its Rococo-style façade, is always referred to as La Maddalena out of respect for the Virgin Mary. Catholics did not want the name Mary to be associated with Mary Magdalene, a sinner who had repented. As architectural tastes evolved, some people wanted to replace the highly decorated wedding-cake façade with a more sombre-looking Neo-Classical one. The façade is best admired while enjoying an ice cream from one of the great ice-cream parlours nearby.

Letting off steam

Visit the **Piazza della Rotonda** *(see p122)*, where kids will find lots of entertainment.

The Lowdown

- 🌐 **Map reference** 12 E2
  Address Palazzo Montecitorio: Piazza di Montecitorio, 00186
- 🚌 **Bus** 25, 81, 116, 119 & 628
- 👫 **Age range** 8 plus
- ⏱ **Allow** 20 mins
- ♿ **Wheelchair access** Yes
- ☕ **Eat and drink** SNACKS Vitti *(Piazza San Lorenzo in Lucina, 00186; 06 687 6304)* is a great café that even serves breakfast with bacon and eggs. *FAMILY TREAT* Trattoria dal Cavalier Gino *(Vicolo Rosini 4, 00186; 06 687 3434; closed Sun & Aug)* offers dishes such as *pasta alla carbonara* and lamb and rabbit *cacciatora* casserole
- 🚻 **Toilets** No

The Lowdown

- **Map reference** 12 E2
- **Address** Piazza della Maddalena, 00186; 06 89 9281
- **Bus** 116
- **Open** 8:30–11:30am & 5–6:30pm Sun–Fri, 9–11:30am Sat
- **Price** Free
- **Age range** 6 plus
- **Allow** 15 mins
- **Wheelchair access** Yes
- **Eat and drink** PICNIC Gelateria della Palma (Via della Maddalena 20, 00186) offers great ice creams. Other popular gelaterie include Giolitti (Via Uffici del Vicario 40), Grom (Via della Maddalena 30) and San Crispino (Piazza della Maddalena 3). Eat it in Piazza della Rotonda. FAMILY TREAT Enoteca al Parlamento Achilli (Via dei Prefetti 15, 00186; 06 687 3446; open daily; www.enotecalparlamento. com) is a classy wine shop that has a Michelin-starred restaurant attached to it
- **Toilets** No

Painting on the ceiling of the nave, Il Gesù

⑯ Il Gesù
God for the masses

Dating from 1568 and 1584, the Gesù church was the seat of the Jesuits in Rome. Its interior with a single, broad, well-lit nave was the first of its kind, designed in 1568, at the height of the Thirty Years' War between Catholics and Protestants. The Catholics were fast losing followers to the Protestants, who let them read their own Bibles, for example, instead of having priests read carefully selected extracts. By providing people with prayer books and filling the nave with enough light to read, the Jesuits hoped to make Catholicism more popular. By the late 17th century, when the interior was decorated, the Thirty Years' War was over, and the church

was riding on a wave of glory. It was in this mood that the ceiling was decorated with triumphant paintings and statues that ridicule the Protestants and heretics.

Letting off steam

The **Piazza del Campidoglio** (see p80) and the **Monte Caprino park** (see p75) are the nearest places for a traffic-free run around.

The Cordonata leading to the Piazza del Campidoglio

The Lowdown

- **Map reference** 12 F4
- **Address** Piazza del Gesù, 00186; 06 697 001
- **Bus** 30, 40, 46, 62, 64, 70, 81, 87, 119, 130, 186, 190, 492, 571, 628, 810 & 916
- **Open** 7am–12:30pm & 4–7:45pm daily
- **Price** Free
- **Age range** 7 plus
- **Allow** 20–30 mins
- **Wheelchair access** Yes
- **Eat and drink** PICNIC Gelateria Origini (Via del Gesù 73, 00186; 06 4547 3915; open daily) makes an amazing ice cream with ricotta, orange and jasmine flowers. Enjoy it in Piazza della Minerva. REAL MEAL Enoteca Corsi (Via del Gesù 88, 00186; 06 679 0821; closed Sun), is more of a trattoria than a wine bar, and serves spaghetti alla carbonara or a rustic soup; puddings are home-made
- **Toilets** No

Picnic under €25; **Snacks** €25–40; **Real meal** €40–80; **Family treat** over €80 (based on a family of four)

Campo de' Fiori and around

Bounded by the Tiber to the south, and linked by the pedestrian Ponte Sisto to Trastevere, the Campo de' Fiori and Piazza Farnese area is mostly pedestrianized and its many sights are within walking distance of each other. Campo de' Fiori itself and the main road, Via de' Giubbonari, get very busy by day and things can get a little wild at night, but other streets remain relatively untouched by the crowds. There are no metro lines crossing the area. The nearest access points by bus are Corso Vittorio Emanuele II and Largo di Torre Argentina.

Piazza Navona & Campo de' Fiori

Campo de' Fiori p130

Places of Interest

SIGHTS

1. Campo de' Fiori
2. Piazza Farnese
3. Palazzo Spada
4. Via Giulia
5. Museo Criminologico
6. Area Sacra di Largo Argentina
7. Jewish Ghetto
8. Fontana delle Tartarughe

EAT AND DRINK

1. Alimentari Ruggeri
2. Antico Forno Roscioli
3. Obicà
4. Roscioli
5. L'Insalata Ricca
6. Sto Bene Roma
7. Trattoria da Sergio alle Grotte
8. Bar Latteria
9. Zoc
10. Antico Bar Mariani
11. Taverna Giulia
12. Coop
13. Bar del Cappuccino
14. Cremeria Romana Gelato Kosher
15. Ba'Ghetto
16. Kosher Bistrot
17. La Taverna degli Amici

SHOPPING

See Palazzo Spada (p132)

WHERE TO STAY

1. Sole al Biscione
2. Hotel Campo de' Fiori
3. Pensione Barrett
4. Little Queen Suite
5. Kame Hall
6. B&B Little Queen
7. Arenula
8. Locanda Cairoli
9. Hotel Ponte Sisto

Narrow side street off Campo de' Fiori

Diners enjoying a meal in Piazza Farnese, near Campo de' Fiori

The Lowdown

- 🚗 **Bus** 30, 40, 46, 56, 60, 62, 64, 70, 81, 87, 116, 119, 130, 186, 190, 492, 571, 628, 810 & 916. **Tram** 8

- ℹ️ **Visitor information** Tourist Information Point, Piazza delle Cinque Lune (near Piazza Navona), 00186; 060608; open 9:30am–7pm daily; *www.turismoroma.it*

- 🛒 **Supermarkets** Coop, Via S Bartolomeo de' Vaccinari 74, 00186. SMA, Via del Monte della Farina 51, 00186. **Markets** Campo de' Fiori market; 7am–2pm Mon–Sat

- ➕ **Pharmacies** Farmacia Arenula: Via Arenula 73, 00186; 06 6880 3278; open 7:30am–10pm Mon–Sat, 6am–10pm Sun

- 🤸 **Nearest play area** There are no playgrounds in this area; Roman children play in piazzas such as Piazza Farnese

0 metres 250

0 yards 250

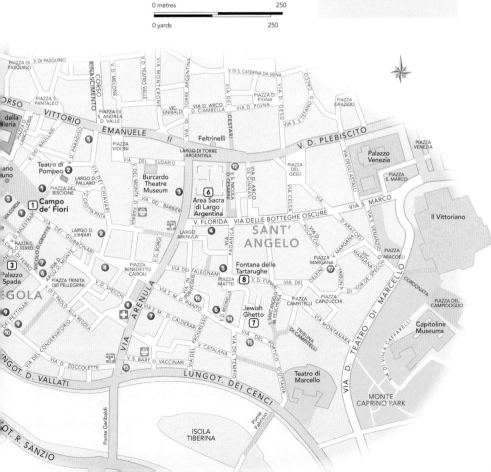

① Campo de' Fiori

Fruit, vegetables and murder most foul

The name *Campo de' Fiori* means "field of flowers". In the Middle Ages it was a meadow, and a horse market was held here. The neighbourhood has a grisly history that kids will love – saunter down the cobbled streets to find where Julius Caesar was murdered, Giordano Bruno was burned at the stake for heresy, painter Caravaggio killed his tennis opponent and goldsmith Benvenuto Cellini murdered a business rival. Today, it is home to central Rome's most appealing food market.

Madonna painting on the piazza

Key Sights

Giordano Bruno Monument A statue marks the spot where the philosopher Bruno was burned at the stake for heresy in 1600.

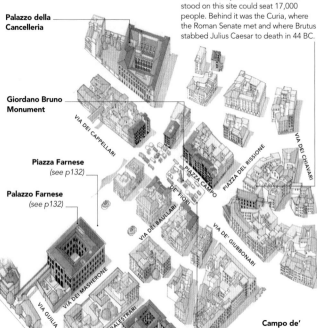

Palazzo della Cancelleria

Teatro di Pompeo The theatre that stood on this site could seat 17,000 people. Behind it was the Curia, where the Roman Senate met and where Brutus stabbed Julius Caesar to death in 44 BC.

Giordano Bruno Monument

VIA DEI CAPPELLARI

Piazza Farnese (see p132)

Palazzo Farnese (see p132)

PIAZZA CAMPO DE' FIORI

PIAZZA DEL RISSIONE

VIA DEI CHIAVARI

VIA DEI BAULLARI

VIA DE' GIUBBONARI

VIA DEI MASHERONE

VIA GIULIA

VIA DEI BALESTRARI

Campo de' Fiori market

VIA DEI PETTINARI

Street names Streets around the Campo de' Fiori are named after the craftsmen that traditionally worked here – look for Via dei Cappellari (hat-makers), Via de' Giubbonari (jerkin-makers), Via dei Balestrari (crossbow-makers), Via dei Baullari (basketmakers) and Via dei Pettinari (comb-makers).

Campo de' Fiori market Surrounded by colourful houses with shutters and pigeons nestling on their sills, the stalls at the food market here sell seasonal fruit and vegetables such as spiky purple artichokes and courgette flowers.

Palazzo della Cancelleria This palace was built by Cardinal Raffaele Riario in the 15th century with the winnings of a single night's gambling.

Prices given are for a family of four

The Lowdown

🌐 **Map reference** 11 C4
Address Campo de' Fiori, 00186

🚗 **Bus** 40, 46, 62, 64 & 116

👫 **Skipping the queue** Prepare to use your elbows to get served at market stalls, since Romans do not really queue!

👫 **Age range** All ages

⏱ **Allow** 2–3 hrs

♿ **Wheelchair access** Yes

🚻 **Toilets** In the cafés, although these are open only to customers; buy an espresso or water at the bar

Good family value?
Nowhere could be better for a family to spend time, and all for the cost of a bag of peanuts.

Letting off steam

If Campo de' Fiori itself gets too hectic amidst the market stalls, stroll down to the more tranquil **Piazza Farnese** (see p132).

Eat and drink

Picnic: under €25; Snacks: €25–40; Real meal: €40–80; Family treat: over €80 (based on a family of four)

PICNIC Alimentari Ruggeri (Campo de' Fiori 1, 00186; 06 6880 1091; open daily) is a great deli with a selection of cheese, salami and ham, plus Marmite and peanut butter for the homesick. Pick up a picnic lunch and head to Piazza Farnese.

Alimentari Ruggeri, purveyor of everything from olive oil to maple syrup

Quiet, open space of Piazza Farnese, a good spot for a cappuccino

SNACKS Antico Forno Roscioli (Via dei Chiavari 34, 00186; 06 686 4045; closed Sun & Jul & Aug: Sat) gets crowded in the evenings, when all kinds of bread, crisp pizza *bianca* and cakes leave the oven. There are hot takeaway dishes, too.
REAL MEAL Obicà (Campo de' Fiori 26, 00186; 06 6880 2366; open daily) is a chic mozzarella bar that serves several gourmet varieties of mozzarella in a tantalizing range of sandwiches and salads.
FAMILY TREAT Roscioli (Via de' Giubbonari 21–22, 00186; 06 687 5287; closed Sun) uses top-quality ingredients to cook up what is said to be Rome's best *spaghetti carbonara*, with organic eggs.

Find out more

DIGITAL www.tinyurl.com/ce9rx8 shows Caesar's murder through interesting clay animation.

Take cover

Visit the **Burcardo Theatre Museum** (Via del Sudario 44, 00186; 06 681 9471; open 9:15am–4:30pm Tue & Thu), which covers 500 years of theatre history. Alternatively, visit **Palazzo Spada** (see p132), or spend time browsing the books and toys at the **Feltrinelli** bookshop (Largo di Torre Argentina 11, 00186; 06 6866 3001; open daily).

Next stop...

TO MARKET OR MURDER
Carry on to the **Palatine Hill** (see pp74–5), scene of more Imperial Roman murders, or cross the Tiber for another great fresh-produce market in **Piazza San Cosimato**.

One of the fountains on Piazza Farnese, topped with irises

② Piazza Farnese
Architecture and frescoes

The elegant Piazza Farnese is a peaceful retreat from the bustle of Campo de' Fiori. The piazza is dominated by two fountains featuring what appear to be giant lilies, but are in fact blue irises – the symbol of the Farnese family.

Overlooking the piazza is the **Palazzo Farnese**. Designed by Antonio Sangallo the Younger and refined by Michelangelo, it now houses the French Embassy. The palazzo's courtyard exemplifies the difference in the styles of the two artists. The lower tiers by Sangallo are faithful copies of elements of ancient Roman architecture that were just being rediscovered. The upper tiers by Michelangelo are far more inventive, reflecting not only his originality, but also his eagerness to further improve upon ancient techniques. The highlight of the palace is the frescoed ceiling in the ambassador's office on the first floor. Painted by Annibale Carracci in 1604, it depicts gods and goddesses falling in love, against an illusionistic background that features fake skies and mock stuccoes. The best time to visit the piazza is at night, when the façade of the palazzo is illuminated, and the chandeliers inside are switched on to reveal the frescoed ceilings.

Letting off steam

To escape the streets for a while, cross the Tiber at **Ponte Sisto** (see p188) and walk along the riverside cycle path to relax and unwind.

③ Palazzo Spada
Mermaids and monsters

Built way back in 1540, Palazzo Spada is one of the most intricately decorated palaces in Rome. It is named after its one-time owner, Cardinal Bernardino Spada, a keen art collector. His collection included the works of artists of the time such as Caravaggio, Artemisia Gentileschi, Lavinia Fontana and Sofonisba Anguissola.

Look at its façade to find Mannerist statues of toga-wearing Romans, medallions, urns, ribbons and swags of flowers, all made of stucco. The courtyard has battling centaurs, mermaids and sea monsters. On the right is what appears to be a long arcade flanked by columns. In reality this gallery is about a quarter of its apparent length, and the statue at the end quite tiny – the result of a crafty optical illusion by the architect Borromini. On guided tours, the guide walks into the gallery and appears to get taller and taller the closer he gets to the end.

Letting off steam

Spot the cats in the palazzo's formal gardens or spend some time browsing for books, toys and music in the **Feltrinelli** bookshop (see p131).

The Lowdown

 Map reference 11 C5
Address Piazza Capo di Ferro 13, 00186; 06 687 4896; http://galleriaspada.beniculturali.it

🚌 **Bus** 46, 56, 62, 64, 70, 81, 87, 492 & 628

🕑 **Open** 8:30am–7:30pm Tue–Sun

💲 **Price** €10–15; under 18s free

🚶 **Skipping the queue** Call 199 757 510 to book tickets

🚩 **Guided tours** 10:30am, 11:30am & 12:30pm first Sun of the month (€24). Book in advance on http://galleriaspada.beniculturali.it or by calling 06 2258 2493

👫 **Age range** 5 plus for perspective; 8 plus for gallery

🕐 **Allow** 1 hr

♿ **Wheelchair access** Only to the Borromini perspective

🍴 **Eat and drink** SNACKS Sto Bene Roma (Piazza Trinita dei Pellegrini 88, 00186; 06 6880 8653; 7am–8pm Mon–Sat) is good spot for sandwiches. Eat it on Piazza Farnese. REAL MEAL Trattoria da Sergio alle Grotte (Vicolo delle Grotte 27, 00186; 06 686 4293; closed Sun) serves all the usual Italian dishes, plus fish

🛍 **Shop** The bookshop on the ground floor sells postcards, art books and posters

🚻 **Toilets** On the ground floor

The Lowdown

🌐 **Map reference** 11 C5
Address Palazzo Farnese: Piazza Farnese, 00186; 06 686 011; www.ambafrance-it.org

🚌 **Bus** 40, 60, 64, 190, 571 & 916

🕑 **Open** Palazzo Farnese: access by tours only; under 15s must be accompanied by parents

🚩 **Guided tours** Palazzo Farnese (€5): 3pm, 4pm & 5pm on Mon, Wed & Fri. Book at least one week in advance on www.inventerrome.com; carry a photo ID

👫 **Age range** Palazzo Farnese: 7 plus

🕐 **Allow** Palazzo Farnese: 45 mins for a tour

🍴 **Eat and drink** SNACKS Antico Forno Roscioli (see p131) offers a good range of breads and pizzas. REAL MEAL L'Insalata Ricca (Via dei Chiavari 85–86, 00186; 06 6880 3656; open daily) serves 50 different kinds of salads as well as hamburgers with chips, pasta, crêpes and suppli

🚻 **Toilets** No

First arch of Michelangelo's unfinished viaduct on picturesque Via Giulia

④ Via Giulia

A cure for sore throats

A perfectly straight, cobbled street lined with Renaissance palaces and churches, Via Giulia was laid out in the early 16th century on the orders of Pope Julius II to link the centre of Rome with St Peter's (see pp204–5). But, due to lack of funds and the pope's death, it could not be completed with a bridge, as planned.

On approaching from Piazza Farnese, look out for an arch covered with creepers. This was intended to be the first arch of a viaduct designed by Michelangelo to link Palazzo Farnese with Villa Farnese on the other side of the Tiber, but was never finished. Just below the arch is a grotesque fountain, the Mascherone.

On one occasion the water dribbling from the mouth of the Mascherone was replaced with wine.

Also on the street is a church decorated with grimacing skulls. This is **Santa Maria dell'Orazione e Morte**, whose priests had the job of collecting the corpses of poor people and giving them a Christian burial. Beyond this is a huge orange building – once the city prison and the church of **San Biagio della Pagnotta**. The church's patron saint is believed to have the power to cure sore throats, and people still visit to be healed by holding two candles to their throats.

Take cover

Shelter in **Antico Bar Mariani** (*Via dei Pettinari 44, 00186; open daily*), or peep inside one of the churches.

The Lowdown

🌐 **Map reference** 11 A3
Address Via Giulia, 00186

🚌 **Bus** C3, 8, 46, 62, 64, 70, 81, 87, 186, 492, 571, 628 & 916

🚹 **Age range** All ages

🕐 **Allow** 30 mins

♿ **Wheelchair access** Yes

🍴 **Eat and drink** PICNIC Bar Latteria (*Via del Gallo 4–5, 00186; 06 686 5091*) is famous for its hot chocolate and milky coffee. Have it on Piazza Farnese. *FAMILY TREAT* Zoc (*Via delle Zoccolette 22, 00186; 06 6819 2515; open daily for dinner & Sun lunch*) serves delicious pumpkin ravioli with melted butter and sage. Also try the soup of spelt, beans and cavolo nero

🚻 **Toilets** In the cafés

Priests walking past the Mascherone fountain on Via Guilia

Picnic under €25; **Snacks** €25–40; **Real meal** €40–80; **Family treat** over €80 (based on a family of four)

Ruins of Republican-era temples at the Area Sacra di Largo Argentina

⑤ Museo Criminologico

Letter on a pair of underpants

Part of the former 19th-century Delle Carceri Nuove prison, this museum takes visitors on a harrowing voyage into the world of crime and punishment. The journey begins with replicas of ancient and medieval instruments of torture made by young offenders in the 1930s, including a spiked torture chair used to punish witches in medieval Nuremberg and a hollow bronze bull to roast offenders in ancient Agrigento. Beyond this is the red hooded cloak used by Rome's 19th-century executioner, Mastro Titta.

Also in the museum is a section devoted to the "science" of criminal physiognomy – it was believed that faces and even the shape of the ears could indicate that someone had criminal tendencies! Do not miss the room of stolen art objects and fake paintings. Finally there is a room full of various objects smuggled into prisons – shoes, a hairbrush and books concealing knives – and letters from prisoners written on underpants and one written on a handkerchief and rolled up inside a cigarette.

Letting off steam

Head towards **Piazza Farnese** (see p132) and enjoy a walk or run around the fountains there.

⑥ Area Sacra di Largo Argentina

Count the cats

In the centre of Largo Argentina are the remains of four temples (A, B, C and D), which date back to the Republican era and are among the oldest in Rome. In Roman times, the area was dominated by an 8-m-(24-ft-) high acrolith of Fortuna Huiusce Diei, Roman goddess of fate. Parts of her body, including a head, are on show at the Centrale Montemartini (see p109). The temple dedicated to Fortuna (Temple B) was circular, and can clearly be seen from the pavement above. The tufa blocks behind it belonged to the vast Curia di Pompeo (see p130). This is where Julius Caesar was murdered. The other temples in this area are rectangular in shape. Behind Temple A are the remains of a marble Roman toilet. The ruins are now home to a sanctuary for abandoned cats.

Letting off steam

Children can play safely in the car-free streets of the **Jewish Ghetto**, or dive back into the bustle of **Campo de' Fiori**.

⑦ Jewish Ghetto

Artichokes and sweet pizza

In 1555, Pope Paul IV, one of the leaders of the Inquisition (see p124), confined Rome's Jews to one area. This area was surrounded by a wall with five gates that were opened at dawn and closed at sunset. The inhabitants of this area were forced to wear a yellow badge. Future popes banned Jews from all trades except selling old clothes and scrap iron. Nowadays, the area is full of narrow streets and alleys and still has a strong Jewish presence, with a synagogue and several restaurants serving Jewish

The Lowdown

- 🌐 **Map reference** 12 E6
  Address Between Via del Portico d'Ottavia, Lungotevere dei Cenci, Via del Progresso and Via di Santa Maria del Pianto, 00186
- 🚗 **Bus** 8, 46, 62, 64, 70, 81, 87, 186, 492, 571, 628 & 916
- 👫 **Age range** All ages
- ⏲ **Allow** 1 hr
- ♿ **Wheelchair access** Yes
- 🍴 **Eat and drink** PICNIC Cremeria Romana Gelato Kosher (*Via del Portico d'Ottavia 1B, 00186; closed Sat*) sells excellent kosher ice creams and sorbets, made with natural ingredients. *FAMILY TREAT* Ba'Ghetto (*Via del Portico d'Ottavia 57, 00186; 06 6889 2868; closed Fri dinner & Sat lunch*) is a kosher restaurant that combines Roman Jewish cuisine with Middle Eastern specialities, mainly from Libya and Israel
- 👫 **Toilets** No

dishes such as *carciofi alla giudia* (deep-fried artichokes) and pizza *dolce* (a singed scone filled with candied fruit).

Not all the sights here are Jewish. The remains of the **Teatro di Marcello** stand at the end of Via Portico d'Ottavia. In the 16th century, the ruins of this theatre were incorporated into a palace, which has now been converted into luxury apartments.

Letting off steam

Let the kids enjoy a game of Poohsticks on **Ponte Fabricio** (*Lungotevere de' Cenci, 00186*), Rome's oldest bridge. Built in 62 BC, this Roman bridge leads to the Isola Tiberina, or Tiber Island, from the end of Via del Portico d'Ottavia.

⑧ Fontana delle Tartarughe

Of dolphins and tortoises

Piazza Mattei is one of the prettiest and quietest piazzas in the *centro storico*. At its centre is the Fontana delle Tartarughe, or tortoise fountain, with sculptures of boys on dolphins. It was created by the Italian architects Giacomo della Porta and Taddeo Landini in 1585, allegedly in a single night. The fountain, however, ran into problems straight away – the pressure of the water

was too low for it to work properly. Consequently the fountain was redesigned. Four of the original eight dolphins were removed and, instead of trying to make the water gush dramatically, the designers settled for a single small jet of water into the basin and a gentle stream of water from each of the remaining dolphins' mouths. In the 1650s, Bernini decided to give each boy a bronze tortoise, which they hold up as if to let the creatures drink from the upper basin.

Letting off steam

Wander the streets of the **Jewish Ghetto**, where kids can enjoy a game of hide-and-seek.

Della Porta's tortoise fountain in Piazza Mattei

The Lowdown

- 🌐 **Map reference** 12 E5
  Address Piazza Mattei, 00186
- 🚗 **Bus** 30, 40, 46, 62, 64, 70, 81, 87, 119, 130, 186, 190, 492, 571, 628, 810 & 916. **Tram** 8
- 👫 **Age range** All ages
- ♿ **Wheelchair access** Yes
- 🍴 **Eat and drink** SNACKS Kosher Bistrot (*Via Santa Maria del Pianto 68/69, 00186; 06 686 4398; www.kosherbistrotcaffe.com*) is perfect for a quick lunch of hamburgers, Jewish-style artichokes, sandwiches and some Middle Eastern dishes. *FAMILY TREAT* La Taverna degli Amici (*Piazza Margana 36–7, 00187; 06 6992 0637; closed Sun pm & Mon*) offers specialities such as zucchini flowers stuffed with ricotta and osso buco (braised veal shanks) and tagliata
- 👫 **Toilets** No

Piazza di Spagna
& Trevi Fountain

Since the 18th century, this area, with popular sights such as the Spanish Steps and Trevi Fountain as well as numerous lesser-known churches and piazzas, has been a favourite with visitors from all over the world. Families can alternate sightseeing with visits to the Pincio Gardens and Villa Borghese. The area also offers plenty of good opportunities for window-shopping and people-watching.

Highlights

Piazza di Spagna
Watch passers-by while sitting on the magnificent Spanish Steps in the Piazza di Spagna, one of the most famous piazzas in Rome (see pp142–3).

Santa Maria del Popolo
Marvel at works by Bernini, Caravaggio and Raphael, and hunt for skeletons in this art-packed church (see pp148–9).

Pincio Gardens
Hire roller skates, a go-kart, bicycle or electric car and have fun riding around the Pincio Gardens (see p151).

Trevi Fountain
Help the poor and guarantee a return to Rome by throwing a coin into this majestic fountain (see pp154–5).

Time Elevator
Let kids see, hear, smell and feel history nibbling at their toes at the Time Elevator (see p156).

Palazzo Barberini
Visit the Galleria Nazionale d'Arte Antica to see Raphael's famous La Fornarina, then gaze up at the spectacular illusionistic ceiling of the palazzo's Grande Salone (see p158).

Above right Fresco in the vault of Santa Maria della Vittoria church
Left Spouting lions on the Fontana dell'Obelisko in Piazza del Popolo, with Santa Maria in Montesanto church and Via del Corso beyond

The Best of...
Piazza di Spagna & Trevi Fountain

The Spanish Steps and Trevi Fountain make the most immediate impact in this area, but there are many other attractions to seek out such as the Quirinal Hill, home to several ingenious churches as well as the Italian president, and the Time Elevator, where children can enjoy a 5D trip through the history of Rome. This wealthy area teems with elegant people, but many of its attractions are free.

A taste of *la dolce vita*

Window-shopping in the designer boutiques along the streets around **Piazza di Spagna** *(see pp142–3)* – most famously Via Condotti *(see p142)* and Via del Babuino – will doubtless appeal to fashionable teenagers, although they will be able to buy more for their money in the mainstream shops that line Via del Corso. Those seeking a lesson in elegance and élan might want to take a seat in one of the cafés on Via Condotti and check out the clothes, manicured nails and make-up of passers-by. Or, head to the cafés of **Piazza del Popolo** *(see p150)*, also popular with the idle rich. To simply watch people enjoying themselves, head to the **Pincio Gardens** *(see p151)* – a favourite with Roman families for a stroll at weekends or on summer evenings.

Right *The nave and altar of Santa Maria del Popolo church*
Below *Families relaxing in the idyllic grounds of the Pincio Gardens in spring*

Ecclesiastical treasure hunt

The churches here house some of the area's great treasures. Step into **Santa Maria del Popolo** (see pp148–9) and see Caravaggio's ground-breaking paintings: The Crucifixion of St Peter and The Conversion of St Paul. Also check out the chapel with two pyramids designed by Raphael and a theatrical sculpture by Bernini, as well as more than the customary number of images of skulls and skeletons. Those in the mood for more chills and thrills could pay a visit to the catacombs below the church of Santa Maria della Concezione on **Via Vittorio Veneto** (see p161), which are decorated with the bones from more than 4,000 skeletons. For a change of tempo, drop into two of the city's sophisticated Baroque churches **San Carlo alle Quattro Fontane** (see p159) by Borromini and **Sant'Andrea al Quirinale** (see p159) by Bernini.

Fountains and piazzas

This area has some of Rome's most striking piazzas and fountains. There is the vast oval **Piazza del Popolo**, with its trick symmetrical twin churches and a lion-and-obelisk fountain; **Piazza di Spagna**, dominated by the famous **Spanish Steps** (see p142); and the huge **Piazza del Quirinale** (see p157), overlooked by the presidential palace and an obelisk flanked by ancient Roman statues of Castor and Pollux leading horses. Even more varied are the area's fountains. Marvel at the Fontana della Barcaccia in **Piazza di Spagna**, designed by Bernini's father, the **Fontana del Tritone** and **Fontana delle Api** on Piazza Barberini (see p160) by Bernini and, most flamboyant of all, the **Trevi Fountain** (see pp154–5), occupying an entire palace wall and half a piazza.

Above The twin churches of Santa Maria dei Miracoli and Santa Maria in Montesanto in Piazza del Popolo *Below* Statue of a Triton guiding a sea horse, Trevi Fountain

Party in the piazza

Plan a trip to Rome in February, during the Carnival, when the focus of attention is the **Piazza del Popolo**. Catch the spectacular equestrian shows, free entertainment from fire-eaters, acrobats and tightrope-walkers, and costumed parades and events for children (such as a gladiator school!). Be sure to pack fancy-dress clothes for children, and be prepared to buy them a bag of *coriandoli* (paper confetti) to throw over each other (and unsuspecting passers-by) so that they can join in the festivities.

Piazza di Spagna and around

Known as the Tridente, this area is defined by three streets – Via di Ripetta, Via del Corso and Via del Babuino – that cut straight through this part of the *centro storico*, converging at Piazza del Popolo like an arrowhead. Much of the area is pedestrianized – Via del Corso is closed to cars, but not buses, in the evenings, and there are plans to further pedestrianize the zone. The main points of interest with young children are the Spanish Steps and the Pincio Gardens. Join in the early evening *passeggiata*, when Romans strut their stuff on the designer shopping streets: Via Condotti, Via del Babuino and Via del Corso.

Piazza di Spagna &
Trevi Fountain

Santa Maria del Popolo
p148

Piazza di Spagna
p142

Azaleas in full bloom on the Spanish Steps, with the Trinità dei Monti church in the background

Places of Interest

SIGHTS
1 Piazza di Spagna
2 Keats-Shelley Memorial House
3 Babington's Tea Rooms
4 Trinità dei Monti
5 Villa Medici
6 Ara Pacis
7 Santa Maria del Popolo
8 Piazza del Popolo
9 Santa Maria dei Miracoli & Santa Maria in Montesanto
10 Pincio Gardens

EAT AND DRINK
1 Salumeria Focacci
2 Vuda Bar
3 Il Margutta Vegetarian Food and Art
4 Edy
5 Carrefour Express, Via Vittoria
6 Da Giggi
7 McDonald's
8 Hostaria al 31
9 Fratelli Fabbi
10 Ciampini al Café du Jardin
11 ReCafé
12 Buccone
13 Antica Osteria Brunetti
14 Dal Pollarolo
15 Mare
16 Café Rosati
17 Babette
18 Cose Fritte
19 La Penna d'Oca
20 Casina dell'Orologio

See also Babington's Tea Rooms (p144)

SHOPPING
1 Il Pesciolino Rosso
2 Vertecchi

WHERE TO STAY
1 Hotel Locarno
2 Casa Montani
3 Hotel de Russie
4 B&B Corso 22
5 Hotel Mozart
6 Hotel del Corso
7 Class House
8 Hotel Panda
9 Portrait Suites
10 B&B Pantheon View
11 Hotel Piazza di Spagna
12 Hotel Hassler Roma
13 Hotel Madrid

0 metres   300
0 yards   300

Bar Canova, a popular restaurant on Piazza del Popolo

The Lowdown

🚗 **Metro** Spagna (Line A) & Flaminio–Piazza del Popolo (Line A). **Bus** 61, 70, 81, 116, 117, 119, 120, 150, 160, 186, 491, 492, 628, 590 & 926. **Tram** 2

ℹ️ **Visitor information** Tourist Information Point, Via Marco Minghetti, off Via del Corso, 00188; 060608; open 9:30am–7pm daily; www.turismoroma.it

🛒 **Market** Via Bocca di Leone: 8am–noon Mon–Sat

🎭 **Festivals** Carnival (on the 5 days before Shrove Tue; see p139). Festa della Primavera (Apr): azaleas cover the Spanish Steps and concerts take place in Trinità dei Monti church

➕ **Pharmacies** Farmacia Trinità dei Monti: Piazza di Spagna 30, 00187; 06 679 0626; open 8:30am–8pm daily. Farmacia Europea: Via della Croce 10–11, 00187; 06 679 1632; open 8:30am–8pm Mon–Sat, 10:30am–7:30pm Sun

🛝 **Nearest play area** Pincio Gardens (see p151)

① Piazza di Spagna
Fancy-dress party on the bow-tie piazza

Overlooked by russet-, cream- and mustard-washed palazzos, the bow-tie-shaped Piazza di Spagna is one of the most famous squares in Rome. The area around the square has been popular with visitors since the days of the Grand Tour – poets Keats, Shelley and Byron, and composers Liszt and Wagner, chose to live here. These days the area is known for its designer clothes shops – an entire day can be spent here watching people walk by in all their designer finery.

Fontana della Baracaccia

Key Sights

Babington's Tea Rooms (see p144)

Piazza di Spagna Known as the Ghetto degli Inglesi (English Ghetto) in the 18th century, Piazza di Spagna has been the meeting place for visitors to Rome for almost three hundred years.

Antico Caffè Greco

Via delle Carrozze In the 18th and 19th centuries, this was where the carriages of wealthy locals and visitors would be repaired.

Via Condotti This cobbled street is the hub of the designer shopping zone.

Spanish Steps

VIA DELLA CROCE

VIA CONDOTTI

VIA DELLA VITE

Trinità dei Monti (see p145)

Keats-Shelley Memorial House (see p144)

Rampa Mignanelli Also known as the secret steps, this flight is located to the side of the Spanish Steps.

Fontana della Barcaccia Designed by Gian Lorenzo Bernini and his father for Pope Urban VIII in 1627, this fountain shows a boat that appears to be sinking. It is decorated with bees from the pope's coat of arms.

Colonna dell'Immacolata

Spanish Steps In 1700, the Bourbon royal family became the rulers of Spain as well as France. It was decided to symbolize their power by linking the French church of Trinità dei Monti with the Spanish Embassy by building the steps. This grand flight of stairs is now a distinctive landmark.

Prices given are for a family of four

Colonna dell'Immacolata Inaugurated in 1857, this Roman column, crowned by a staue of the Virgin Mary, commemorates the proclamation of the doctrine of the Immaculate Conception.

Antico Caffè Greco Started by Greek national Nicola di Madalena in 1760, the legendary Caffè Greco was a favourite with composers and poets such as Liszt, Wagner, Byron and Keats.

The Lowdown

🌐 **Map reference** 4 H4
Address Piazza di Spagna, 00187

🚗 **Metro** Spagna (Line A).
Bus 116, 117, 119 & 590

👥 **Skipping the queue** The piazza and its cafés get very busy on weekends and in the early evening. The quietest time to visit is early morning

👫 **Age range** 5 plus

⏱ **Allow** 1 hr

♿ **Wheelchair access** Yes (not on the steps)

🚻 **Toilets** In the cafés, although these are open only to customers; buy an espresso or water

Good family value?
While the main attractions here can be seen for free, this is one of the most expensive parts of Rome to dine and shop in, so if on a budget make sure kids are well fed before visiting the area.

Letting off steam

Children can usually find space to run up and down the steps, even at busy times! It is a pleasant and short walk from Trinità dei Monti to the **Pincio Gardens** (see p151), and beyond to **Villa Borghese** (see pp168–9).

A path through the scenic Pincio Gardens in autumn

Eat and drink

Picnic: under €25; Snacks: €25–40; Real meal: €40–80; Family treat: over €80 (based on a family of four)

PICNIC Salumeria Focacci (Via della Croce 43, 00187; closed Sun) offers a selection of hams, salami, cheese, smoked salmon and other smoked fish, as well as a luscious selection of olives, sundried tomatoes, anchovies and other sott'olii (delicacies preserved in oil). Picnic at the Pincio Gardens.
SNACKS Vuda Bar (Via della Vite 71–72, 00187; 06 679 2976; open daily; www.vudahotels.it), located on the ground floor of Hotel Homs, serves a decent selection of pastas and salads, risotto agli scampi (with prawns), good sandwiches and great coffee. The place is very popular with the locals working in the neighbourhood.
REAL MEAL Il Margutta Vegetarian Food and Art (Via Margutta 118, 00187; 06 3265 0577; open daily) is a chic vegetarian restaurant full of vividly coloured furniture and vibrant paintings. The weekday buffet brunch in its more relaxed lounge-café area offers good value and the weekend brunch is accompanied by live music.
FAMILY TREAT Edy (Vicolo del Babuino 4, 00187; 06 3600 1738; closed Sun) is a family-run restaurant untouched by time, fads and fashions, tucked into a quiet alley

not far from Piazza di Spagna. The tagliatelle with artichokes and ricotta, and the home-made tiramisù served here are delicious.

Shopping

Il Pesciolino Rosso (Via Bocca di Leone 49, 00187; 06 6992 2059) is a lovely upmarket toyshop with plenty of small toys and craft activities suitable for trying in a hotel room. **Vertecchi** (Via della Croce 70, 00187; www.vertecchi.com) is one of the city's best-equipped art supplies and stationery shops.

Find out more

DIGITAL Read the news report on one of the people who drove down the Spanish Steps at www.tinyurl.com/7k4v39x, or complete a digital jigsaw puzzle of the Spanish Steps at www.tinyurl.com/7bwqwp5.
FILM In the romantic comedy Roman Holiday (1953), runaway princess Audrey Hepburn sits on the Spanish Steps eating an ice cream. It is here that journalist Gregory Peck "accidentally" runs into her, starting a day-long romance.

The library inside the Keats-Shelley Memorial House

Take cover

Shelter in **Babington's Tea Rooms** (see p144) or at the **Antico Caffè Greco**, making an expensive cup of tea or coffee last as long as you can, or see how long it is possible to keep the kids interested at the **Keats-Shelley Memorial House** (see p144).

Next stop...

FAR FROM THE MADDING CROWD The best place for families after Piazza di Spagna is the **Villa Borghese**, a short walk away. Choose between its museums, the zoo or just a run around the park.

A room in the Keats-Shelley Memorial House, furnished as it was when Keats lived there

② Keats-Shelley Memorial House

A Romantic death

In November 1820, the English poet John Keats came to stay in this dusky pink house, the Casina Rosa, on the corner of the Spanish Steps. Keats was suffering from consumption and was sent to Rome by his doctor, in the hope that the warm, dry climate

The Lowdown

🌐 **Map reference** 5 A4
Address Piazza di Spagna 26, 00187; 06 678 4235; www. keats-shelley-house.org

🚗 **Metro** Spagna (Line A). **Bus** 116, 117, 119 & 590

🕐 **Open** 10am–1pm & 2–6pm Mon–Sat

💶 **Price** €10–18; under 6s free

Guided tours Only for groups

👫 **Age range** 8 plus

⏱ **Allow** 1 hr

♿ **Wheelchair access** No

🍽 **Eat and drink** *PICNIC* Carrefour Express (*Via Vittoria 32, 00187; closed Sun*) is the ideal place to pick up picnic provisions. Eat on the Spanish Steps. *FAMILY TREAT* Da Giggi (*Via Belsiana 94/a, 00187; 06 679 1130; closed Tue; www. trattoriadagiggi.it*) has been dishing out Roman specialities such as *spaghetti alla carbonara, abbacchio* (lamb) and *maialino* (suckling pig) since the 1960s

🛍 **Shop** The shop on the first floor sells posters, prints, T-shirts and fridge magnets

👫 **Toilets** Yes, on the first floor

would help him recover. But the ship from England was delayed by storms, and, by the time Keats and his friend Joseph Severn arrived, the weather had turned cold. Keats was further weakened by a starvation diet of anchovies and a piece of bread every day, and died the following February. His death inspired poet Percy Bysshe Shelley to write the poem *Mourn not for Adonais*. In July 1822, Shelley himself was drowned in a boating accident. Keats, Shelley and Severn are all buried at the Protestant cemetery in Testaccio (*see p108*).

In 1906, the house was bought by an Anglo-American association and preserved as a memorial and library in honour of English Romantic poets. The museum is furnished as it would have been in Keats' time and houses a collection of memorabilia associated with him and other key Romantic figures. However, all the original furniture was burned on the pope's orders after Keats died.

Letting off steam

Race up the **Spanish Steps** and down the **Rampa Mignanelli** to have some fun.

③ Babington's Tea Rooms

Teatime

It is inevitably crowded with tourists from all over the world, but few want to leave Piazza di Spagna without a taste of Babington's. In 1893, two young Englishwomen, Anna Maria and Isabel Cargill

The Lowdown

🌐 **Map reference** 4 H4
Address Piazza di Spagna 23, 00187; 06 678 6027; www. babingtons.com

🚗 **Metro** Spagna (Line A). **Bus** 116, 117, 119 & 590

🕐 **Open** 10am–9:30pm daily

👫 **Skipping the queue** Queues are hard to avoid, but try going early for breakfast

👫 **Age range** All ages

♿ **Wheelchair access** Yes

🍽 **Eat and drink** *REAL MEAL* Babington's offers authentic English breakfast as well as scones and jam, sandwiches, cakes, salads, omelettes and kedgeree. For a splash out, try their sumptuous Champagne brunch. Ice creams, including Babington's Earl Grey tea sorbet, are available too. The kids' menu includes soft-boiled eggs and toast soldiers

🛍 **Shop** The shop in the café stocks tea, marmalade, teapots, cups and saucers

👫 **Toilets** Yes

Babington, came to Rome with £100, intending to start a business. As Rome was full of English people, they decided to set up an authentic English tea room – at that time the only place people could buy tea in Rome was from a pharmacy! It was so successful that they soon set up another branch on St Peter's Square which is, however, no longer open. There are now three branches of Babington's in Tokyo.

Letting off steam

Hire go-karts and skates in the **Pincio Gardens** (*see p151*) to have some fun with kids.

Display window at the famous Babington's Tea Rooms

④ Trinità dei Monti
Michelangelo's wardrobe artist

The best thing about the church of Trinità dei Monti is the view of Rome from the platform in front of its twin bell-towered façade. The church's interior has two paintings by Daniele di Volterra, a pupil of Michelangelo. Volterra was given the job of painting clothes on the nude figures of *The Last Judgment* in the Sistine Chapel, when Pope Pius IV objected to their nudity. This earned Volterra the nickname of "Il Braghettone" (the breeches-maker). Look out for the swirling drapery around the figures in his *Descent from the Cross* (1545) here. The figure on the far right in his *Assumption of the Virgin* (1555) is believed to be Michelangelo.

Façade of the Trinità dei Monti church with the Spanish Steps in the foreground

Letting off steam

The **Pincio Gardens** are just along the road from here, an ideal place to unwind with kids.

Above A Tourist Angel on a Segway, Pincio Gardens ***Below*** Assumption of the Virgin, *Trinità dei Monti*

The Lowdown

- 🌐 **Map reference** 5 A4
  Address Piazza Trinità dei Monti, 00187; 06 679 4179
- 🚗 **Metro** Spagna (Line A).
  Bus 116, 117, 119 & 590
- 🕐 **Open** 6:30am–8pm Tue, Wed & Fri–Sun, 6:30am–midnight Thu
- 👫 **Age range** 10 plus
- ♿ **Wheelchair access** Limited
- 🍴 **Eat and drink** SNACKS McDonald's *(Piazza di Spagna 46–7, 00187; 06 6992 3613; open daily)* offers its usual fast food fare. *FAMILY TREAT* Hostaria al 31 *(Via delle Carrozze 31, 00187; 06 678 6127; closed Sun; www. hostariaal31.com)* serves slow food: artichoke risotto or lentil soup followed by roast suckling pig for lunch
- 🚻 **Toilets** No

The imposing cream and brown building of Villa Medici on Pincio Hill

⑤ Villa Medici

A prison and a school

Built in 1540 and bought by the Cardinal Ferdinando de' Medici in 1576, this villa was used as a prison for those who fell foul of the Inquisition. Its most famous prisoner was scientist Galileo Galilei, who is remembered in an inscription on a column just beyond the villa.

The villa is now home to the Académie de France à Rome, which was founded by Louis XIV in 1666 to give a few select painters the chance to study in Rome. Nicolas Poussin was one of the first advisors to the academy and French Neo-Classical painter Ingres was a director. Alumni include eminent French painters such as Fragonard

and Boucher. After 1803, when the academy moved from Palazzo Mancini on Via del Corso to the Villa Medici, musicians were also admitted; renowned French composers Berlioz and Debussy came to Rome as students of the academy.

The highlight of the villa is the Stanza degli Uccelli, a pavilion in the garden frescoed with birds, flowers, fruit and trees. The garden also features an Egyptian obelisk standing on four bronze tortoises and an unsettling group of statues, the Niobidi, laid out on the lawn. The story – a Greek myth – goes that Niobe was so proud of having 14 children that she persuaded the people of her town to stop worshipping the goddess Leto, mother of only two, and to worship

her instead. As punishment, Leto commanded her twin son and daughter, Apollo and Artemis, to shoot Niobe's children with arrows.

Nowadays the villa is used for exhibitions and concerts, and the grounds and some of the interior can be visited on guided tours. The views are spectacular, stretching right over the city to St Peter's and the Alban hills beyond.

Letting off steam

Less than a 5-minute walk away are the **Pincio Gardens** *(see p151)*, one of the best places to relax in the whole of central Rome.

Fountain with Queen Christina's cannon-ball still in it, in front of the Villa Medici

The Lowdown

🌐 **Map reference** 4 H3
Address Viale Trinità dei Monti 1, 00187; 06 676 1223; www.villamedici.it

🚗 **Metro** Spagna (Line A). **Bus** 116, 117, 119 & 590

🕐 **Open** Interiors can be visited only during concerts, exhibitions and film screenings. Gardens can be visited by tour only, Tue–Sun

💶 **Price** €24–36; under 10s free

Skipping the queue Book in advance for tours

Guided tours In English, Italian and French; check website for details

🚹 **Age range** 9 plus

⏱ **Allow** 1 hr for a guided tour mainly of the garden

♿ **Wheelchair access** Yes, to the Stanza degli Uccelli

🍴 **Eat and drink** PICNIC Fratelli Fabbi *(Via della Croce 27, 00187; 06 679 0612; closed Sun)* is the right place to shop for wine, ham and cheese. Enjoy a picnic lunch in the Pincio Gardens. *FAMILY TREAT* Ciampini al Café du Jardin *(Piazza Trinità dei Monti 1, 00187; 06 678 5678; summer: daily; winter: Thu–Tue)* serves delicious *cornetti* (croissants), cappuccino and other coffees, a variety of pasta dishes, grilled meat and ice creams

🛍 **Shop** The bookshop, Electa, near the exhibition area, sells art books

🚻 **Toilets** Next to the exhibition area

⑥ Ara Pacis

Imperial children

Constructed under Emperor Augustus, the Ara Pacis, or Altar of Peace, is one of the most significant monuments of ancient Rome. It was erected in 9 BC to celebrate the peace and prosperity Augustus had brought to the Roman Empire after his victorious campaigns in Gaul and Spain. Since 2006 it has been

The Lowdown

- 🌐 **Map reference** 4 G4
  Address Lungotevere in Augusta, 00186; 060608; www.arapacis.it
- 🚗 **Bus** 70, 81, 117, 119, 186, 492, 628 & 926
- 🕐 **Open** 9am–7:30pm daily
- Ⓖ **Price** €21–38; EU under 18s €8.50; under 6s free
- 👕 **Skipping the queue** Call 060608 or book in advance at www.ticketclic.it
- 🎧 **Guided tours** Audioguides (€4.50) available from the ticket desk in Italian, English, French and Spanish
- 👫 **Age range** 7 plus
- ⏱ **Allow** 45 mins
- ♿ **Wheelchair access** Yes
- ☕ **Eat and drink** PICNIC ReCafé (Piazza Augusto Imperatore 36, 00186; 06 6813 4730; open daily; www.recafe.it) is a modern café and restaurant that serves Neapolitan pizza, pagnotelle (baked bread rolls with the filling inside), salads or a cake and coffee. REAL MEAL Buccone (Via di Ripetta 19, 00186; 06 361 2154) is an enoteca (wine shop/bar) that offers a selection of first and second courses at lunch and dinner
- 🚻 **Toilets** Behind the altar

encased in an ultramodern building of glass and travertine designed by New York architect Richard Meier.

Carved along the sides of the altar are figures in a long procession – lictors (guards), augurs (soothsayers) and flamines (priests) – followed by Augustus and his family members, including several children. A scale model of the Ara Pacis with a key helps to identify the characters, while a huge Caesar family tree makes it easier to work out who is related to whom.

Visible from the Ara Pacis is an overgrown brick cylinder that is actually the **Mausoleum of Augustus**, where the emperor and his family were buried. The mausoleum is currently undergoing restoration and there are plans to reopen it – exactly 2,000 years after Augustus died in AD 14 – as part of a pedestrianized Tridente zone.

Letting off steam

There is space to run around and fountains for cooling fingers and toes outside the **Ara Pacis**.

Above Overgrown ruins of the Mausoleum of Augustus **Below** The altar inside the Ara Pacis

⑦ Santa Maria del Popolo
Demons and skeletons

According to legend, the church of Santa Maria del Popolo occupies the site where Emperor Nero's nurse and girlfriend secretly buried his body after his death. They planted walnut trees over the grave, and for centuries the ravens nesting there were believed to be demons fleeing from Nero's soul. In 1099, the pope decided to exorcize the site, dug up the walnut trees and had a chapel built. Santa Maria del Popolo replaced this chapel in the late 15th century, and over the years popes and aristocrats commissioned artists such as Raphael, Pinturicchio, Caravaggio and Bernini to paint many of the church's excellent works.

Façade of Santa Maria del Popolo

Key Features

Stained-glass windows

Cerasi Chapel The chapel is famous for two canvases by Caravaggio – *The Conversion of St Paul*, which shows the saint sprawled on the ground under the rump of a horse, and *The Crucifixion of St Peter*, in which the saint looks in horror at the nail that skewers his hand.

Chigi Chapel

The Kneeling Skeleton

Apse frescoes The frescoes on the apse ceiling were painted by Pinturicchio. In the centre is the Madonna, in the circular medallions are the four Evangelists and in the four curvy lozenges are four *Sibyls*. The borders depict fantastic freakish beasts – bring binoculars to see them.

Daniel* and *Habakkuk This is a dramatic two-part sculpture by Bernini, with Daniel in a niche on one side of the chapel, and Habakkuk and the angel in a niche on the other side.

Della Rovere Chapel Look for the *Adoration of the Shepherds* painted by Pinturicchio in 1490. The fresco shows Mary and Joseph in front of a hut with baby Jesus lying on a little pile of hay. The shepherd in front is Cardinal della Rovere, who commissioned the paintings.

The Kneeling Skeleton In Dan Brown's novel *Angels and Demons*, this plaque covers the fictional Demon's Hole and is the site of the murder of a cardinal.

The Lowdown

🌐 **Map reference** 4 G2 **Address** Piazza del Popolo 12, 00187; 06 361 0836

🚗 **Metro** Flaminio-Piazza del Popolo (Line A). **Bus** 61, 120, 150, 160 & 491. **Tram** 2

🕐 **Open** 7am–12:30pm & 4–7pm Sun–Thu, 7:30am–7pm Fri & Sat

€ **Price** Free. €1 to illuminate Cerasi Chapel for a minute

👫 **Age range** 7 plus

🕐 **Allow** 30 mins

🚻 **Toilets** No

Stained-glass windows Created by the French artist Guillaume de Marcillat, the stained-glass windows behind the altar were the first in Rome. Watch how the light from outside makes the haloes glow.

Chigi Chapel Created by Raphael in 1513 for banker Agostino Chigi, the Chigi Chapel is a daring fusion of pagan and Christian imagery. Inside are the pyramid-shaped tombs of Chigi and his brother.

Good family value?
Entry to Santa Maria del Popolo is free and there is plenty for children to see.

Prices given are for a family of four

Children playing on the fountain at the centre of Piazza del Popolo

Letting off steam

Run around the **Piazza del Popolo**, climb up to the **Pincio Gardens** (see p151) for a bike or go-kart ride, or walk to the nearby gardens of **Villa Borghese** (see pp168–9).

Eat and drink

Picnic: under €25; Snacks: €25–40; Real meal: €40–80; Family treat: over €80 (based on a family of four)

PICNIC Fratelli Fabbi (see Villa Medici, p146).
SNACKS Antica Osteria Brunetti (Via Angelo Brunetti 10, 00186; 06 6452 1062; closed Sun) is a great find for a cheap family lunch. It specializes in oven-baked pasta dishes and has a special lunch menu for €10.
REAL MEAL Dal Pollarolo (Via di Ripetta 4–5, 00186; 06 361 0276; closed Thu & Aug) is inexpensive and serves pasta alla checca (elbow-shaped pasta with raw tomato, basil, capers, olives and fennel seeds) in summer and good, crisp pizza in the evenings.

FAMILY TREAT Mare (Via di Ripetta 242, 00186; 06 8901 7481; open daily) serves fresh seafood raw in dishes such as a carpaccio of prawns, or a plate of oysters, scampi and prawns served with pink grapefruit and coconut, or cooked, in dishes such as the delicious paccheri al sugo di scorfano (handmade pasta dressed with a sweet, sticky, intense sauce of scorpion fish).

Shopping

There are no shops in the immediate vicinity, but the shopping areas of **Piazza di Spagna** (see pp142–3) and **Via del Corso** are just a short walk away.

Clothes and accessories on display in a shop window on Via del Corso

Next stop...
CARAVAGGIOS AND SIBYLS
Check out more Caravaggios at **Sant'Agostino** (see p119) and at **San Luigi dei Francesi** (see p118). See Sibyls – this time by Raphael – at the church of **Santa Maria della Pace** (see pp120–21).

Tank with fresh seafood to choose from, Mare restaurant

⑧ Piazza del Popolo

Welcome to Rome...

The huge, oval Piazza del Popolo has an Egyptian obelisk flanked by water-spouting lions in its centre and a grand stone gate where the Via Flaminia, which runs all the way to the Adriatic Sea, enters the city. The outer face of the gate was decorated by Michelangelo with stone bobbles copied from the coats of arms of the Medici Pope who commissioned it. The inner face, decorated with "Chigi" jelly moulds and stars, was created by Bernini in 1655 on the orders of Pope Alexander VI Chigi. Chigi wanted to impress Queen Christina of Sweden, who had just converted to Catholicism and was coming to live in Rome.

In the 18th and 19th centuries, hundreds of wealthy (and many famous) travellers entered Rome through the piazza gate. However, their first taste of Rome may well have been terrifying – Piazza del Popolo was a place of execution, and the English poet Lord Byron arrived in 1871 to see three

The Egyptian obelisk in the centre of the enormous Piazza del Popolo

criminals being beheaded. Others made their entry to witness riderless horse races down the Via del Corso, in which the horses were given spiked saddles and fed stimulants to make them run faster.

Take cover

Visit **Babington's Tea Rooms** (see p144) to enjoy premium tea or coffee with the family.

⑨ Santa Maria dei Miracoli & Santa Maria in Montesanto

Twin tricks!

Located at the southern end of Piazza del Popolo are two 17th-century churches, cleverly designed by local architect Carlo Rainaldi. Thanks to him it seems that the three streets cutting down through the centro storico, known as "Il Tridente", form a perfect triangle, when they actually do not. To give the appearance of symmetry, it was essential that the twin churches looked identical despite the fact that the site on the left was narrower. So Rainaldi gave Santa Maria dei Miracoli (on the right) a circular dome, and Santa Maria in Montesanto an oval one to squeeze it into the narrower space, while keeping the sides of the supporting drums that faced the piazza identical. Stand in the centre of the piazza, in front of the obelisk, to judge this visual trick.

Letting off steam

These days **Piazza del Popolo** is traffic-free and perfect for a run from fountain to fountain. For extended outdoor play or a picnic, head to **Pincio Gardens**.

The Lowdown

🌐 **Map reference** 4 G3
Address Piazza del Popolo, 00187

🚗 **Metro** Flaminio-Piazza del Popolo (Line A). **Bus** 61, 120, 150, 160 & 491. **Tram** 2

👫 **Age range** 8 plus

⏱ **Allow** 15 mins

♿ **Wheelchair access** Yes

🍴 **Eat and drink** SNACKS Cose Fritte (Via di Ripetta 3, 00186; 06 321 9257; closed Sun) is the place for all things deep-fried, such as fish, potatoes, meatballs, courgette flowers and pineapple. FAMILY TREAT La Penna d'Oca (Via della Penna 53, 00186; 06 320 2898; closed Tue & Jan) is a welcoming little restaurant that has a tempting menu ranging from stuffed courgette flowers to spaghetti alle vongole (pasta with clams)

🚻 **Toilets** No

A tempting display counter in Babington's Tea Rooms

The Lowdown

🌐 **Map reference** 4 G3
Address Piazza del Popolo; 00187

🚗 **Metro** Flaminio-Piazza del Popolo (Line A). **Bus** 61, 120, 150, 160 & 491. **Tram** 2

👫 **Age range** All ages

⏱ **Allow** 30 mins

♿ **Wheelchair access** Yes

🍴 **Eat and drink** REAL MEAL Café Rosati (Piazza del Popolo 4, 00187; 06 322 5859; open daily) is a good option for a fancy lunch of tagliolini with lobster or a gran fritto of seafood in a great locality. To save money, eat breakfast standing at the bar inside with those in the know. FAMILY TREAT Babette (Via Margutta 1/d/3, 00187; 06 321 1559; closed Mon lunch) offers a great buffet at lunchtime and is a nice place for an afternoon tea or Sunday brunch

🚻 **Toilets** No

⑩ Pincio Gardens

Beautiful greens

Located above Piazza del Popolo on a hillside, the Pincio Gardens have been so skilfully terraced and richly planted with trees that, from below, the zigzagging road climbing to the gardens is almost invisible. Laid out in the early 19th century by Italian architect Giuseppe Valadier, its broad tree-lined avenues were frequented in the evenings by the wealthy of Rome, who came here to take a stroll or ride in their carriages.

One of the most striking features of the park is an Egyptian-style obelisk that Emperor Hadrian erected on the tomb of his lover, Antinous. Other attractions include a 19th-century water clock designed by a Dominican monk, which was displayed at the Paris Exhibition of 1889, and the Teatro dei Burattini, Rome's main puppet theatre.

These days the park is still well visited, especially on weekends, and, although many still stroll in their finery, carriages have been replaced by bikes, four-wheeler rickshaws, electric golf-carts, electric bikes, go-karts and roller-skates – all of which are available for hire. The panorama is particularly beautiful at sunset, the ideal time to take a stroll.

Take cover

There are activities for children in the **Casina di Raffaello** *(see p168),* an indoor play area in the nearby Villa Borghese.

Above Children go-karting in the Pincio Gardens *Below* Nineteenth-century water clock in the Pincio Gardens

The Lowdown

🌐 **Map reference** 4 H2
Address Salita del Pincio, 00187

🚗 **Metro** Flaminio-Piazza del Popolo (Line A). **Bus** 61, 120, 150, 160 & 491. **Tram** 2

👫 **Age range** All ages

Activities Hire bikes, four-wheeler rickshaws, electric golf-carts, go-karts and skates. Watch puppet shows at the Teatro dei Burattini (*www.sancarlino.it*)

⏱ **Allow** 1–2 hrs

♿ **Wheelchair access** Yes

☕ **Eat and drink** PICNIC Carrefour Express (*Via della Vittoria 22/a, 00187; closed Sun*) is the best place to shop for a picnic lunch, which you can eat at leisure in the lush gardens. REAL MEAL Casina dell'Orologio (*Viale Bambini, 00187; 06 679 8515, open daily*) is a kiosk café ideal for a panino or light lunch

🚻 **Toilets** Along the Salita del Pincio

Trevi Fountain and around

The fabulous Trevi Fountain is the obvious main attraction here and can be easily reached on foot from Via del Corso and Via del Tritone. The Quirinal Hill itself has less immediate appeal, and is only worth exploring with older children interested in seeing more work by Bernini and Borromini, or the formidable art collection of the Palazzo Barberini. However, this area is easy to access – there is a metro station on Piazza Barberini, and the busy main roads cutting across the area are well served by buses.

Piazza di Spagna & Trevi Fountain

Trevi Fountain p154

The Trevi Fountain illuminated at night

Places of Interest

SIGHTS

1. Trevi Fountain
2. Time Elevator
3. Museo delle Paste Alimentari
4. Piazza del Quirinale
5. Palazzo Barberini
6. Sant'Andrea al Quirinale
7. Santa Maria della Vittoria
8. Fontana del Tritone
9. Via Vittorio Veneto

EAT AND DRINK

1. Fratelli Ciavatta
2. La Prosciutteria
3. Sora Lucia
4. Le Tamerici
5. Il Bibo
6. Bistrot Quirino
7. Sandwicheria al Nazareno
8. Vineria Il Chianti
9. Hostaria Piccolo Arancio
10. Terrazza Barberini
11. Mr Chow
12. Coop
13. Gelateria Verde Pistacchio
14. Fratelli Ghezzi
15. Trimani
16. Forno Cerulli
17. Colline Emiliane
18. Palombi
19. Hamasei

WHERE TO STAY

1. Hotel Elite
2. Boscolo Exedra Rome
3. Hotel Julia
4. Villa Spalletti Trivelli
5. Hotel Accademia
6. Hotel dei Borgononi
7. Hotel Erdarelli

0 metres 300
0 yards 300

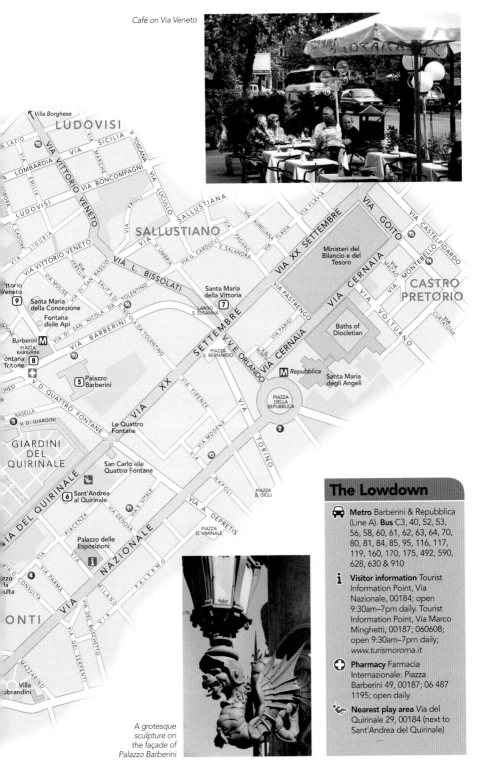

Café on Via Veneto

Villa Borghese

LUDOVISI

VIA SICILIA

VIA LAZIO

VIA TOSCANA

VIA MARCHE

VIA LOMBARDIA

VIA EMILIA

VIA BONCOMPAGNI

VIA VITTORIO VENETO

LUDOVISI

VIA LIGURIA

VIA FRIULI

VIA LUCULLO

SALLUSTIANA

VIA FLAVIA

VIA GOITO

VIA CASTELFIDARDO

SALLUSTIANO

VIA AURELIANA

VIA FLAVIA

VIA PAGANO

VIA MONTEBELLO

VIA UMBRIA

VIA G. CARDUCCI

V. SALANDRA

VIA XX SETTEMBRE

Ministeri del Bilancio e del Tesoro

VIA MACAO

CASTRO PRETORIO

VIA VITTORIO VENETO

VIA L. BISSOLATI

VIA MOLISE

VERGILIA

VIA DI SAN BASILIO

SALITA DI S. NICOLA DA TOLENTINO

Santa Maria della Vittoria

VIA PASTRENGO

VIA CERNAIA

VIA VOLTURNO

Baths of Diocletian

VIA CURATONE

Santa Maria della Concezione

9

Fontana delle Api

VIA DI S. NICOLA DA TOLENTINO

LARGO S. SUSANNA

7

SETTEMBRE

V. V. E. ORLANDO

VIA PARIGI

Barberini M

VIA BARBERINI

PIAZZA BARBERINI

PIAZZA S. BERNARDO

VIA CERNAIA

M Repubblica

Santa Maria degli Angeli

8

ntana Tritone

10

5 Palazzo Barberini

VIA XX

VIA FIRENZE

PIAZZA DELLA REPUBBLICA

2

RASELLA

V. D. QUATTRO FONTANE

Le Quattro Fontane

VIA

VIA MODENA

VIA TORINO

3

V. D. GIARDINI

VIA A. DEPRETIS

GIARDINI DEL QUIRINALE

San Carlo alle Quattro Fontane

VIA

13

PIAZZA B. GIGLI

VIA DEL QUIRINALE

6 Sant'Andrea al Quirinale

PIACENZA

VIA GENOVA

V. S. VITALE

VIA A. DEPRETIS

PIAZZA D. VIMINALE

Palazzo delle Esposizioni

VIA NAZIONALE

PIAZZA D. VIMINALE

ONTI

VIA D. CONSULTA

VIA PARMA

VIA MILANO

VIA PALERMO

VIA DEL BOSCHETTO

VIA MAZZARINO

VIA DEL SERPENTI

Villa Aldobrandini

A grotesque sculpture on the façade of Palazzo Barberini

The Lowdown

🚗 **Metro** Barberini & Repubblica (Line A). **Bus** C3, 40, 52, 53, 56, 58, 60, 61, 62, 63, 64, 70, 80, 81, 84, 85, 95, 116, 117, 119, 160, 170, 175, 492, 590, 628, 630 & 910

ℹ️ **Visitor information** Tourist Information Point, Via Nazionale, 00184; open 9:30am–7pm daily. Tourist Information Point, Via Marco Minghetti, 00187; 060608; open 9:30am–7pm daily; www.turismoroma.it

➕ **Pharmacy** Farmacia Internazionale: Piazza Barberini 49, 00187; 06 487 1195; open daily

🛝 **Nearest play area** Via del Quirinale 29, 00184 (next to Sant'Andrea del Quirinale)

① Trevi Fountain
Sweet water and sea horses

Built in 1762 by Italian architect Nicola Salvi in the flamboyant Rococo style, the Trevi Fountain is a creamy travertine extravaganza of rearing sea horses, conch-blowing Tritons, craggy rocks and flimsy palm trees set into the side of a palace. The fountain's waters come from the Acqua Vergine, a Roman aqueduct built in 19 BC, and fed by springs 22 km (14 miles) from the city. Surprisingly, Trevi, the most famous fountain in Rome, is tucked away on the tiniest piazza. The narrow streets and alleyways surrounding it are glutted with gaudy souvenir shops and takeaway pizzerias that echo with the sound of gushing water.

A Triton and sea horse, Trevi Fountain

Key Features

Relief One of the reliefs on the first storey of the palazzo shows a young girl named Trivia – after whom the aqueduct was named – pointing to the spring from which the water flows.

Palazzo Poli The Trevi Fountain is built into the wall of the Palazzo Poli, the central part of which was demolished to make room for the fountain.

Tritons Neptune's chariot is pulled by two sea horses – one wild, one calm; reflecting the changing moods of the sea – each led by a Triton.

Neptune

Tritons

The fountain's pool

The Lowdown

🌐 **Map reference** 12 G2
Address Piazza di Trevi, 00187

🚗 **Bus** C3, 53, 63, 80, 81, 85, 117, 119, 160, 175, 492, 628 & 630

👪 **Skipping the queue** Visit in the early morning to avoid crowds

👫 **Age range** 4 plus

🕐 **Allow** 20 mins

♿ **Wheelchair access** Yes

🚻 **Toilets** No

Good family value?
Looking at the fountain is free, and it is dramatic enough to appeal to children of all ages. Bring small change to ensure that children do not throw a fortune into the fountain's waters!

The fountain's pool The fountain contains about 3 million litres (66,000 gal) of water. Although it was once reputed to be the sweetest water in Rome, it is now treated with a cocktail of chemicals. Legend says that throwing a coin into the fountain guarantees a return to Rome, and around €3,000 is thrown into the fountain daily.

Neptune In this statue designed by Pietro Bacci, the sea god Neptune is shown riding his conch-shell chariot.

Amphitheatre The fountain is provided with a tier of steps in front – as if it were part of an amphitheatre.

Letting off steam

The nearest places where children can have a run around are **Piazza del Quirinale** (see p157) and the small garden with a playground next to **Sant'Andrea al Quirinale** (see p159). The **Pincio Gardens** (see p151) and **Villa Borghese** (see pp168–9) are further away, but worth the walk for anyone with a few hours to spare.

A family enjoying an electric cart ride in Pincio Gardens

Eat and drink

Picnic: under €25; Snacks: €25–40; Real meal: €40–80; Family treat: over €80 (based on a family of four)

PICNIC Fratelli Ciavatta (*Via del Lavatore 31, 00187; 06 679 2935; closed Sat pm in summer*) is a great place to pick up ingredients for a picnic on the piazza. A historic grocery and deli, it is well regarded for its cheeses, salamis and hams, which come from all over Italy.
SNACKS La Prosciutteria (*Via della Panetteria 34, 00187; 06 678 6990*) sells gourmet Italian ingredients and specializes in cured meats. The quaint place also makes a variety of delicious sandwiches and serves fabulous cheese and meat platters.
REAL MEAL Sora Lucia (*Via della Panetteria 12, 00187; 06 679 4078; closed Mon*) is a small, family-run trattoria that seems unaffected by the passage of time. Simple food

such as *pasta e fagioli* (with beans), *spaghetti alla carbonara* (with bacon and egg), lasagne or veal escalope should please most kids. The tiramisù is also delicious.
FAMILY TREAT Le Tamerici (*Vicolo Scavolino 79, 00187; 06 6920 0700; closed Sun; www.letamerici.com*), with its tasteful interior and excellent seafood, seems very far away from the chaos around the fountain. Try the fresh pasta with prawns, courgette and pistachios, or tuna with olives, capers and sundried tomatoes. Do not miss their pistachio ice cream.

Find out more...

DIGITAL *www.tinyurl.com/ltaxurd* is an online shuffle puzzle game that uses an image of the Trevi Fountain.
FILM The fountain sprang to fame after its role in the 1950s film *La Dolce Vita* by Federico Fellini. Film star Anita Ekberg is shown walking home at night with a stray cat on her head. She comes across the fountain and decides to go for a swim! The fountain also featured in the 1954 film *Three Coins in the Fountain*, which revolved around three American women searching for romance in Rome.

Take cover

Time Elevator (see p156) is the ideal place to go to on a very hot afternoon or a rainy day.

Next stop...

ACQUA VERGINE For a quick, cool trip underground, visit **La Città dell'Acqua** (*Vicolo del Puttarello 25, 00187; 339 778 6192; closed Mon & Tue*) to see a short section of the Acqua Vergine aqueduct and the ruins of an ancient Roman apartment block discovered in 2001.

KIDS' CORNER

Take a closer look...
1 What is strange about the bodies of Neptune's sea horses?
2 What do the Tritons have instead of legs?
3 What is Neptune's chariot made of?
4 What are the Tritons using as musical instruments?

....

Answers at the bottom of the page.

Coins for the poor
The money thrown into the fountain is collected and funds a supermarket where the poor of Rome can get essential food for free.

Red paint artist
In 2010, controversial artist and activist Graziano Cecchini, protesting at the €15 million budget for the Rome Film Festival, threw red paint into the Trevi Fountain. His other actions include releasing 500,000 coloured balls down the Spanish Steps and, in September 2011, unrolling 20 m (66 ft) of clingfilm outside Palazzo Chigi to create a transparent wall on which he wrote "Don't waste time, resign", a message to the then Prime Minister Berlusconi. See him in action at *www.tinyurl. com/7ju3a6v*.

BIG NOSES
In Rome, a small drinking fountain – of which there are hundreds – is known as a *nasone*, or big nose!

....

Answers: 1 They have fish tails and birds' wings. **2** Fish tails. **3** A conch shell. **4** More conch shells.

The elegant dining area at Le Tamerici

The Time Elevator, where viewers can take a virtual trip through Roman history

② Time Elevator
Relive Rome

A multimedia cinema that presents 3,000 years of Roman history through vivid technology, the Time Elevator is not only fun, but educational too, making it an ideal rainy day activity. The multisensory experience takes visitors on a palpable journey through time, right from the days of Rome's foundation, through the glorious days of the ancient Roman Empire, up to the period of the Renaissance with its masterpieces of architecture and art. The high-adrenaline trip culminates in a virtual aerial flight over the Rome of today.

The flight simulator has three panoramic screens with seats on special moving platforms and individual surround-sound headsets, which bring alive events such as the legend of Romulus and Remus, the betrayal of Julius Caesar at the hands of Brutus and virtually reconstruct historical Roman monuments such as the Colosseum (*see pp70–71*) and the Baths of Caracalla (*see p230*). Special effects simulate the sensation of winds blowing, water dripping and mice nibbling at your toes!

If kids have had enough of history, look out for screenings such as *Escape from Bane Manor* or, for those with a scientific bent of mind, *An Ode to Life*, a spectacular 3D film on nature.

Letting off steam

Kids can run about in the gardens of **Villa Aldobrandini** (*Via IV Novembre, 00187*), **Piazza del Quirinale** (*see opposite*) or in the garden on Via del Quirinale.

The Lowdown

- 🌐 **Map reference** 12 G3
- 📍 **Address** Via SS Apostoli 20, 00187; 06 6992 1823; *www.time-elevator.it*
- 🚌 **Bus** 40, 60, 64, 70, 117 & 170
- 🕐 **Open** 10:30am–8:15pm daily; movie screenings every hour
- 💲 **Price** €24–42
- 🎟 **Skipping the queue** Book at *www.time-elevator.it*
- 👫 **Age range** 7 plus
- ⏱ **Allow** 45 mins
- ♿ **Wheelchair access** Yes, but not to toilets
- 🍽 **Eat and drink** SNACKS Il Bibo (*Piazza SS Apostoli 58, 00187; 06 678 2419; open daily*) is a nice place for a snack or sandwich. REAL MEAL Bistrot Quirino (*Via delle Vergini 7, 00187; 06 9887 8090; open from 8am till last theatre show*), inside the Teatro Quirino, is great for breakfast, brunch and dinner
- 🛍 **Shop** There are shops selling books and souvenirs near the ticket office
- 🚻 **Toilets** Near the exit

③ Museo delle Paste Alimentari
Pasta perfect!

If devotion to pasta can be showcased, this museum does it effectively – from its history, to how pasta is made, the machines used to mix and dry it, and how the myriad pasta shapes came to be.

Legend says that Marco Polo brought pasta to Italy from China. This is probably untrue – it is more likely that pasta was introduced by the Arabs when they invaded Italy in the 8th century and discovered that Italy had the perfect climate for growing durum wheat, which produces the best kind of flour for making pasta. Pictures in the museum document the history of pasta eating – it was originally eaten with the fingers. Also, there was no tomato sauce as tomatoes were not brought to Italy until the 16th century.

Lettting off steam

Head to **Piazza del Quirinale** for a run around or continue along Via del Quirinale to the garden with a playground next to **Sant'Andrea al Quirinale** (*see p159*).

The Lowdown

- 🌐 **Map reference** 12 H2
- 📍 **Address** Piazza Scanderbeg 117, 00187; 06 699 1120; *www.museodellapasta.it*
- 🚇 **Metro** Barberini (Line A). **Bus** 52, 53, 61, 62, 63, 71, 95, 175, 492 & 630
- 🕐 **Open** Closed for renovation, check website before planning a visit
- 💲 **Price** €22–25 (inclusive of tours); under 18s €7
- 👫 **Age range** 5 plus
- ⏱ **Allow** 45 mins
- ♿ **Wheelchair access** Partial (special guided tours available)
- 🍽 **Eat and drink** PICNIC Sandwicheria al Nazareno (*Largo del Nazareno, 00187; 06 6979 7805; www.lasandwicheria.it*) is a friendly sandwich joint. Guests can choose their favourite fillings and sauces. FAMILY TREAT Vineria Il Chianti (*Via del Lavatore 81–82/a, 00187; 06 678 7550; www.vineriailchianti.com*) is a traditional trattoria serving hearty Tuscan dishes, accompanied by good wine

Façade of Bernini's Sant'Andrea al Quirinale church

Piazza del Quirinale, with the Roman presidential palace to the right

④ Piazza del Quirinale

A presidential piazza

Located on the Quirinal Hill, the highest of Rome's seven hills, Piazza del Quirinale has buildings on three sides and an open fourth side, which offers splendid views of the city. The centrepiece of the piazza is a fountain spilling into an ancient basin beneath an obelisk. The massive granite basin was once a cattle trough in the Roman Forum, and the obelisk was one of a pair that originally flanked the entrance to the **Mausoleum of Augustus** *(see p147)*. On either side of the fountain are ancient Roman statues of the Dioscuri Castor and Pollux – patrons of horsemanship – each with a disproportionately small horse.

Pope Gregory XIII chose this site to build a papal summer residence and the **Palazzo del Quirinale**, as it is known, assumed its present form in the 1730s. The huge orange building is now home to the Italian president. On the other side of the piazza, the palace's stables, or Scuderie, have been turned into a space for temporary art exhibitions. The flamboyant palazzo between them is the **Palazzo della Consulta**, seat of the Corte Costituzionale, the supreme court for consitutional matters – what goes on inside may be very boring, but the façade is rather interesting.

Take cover

Visit **Time Elevator** and enjoy looking at Roman history, with the family, through the prism of interactive technology.

The Lowdown

🌐 **Map reference** 12 H3
Address Palazzo del Quirinale: Piazza del Quirinale, 00187. Palazzo della Consulta: Piazza del Quirinale, 41, 00187. Scuderie: www.scuderiequirinale.it

🚌 **Bus** 71, 116 & 117

♿ **Wheelchair access** Yes

☕ **Eat and drink** PICNIC Fratelli Ciavatta *(see p155)* stocks all the ingredients for a nice picnic lunch, which can be enjoyed on the piazza or in the gardens next to Sant'Andrea on Via del Quirinale. **REAL MEAL** Hostaria Piccolo Arancio *(Vicolo Scanderbeg 112, 00187; 06 678 6139; closed Mon)* is a simple, cosy place for lunch, on the hill leading up to Piazza del Quirinale from the Trevi Fountain. Try the pumpkin ravioli

🚻 **Toilets** No

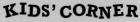

⑤ Palazzo Barberini

House of high art

Home to the Galleria Nazionale d'Arte Antica, Palazzo Barberini holds one of the best collections of art in Rome, with paintings from the 13th to the 16th centuries including notable works by Filippo Lippi, El Greco and Caravaggio. Designed by architect Carlo Maderno, the palace was originally built in 1627 to serve as a grand palace for the family of Pope Urban VIII Barberini. Maderno died in 1629 and Bernini took over, assisted by Borromini.

The oldest pieces in the collection, on the ground floor, are icons and crucifixes – in most of them Christ appears as a symbol, stiff and triumphant, rather than as a human being. On the same floor are paintings that show how Renaissance artists began to imagine lives for biblical figures, instead of just painting them as symbols. In the *Birth of John the Baptist* by the Maestro dell'Incoronazione di Urbino, an elderly Elizabeth is being fed soup, wine and a tiny roast bird after giving birth. Set in a Renaissance room with a garden visible through the window is the *Annunciation with Two Kneeling Donors* by Filippo Lippi. The angel and Mary cast shadows, and through an open door a man and woman can be seen talking. It is almost if the Annunciation is happening in the kind of room Lippi's patrons would have lived in. In the same exhibition room is a very peculiar *Madonna and Child*, also by Lippi – for some reason the baby is absolutely hideous!

The first floor has the palazzo's most famous painting – Raphael's *La Fornarina*, said to be a portrait of his mistress, a baker's daughter from Trastevere. There is also a version of *Henry VIII* by Hans Holbein and three paintings by Caravaggio – one of *St Francis*; one of *Narcissus*, who fell in love with his own reflection; and the third of *Judith beheading Holofernes*. Also on the same floor is the most striking of the many sumptuously decorated rooms – the Gran Salone. Its vast ceiling is covered with an illusionistic fresco by the Italian painter Pietro da Cortona. Do not miss the fantastic sinuous oval staircase by Borromini.

Letting off steam

Head to **Trinità dei Monti** *(see p145)* and the Spanish Steps, or visit the **Pincio Gardens** *(see p151)* for more open space and greenery.

Trinità dei Monti church at the top of the Spanish Steps, Piazza di Spagna

The Lowdown

🌐 **Map reference** 5 B4
Address Via delle Quattro Fontane 13, 00184; 06 482 4184; *http://galleriabarberini. beniculturali.it*

🚗 **Metro** Barberini (Line A). **Bus** 52, 53, 56, 58, 60, 61, 95, 116, 175, 492 & 590

🕐 **Open** 8:30am–7pm Tue–Sun

💲 **Price** €14–21; under 18s free

👫 **Skipping the queue** Book in advance via the website, although queues are rare

🗺 **Guided tours** Audioguides in Italian, English and French (€2.50) on the ground floor. Book in advance to access 18th-century apartments on 3rd floor

👫 **Age range** 8 plus

👫 **Activities** Interactive computer guides available in Italian and English

⏱ **Allow** 1 hr

♿ **Wheelchair access** Yes

☕ **Eat and drink** SNACKS Terrazza Barberini *(Via Barberini 16/a, 00187; 06 4201 4596; open daily; www.terrazzabarberini.it)* is nice for a quick sandwich or pastry before or after visiting the palazzo. REAL MEAL Mr Chow *(Via Genova 29a, 00184; 06 488 4412; open daily)* offers great Chinese food. Try the pork with soya beans and peppers

🛍 **Shop** Gift shops selling mugs and T-shirts, and a bookshop (both on the first floor)

🚻 **Toilets** On the ground floor

The Baroque trompe l'oeil fresco on the ceiling of the Palazzo Barberini

Prices given are for a family of four

⑥ Sant'Andrea al Quirinale

A little architectural trickery

Designed by Bernini and known as the "Pearl of the Baroque" because of its beautiful roseate marble interior, Sant'Andrea al Quirinale is possibly the most theatrical church in Rome. Bernini combined architecture, painting and sculpture to re-enact the martyrdom and subsequent journey to heaven of St Andrew. The church is oval in shape and set on its short axis so that the first thing that people see upon entry is the high altar niche in which sculpted angels appear to be positioning a painting of the saint being crucified on his diagonal cross. Higher up is a statue of the saint floating on a cloud, as if he has just slipped through the gap in the broken pediment behind him, on his way to heaven.

San Carlo alle Quattro Fontane, further along Via del Quirinale, is a tiny, enchanting church by Bernini's bitter rival, Borromini. It has a springily curved façade, and column capitals licked by curling fronds and tongues of foliage. Inside, an octagonal courtyard leads to the oval church. Look up at the oval dome. Its coffering of crosses, hexagons and octagons get smaller as they reach the top, creating the illusion that the dome is higher than it really is. Before leaving the area, check out the four fountains that gave the church – and the street – its name. The fountains are attached to buildings at each of the four corners

Impressive stuccowork on the dome of Sant'Andrea al Quirinale

of the crossroads. Attached to each fountain is a reclining deity, two goddesses (probably Juno and Diana) and two river gods, the Tiber and, possibly, the Arno.

Letting off steam
There is a small playground in the gardens next to **Sant'Andrea al Quirinale** where children can have some fun.

The Lowdown

- **Map reference** 5 B5
  Address Sant'Andrea al Quirinale: Via del Quirinale 29, 00184; 06 487 4565. San Carlo alle Quattro Fontane: Via del Quirinale 23, 00187; 06 488 3261
- **Metro** Barberini (Line A). **Bus** 71, 116 & 117
- **Open** Sant'Andrea al Quirinale: 8:30am–noon & 2:30–6pm Tue–Sun. San Carlo alle Quattro Fontane: 10am–1pm & 3–6pm Mon–Fri, 10am–1pm Sat & Sun
- **Age range** 10 plus
- **Allow** 20 mins each
- **Wheelchair access** Yes
- **Eat and drink** PICNIC Coop (Via in Arcione 70, 00184; open 8am–9pm Mon–Sat, 9am–9pm Sun) is the handiest supermarket for buying picnic supplies. Eat in the garden next to Sant'Andrea. SNACKS Gelateria Verde Pistacchio (Via Nazionale 239, 00184; open daily) serves good, home-made ice cream, crêpes, smoothies, ice cream frappé and hot chocolate from behind a counter made out of an old VW van
- **Toilets** No

Façade of the San Carlo alle Quattro Fontane church

KIDS' CORNER

Can you find…
Lie down on the huge padded bench in the Gran Salone in Palazzo Barberini and look up at Pietro Da Cortona's fresco. See if you can spot:
1 Bees similar to the ones on the Barberini family's coat of arms
2 A figure about to fall into the room
3 People sitting and standing on clouds
4 Stone figures who start to seem real the longer you stare at them

DESIGN DEMANDS
The design of San Carlo alle Quattro Fontane was considered so revolutionary that requests poured in from as far away as India for a copy of its plans.

Fairy-tale palazzo
In the 19th century, an American sculptor called William Westmore Story lived in an apartment in Palazzo Barberini with his wife and children. One Christmas they had a children's party, which featured family friend Hans Christian Andersen reading his story *The Ugly Duckling*, and the English poet Robert Browning reading *The Pied Piper* while Story played the flute and the children processed around the Gran Salone.

Baroque ceiling of Santa Maria della Vittoria church

⑦ Santa Maria della Vittoria

A theatre of stone

The modest-looking façade belies the lavish interiors of Santa Maria della Vittoria, one of the most elaborately decorated churches in Rome. The intimate Baroque church is lit by candles and caked with stucco, coloured marbles and gold. It contains one of Bernini's most famous statues, the *Ecstasy of St Teresa*, in the Cornaro Chapel. The sculpture shows St Teresa lying on a cloud, watched by an angel who seems about to stab her. The chapel was designed to resemble a miniature theatre, complete with an audience consisting of sculptures of the benefactor, Cardinal Federico Cornaro, and his ancestors.

Letting off steam

There is ample space for kids to run around in the gardens of the **Baths of Diocletian** (see p99).

⑧ Fontana del Tritone

Thirsty bees

One of Bernini's liveliest creations, the Fontana del Tritone on busy Piazza Barberini features the sea god Triton blowing a spindly column of water through a conch shell, supported by four goggle-eyed acrobatic dolphins standing on their heads. It was commissioned by Pope Urban VII Barberini shortly after the completion of his palace on the ridge above. Entwined among the dolphins' tails are the papal keys, the papal tiara and a shield featuring chubby Barberini bees.

A more modest creation by Bernini, the **Fontana delle Api** is tucked away in a corner of Piazza

Barberini. It features *api* (bees), scuttling like crabs, as if to take a sip of the water that dribbles down into the fountain basin.

Take cover

Those who dare can seek shelter among the bones in the spooky catacombs of **Santa Maria della Concezione** (see *opposite*).

Above *A bone-encrusted shrine, Santa Maria della Concezione* **Below** *The dolphins in Bernini's Fontana del Tritone*

The Lowdown

🌐 **Map reference** 5 C4
Address Via XX Settembre 17, 00187; 06 4274 0571

🚇 **Metro** Repubblica (Line A).
Bus 60, 61, 62, 84, 85, 175, 492, 590 & 910

🕐 **Open** 8:30am–noon & 3:30–6pm daily

👫 **Age range** 10 plus

⏱ **Allow** 20 mins

♿ **Wheelchair access** Yes

🍴 **Eat and drink** SNACKS Fratelli Ghezzi (*Via Goito 32, 00185; 06 494 1215; closed Sat pm & Sun*) sources its own hams, salamis and cheeses. It has a selection of hot dishes such as lasagne and pasta *al forno* (oven baked) to take away. *FAMILY TREAT* Trimani (*Via Cernaia 37/b, 00185; 06 446 9630; closed Sun*) serves fabulous quiche with *escarole*. The wines are exceptional

👫 **Toilets** No

The Lowdown

🌐 **Map reference** 5 B4
Address Piazza Barberini, 00187

🚗 **Metro** Barberini (Line A).
Bus C3, 52, 53, 62, 63, 80, 85, 116, 160, 175, 492, 590 & 630

👫 **Age range** 5 plus

♿ **Wheelchair access** Yes

🍴 **Eat and drink** PICNIC Forno Cerulli (*Via di San Nicola da Tolentino 15, 00187*) is a little bakery that has been cheering Romans up with its *pizza al taglio* (rectangular slices of pizza to takeaway) for over 80 years. *FAMILY TREAT* Colline Emiliane (*Via degli Avignonesi 22, 00187; 06 481 7538; closed Sun dinner & Mon*) is perfect for a hearty meal, serving dishes from the Emilia-Romagna region, whose capital is Bologna. It is, therefore, the perfect place to try an authentic *tagliatelle bolognese*

👫 **Toilets** No

Passers-by on one of Rome's most famous streets, Via Vittorio Veneto

⑨ Via Vittorio Veneto

Life and death

Lined in its upper reaches with exuberant hotels and canopied pavement cafés, Via Veneto was laid out in 1879 over a large estate sold by the Ludovisi family. In the 1960s Via Veneto was the most glamorous street in Rome, its luxury hotels and cafés patronized by film stars and plagued by paparazzi. It had a starring role in Federico Fellini's film *La Dolce Vita* (1960) – literally "the sweet life".

At the foot of Via Veneto is the plain, unassuming church of **Santa Maria della Concezione**. The catacombs below the church, now a museum, belonged to the Capuchin

Order, whose object was to make people confront the reality of death. They dismantled thousands of skeletons belonging to their departed brothers and used the bones to decorate the walls of the church's labyrinthine underground chapels. Vertebrae are wired together to make sacred crowns, and clothed skeletons lie in niches constructed from pelvic bones that look like layers of sliced mushrooms. At the exit, an inscription in Latin translates as "What you are, we used to be. What we are, you will be."

Letting off steam

The open spaces of **Villa Borghese** (see pp168–9) park, about 5 minutes away from Via Vittorio Veneto, is a great place for kids, with lots of space for running.

The Lowdown

🌐 **Map reference** 5 B4
Address Capuchin museum and crypt under Santa Maria della Concezione: Via Vittorio Veneto 27, 00187; 06 8880 3695; www.cappucciniviaveneto.it

🚇 **Metro** Barberini (Line A). **Bus** C3, 52, 53, 62, 63, 80, 85, 116, 160, 175, 492, 590 & 630

🕐 **Open** Museum & crypt: 9am–7pm daily

💶 **Price** Museum & crypt: €12–20

👫 **Skipping the queue** Visit in the early morning

👪 **Age range** Capuchin museum and Santa Maria della Concezione: 8 plus

⏱ **Allow** 30 mins

♿ **Wheelchair access** No

🍴 **Eat and drink** SNACKS Palombi (*Via Vittorio Veneto 114, 00187; closed Sun*) is a classic from the days of *La Dolce Vita*, serving tea, coffee, cakes, muffins and savouries.
FAMILY TREAT Hamasei (*Via della Mercede 35/36, 00187; 06 679 2134; closed Mon*) is one of the best Japanese restaurants in Rome. Eat sushi at the bar, or sit down for more substantial fare such as tempura or teppanyaki

🚻 **Toilets** No

Picnic under €25; **Snacks** €25–40; **Real meal** €40–80; **Family treat** over €80 (based on a family of four)

Villa Borghese
& Northern Rome

With its zoo, boating lake, woods, playgrounds and miniature train rides, Villa Borghese park is a paradise for families. Close by are the city's most innovative children's parks, hands-on Explora and high-tech Technotown. Within the park, elaborate Renaissance mansions house world-class art museums – nowhere else in Rome is it so easy to combine a morning of high culture with a relaxing afternoon in the park.

Villa Borghese
& Northern Rome

The
Vatican

Piazza di Spagna
& Trevi Fountain

Piazza Navona
& Campo
de' Fiori

Trastevere &
Janiculum Hill

Ancient
Rome

Highlights

Villa Borghese
Explore Villa Borghese – walk or bike through its grounds, go boating or watch horses in the Galoppatoio (see pp168–9).

Cinema dei Piccoli and the Globe Theatre
Watch a children's film at the Cinema dei Piccoli and plays by Shakespeare at Rome's very own Globe Theatre (see p168).

Villa Giulia
See exquisite Etruscan treasures and a reconstructed tomb on a visit to Villa Giulia (see pp170–71).

Explora
Bake cookies, become a news presenter on TV and play games at Rome's innovative children's museum (see p173).

Museo e Galleria Borghese
Gaze in wonder at the city's finest collection of sculptures by Bernini, which give the impression that he found carving stone as easy as carving butter (see pp174–5).

Bioparco
Observe lemurs doing yoga and hippos being fed at Rome's conservation-minded zoo (see pp176–7).

Above right Children with their heads in lemur cut-outs, Bioparco
Left Families boating on the lake at Villa Borghese, with the 19th-century Temple of Aesculapius in the background

The Best of...
Villa Borghese & Northern Rome

Families could easily spend several days in and around Villa Borghese, visiting one major museum or children's attraction per day, and spending the rest of the time exploring the park, picnicking, boating on the lake or going for a bike ride. Other than the obvious favourites with children – Bioparco, Explora and Technotown – the collections of Villa Giulia, which bring the Etruscan world vividly to life, and MACRO are great too.

Indoor fun

In and around **Villa Borghese** (see pp168–9) are several of the city's finest indoor attractions for children. Experiment with water, or bake – and eat – cookies in **Explora** (see p173), a hands-on science museum aimed at children under ten. Explore the world of virtual reality in **Technotown** (see pp178–9), dedicated to introducing new technology to children and teenagers. For more traditional entertainment, visit the kids' play centre at the **Casina di Raffaello** (see p168); the world's smallest cinema, the **Cinema dei Piccoli** (see p168); and the park's engaging and imaginative puppet theatre, the **Teatro San Carlino** (see p168). In summer, older children might be interested in catching a Shakespeare production in the **Globe Theatre** (see p168).

Left Family riding past the Fontana dei Cavalli Marini, Villa Borghese **Below** A colourful activity room in Explora, the excellent children's museum

Above A painting in the loggia of Villa Giulia, known for its impressive collection of Etruscan art

Outdoor fun

As well as formal gardens, fountains and ornamental lakes, **Villa Borghese** has a stretch of wild woodland, perfect for kids who need to break free from the constraints of city life for a while. If they still have energy to burn, there are bikes, go-karts and skates to rent at various points around the park, and rowing boats for hire on the main lake. Walk into Rome's zoo, the **Bioparco** *(see pp176–7)*, which deftly balances the joys of seeing animals up close with the ethics of conservation. Get exhausted playing games in the **Arca della Conservazione** *(see p177)* – a huge playground in a boat. For kids in need of downtime, the **Villa Torlonia** park *(see p178)* is another good option.

Art – ancient and modern

Stop by **Villa Giulia** *(see pp170–71)*, not only home to one of the best collections of Etruscan art in the world, but also one of the most absorbing, thanks to imaginative displays and thought-provoking information boards. To see an unmatched collection of sculptures by Bernini, visit the **Museo e Galleria Borghese** *(see pp174–5)*, which also offers regular family tours with excellent art activities for children. As an antidote for eyes tired of the old, get a taste of Rome's modern and contemporary art collections and architecture. The smashed mirror floor and scrubbing brush sculptures in **Galleria Nazionale d'Arte Moderna** *(see p172)*, the

bathrooms with infinity mirrors and illuminated washbasins in **MACRO** *(see p179)* and the collection of surreal De Chirico paintings in **Museo Carlo Bilotti** *(see pp172–3)* are guaranteed to provoke lively reactions.

Free for all

The open spaces of the **Villa Borghese** park are free, offering plenty of opportunities for children to stage races, play hide-and-seek and enjoy picnic lunches. Visitors can also walk around **Coppedè** *(see p177)*, one of Rome's most whimsical neighbourhoods, or watch horses galloping around the **Galoppatoio** *(see p168)*.

Right Actors in costume enacting a scene from Pinocchio in the Teatro San Carlino, Villa Borghese

Villa Borghese and around

There are few places in the world where it is possible to weave together a day in a park with high culture as easily as at the Villa Borghese. The park is at its busiest at weekends and during the summer holidays. At these times, book in advance for a puppet show and arrive early or during lunchtime when there are plenty of bikes, roller-skates and other means of transport left to hire. If children are reluctant to walk far, take the miniature train or the minibus that traverse the park. Other sights are within walking distance; however, the walk to MACRO and Villa Torlonia is quite a trek, with lots of busy roads to cross – so much more relaxing to jump on to a bus.

Villa Borghese & Northern Rome

Bioparco
p176

Museo e
Galleria
Borghese
p174

Villa Giulia
p170

Villa Borghese
p168

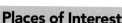

0 metres 300

0 yards 300

Places of Interest

SIGHTS

1. Villa Borghese
2. Villa Giulia
3. Galleria Nazionale d'Arte Moderna
4. Museo Carlo Bilotti
5. Explora
6. Museo e Galleria Borghese
7. Bioparco
8. Musei di Villa Torlonia
9. Technotown
10. MACRO

EAT AND DRINK

1. Salumeria Focacci
2. Vyta Santa Margherita
3. Carrefour Express, Via Flaminia
4. Villa Giulia Café
5. Casina del Lago
6. Caffè dei Pittori
7. Carrefour Express, Via Vittoria
8. Picnic
9. Caffè del Ninfeo
10. Bioparco Cafeteria
11. Ristorante Mascagni
12. TUODI
13. Limonaia
14. Pizza al Taglio

See Galleria Nazionale d'Arte Moderna
(p172), Explora (p173) & MACRO (p179)

WHERE TO STAY

1. Aldrovandi Villa Borghese
2. Parioli House
3. Il Bacio delle Stelle
4. Hotel Rome Garden
5. Almacromondo

A zoo train at Villa Borghese

The Lowdown

🚗 **Metro** Flaminio & Spagna (Line A) & Bologna (Line B). **Bus** C3, 3, 6, 36, 52, 53, 60, 61, 62, 80, 84, 88, 90, 92, 95, 116 (through the park), 120, 140, 150, 160, 204, 217, 348, 360, 490, 491, 495, 628, 910 & 926. **Tram** 3 & 19

ℹ️ **Visitor information** Tourist Information Point, Via Marco Minghetti (on the corner with Via del Corso), 00187; 060608;

open 9:30am–7pm daily; www.turismoroma.it

🍴 **Market** Mercato Rionale, Via Flaminia 60–65, 00197; Mon–Sat am

🎭 **Festivals** Estate Romana (summer); cinema, theatre and puppet shows at different venues across the Villa Borghese park. International Horse Show (May); horse shows on Piazza di Siena

➕ **Pharmacies** Farmacia Guarnacci, Via Flaminia 5, 00196; 06 361 0905; open 8:30am–8pm Mon–Fri (till 7:30pm in winter), Sat am only; www.tinyurl.com/kcofxrw

🛝 **Nearest play areas** Casina di Raffaello (see p168). Viale Esculapio, 00197

Children playing in the park at Villa Borghese

Stone carving outside the Galleria Borghese

Colonnaded interior of Villa Borghese

① Villa Borghese
Mythological theme park

One of Rome's largest parks, Villa Borghese was created by Cardinal Scipione Borghese as a 17th-century theme park, with ingenious fountains, exotic bird enclosures and a mechanical talking satyr with rolling eyes and a lolling head. The original attractions have all long gone – instead there are artificial ponds, mock temples, a children's play centre, a zoo and two fine museums, one devoted to the works of 17th-century sculptor Gianlorenzo Bernini; the other, to Etruscan finds.

Statue in Museo e Galleria Borghese

Key Sights

Villa Giulia (see pp170–71)

Galleria Nazionale d'Arte Moderna (see p172)

Bioparco (see pp176–7)

① **Casina di Raffaello** A tiny house dedicated to younger children, it has a play area and reading corner inside, and a playground outside.

Piazzale Flaminio entrance

② **Boating lake and island** Hire a boat and row down to the 18th-century temple on an island at the centre of this artificial lake.

③ **Globe Theatre** London's Globe Theatre was reconstructed here in just three months! Every summer, the theatre showcases Shakespeare's plays in Italian.

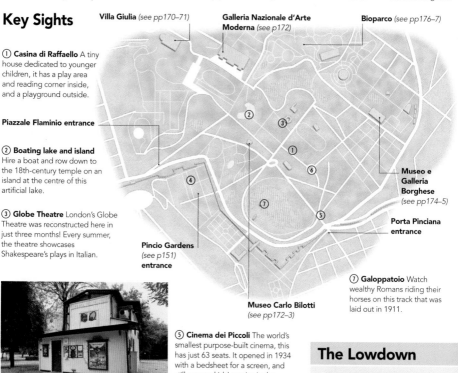

Museo e Galleria Borghese (see pp174–5)

Porta Pinciana entrance

Pincio Gardens (see p151) entrance

⑦ **Galoppatoio** Watch wealthy Romans riding their horses on this track that was laid out in 1911.

Museo Carlo Bilotti (see pp172–3)

⑤ **Cinema dei Piccoli** The world's smallest purpose-built cinema, this has just 63 seats. It opened in 1934 with a bedsheet for a screen, and still screens kids' movies in the afternoons, usually in Italian.

④ **Teatro San Carlino** The performances in this wonderful little puppet theatre often feature live music. Look out for well-known stories such as *Pinocchio* that can be understood by non-Italian speakers.

Prices given are for a family of four

⑥ **Temple of Diana** This circular Neo-Classical temple is one of the garden's follies.

The Lowdown

🌐 **Map reference** 5 A1
Address Entrances at Piazzale Flaminio, Porta Pinciana & Pincio Gardens, 00197. Casina di Raffaello: Piazza di Siena; *www. casinadiraffaello.it*. Globe Theatre: Largo Aqua Felix; *www. globetheatreroma.com*. Teatro San Carlino: Viale dei Bambini; 06 6992 2117; *www.sancarlino. it*. Cinema dei Piccoli: Viale della Pineta 15; 06 855 3485; *www. cinemadeipiccoli.it*

🚇 **Metro** Flaminio-Piazza del Popolo & Spagna (Line A). **Bus** C3, 53, 61, 88, 95, 116, 120, 150, 160, 490, 491 & 495. **Tram** 3 & 19

🕐 **Open** Park: sunrise–sunset. Casina di Raffaello: 9am–6pm

Letting off steam

With biking, roller-skating, go-karting and boating on offer, there is no shortage of ways in which kids can burn off excess energy. Best of all is the wilder, wooded part of the park between Viale di Valle Giulia and the Bioparco, where kids can run free.

Eat and drink

Picnic: under €25; Snacks: €25–40; Real meal: €40–80; Family treat: over €80 (based on a family of four)

PICNIC Salumeria Focacci (Via della Croce 43, 00187; closed Sun) sells salami, ham, cheese, smoked salmon and other smoked fish. Eat in the park.

SNACKS Vyta Santa Margherita (Casa del Cinema, Largo Marcello Mastroianni 1, 00187; 06 4201 6224) has tables under a portico and a lawn in front, which means kids can play while adults linger over lunch. It serves a delicious brunch on Saturdays and Sundays.

Contemporary decor in the Caffè delle Arti, Galleria Nazionale d'Arte Moderna

Children enjoying pony rides in the Galoppatoio

REAL MEAL Zero100 (Via Flaminia 82, 00187; 366 615 9380; closed Mon, Sun pm) in Explora (see p173) is by far the best place in the area for a decently priced lunch.

FAMILY TREAT Caffè delle Arti (Via Gramsci 73; 06 3265 1236) in the Galleria Nazionale d'Arte Moderna (see p172) is perfect for a brunch of antipasto misto, salad and sea bass fillet with capers and lemon.

Take cover

Duck into **Casina di Raffaello**, a children's play area and activity centre or catch a film at **Cinema dei Piccoli**.

Next stop...

FUN ACTIVITIES FOR KIDS

When everyone has had enough of the park's open spaces, visit the **Bioparco** (see pp176–7), the zoo in Villa Borghese, or head to the hands-on children's museum **Explora** (see p173). A tram ride away is **MAXXI** (see pp224–5), which showcases the best of contemporary Rome.

Tue–Sun (till 3:30pm in winter), 10am–7pm Sat, Sun & hols (till 6pm in winter). Globe Theatre: guided tours & performances only. Cinema dei Piccoli: for shows only

Price Casina di Raffaello: free; €7 per child for organized activities. Globe Theatre: standing €36–46; seats €42–62. Teatro San Carlino: €48–58. Cinema dei Piccoli: €24–34

Guided tours Globe Theatre: Jul & Aug: 7:30pm Sat & Sun; book tickets for performances (inclusive of tour) at www. greenticket.it and tour tickets by calling 060608

Age range All ages; Casina di Raffaello: under 10s

Activities Bikes, go-karts, roller-skates, electric bikes and golf carts can be rented at various points in the park. Boats (€12 for 20 mins) can be rented for rides on the lake

Allow All day in summer, 1 hr per gallery in winter

Wheelchair access Yes

Café Several around the park

Toilets In the cafés

Good family value?

The park itself may be free, but the activities can add up and make a visit to Villa Borghese expensive.

KIDS' CORNER

FULL CIRCLE

The design of Shakespeare's Globe Theatre was based on Rome's Colosseum! It is thought the architects believed that basing it on a Roman amphi-theatre would give it an air of respectability – theatres in Shakespeare's time were very rowdy, and frequented mostly by the lower classes.

Can you find...

Ask your parents where in Villa Borghese park they can...
1 Step back into Tudor London?
2 Find an underground tunnel to the Spagna metro station?
3 Watch a film in the world's smallest cinema?

Answers at the bottom of the page.

Pines of Rome

Download the famous piece of music "The Pines of Rome" onto an iPod or mp3 player and lie down listening to it under the pines of Piazza Siena, near Casina di Raffaello, which is where Ottorino Respighi was inspired to compose it in 1924. Close your eyes, let your mind and imagination wander, and see what the music makes you think of. If you're feeling creative, write down or draw your daydream.

Answers: 1 The Globe Theatre. **2** Under the Galoppatoio. **3** Cinema dei Piccoli.

② Villa Giulia
Treasures from tombs

A 16th-century villa with a beautiful garden, Villa Giulia is home to a collection of Etruscan art. The Etruscans, who lived in central Italy before the Romans, mined metals, which they traded for ceramics and luxury objects made by the Greeks and Phoenicians. The collection includes several important pieces that were returned to Italy after being illegally excavated and sold to collectors and museums. Since most finds come from the tombs of the rich, not much is known about ordinary Etruscans.

Piece of clothing, Villa Giulia

Key Sights

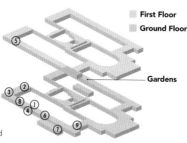

First Floor
Ground Floor

Gardens

① **Lion Sarcophagus (Room 10)** On the lid of this terracotta sarcophagus are four roaring lions with their mouths held open by muzzles. The sarcophagus was huge – it had to be cut into two to be fired in a kiln.

② **Writing on Gold (Room 13b)** The oldest examples of writing in Italy, the three 6th-century BC gold sheets dedicated to the goddess Astarte are written in Etruscan and Phoenician.

③ **Euphronius Vase (Room 13a)** Dating from the 6th century BC, this Greek vase was returned to Italy from the Metropolitan Museum in New York in 2008, and shows Hypnos, the god of sleep, and Thanatos, the god of death.

④ **Hydria (Room 10)** This black hydria (pot used for carrying water) was imported from Greece by the Etruscans and depicts a panther and lion attacking a mule.

⑥ **Ex Voto (Room 5)** These are models of parts of the body – including faces, feet, a uterus and various internal organs – that were probably offered to Etruscan gods by the ailing, in the hope that they would be healed.

⑦ **Tomb of the Funeral Couch (Room 8)** The painted 5th-century BC tomb from Tarquinia has been rebuilt in the basement. Frescoes on it show a banquet with people dancing, acrobats riding horses and youths engaging in sports.

⑤ **Ficoroni Cist (Room 15)** This 4th-century BC bronze coffer, decorated with scenes from the story of Jason and the Argonauts, was used by rich women for storing mirrors, cosmetics and accessories.

Prices given are for a family of four

⑧ **Sarcophagus of the Spouses (Room 12)** When excavated in 1881, this magnificent 530–520 BC sarcophagus was in 400 pieces. Now reconstructed, it depicts the tender, lifelike figures of a married couple and is the museum's most famous work of art.

⑨ **Attic Vase (Room 1)** Illegally excavated at Vulci, this stunning 500–450 BC black vase has a single red figure on each side. On one side is a musician playing a cithera (a kind of harp) and on the other is a youth listening to him.

The Lowdown

🌐 **Map reference** 2 E6
Address Piazzale di Villa Giulia 9, 00196; 06 320 1706; www.villagiulia.beniculturali.it

🚋 **Tram** 3 & 19

🕙 **Open** 8:30am–7:30pm Tue–Sun

💲 **Price** €16–24; under 18s free

🚩 **Guided tours** Audioguides (€5) in Italian and English

👫 **Age range** 6 plus

⏱ **Allow** 1–2 hrs

♿ **Wheelchair access** Yes

🍴 **Café** Yes (see opposite)

🛍 **Shop** Books for children (mostly in Italian) and gifts including Etruscan-themed bookmarks and T-shirts, and erasers with Latin epigrams are available in the shop on the ground floor

🚻 **Toilets** On the ground floor

Good family value?
Villa Giulia is very reasonably priced and its collections are well presented. The grounds and café make it easy for families to relax in between seeing exhibits.

Greenery on either side of a path leading to Villa Giulia

Letting off steam

Relax in or wander around the villa's gardens or walk across to **Villa Borghese** *(entrance on Via Valmichi)*. Hire a bike from near the entrance or play a game of hide-and-seek and picnic in the nearby woods – this is one of the wilder parts of the Borghese estate.

Eat and drink

Picnic: under €25; Snacks: €25–40; Real meal: €40–80; Family treat: over €80 (based on a family of four)

PICNIC Carrefour Express *(Via Flaminia 78, 00197; closed Sun)* provides all the ingredients for a great picnic lunch. Picnic in the gardens or wander into the Borghese park. **SNACKS Villa Giulia Café** offers tables on a terrace shaded by orange trees or in a greenhouse, which make a lovely setting for a coffee and pastry or cold drinks and delicious sandwiches.

REAL MEAL Caffè delle Arti in the Galleria Nazionale d'Arte Moderna *(see p172)* serves a fixed-price lunch menu of one *primo* (usually a pasta dish), a mini-dessert, a glass of wine or soft drink and water.
FAMILY TREAT Caffè delle Arti *(Galleria Nazionale d'Arte Moderna)* is a fine choice for a proper treat, too. Sit on its beautiful travertine terrace and choose from dishes such as home-made ravioli, spinach, bacon and crouton salad, or veal with orange and rosemary.

Find out more

DIGITAL Find out more about the Etruscans at *www.kidspast.com/world-history/0077-etruscan-rulers.php* or at *www.tinyurl.com/c4ylwvl*. There is more about illegal excavations and trade in looted objects at *www.tinyurl.com/cnvgo79*.
FILM Some of the action in *The Twilight Saga: New Moon* (12 plus) is set among the Etruscan sights of the Tuscan town of Volterra, and features a coven of Etruscan-inspired Volturi vampires.

Next stop...

VILLA PONIATOWSKI Villa Giulia's vast collection continues in the adjacent Villa Poniatowski *(Piazzale di Villa Giulia 9, 00196; 06 322 6571; www.villagiulia.beniculturali. it)*. It opened to the public in January 2012. Exhibits include finds from Umbria and northern Lazio, including a tomb carved from a tree trunk, exquisite gold jewellery and elaborate containers for make-up and perfume.

Children posing for photographs on a tree trunk, Villa Borghese

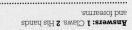

The façade of the Galleria Nazionale d'Arte Moderna

③ Galleria Nazionale d'Arte Moderna

But excuse me, is this hat stand art?

Rome's gallery of 19th- and 20th-century art makes its first impact with a stunning cracked-mirror floor designed by the contemporary Italian artist Alfredo Pirri. The collections are spread over two floors. On the ground floor is a section called "Excuse me, is this art?", which includes several pieces by French Surrealist Marcel Duchamp that make imaginative use of coat hooks, hat stands and a spade. In the same section are pierced *(Buchi)* and slashed *(Tagli)* canvases created by Lucio Fontana in the 1950s.

Paintings include *Ritratti* (portraits) by 20th-century Italian painter Felice Casorati, showing five generations of a family with their black cat; *Watery Paths* by the American Abstract Expressionist Jackson Pollock and the scribbly *Second Voyage to Italy* by American

artist Cy Twombly, who lived in Rome for 50 years. Sculptures include *Coppa Chimerica*, a curvaceous abstract bronze by Dadaist Jean Arp; two skinny scrunched bronzes of women by the Swiss-born Alberto Giacometti and a classic *Figura Distesa* or *Forma Esterna* by British sculptor Henry Moore. Room 40 is devoted to the Italian artist Pino Pascali, who died at the age of 33; exhibits include a caterpillar made of floor brushes.

The most interesting pieces by earlier artists are in Rooms 34–38 on the second floor, which display works by Futurists such as Gino Severini, Mario Sironi and Giacomo Balla. Exhibits include a haunting self-portrait by Giorgio de Chirico and vibrant scenes of everyday life and erupting volcanoes by the Sicilian Renato Guttuso.

Letting off steam

There are bicycles for hire at the nearby entrance to **Villa Borghese** *(see pp168–9)*, and the wooded part of the park – perfect for fun games such as hide-and-seek – is just a short walk away.

④ Museo Carlo Bilotti

The perfume-maker in the orange warehouse

Carlo Bilotti was an American-Italian perfume executive and a collector of contemporary art from artists ranging from Surrealist Giorgio de Chirico to pop artists Andy Warhol and Roy Lichtenstein and Damien Hirst. In 2003, Bilotti approached the mayor of Rome with the idea of a museum to house part of his art collection. Three years later the Museo Carlo Bilotti opened in what had been a dilapidated *villetta* (chalet) used for storing oranges on the Borghese estate.

The permanent collection consists of just 22 works, 18 of which are paintings, sculptures and sketches by De Chirico. Do not miss *Mistero e Malinconia di una Strada* (1960s), which shows a girl with a hoop in a bleak futuristic city. Other works on show are a portrait of Bilotti's wife and daughter – who died of cancer at the age of 20 – by Andy Warhol, the bronze *Grande Cardinale* (outside the museum) by Giacomo Manzù, *Summer* by the Futurist artist Gino Severini and a portrait of Bilotti by the American artist Larry Rivers. The museum is also a venue for contemporary art and photography exibitions.

Letting off steam

Go for a row on the lake, or to the **Casina di Raffaello** *(see p168)* playground for a run around.

Visitors boating on the lake at Villa Borghese

The Lowdown

🌐 **Map reference** 2 F6
Address Viale delle Belli Arti 131, 00197; 06 322 981; www.gnam.beniculturali.it

🚌 **Bus** 3. **Tram** 19

🕐 **Open** 8:30am–7:15pm Tue–Sun

💲 **Price** €16–32; under 18s free

👪 **Age range** 5 plus

🧗 **Activities** Check the website

⏱ **Allow** 1.5 hrs

♿ **Wheelchair access** Yes, from Via Gramsci

🍴 **Eat and drink** REAL MEAL/FAMILY TREAT Caffè delle Arti is GNAM's café-restaurant – perfect for a snack, lunch or full meal. Enjoy an energy drink or indulge in an *antipasto misto* of fried prawns, *suppli*, broccoli croquettes, spinach and chicory, followed by a radicchio, goat's cheese and pear salad and sea bass fillet with capers and lemon

🛍 **Shop** The bookshop on the ground floor has a children's corner with books and creative toys

🚻 **Toilets** In the basement

The Lowdown

🌐 **Map reference** 5 A2
   Address Viale Fiorello La
   Guardia, 00197; 060608; www.
   museocarlobilotti.it

🚇 **Metro** Flaminio-Piazza del
   Popolo (Line A). **Bus** 116

🕐 **Open** summer: 1–7pm
   Tue-Fri (winter: 10am–4pm);
   10am–7pm Sat & Sun

💰 **Price** Free. Admission charge
   during exhibitions only

👫 **Age range** 10 plus

⏱ **Allow** 30 mins

♿ **Wheelchair access** Yes

🍴 **Eat and drink** PICNIC (see p169).
   SNACKS Casina del Lago (Villa
   Borghese; 06 8535 2623; summer:
   open daily; winter: Tue–Sun; 10
   per cent discount with museum
   ticket) is a charming little park
   café with a great outdoor seating
   arrangement. Their terrace can
   be used all year as it is heated.
   Pastries, sandwiches and simple
   pasta and rice dishes are available

🛍 **Shop** The shop near the exit sells
   art books and posters

🚻 **Toilets** Yes

⑤ Explora

Check out the checkout, then bake some cookies

Rome's children's museum offers
plenty of activities, but it is not so
big as to be overwhelming. The
emphasis is on hands-on activities
and learning through play – there
is a supermarket with working cash
registers and weighing scales, a
TV studio where kids can play at
being news presenters and a water
play area with pumps, hosepipes
and waterproof overalls. Other
installations range from paper-
making to the chance to climb
inside an igloo-like womb and
listen to the sounds in an expectant
mother's tummy. All facilitators
speak English, but most activities
are based on "doing" rather
than "listening" in any case.

The museum also offers a
Kitchen Studio, where children can
learn about nutrition while making
and eating biscuits, and ice cream
in summer, and a series of changing
interactive exhibitions. Recent exhibitions have been dedicated to the
inventions of Archimedes and to
mathematics without numbers.
The museum operates by letting

children in at set times for a set
session; the café and playground
mean there is plenty to keep
children busy while they wait.

Letting off steam

Explora has a café, a restaurant-
pizzeria and a small, but good,
adventure playground where kids
can play, eat and relax before or
after shifts.

One of the play areas in the children's museum, Explora

The Lowdown

🌐 **Map reference** 4 G1
   Address Via Flaminia 82, 00196;
   06 361 3776; www.mdbr.it

🚇 **Metro** Flaminio-Piazza del
   Popolo (Line A). **Bus** 6, 88,
   92, 204, 490, 495 & 628.
   Tram 2 & 19

🕐 **Open** Tue–Sun, by tours only

💰 **Price** €26–32; under 3s €3

👫 **Age range** under 10

🧑 **Activities** Kitchen Studio:
   10:45am–3:45pm Sat, Sun & hols;
   book in advance via the website

⏱ **Allow** 1hr 45mins

♿ **Wheelchair access** Yes

🍴 **Eat and drink** SNACKS Explora's
   café-restaurant-pizzeria is perfect
   for a quick snack after or before
   activities. REAL MEAL Caffè dei
   Pittori (Via Flaminia 57–59,
   00196; 06 320 0803; closed Sun),
   a lively, canteen-like café, serves
   pastries and sandwiches
   throughout the day

🚻 **Toilets** On the ground floor

⑥ Museo e Galleria Borghese
Greek gods and a maggot hole

Cardinal Scipione Borghese created Villa Borghese in the 17th century as an elaborate party venue. He was an extravagant patron of the arts and filled the villa with sculptures by Bernini and exotic antique statues. Today it houses the superb private Borghese collection of sculptures and paintings, divided into two sections: the sculptures on the ground floor and the paintings on the first. The highlights of the collection are the pieces by Bernini based on Greek mythology – in which he seemed determined to prove that he could carve stone into anything he wanted.

The garden outside the museum

Key Exhibits

① **Pauline Borghese (1808)** Napoleon Bonaparte's sister, Pauline, was married to Camillo Borghese. This sculpture by Antonio Canova depicts her as Venus.

② **Apollo and Daphne (1628)** Bernini's most famous masterpiece shows the nymph Daphne turning into a laurel tree to escape from the sun god Apollo.

③ **Gladiator Mosaic** The floor is decorated with fragments of a gory 4th-century mosaic, found in an aristocratic Roman villa; scenes depict a gladiator fighting leopards.

Prices given are for a family of four

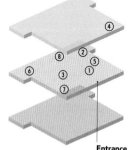

- First Floor
- Ground Floor
- Basement

Entrance

④ **Sacred and Profane Love (1515)** In this famous painting by Titian, the same model seems to have been used to represent both kinds of love.

⑤ **David (1623–1624)** Bernini's David has a furrowed brow and pursed lips and holds a taut catapult as if he is just about to use the full force of his body to launch a stone to kill the giant Goliath.

⑥ **Aeneas and Anchises (1619)** This statue by Bernini shows Aeneas escaping from Troy with his father, Anchises, on his back and his young son at his side.

⑦ **Caravaggio's Boy with a Basket of Fruit (1593)** Caravaggio's fruit are very realistic – the grapes are over-ripe, the vine leaves flecked with brown, and there is a maggot hole in the apple. The young man in the painting is the artist himself.

⑧ **Pluto and Proserpine (1621)** Bernini's sculpture shows Pluto (Hades), god of the Underworld, abducting Proserpine (Persephone), the daughter of Ceres. According to Greek mythology, she spent half the year in the Underworld, and the other half on earth. Spring was believed to occur when she emerged from hell; autumn, when she went back.

The Lowdown

🌐 **Map reference** 5 B2
Address Piazzale del Museo Borghese 5, 00197; 06 32810; http://galleriaborghese. beniculturali.it

🚗 **Metro** Spagna (Line A). **Bus** 52, 53 & 910

🕐 **Open** 9am–7pm Tue–Sun; book in advance on 06 32810 or via the website

💶 **Price** €22–38; EU under 18s €2; under 6s free. First Sunday of the month: free

🧍 **Skipping the queue** Arriving 30 mins before the allotted entry time is obligatory, but to avoid queues arrive earlier

🎧 **Guided tours** Audioguides (€5) in Italian, English, French, German and Spanish

👫 **Age range** 7 plus

🧍 **Activities** Workshops for kids in Italian: 4:30pm Sat, 10am Sun; call 06 32810 for information & bookings (obligatory)

⏱ **Allow** 90 mins

♿ **Wheelchair access** Partial. No access to first floor, as the lift is antique and very small

☕ **Café** Yes

🛍 **Shop** The bookshop in the basement stocks books in Italian and English

🚻 **Toilets** On the utilities floor

Good family value?
The stunning collection is well worth the entry fee. Bernini's sculptures have a very immediate appeal for children, and Greek myths help bring alive anything that Bernini doesn't.

Letting off steam

Let kids have a spin on Villa Borghese's carousel, play in the playground at the **Casina di Raffaello** (see p168) or enjoy a dodgem car session in the little playground near **Cinema di Piccoli** (see p168). Those visiting the gallery in the morning may find the **Bioparco** (see pp176–7) perfect for an absorbing afternoon.

Children reading an information board at Bioparco, Villa Borghese

Eat and drink

Picnic: under €25; Snacks: €25–40; Real meal: €40–80; Family treat: over €80 (based on a family of four)

PICNIC Carrefour Express (Via Vittoria, 00197; closed Sun) sells ingredients for sandwiches. Enjoy a picnic lunch in the Villa Borghese grounds.
SNACKS Picnic (Piazzale delle Canestre, 00197; 366 446 9901; open daily) provides gourmet picnics including hampers and blankets. For those who prefer to eat in, choices range from English breakfasts, salads and sandwiches, to more substantial dishes such as pizzas or steaks.
REAL MEAL Vyta Santa Margherita (see p169) offers a good buffet lunch.
FAMILY TREAT Caffè delle Arti (see p169) serves a superb radicchio, goat's cheese and pear salad, and sea bass with capers and lemon.

Find out more

DIGITAL www.mrdonn.org has simple, appealing retellings of Greek myths, including several stories about Pluto and Persephone (the Greek name for Proserpine). There are also some entertaining ancient Greek-themed games, including a personality quiz to find out which Greek god or hero kids most resemble, as well as a link to a game which helps kids create their own Greek myth.

Take cover

For a child-friendly indoor experience after a visit to the gallery, head for the **Casina di Raffaello**, or take in a film at the **Cinema dei Piccoli**.

Next stop...

BERNINI HUNTING To see more works by Bernini, take bus 52 to Piazza Barberini to see **Fontana del Tritone** and **Fontana delle Api** (see p160). Continue on foot to **Sant'Andrea al Quirinale** (see p159) and **Santa Maria della Vittoria** (see p160) to see architecture, paintings and sculptures created by him. For a full Bernini extravaganza, visit **St Peter's** (see pp204–5) to see his curly-wurly baldacchino.

Bernini's Fontana del Tritone, Piazza Barberini

⑦ Bioparco
Back to the ark

When it opened in 1908, the Bioparco was designed as a place where animals and their antics were considered to be there solely for the entertainment of the public. Today the zoo's mission is far more responsible and much of its work is dedicated to research and the preservation of animals in danger of extinction. The zoo houses more than 1,300 animals ranging from lions, hippos and elephants to snakes and crocodiles, and offers excellent information boards and a little train, as well as the opportunity to watch animals being fed at weekends.

Mini train at the Bioparco

Key Sights

① **Brown Bears** The Bioparco has three brown bear siblings who love to sleep all day in winter, and play in water and search for food in summer. Information boards explain how to look out for signs of bears in the wild.

Entrance

Shop and café

Reptile House

② **Elephants** The zoo's two elephants were taken from the wild 40 years ago when they were two-year-olds; at the time, such practices were common.

③ **Ring-tailed Lemurs** These entertaining primates like to sunbathe in a cross-legged yoga position.

④ **Armadillos** Two of the zoo's armadillos have been named Charles and Emma, after Darwin and his wife.

⑤ **Black Lemurs** Twin black lemurs, weighing 50 g (2 oz) each, were born in March 2011. Roman children voted to choose their names: Apollo and Aphrodite.

⑥ **Children's Farm** There are several opportunities for children to meet and pet the animals on the small children's farm.

The Lowdown

🌐 **Map reference** 5 A1
Address Piazzale Giardino Zoologico, 00197; 06 360 8211; www.bioparco.it

🚗 **Metro** Flaminio-Piazza del Popolo & Spagna (Line A). **Bus** 3, 52, 53, 217, 360, 910 & 926. **Tram** 3 & 19

🕐 **Open** late Oct–late Mar: 9:30am–5pm daily; late Mar–late Oct: 9:30am–6pm daily; till 7pm Sat & Sun in Apr–Sep

€ **Price** €30–54; under 12s €12, children under 1 m (3 ft) tall free

🚶 **Skipping the queue** Book via website or by calling 063608211. Tickets valid for 60 days

🪧 **Guided tours** Check the website for special tours

👫 **Age range** All ages

👫 **Activities** Check the website for feeding times and for events ranging from face-painting to workshops, night safaris and a summer school

⏱ **Allow** 4–5 hrs

♿ **Wheelchair access** Yes

☕ **Café** Yes

🛍 **Shop** The bookshop near Bioparco Cafeteria sells books, gadgets and soft toys

🚻 **Toilets** Near the entrance

Good family value?
Entry is expensive, but this is one of the best-value sights for children in Rome, with the city's most absorbing playground, the Arca della Conservazione, as well as the zoo.

Open-air theatre near the Arca della Conservazione, Bioparco

Letting off steam

The **Arca della Conservazione** is a wooden boat with slides, swings, climbing frames and ropes, and may turn out to be as popular with children as the animals themselves. Adjoining this is a small open-air theatre where there are temporary exhibitions and occasional theatre performances and workshops.

Eat and drink

Picnic: under €25; Snacks: €25–40; Real meal: €40–80; Family treat: over €80 (based on a family of four)

PICNIC Carrefour Express *(see p175)* stocks everything for a picnic. There is a picnic area right by the lake – great for flamingo-watching.
SNACKS Caffè del Ninfeo *(06 321 1388; open daily for lunch)* looks over the lemur enclosure. Watch the playful creatures while eating hamburgers, sausages or toasted ham and cheese sandwiches, followed by ice cream.
REAL MEAL Bioparco Cafeteria *(06 321 1388; open daily for lunch)*, near the entrance, has simple, reasonably priced meals – *pasta al pomodoro*, chicken escalopes and ice creams for dessert.
FAMILY TREAT Ristorante Mascagni *(06 321 1388; open daily for lunch)*, founded in 1926, is the smartest of the zoo's eating places. Children may like the simple dishes such as *pasta al pomodoro* and lasagne, while parents will enjoy typical Roman dishes.

Find out more

DIGITAL The Bioparco website (in both English and Italian) has excellent sections (in Italian only)

for children, including a puzzle and wallpaper downloads – older children will find plenty to interest them throughout the site. There is also a Bioparco app for smartphones, currently in Italian only, downloadable from the website.

Take cover

The **Reptile House**, a conservation centre for reptiles, amphibians and invertebrates, is home to terrifying giant millipedes and brilliant-green tree frogs as well as crocodiles and chameleons. Its tropical forest zone is a great place to take cover on a cold, rainy day.

Next stop...

COPPEDÈ A short walk from the Bioparco is Coppedè. A fantastical combination of different historic styles, the buildings in this district feature Art Nouveau decorations, medieval frescoes, gargoyles and grotesque fountains and chandeliers.

Reptile House at the Bioparco

⑧ Musei di Villa Torlonia

A dictator in a gingerbread house

A large park with several villas, Villa Torlonia was created in the 19th century for a wealthy banker, Prince Giovanni Torlonia. It sprang to fame in the 1920s, when Torlonia's nephew rented it out, for the tiny sum of one lira per year, to Fascist dictator Benito Mussolini. The villa remained Mussolini's main residence until 1943, when he was ousted from power. The grounds were then turned into a public park, but the buildings fell into disrepair. It was only in the 1990s that it was decided to restore them. The grounds now house several minor museums, as well as Rome's innovative science space, Technotown. To find out more about the life of the Mussolini family, visit the **Casino Nobile**, where exhibits include the bed in which Mussolini slept and the anti-air-raid and anti-gas bunkers that he constructed, as well as old film footage on the villa and Mussolini's residence. The interiors reflect 19th-century taste – a pick-and-mix of styles ranging from mock-Etruscan to mock-Gothic, with a mock-Egyptian room complete with hieroglyphic decorations.

It is a lovely walk through the grounds to the diminutive **Casina delle Civette**, literally "little house of owls", which looks like a fairy-tale gingerbread house and was designed as a retreat to which the Torlonia family could escape to avoid their formal lives in the main villa. It was almost destroyed by vandalism, fire and the Allied troops who occupied it after the fall of Mussolini. Today its stained glass, enamelled-tile roofs and delicate wrought iron and stucco have been painstakingly restored.

Letting off steam

There is plenty of space for a run about and picnic in the beautiful tree-shaded park of **Villa Torlonia**.

⑨ Technotown

A 3D high

A pleasant walk across the Villa Torlonia park takes visitors to Technotown, an interactive space dedicated to new technology. Although, at present, visits are guided by facilitators who speak only Italian, language is not really a barrier, as the installations speak for themselves. Highlights include Sbong!, a virtual ball game, and Adventures in 3D, where visitors get to experience a tsunami in three dimensions, before going on a 3D space trip in which challenges include flying between the rings of Saturn and avoiding falling into a black hole. Three-dimensional antics continue at Scultorobot – an imaging device that can take a photo, rotate it to show it in profile and finally

The Casina della Civette, one of the museums in the Musei di Villa Torlonia

The Lowdown

🌐 **Map reference** 6 F1
Address Via Nomentana 70, 00161; 060608; www. museivillatorlonia.it

🚗 **Metro** Bologna (Line B). **Bus** 36, 60, 62, 84, 90 & 140. **Tram** 3

🕐 **Open** 9am–7pm Tue–Sun (last adm: 45 mins before closing). Park: dawn–dusk daily

💶 **Price** Casino Nobile: €15–28; EU under 18s €5.50; under 6s free. Casina delle Civette: €12–22; EU under 18s €3; under 6s free. Casino Nobile & Casina delle Civette: adults €19–34; EU under 18s €6.50; under 6s free

🚩 **Guided tours** Audioguides (€3.50) available in Italian, French & English

👫 **Age range** Casino Nobile: 10 plus. Casina delle Civette: 6 plus

⏱ **Allow** Casino Nobile: 30 mins. Park and Casina delle Civette: 1 hr

♿ **Wheelchair access** Yes

🍴 **Eat and drink** PICNIC TUODI *(Via Zara 24, 00198; closed Sun)*, a supermarket, offers a variety of food items suitable for a picnic. Eat at the park. REAL MEAL Limonaia *(Via Spallanzani 1/a, 00161; 06 440 4021; open daily)* is a café and restaurant housed in the orangery adjoining Technotown. Visit for a sandwich, pizza or crunchy crostini topped with melted taleggio cheese and speck, and a slice of delicious cake. Try child-friendly daily specials such as sausage and potatoes or hamburger and chips

🚻 **Toilets** In the museums

The Lowdown

🌐 **Map reference** 6 F2
Address Via Lazzaro Spallanzani 1/a, 00161; 060608; www. technotown.it

🚗 **Metro** Bologna (Line B). **Bus** 36, 60, 62, 84, 90 & 140

🕐 **Open** summer: 6:30am–11:30pm Tue–Sun; winter: 9:30am–7pm Tue–Sun. Booking obligatory

💶 **Price** €32 for one activity

🚩 **Guided tours** Tours compulsory; check the website for details

👫 **Age range** 4 plus

🎭 **Activities** Check the website for details of talks and demonstrations

⏱ **Allow** Percorso Junior: 40 mins. Percorso Basic: 80 mins. Percorso Educational: 140 mins. Park: 1 hr

♿ **Wheelchair access** Yes

🍴 **Eat and drink** PICNIC Pizza al Taglio *(Via Nomentana 48, 00161; open daily)* is perfect for a slice of pizza with fresh mozzarella. REAL MEAL Limonaia *(see Musei di Villa Torlonia)*

🛍 **Shop** The shop near the entrance has an exciting selection of science toys and books

🚻 **Toilets** Near the entrance

An exhibit at MACRO, housed in a former beer factory

sculpt it in polystyrene. Kids are also given the chance to get hands-on experience with new materials such as metals with memory and elastic foam, before finding out how to make superheroes fly and magicians disappear on a virtual film set.

Letting off steam
Pick up lunch and find a shaded spot to relax and picnic in the surrounding **Villa Torlonia** park.

⑩ MACRO
Alice in Macroland
The Museo d'Arte Contemporanea Roma (MACRO) has two branches – one in Testaccio (see p108) and the other in this converted 20th-century Peroni beer factory. Coloured lights, glass, exposed steel, transparent lifts and oversized doors may make a child – or adult – feel like a tiny, awestruck Alice in a contemporary wonderland. This sense of wonder is only enhanced on discovering the table lamps in the café that light up as they are lifted, infinity mirrors and translucent washbasins illuminated from within in the bathrooms and a courtyard which appears to be at street level – until the moment the visitor realizes that he or she is walking on glass with the ground far below.

Although MACRO has a permanent collection, the style is that of a contemporary gallery with an ever-changing series of exhibitions and installations. There are free screenings of oddball, experimental and arthouse shorts in a niche just off the atrium, and the shop – devoted to contemporary design – is excellent. A café, a terrace restaurant and a packed programme of events and exhibitions makes this a perfect choice for a rainy day – or for kids fed up with history.

Letting off steam
Take tram 3 to **Villa Borghese** (see pp168–9) park, or walk to **Villa Torlonia**.

The Lowdown

🌐 **Map reference** 5 D2
Address Via Nizza 138, 00198; 060608; www.museomacro.org

🚌 **Bus** 80, 88 & 348

🕐 **Open** 10:30am–7:30pm Tue–Sun

🎫 **Price** Exhibitions: €27–50; under 6s free

👥 **Skipping the queue** Book in advance for major exhibitions at http://ticket.museiincomuneroma.it to avoid long queues at the booking counter

🎧 **Guided tours** Reservation required

👫 **Age range** 4 plus

👪 **Activities** Interactive sessions and activities, usually based around one of the exhibitions, for families with children aged 6–12 on Sundays at 11am and 4pm. For bookings, email didattica.macro@gmail.com

⏱ **Allow** 1 hr

♿ **Wheelchair access** Yes

🍴 **Eat and drink** SNACKS MACRO's café offers coffee, sandwiches and pastries. REAL MEAL MACRO138, on a dramatic terrace, serves a stylish blend of traditional and creative cuisine and makes its own bread, cakes and ice cream

🛍 **Shop** The shop on the ground floor sells toys and has a good range of illustrated books for children in many languages

🚻 **Toilets** On the ground floor

Trastevere
& Janiculum Hill

Across the Tiber, the vibrant streetlife of Trastevere paints a contrasting picture to the peaceful Janiculum Hill above it. For centuries a working-class area, Trastevere is now one of Rome's most fashionable districts, with a maze of narrow streets full of traditional markets and *trattorie* that coexist with modern galleries and shops. The Janiculum Hill provides respite from the chaos of the city as well as splendid views.

Highlights

Santa Maria in Trastevere
Admire the magnificent mosaics in Rome's oldest church, the Santa Maria in Trastevere (see pp186–7).

West and East of Viale di Trastevere
Explore Trastevere's enticing tangle of streets and piazzas, leaving plenty of time for window-shopping and people-watching (see pp188–9).

Janiculum Hill
Climb up the Janiculum Hill for panoramic views of Rome, followed by a puppet show and a picnic (see pp190–91).

Galleria Nazionale d'Arte Antica
Visit the sumptuously decorated halls of the Palazzo Corsini, full of intriguing art (see p192).

Villa Farnesina
Wonder at the exquisitely painted pergola and frescoed horoscopes at the Villa Farnesina, to the accompaniment of classical music (see pp192–3).

Villa Doria Pamphilj
Take a break from city life at Rome's largest park, the Villa Doria Pamphilj, and perhaps enjoy a meal at its pretty Provençal-style bistro (see p195).

Above right Colourful carousel horses, Janiculum Hill
Left People enjoying a walk down a typical street in Trastevere

The Best of...
Trastevere & Janiculum Hill

Sightseeing, shopping, people-watching and walks in the park can all be easily combined in Trastevere. There are beautiful mosaics in Santa Maria in Trastevere and sculptures in Santa Cecilia in Trastevere, while a visit to the exquisite Villa Farnesina and Bramante's refined Tempietto brings a tangible sense of Renaissance Rome. The area's many parks include the Janiculum Hill, Villa Sciarra, Villa Doria Pamphilj and the Botanical Gardens, while several piazzas are traffic-free.

Escape to the greenery

The green spaces on the fringes of Trastevere are ideal for winding down after a tiring day of sightseeing. Walk up the **Janiculum Hill** *(see pp190–91)* for fantastic views of the city, stopping by at the tranquil **Botanical Gardens** *(see p193)*. Once part of the **Palazzo Corsini** *(see p192)*, it is the perfect escape from the heat – full of shade and perfect for a picnic and games. Escape the madding crowds at **Villa Doria Pamphilj** *(see p195)*, Rome's largest park and one of the few places in the city where the sound of traffic seems a world away. The intimate and beautifully landscaped park of **Villa Sciarra** *(see p194)* is also a great picnic spot and has a playground too.

*Right A family taking in views of Vatican City from the Janiculum Hill **Below** Wide, open spaces of Villa Doria Pamphilj – green and relaxing*

Above Spectacular 12th-century mosaics in Santa Maria in Trastevere church

On a budget

Head to the area **West of Viale di Trastevere** *(see p188)* and explore the tangle of medieval streets at random, letting children decide when to turn right and left. Discover tiny alleyways and intimate piazzas crying out to be photographed. Armed with a picnic lunch, spend an entire day exploring the **Janiculum Hill**, then head to either **Villa Sciarra** or **Villa Doria Pamphilj**, without being tempted to spend a euro. On Sundays, search for bargains in the huge flea market at **Porta Portese** *(see p189)* and in the months of January and July, buy clothes and shoes at prices that are a fraction of the original. For a change of scene, visit **Santa Maria in Trastevere** *(see pp186–7)* at night and admire the illuminated mosaics on the façade.

Palaces and villas

Get children to spot exotic vegetables on the vaults of the Sala di Psiche, and figure out the horoscopes represented on the walls of the Sala di Galatea at **Villa Farnesina** *(see pp192–3)*, a palace with beautiful grounds and enticing frescoes. Visit the splendid Palazzo Corsini, which houses the **Galleria Nazionale d'Arte Antica** *(see p192)*, with an amazing collection of art from the 18th and 19th centuries. Families who visit early in the morning may well have the entire place to themselves – imagine what it would be like to live among such splendour.

Quirky sights

Wander through the eclectic streets of **Trastevere** *(see pp188–9)* counting the quirky sights on the way – the world's first police and fire station, the house where Italian painter Raphael's beloved Margherita Luti lived and a pharmacy where children can see an antidote to snake bites invented by Emperor Nero's doctor. Cross the **Ponte Sisto** *(see p188)*, a foot-bridge across the Tiber incorporating a 16th-century flood-warning device. Up on the **Janiculum Hill**, unique sights include a lighthouse that beams out the colours of the Italian flag; a statue of a baby-carrying, gun-toting war heroine; and, concealing a huge water tank, the façade of a house in which Michelangelo once lived.

Left Crossing the Tiber on the pedestrian bridge, Ponte Sisto

Santa Maria in Trastevere and around

The bustling Trastevere neighbourhood can be reached by bus or tram, but the nicest (and often quickest) way to reach the area from the *centro storico* is to walk across a bridge – Ponte Garibaldi, Ponte Sisto, Ponte Fabricio and Ponte Cestio are all convenient. Climbing the Janiculum Hill from either the Vatican or Trastevere is fun – and much easier than might be expected, as flights of steps provide many shortcuts between the winding roads. Other sights are all within a hop and a skip of each other at the foot of the hill. Below the Janiculum, the busy Lungotevere is served by several buses, useful as swift access to – or a speedy escape from – St Peter's and the Vatican.

Trastevere &
Janiculum Hill

Janiculum Hill
p190

Santa Maria
in Trastevere
p186

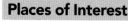

Fountain in
Piazza di Santa
Maria in
Trastevere

VILLA
ABAMELEK

Places of Interest

SIGHTS
1. Santa Maria in Trastevere
2. West of Viale di Trastevere
3. East of Viale di Trastevere
4. Janiculum Hill
5. Galleria Nazionale d'Arte Antica
6. Villa Farnesina
7. Botanical Gardens
8. Fontana dell'Acqua Paola
9. San Pietro in Montorio and Tempietto
10. Villa Doria Pamphilj

EAT AND DRINK
1. Forno La Renella
2. La Boccaccia
3. Augusto
4. Glass Hostaria
5. Ditta Trinchetti
6. Da Lucia
7. Convivium
8. Panetteria Romana e Spaccio di Paste
9. Carpe Diem al Gianicolo
10. Antico Arco
11. Luna e L'Altra
12. Zi'Mberto
13. Da Giovanni
14. La Scala in Trastevere
15. Terrazza San Pancrazio
16. Il Baretto
17. Antica Pesa
18. DOC
19. Vivi Bistrot

SHOPPING
1. Open Door Bookshop
2. Polvere di Tempo
3. Vetro Soffiato

WHERE TO STAY
1. Orsa Maggiore
2. Buonanotte Garibaldi
3. Hotel Santa Maria
4. Villa della Fonte
5. Residenza Santa Maria
6. Maria-Rosa Guesthouse
7. Kimama
8. Il Boom
9. Casa Cibella

Villa Doria
Pamphilj

Vivi Bistrot
1.25 km

PIAZZA SAN
PANCRAZIO

The Lowdown

🚌 **Bus** H, 8, 23, 44, 75, 115, 125, 271, 280, 710, 780, 870 & 984. **Tram** 8

ℹ️ **Visitor information** Tourist Information Point, Piazza Sonnino, 0015; 060608; open 10:30am–8pm daily; www.turismoroma.it

🍴 **Supermarkets** Conad: Viale di Trastevere 62, 00153. Supermercato Panella: Via Natale del Grande 19, 00153. Supermercato TODIS: Via Natale del Grande 23, 00153. Drogheria Innocenzi: Piazza San Cosimato 66, 00153.

Markets Piazza San Cosimato market: Mon–Sat am. Porta Portese market: Piazza di Porta Portese, 00153; Sunday am

🎭 **Festivals** Festa de' Noantri (Jul); involves street parties, fireworks and performances in dialect. A statue of Madonna del Carmine is carried through Trastevere to the church of San Grisogono, where it stays for eight days, before returning with another procession

➕ **Pharmacies** Farmacia Istituto San Gallicano: Via di San Gallicano 23, 00153; 06 589 5764; open summer: 8:30am–1pm &

4:30–8pm, till 7:30pm in winter Mon–Sat. Farmacia Sant'Agata di Sarcinelli Maurizio: Piazza Sidney Sonnino 47, 00153; 06 580 3715; open 8:30am–8pm Mon–Sat, noon–8pm Sun.

🛝 **Nearest play areas** Villa Sciarra, Via Calandrelli, 00153. Villa Doria Pamphilj, Via Vitellia, 00152. Piazza San Cosimato, 00153.

🚻 **Public toilets** Via Portuense, by Ponte Sublicio. Piazzale Giuseppe Garibaldi. Via Sergio I, by Castel Sant'Angelo. At the Via Aurelia Antica entrance, by Vivi Bistrot and the playground in Doria Pamphilj

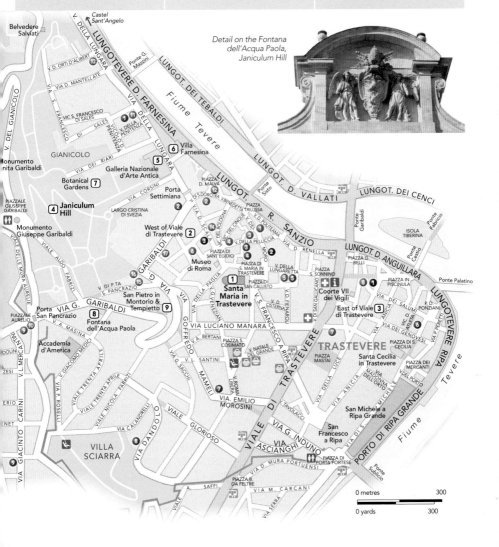

Detail on the Fontana dell'Acqua Paola, Janiculum Hill

0 metres 300
0 yards 300

① Santa Maria in Trastevere
Holy bath water

Located on lively, traffic-free Piazza di Santa Maria in Trastevere, the basilica of Santa Maria is probably the first official Christian church to have been built in Rome. According to legend, a fountain of oil miraculously bubbled up here at the precise moment that Jesus was born and, in the 3rd century, Pope Callixtus I built a church on the site. The present church was built in the 12th century and was the first in the city to be dedicated to the Virgin Mary. Try to see it at least once at night, when the glittering mosaics on the façade are illuminated.

Façade of Santa Maria church

Key Features

Façade Mosaic On the façade is a 12th-century mosaic showing the Madonna feeding baby Jesus, flanked by ten women holding lamps. The veiled women whose lamps have gone out are probably widows. Kneeling on either side of the Madonna are two unidentified figures – probably those of the donors who provided funds for the building of the church – so tiny that were they to stand, they would barely reach the Virgin's knees.

Cappella Altemps

The bell tower The tower dates from the 12th century. At the top is a small mosaic of the Virgin Mary.

Cavallini Mosaics

Coronation of the Virgin

Columns in the Nave The nave is lined with 22 huge granite columns filched from the Baths of Caracalla (see p230).

Narthex A miscellany of ancient inscriptions adorn the wall of the narthex.

Cappella Altemps An 8th-century Byzantine fresco in this chapel shows the Madonna as the queen of heaven, dressed like a contemporary empress with a pearly diadem. Kneeling at her feet is Pope John VII.

Coronation of the Virgin This 12th-century mosaic represents the Virgin Mary as the Bride of Christ, young, beautiful and sumptuously dressed, speckled with gold and gloriously glinting, as if at her wedding.

Cavallini Mosaics Pietro Cavallini created these realistic scenes, from the life of the Virgin, in the lower apse, in the 13th century. In the Nativity scene, the newborn baby's nurse checks the temperature of the bath water with her fingers, while other servants offer the mother food and drink.

The Lowdown

🌐 **Map reference** 8 F2
Address Piazza di Santa Maria in Trastevere, 00153; 06 581 4802

🚗 **Bus** H, 115, 125 & 780. **Tram** 8

🕐 **Open** 7:30am–9pm daily

💲 **Price** Free

👫 **Age range** 7 plus

⏱ **Allow** 20–30 mins

♿ **Wheelchair access** Yes

🚻 **Toilets** No

Good family value?
Santa Maria is free and its mosaics have plenty of detail for older children to seek out. Younger kids can play under supervision on the piazza outside.

Prices given are for a family of four

Visitors relaxing around the fountain in Piazza di Santa Maria in Trastevere

Letting off steam

Enjoy the traffic-free spaces on **Piazza di Santa Maria in Trastevere**, or go to the playground and market in nearby **Piazza San Cosimato** (00153). Buses 44 and 75 go up to the park at **Villa Sciarra** (see p194), not far away.

Eat and drink

Picnic: under €25; Snacks: €25–40; Real meal: €40–80; Family treat: over €80 (based on a family of four)

PICNIC Forno La Renella (Via del Moro 15–16, 00153; 06 581 7265; open daily) is the place where Romans from all over the city come to seek out pizza, focaccia and bread. Picnic in the Botanical Gardens (see p193) or take a bus (44 or 75) up to Villa Sciarra.
SNACKS La Boccaccia (Via di Santa Dorotea 2, 00153; open daily) offers great pizza by the slice.
REAL MEAL Augusto (Piazza de Renzi, 15, 00153; 06 580 3798; open daily) is a typical trattoria serving traditional dishes such as pasta cacio e pepe, sausages and lamb at very reasonable prices.
FAMILY TREAT Glass Hostaria (Vicolo del Cinque 58, 00153; 06 5833 5903; closed Mon; www.glass-restaurant.it) has minimalist decor, good service and exquisite inventive modern international food. Try the sumac-crusted lamb, or grilled calamari with bok choy and kombu.

Shopping

The **Open Door Bookshop** (Via della Lungaretta 23, 00153; closed Sun) has a good selection of second-hand books for kids, mostly in English. **Polvere di Tempo** (Via

del Moro 59, 00153) sells replicas of ancient time-measuring instruments, most of them handmade by the owner. **Vetro Soffiato** (Via della Scala 11, 00153; closed Sun) is an Aladdin's cave of glass beads – buy them individually to string at home, or have a necklace made to order on the spot.

Find out more

DIGITAL Kids can learn a lot from the wise virgins, though they may have to make different kinds of preparations. For inspiration, listen to "Be Prepared" from *The Lion King* at *www.tinyurl.com/yf2goyg*. "Be Prepared" is also the motto of the Scout Association; adults may prefer the Tom Lehrer version of the song at *www.tinyurl.com/5to4sm*.

Façade of the Santa Cecilia in Trastevere church

Next stop...

CHURCHES AND VIEWS There is a fresco by Pietro Cavallini in the nearby church of **Santa Cecilia in Trastevere** (see pp188–9). Visit **Santa Maria in Domnica** (see p72) and **Santa Prassede and Santa Pudenziana** (see p97) to look at more mosaics. Or get some fresh air and good views by walking up the **Janiculum Hill** (see pp190–91).

KIDS' CORNER

Look carefully...

1 Can you see which of the lamps are lit on the mosaic façade?
2 In the narthex, can you find:
(a) Two peacocks drinking from a vase?
(b) Other birds?
(c) A boat?
(d) A barrel?
3 Inside the church, can you find a mosaic of a shepherd boy playing pipes to sheep?

Answers at the bottom of the page.

BE PREPARED

The ten virgins on the façade represent Jesus's story of the wise and foolish virgins, a parable about the importance of always being prepared – the wise virgins took supplies of oil with them, while the foolish ones did not.

Wine or God?

After Pope Callixtus built his church, local tavern-keepers protested, claiming the site was theirs. The emperor, Alexander Severus, however, decided that a church was preferable to taverns, and the building became the first official place of Christian worship in the city.

Answers: 1 On the right side, the third, fourth and fifth. On the left side, the second and third. **2** They are all to the left of the left-hand door; **3** In the corner of the mosaic to the left of the central window in the apse.

Ponte Sisto bridge with the dome of St Peter's in the background

② West of Viale di Trastevere

Mystic medicines and busy street life

The elegant, four-arched **Ponte Sisto** has linked Trastevere with the Campo de' Fiori (*see pp130–31*) district since the 16th century. Commissioned by Pope Sixtus IV and built by Italian architect Baccio Pontelli, it remains the most evocative approach to the Tiber's left bank and is busy day and night with people hurrying, strolling, chatting, cycling, scootering and sometimes even skating. The bridge is pierced by an *oculus* (eye), designed to warn Romans when the water level

of the Tiber gets dangerously high. Ponte Sisto also serves as an aqueduct, carrying water across the river from the Fontana dell'Acqua Paola (*see p194*) on the Janiculum Hill. To the west of Ponte Sisto is a 16th-century city gate, the **Porta Settimiana**. Overlooking it is Casa della Fornarina (*see p190*), a modest house, which now houses a restaurant. It is thought to have been home to Margherita Luti, the baker's daughter with whom master painter Raphael fell in love.

From here, stroll down to Via della Scala, one of Trastevere's main pedestrian thoroughfares, lined with shops, restaurants and cafés. Located here is the **Antica Farmacia Santa Maria della Scala**, run by

Carmelite monks, and first opened to the public in the 17th century. The pharmacy became famous among the Grand Tourists of the 18th and 19th centuries for its *acqua della scala* (anti-plague water). This is no longer on sale, but calling in advance helps gain access to the original pharmacy on the first floor. Here visitors can see alembics, distillation equipment, pestles and mortars and a device for making pills, along with a vase containing theriac, a supposed cure for snake bites.

Further along Via della Scala is the **Museo di Roma**, which hosts photography exhibitions occasionally. A short walk beyond is **Piazza di Santa Maria in Trastevere** (*see pp186–7*), the traditional heart of the neighbourhood.

Letting off steam

Piazza Trilussa on the left bank has space for kids to run around and have fun, and there is a basic playground in **Piazza San Cosimato**.

③ East of Viale di Trastevere

Of strict vigils and flea markets

The neighbourhood to the east of Viale di Trastevere is considerably less gentrified than that to the west, although quirky new shops and places to eat and drink are opening all the time. Begin with an inspection of the world's oldest police station, the **Coorte VII dei Vigili**. Like the modern Carabinieri, ancient Rome's policemen were part of the army. Their duties included firefighting, demolishing dangerous buildings and patrolling the streets at night on the lookout for thieves and runaway slaves. The *vigili* (municipal police officers) were nicknamed *spartoli*, or little buckets, as they patrolled the streets carrying buckets of water. All that can be seen today is a scruffy red building on Via della VII Coorte, with a Roman-looking wall around the corner on Via del Montefiore.

A short walk from here leads to the church of **Santa Cecilia in Trastevere**, which stands above the house where St Cecilia lived – and was martyred – in the 3rd century. A church was built on the site in the 9th century and, although

The Lowdown

🌐 **Map reference** 8 F2
Address Trastevere, 00153. Ponte Sisto: Piazza Trilussa. Porta Settimiana: Via di Porta Settimiana 8. Antica Farmacia Santa Maria della Scala: Piazza della Scala 23; 06 580 6233 or 06 580 6217. Museo di Roma: Piazza Sant'Egidio 1B; 060608; www.museodiromaintrastevere.it

🚌 **Bus** H, 23, 125, 271, 280 & 780. **Tram** 8

🕐 **Open** Antica Farmacia Santa Maria della Scala: book in advance. Museo di Roma: 10am–8pm Tue–Sun

💶 **Price** Antica Farmacia di Santa Maria della Scala: €5 per person for tours (minimum 5 people or pay the minimum price of €25). Museo di Roma: €12–22, expect to pay more during exhibitions; under 6s free

🎫 **Guided tours** Antica Farmacia Santa Maria della Scala: book to see the old pharmacy. Museo di Roma: guided tours; call 060608 to book

👫 **Age range** Antica Farmacia Santa Maria della Scala: 5 plus; Museo di Roma: 10 plus

⏱ **Allow** West Trastevere area: 1–2 hrs. Antica Farmacia Santa Maria della Scala: 30 mins

🍽 **Eat and drink** REAL MEAL Da Lucia (Vicolo del Mattonato 2, 00153; 06 580 3601; closed Mon) is a lovely old trattoria with outdoor seating. The speciality is spaghetti cacio e pepe. FAMILY TREAT Ditta Trinchetti (Via della Lungaretta 76, 00153; 06 5833 1189; open daily) is a fabulous tavola calda and deli serving Puglian burrata (mozzarella marinated in cream), sandwiches, salads and hot bean soup

🚻 **Toilets** In Piazza Sidney Sonnino

Tomb of Santa Cecilia, Santa Cecilia in Trastevere

there are very few signs of it today, it still exists, hidden beneath the 18th-century makeover. Tapping on the pillars in the aisle reveals that they are hollow – with the original columns still encased inside. In the 1260s the original church was covered with what must have been some of the first frescoes of the early Renaissance, by Italian painter Pietro Cavallini; surviving fragments of *The Last Judgment* can be seen in the adjacent cloister.

In 1599 St Cecilia's tomb in the Catacombs of San Callisto *(see p228)* was opened, and inside, wrapped in a gown shot with gold and a green silk veil, was her perfectly preserved body. On contact with air, the body began to disintegrate, but not before sketches were made, which sculptor Stefano Maderna used to create a statue of the saint, lying on her side with her head turned away to reveal her wounded neck. This is now displayed in a niche below the high altar. Below the church are Roman houses, and the remains of a tannery, complete with vats.

Opposite the church is a small children's printing press called **Nuove Edizioni Romane**, with an interesting range of illustrated books in Italian.

Not far away is **Piazza di Porta Portese**, which turns into a huge and famous flea market on Sundays.

Letting off steam

Walk to **Piazza di Santa Cecilia**, which is a great place for children to let their hair down.

The Lowdown

- 🌐 **Map reference** 8 G2
  Address Trastevere, 00153. Santa Cecilia in Trastevere: Piazza di Santa Cecilia; 06 589 9289. Nuove Edizioni Romane: Via di Santa Cecilia, 18. Porta Portese market: Piazza di Porta Portese
- 🚌 **Bus** 23, 44, 125 & 280
- 🕐 **Open** Santa Cecilia in Trastevere: 10am–1pm & 4–7pm daily. Nuove Edizioni Romane: 9am–7:30pm Mon–Fri, 10am–1:30pm Sat & Sun
- 💶 **Price** Santa Cecilia in Trastevere: Donations requested
- 🎫 **Guided tours** The baths where Cecilia died are open on request (06 4549 2739)
- 👫 **Age range** 7 plus
- ⏱ **Allow** 30 mins
- ☕ **Eat and drink** SNACKS Convivium *(Via Cardinale Marmaggi 12; 06 8660 5560; closed Mon)* sells pizza by the slice, *suppli*, and other traditional fried specialties for a quick snack. REAL MEAL Panetteria Romana e Spaccio di Paste *(Via della Lungaretta 31, 00153; 06 5831 0598; open daily)* is a great place for a hot lunch where one can choose dishes from the fabulous *tavola calda*
- 🛍 **Shop** Kids will enjoy visiting the traditional bakery at No. 21, Via della Luce
- 🚻 **Toilets** No

Nuove Edizioni Romane, the children's printing press

Picnic under €25; **Snacks** €25–40; **Real meal** €40–80; **Family treat** over €80 (based on a family of four)

④ Janiculum Hill
Lights, battles and a moving house

It is hard to imagine that in 1849 the Janiculum was the scene of a fierce battle between the French – backing the pope – and Italian Republicans led by Giuseppe Garibaldi. Today, there is no better antidote to a morning at the Vatican than a leisurely walk up the Janiculum Hill. The views of Rome from the top are tremendous, and the Passeggiata Gianicolense, with its several belvederes, a picnic area, refreshment vans and a seasonal puppet theatre, has long been a favourite spot for a lazy early evening stroll.

Puppets at Piazzale Garibaldi

Key Sights

Tasso's Oak Struck by lightning in 1843, this tree trunk, held together by metal braces, is all that remains of the oak under which the Renaissance poet Torquato Tasso liked to sit.

Manfredi Lighthouse Built in 1911, this was a gift to the city of Rome from Italians living in Argentina. At night, the lighthouse beams out red, green and white lights – the colours of the Italian flag.

Villa Farnesina (see pp192–3)

Galleria Nazionale d'Arte Antica (see p192)

Monument to Anita Garibaldi

Porta Settimiana (see p188)

Piazzale Giuseppe Garibaldi

Casa della Fornarina

Michelangelo's House

Botanical Gardens (see p193)

Piazzale Giuseppe Garibaldi Dominated by a monument to Garibaldi, this large, open piazza is a favourite with Roman kids for candyfloss and a puppet show. To mark the 150th anniversary of the Italian Republic, a new low wall inscribed with the country's constitution was created in 2011.

Casa della Fornarina This house supposedly belonged to La Fornarina, a baker's daughter, with whom Raphael fell in love. Raphael's most famous portrait of her is in the Palazzo Barberini (see p158).

Monument to Anita Garibaldi Anita, Garibaldi's wife, lies buried beneath this statue, which depicts her riding into war with a baby tucked under one arm and a pistol in the other.

Prices given are for a family of four

The Lowdown

🌐 **Map reference** 8 E2
Address 00165

🚗 **Bus** 115 & 870

👫 **Age range** All ages

🤸 **Activities** A puppet theatre (338 756 4534; Sat & Sun am; donations requested; www.iburattinidelgianicolo.it) on Piazzale Giuseppe Garibaldi provides great entertainment for kids

⏱ **Allow** 2 hrs

♿ **Wheelchair access** No

☕ **Café** Mobile refreshment vans on Piazzale Garibaldi

🚻 **Toilets** In the cafés, although these are open only to customers; buy an espresso or water

Good family value?
A trip up the Janiculum Hill is worth the effort – and anyone who walks and carries a picnic could have a day out without spending a euro.

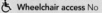

Snack van on the Janiculum Hill, with various foods and beverages on display

Letting off steam

Kids with plenty of excess energy to burn off, even after walking up the Janiculum Hill, can run around safely on **Piazzale Giuseppe Garibaldi** and around the picnic area on **Belvedere Salviati** (near Tasso's Oak).

Eat and drink

Picnic: under €25; Snacks: €25–40; Real meal: €40–80; Family treat: over €80 (based on a family of four)

PICNIC There are no handy shops on the Janiculum. However, if coming from the Vatican (see pp202–3), pick up made-to-order sandwiches from **Alimentari** (Borgo Pio 27, 00193; closed Sun) and if coming from Trastevere (see pp180–97), pick up a picnic lunch at the market in **Piazza San Cosimato**. Eat in the picnic area on Belvedere Salviati.

SNACKS Mobile vans (Piazzale Giuseppe Garibaldi, 00153) sell sandwiches, drinks and ice creams.

REAL MEAL Carpe Diem al Gianicolo (Via di San Pancrazio 3, 00152; 06 580 0896; closed Tue) serves pizzas and pasta, and is one of very few places to eat at the top of the hill.

FAMILY TREAT Antico Arco (Piazzale Aurelio 7, 00152; 06 581 5274; open daily for lunch & dinner) is one of the best and most consistent of Rome's restaurants. Try the onion flan with aged parmesan fondue, home-made ravioli with sea bass, squid, broccoli and leeks, *ricciola* (amberjack) tartare with ginger and lime, or crème caramel with lemongrass served with a warm banana crumble.

Find out more

DIGITAL To read about the exploits of Garibaldi, go to *www.tinyurl.com/cwnbgq2*.

FILM Roberto Rossellini's drama *Garibaldi* (1961; released as *Viva l'Italia!* in English) is a historical drama based on the life of the hero.

Take cover

There is nowhere to take cover on the hill. If it rains, jump on bus 870 to **Castel Sant'Angelo** (see pp214–15) and spend a couple of hours in the castle.

Next stop...

FOUNTAIN, CHURCH AND VIEWS Head down into Trastevere along Via Garibaldi, taking in views from the **Fontana dell'Acqua Paolo** and Bramante's **Tempietto** (see p194) on the way. Head to **Il Vittoriano** (see p84) and take the elevator to the top for more views of Rome.

Castel Sant'Angelo overlooking Ponte Sant'Angelo

A hall in the Palazzo Corsini, home to the Galleria Nazionale d'Arte Antica

⑤ Galleria Nazionale d'Arte Antica

Artful gore and bronze animals

The splendid Palazzo Corsini, with enticing views over the magnificent Botanical Gardens, houses the Galleria Nazionale d'Arte Antica, popularly known as the Galleria Corsini. The gallery showcases the outstanding paintings collected in the 18th century by Neri Corsini.

The Lowdown

- 🌐 **Map reference** 11 A6
- **Address** Via della Lungara 10, 00165; 06 6880 2323; http://galleriacorsini.beniculturali.it
- 🚌 **Bus** 23, 125 & 280
- ⏱ **Open** 8am–7:30pm Tue–Sun
- 💲 **Price** €10–15; under 18s free
- 🚩 **Guided tours** By appointment
- 👫 **Age range** 9 plus
- 🏃 **Activities** Occasionally, especially around Christmas and school holidays
- ⏲ **Allow** 40 mins
- ♿ **Wheelchair access** Yes
- 🍴 **Eat and drink** SNACKS Luna e L'Altra *(Via San Francesco di Sales 1, 00165; 06 6889 2465; closed Sun; www.casainternazionaledelle donne.org)* has a café that serves ethnic and organic food and has plenty of space for kids to run around. REAL MEAL Zi'Mberto *(Piazza della Malva 11, 00153; 06 581 6643; closed Mon)* offers *spaghetti alla carbonara* and steak – try the *tagliata* with mushrooms
- 🛍 **Shop** The bookshop on the first floor sells books and postcards
- 🚻 **Toilets** On the first floor

Both collection and palace were sold to the Italian state in 1883. Several paintings in the gallery are a little gory, notably, the 17th-century artist Salvatore Rosa's anatomically accurate rendition of Prometheus having his guts pecked out by an eagle. The squeamish may prefer the 18th-century bronzes in the Galleria del Cardinale of a boy strangling a snake and two boys holding a parrot and sitting on a goat. Kids might also be amused by the portrait of Queen Christina of Sweden as the goddess Diana, on display in the room in which she died in 1689 after living here for 30 years. Besides the painting of a young *St John the Baptist* by Caravaggio, it is the collection of 18th-century still lifes, in the Camera Verde, with their minute attention to detail, that are most fascinating. Spot the fly on a peach in Pfeiffer's *Natura Morta*.

Letting off steam

Carry a picnic lunch to the **Botanical Gardens**, where kids can run around and play games.

The Lowdown

- 🌐 **Map references** 11 B5
- **Address** Via della Lungara 230, 00165; 06 6802 7268; www.villafarnesina.it
- 🚌 **Bus** H, 8, 23, 271 & 280
- ⏱ **Open** 9am–2pm Mon–Sat
- 💲 **Price** €20–30; under 14s free
- 🚩 **Guided tours** 12:30pm Mon, Fri & Sat; 12:30pm (with live music, 2nd Sun of month, book in advance), 3pm & 4pm (2nd Sun of month)
- 👫 **Age range** 7 plus
- ⏲ **Allow** 1–2 hrs

⑥ Villa Farnesina

Music and art

A perfect example of Renaissance architecture, elegant Villa Farnesina was built in the early 16th century for Agostino Chigi, a fabulously rich banking tycoon, and served as a sophisticated retreat where he could entertain and hold magnificent banquets. After Chigi died in 1520, his business collapsed, the villa was abandoned and its statues, furniture and paintings sold. Fortunately, the best artworks – two loggias frescoed by Raphael – could not be moved.

Begin with the glassed-in Loggia of Cupid and Psyche, which was originally designed to resemble a pergola. Scenes from the love story of Cupid and Psyche appear on trompe l'oeil tapestries (look carefully and it is possible to see the fake

Fresco in the Loggia of Cupid and Psyche, Villa Farnesina

- ♿ **Wheelchair access** Yes
- 🍴 **Eat and drink** PICNIC Forno La Renella *(see Santa Maria in Trastevere, p187)*. REAL MEAL Da Giovanni *(Via della Lungara 41/a, 00165; 06 686 1514; closed Sun)*, a trattoria, offers dishes such as chickpea soup, pasta and wine – for the price of a snack
- 🛍 **Shop** The bookshop has an excellent guidebook to the villa (in Italian) for children
- 🚻 **Toilets** Yes

hooks) against an illusionistic sky framed by illusionistic ribs garlanded with foliage, fruit, vegetables and flowers. Although designed by Raphael, it was painted by his pupils.

The second one, the Loggia of Galatea, is named after the one painting that Raphael completed here – the famous *Triumph of Galatea*. It shows Galatea, a beautiful woman with strawberry-blonde hair streaming in the wind, as she rides the sea in a shell drawn by dolphins surrounded by Tritons and Nereids.

Above the door to the immediate left of this fresco is a portrait of the one-eyed giant, Polyphemus, sitting with his dog and gazing out to sea after having fallen hopelessly in love with Galatea. It was long believed that the blue drapes had been painted on after a woman was shocked by the giant's naked body. However, a recent restoration revealed that there was no body underneath the drapery.

The upper walls of the room are devoted to horoscopes, one of Chigi's main interests, while the panels on the ceiling depict the story of Perseus and Medusa as well as the story of the nymph Callista who was turned into a bear by Juno, and then into a constellation of stars by Jupiter.

Letting off steam

Stroll around the villa's formal garden, laid out in geometrical patterns with trees, box hedges and rose bushes, and across to its lawns, shaded by pines and cedars and overlooked by the glassed-in loggia.

⑦ Botanical Gardens

The perfect escape

Rome has a long history of gardens, dating back to the 13th century, when a garden of medicinal plants was cultivated within the walls of the Vatican. Since then, there have been several botanical gardens in the city, but it was only in 1883 that the University of Rome was given this permanent site – perfectly located between the Janiculum Hill and the Tiber – away from the chaos of the city.

The tranquil gardens contain more than 7,000 plant species from all over the world. Although peaceful,

lush, full of shade and perfect for a picnic or to get away from the heat, the gardens are not very well maintained – many of the fountains are dry and the greenhouses dilapidated. There is, however, plenty of space to run around, including an avenue of palms, a Japanese garden and a rustling bamboo grove.

Take cover

If it rains, make a dash for the **Villa Farnesina**, with its beautiful paintings and frescoes by Raphael and his pupils.

A fountain in the Botanical Gardens, at the foot of the Janiculum Hill

The Lowdown

- 🌐 **Map reference** 11 A6
- **Address** Largo Cristina di Svezia 24, 00165; 06 4991 7107; https://web.uniroma1.it/ortobotanico
- 🚌 **Bus** H, 8, 23, 271 & 280
- 🕐 **Open** Summer: 9am–6:30pm Mon–Sat; winter: 9am–5:30pm Mon–Sat. Hothouses: 9am–1:30pm Mon–Sat
- 💶 **Price** €16–36; under 6s free
- 🚩 **Guided tours** Book tours online via the website (free)
- 👫 **Age range** All ages
- ⏱ **Allow** 1–2 hrs
- ♿ **Wheelchair access** Yes
- 🍴 **Eat and drink** PICNIC (*see the Janiculum Hill, p191*). FAMILY TREAT La Scala in Trastevere (*Piazza della Scala 58, 00153; 06 580 3763; open daily*) is a friendly place offering excellent Mediterranean cuisine with a focus on fish and some meaty creations. For something truly special, try one of their truffle recipes
- 🚻 **Toilets** In the orangerie

Picnic under €25; **Snacks** €25–40; **Real meal** €40–80; **Family treat** over €80 (based on a family of four)

The Fontana dell'Acqua Paola on the Janiculum Hill

⑧ Fontana dell'Acqua Paola

From lake to fountain

Built into a wall like a miniature Trevi Fountain (see pp154–5), the Fontana dell'Acqua Paola is best visited at night, when it is illuminated and its marble columns – taken from the original St Peter's Basilica – and statues gleam with the light bouncing off its waters. The fountain's source is Lake Bracciano, to the northwest of Rome, connected to the city via an aqueduct built by Trajan in AD 109. In ancient times the water powered the many flour mills that existed in this area. Just below the fountain, on the other side of the road, are a flight of steps that lead to the Tempietto.

The Lowdown

- 🌐 **Map reference** 8 E2
  Address Via Garibaldi, 00153
- 🚌 **Bus** 44, 75 & 125
- 👫 **Age range** All ages
- ⏱ **Allow** 10 mins
- ♿ **Wheelchair access** Yes
- 🍽 **Eat and drink** PICNIC Forno La Renella (see p187) offers excellent bread and pizza – try the latter with just salt and oil, or with sausage and potato. Eat at the top of the steps leading down to San Pietro in Montorio. REAL MEAL Terrazza San Pancrazio (Via di Porta San Pancrazio 32, 00153; 345 403 5679) serves delicious aperitivo buffets and light dinner options, including sushi
- 👫 **Toilets** No

Take cover

If it starts raining, jump on to bus 125 or run down the steps that cut across the bends of Via Garibaldi to Trastevere and shelter in a café or visit **Villa Farnesina** (see pp192–3) or **Santa Maria in Trastevere** (see pp186–7).

⑨ San Pietro in Montorio and Tempietto

Temple within a church

Founded in the Middle Ages, San Pietro in Montorio is Rome's Spanish church, rebuilt by order of Ferdinand and Isabella of Spain at the end of the 15th century. It was decorated by some of the most outstanding artists of the time, including Giorgio Vasari.

Secreted away behind a gate in a tiny courtyard alongside the church is the Tempietto or "little temple". Possibly the most famous and certainly the most quintessential Renaissance building in Rome, the Tempietto was built by Bramante in 1501 on the site where St Peter was believed to have been crucified. It is a perfectly circular Doric temple, whose design and proportions adhere precisely to those laid down by the ancient Roman architectural writer, Vitruvius. His book, *De Architettura*, describing Roman buildings and building techniques, became the driving force behind the revival of Classical architecture during the Renaissance. The Tempietto was the first building to be based entirely on these principles.

The Lowdown

- 🌐 **Map reference** 8 E2
  Address Piazza San Pietro in Montorio, 00153; 06 581 3940
- 🚌 **Bus** 44, 75 & 125
- ⏱ **Open** San Pietro in Montorio: summer: 8am–noon & 3–4pm daily. Tempietto: 9:30am–12:30pm & 2–6:30pm Tue–Fri, 9am–3pm Sat
- 💲 **Price** Free
- 👫 **Age range** 9 plus
- ⏱ **Allow** 20 mins
- ♿ **Wheelchair access** No
- 🍽 **Eat and drink** SNACKS Il Baretto (Via Garibaldi 27/g, 00153; 06 589 6055; open daily) is a trendy bar that also serves warm dishes for lunch and aperitivos for dinner. FAMILY TREAT Antica Pesa (Via Giuseppe Garibaldi 18, 00153; 06 580 9236; closed Sun; www.anticapesa.it) creates traditional Roman food with a sophisticated twist, along with inventive dishes such as the lightly smoked prosciutto crudo (cured ham) served with a crunchy puff-pastry parcel filled with melting buffalo mozzarella. Desserts include chestnut millefeuille and tiramisu
- 👫 **Toilets** No

Letting off steam

Walk down to the **Villa Sciarra** (Via Calandrelli, 00153; open dawn–dusk daily). Shaded by trees and set on a hill above a steep valley, it is Rome's most romantic park. With a small children's playground, a scattering of follies and fountains, and an ornamental pond, it is the perfect place for a picnic on a hot summer day.

Bramante's Tempietto, the most famous Renaissance building in Rome

Top Formal gardens, Villa Doria Pamphilj
Above Umbrella pines in Villa Doria Pamphilj

⑩ Villa Doria Pamphilj

The perfect getaway

A vast expanse of rolling hills, lakes and ancient pines, this is the largest, and probably the most beautiful park in Rome and one of the few places in the city where, at times, it is possible to be out of earshot of traffic. Created as a summer retreat for the Doria Pamphilj family in the 17th century, the park comprises several villas, including the Casino del Buon Respiro, surrounded by formal gardens. Close to the entrance on Via Vitellia is a children's playground.

Take cover

Find shelter in Vivi Bistrot if it drizzles or rains for a short period of time. If the weather gets really bad, take bus 115 from Via di Porta San Pancrazio to the heart of Trastevere.

The Lowdown

🌐 **Map reference** 7 B3
Address Entrances at Via Aurelia Antica and Via Vitellia, 00165; 06 679 7323
🚌 **Bus** 115, 710, 870 & 984
🕐 **Open** dawn–dusk daily
💶 **Price** Free
👫 **Age range** All ages
👪 **Activities** Occasional child-friendly exhibitions at the Casa Dei Teatri within the park. Check www.060608.it for details
⏱ **Allow** 2 hrs
♿ **Wheelchair access** Yes
🍴 **Eat and drink** PICNIC DOC (*Via Fonteiana 28/a, 00152; closed Sun*) is the closest supermarket. Put together a picnic meal and eat it at the park. REAL MEAL Vivi Bistrot (*Via Vitellia 102, 00165; www.vivibistrot.com; open daily*) is a Provencal-style café-restaurant complete with a lavender garden. It is worth a visit for breakfast, brunch, lunch, tea, apéritifs or dinner. There are also kids' menus
🚻 **Toilets** At the Via Aurelia Antica entrance, by Vivi Bistrot and the playground in Doria Pamphilj

Vivi Bistrot, the restaurant in Villa Doria Pamphilj park

KIDS' CORNER

Nature's soundtrack

Walk into the middle of the park at Villa Doria Pamphilj and you will be in what is possibly the quietest spot in Rome. But how quiet is it really? Take a piece of paper and a pencil, close your eyes for five minutes and write down everything you can hear.

Circular buildings
Buildings that are circular like the Tempietto have always fascinated architects. Can you design a house in which everything is circular?

CAESAR'S GARDEN

Julius Caesar had a wonderful garden, which stretched right down to the banks of the Tiber, in the area where Villa Sciarra is today. It is said that Cleopatra was his guest here.

Floating mills

In ancient Rome, there were several mills on the Janiculum Hill, which were powered by water from Trajan's aqueduct. In AD 573, the Visigoths cut off all 14 of Rome's aqueducts, leaving the city without fresh water – and without mills to make flour to make bread. The mills were then moved down to the Tiber and rebuilt on rafts anchored to the pylons of bridges. These floating mills survived for centuries – the last were destroyed in the great flood of 1870.

Picnic under €25; **Snacks** €25–40; **Real meal** €40–80; **Family treat** over €80 (based on a family of four)

The Vatican

The residence of the pope since 1377 and one of the most impressive and monumental parts of Rome, the Vatican City became an independent state in 1929. Decisions taken here have long shaped the destiny of Europe and have affected the lives of Catholics throughout the world. The pope makes weekly addresses to the crowds here, while the great basilica of St Peter's and the magnficent collections of the Vatican Museums draw visitors from all over the world.

Highlights

Vatican City
Take a guided tour around the Vatican Gardens and then stop by the tower from which the Vatican's radio and TV are broadcast *(see pp202–203)*.

St Peter's
Climb up to the cupola of St Peter's to get a bird's-eye view of the Vatican and see Bernini's symmetrical colonnade *(see pp204–205)*.

Vatican Museums
Take an audiotour of the Vatican Museums and visit the spectacular Raphael Rooms *(see pp206–213)*.

Sistine Chapel
Crane your neck and try to solve the mysteries of the ceiling frescoes by Michelangelo in the Sistine Chapel *(see pp208–209)*.

Egyptian Museum
See mummies, mummy-cases and an ancient Egyptian nit-comb in the Vatican's Egyptian Museum *(see p212)*.

Castel Sant'Angelo
Let kids travel back in time as they explore the ramparts, prisons and the spectacular terrace, and imagine defending Rome from attack in Castel Sant'Angelo *(see pp214–15)*.

Above right View of St Peter's from Castel Sant'Angelo
Left Interior of Michelangelo's dome, lavishly decorated with mosaics and stuccowork, St Peter's

The Best of...
The Vatican

There is plenty to interest children in the Vatican, but the sheer number of things to see, combined with the crowds, can be overwhelming; the Cortile della Pigna and the green spaces outside the Vatican Museums' pizzeria are good places to rest, while Castel Sant'Angelo is another altogether less demanding destination, with plenty to fire imaginations, and space in the nearby Parco Adriano for children to play.

Weeping angels, chubby cherubs and divine superheroes

Kids will enjoy looking for angels and divine superheroes in the **Vatican City** (see pp202–203). Start with Bernini's angels – popularly known as the breezy maniacs – on the Ponte Sant'Angelo. Walk into **Castel Sant'Angelo** (see pp214–15) and spot angels everywhere – on the roof and on Segways outside giving out information to tourists. Find the bored, obese cherubs supporting Holy Water stoups by the entrance to **St Peter's** (see pp204–205) and a smiling baby on Bernini's baldacchino. Visit the **Vatican Museums** (see pp206–213) to see angels on rescue missions in *The Liberation of St Peter*, divine thief-busting superheroes in Raphael's *The Expulsion of Heliodorus from the Temple* and fragments of an angelic orchestra by Melozzo da Forlì in the Pinacoteca.

Right Bernini's colossal baldacchino, St Peter's **Below** Castel Sant'Angelo and the Ponte Sant'Angelo at night

The smallest country in the world

Follow the walls around the **Vatican City** to
see how small the state really is – it is fun to
time the walk, and the mathematically minded
can attempt to calculate the length of the
border with a pedometer. For good views of
Piazza San Pietro and the colonnades as well
as the rest of the state, climb to the cupola of
St Peter's – those who cannot face the steep,
narrow and invariably crowded staircase should
climb to the top of **Castel Sant'Angelo** and
look across to try to spot the Papal heliport and
railway station. The souvenir shop on **St Peter's**
roof sells postcards and Vatican City stamps,
which can be mailed from the adjacent
yellow postbox.

Money and power

The wealth and power of the papacy is clear
from the extravagant buildings and exquisite
works of art that it has amassed over the
centuries. When planning **St Peter's**, there was
no doubt in the minds of the popes and their
architects that it had to be the biggest church
in the world. In fact, it still is, with a volume
estimated at 1,200,000 cubic metres (42 million
cubic feet). There is ample evidence, too, that
the popes felt they could do whatever they
liked: Pope Urban VIII ordered the bronze roof
tiles of the **Pantheon** *(see pp122–3)* to be
melted down to create the *baldacchino* in
St Peter's, and Pope Julius II insisted that
Raphael paint over frescoes by the brilliant
Piero della Francesca in the suite that became
known as the **Raphael Rooms** *(see p211)*.

Sprint to the Sistine Chapel

For a chance to explore the **Sistine Chapel** *(see
pp208–210)* before it gets crowded, buy tickets
online for 9am when the museums open, but

*Above Piazza San Pietro flanked by Bernini's colonnades
Below A fresco and vaulted ceiling in one of the chambers in
the Raphael Rooms*

arrive even earlier to get to the front of the
queue. Then follow signs straight to the **Sistine
Chapel**, ignoring everything else and walk as
fast as is possible. This can be quite fun for kids
who like a challenge. Once inside, help children
discover the story of the Book of Genesis in
the central panels and let them search for
details – opera glasses or small binoculars will
be a huge help, or hunt for Michelangelo's
gruesome self-portrait in *The Last Judgment*.

Vatican City and around

The Vatican area is easily accessible on foot from the *centro storico* via the pedestrian Ponte Sant'Angelo, which leads to the Castel Sant'Angelo. A short walk away are the Vatican Museums and St Peter's. The area is also well served by buses, trams and metro Line A, which stops at Ottaviano San Pietro for the Vatican. Nearby, Via Ottaviano and Via Cola di Rienzo are major high-street shopping areas. The area is almost always busy – start your day before St Peter's opens to avoid the crowds.

The Vatican

Vatican Museums p206

Vatican City p202

St Peter's p204

Castel Sant'Angelo p214

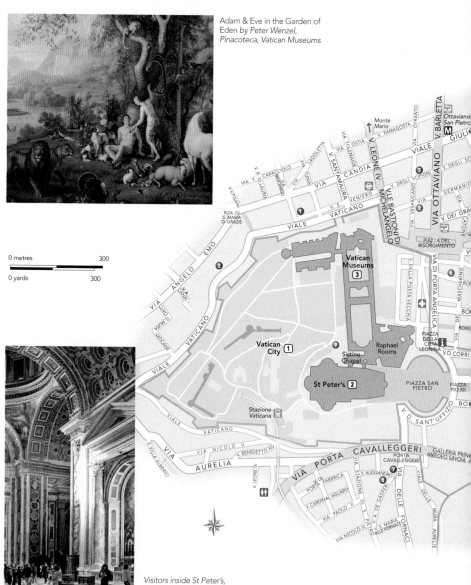

Adam & Eve in the Garden of Eden by Peter Wenzel, Pinacoteca, Vatican Museums

0 metres 300

0 yards 300

Vatican Museums **3**

Vatican City **1**

Raphael Rooms

Sistine Chapel

St Peter's **2**

Stazione Vaticana

Visitors inside St Peter's, dwarfed by its size

Places of Interest

SIGHTS
1. Vatican City
2. St Peter's
3. Vatican Museums
4. Castel Sant'Angelo

● **EAT AND DRINK**
1. Alimentari
2. Fa-bio
3. Er Sor Guido
4. Hostaria da Cesare
5. Franchi Gastronomia
6. Pizza Rosticceria Vecchio Borgo
7. De' Penitenzieri
8. Borgo Antico
9. Caffetteria Sistina
10. Coop Tirreno
11. Antico Caffè di Marte
12. Simposio

See also Vatican Museums (p207) & Castel Sant'Angelo (p215)

● **SHOPPING**
See St Peter's (p205)

● **WHERE TO STAY**
1. B&B Musei Vaticani
2. Vaticano 68
3. Gli Artisti
4. A Le Stanze di Frederica
5. A Roma San Pietro
6. Ted's Vatican
7. Alle Fornaci di San Pietro
8. Residenza Madri Pie

Bronze statue of an angel on the Terrazza dell'Angelo, Castel Sant'Angelo

The Lowdown

🚇 **Metro** Ottaviano San Pietro & Lepanto (Line A). **Bus** 23, 34, 40, 46, 49, 62, 64, 81, 87, 271, 280, 492, 926, 982 & 990. **Tram** 19

ℹ️ **Visitor information** Tourist Information Point, Largo del Colonnato 1, 00193; 060608; open 9am–6pm daily; www.turismoroma.it. Tourist Angels on Segways outside the castle

🛒 **Supermarket** Carrefour Express, Via Sebastiano Veniero 10a, 00192; open 8am–8:30pm daily

🎉 **Festivals** Festa di San Giuseppe (19 Mar): St Joseph's Day with an address by the pope. The pope presides over Mass in the basilica at Easter, Christmas & other major Christian festivals. Check www.tinyurl.com/ycku56v for the Vatican festival calendar

➕ **Pharmacy** Farmacia Vaticana: Via di Porta Angelica, 00193; 06 6988 9806; open 8:30am–6pm Mon–Fri & 8:30am–1pm Sat. An ambulance is always in attendance on Piazza San Pietro

🛝 **Nearest play area** Parco Adriano, below Castel Sant'Angelo

🚻 **Public toilets** Via Sergio I, 00165

① Vatican City
Miniature state

With an area of just 0.3 sq km (0.1 sq mile) and a population of 800 people, the Vatican City is the smallest country in the world. The borders of the state are marked by the walls that encircle the papal palaces and gardens, the colonnade that surrounds Piazza San Pietro and by a white line between the end of the piazza and the beginning of Via della Conciliazione. The Vatican has its own railway station, police force, heliport, post office, radio station and newspaper. Take a lift or climb stairs to the roof of St Peter's, the best place from which to view the whole of this tiny state.

Fountain, Piazza San Pietro

Key Sights

Vatican Railway Station The Vatican has the shortest national railway line in the world. Just 300 m (1,000 ft) long, it is used mostly for freight, and connects with the Italian railway network.

Papal Heliport

Radio Vaticana The Vatican's radio, TV and web TV are broadcast in 39 languages from this tower, part of the Leonine Wall built in AD 847.

Vatican Gardens

Obelisk The Egyptian obelisk in the centre of Piazza San Pietro originally decorated the Circus that Caligula and Nero had built on the land now occupied by the Vatican.

Vatican Museums (see pp206–13)

St Peter's (see pp204–5)

Sistine Chapel This chapel (see pp208–10), with its famous ceiling, is where cardinals convene to elect the new pope.

Papal Audience Chamber The pope meets with an audience here on most Wednesday mornings.

Apostolic Palace The pope appears on the balcony of the Apostolic Palace – his official residence – at noon on Sundays to give the gathered crowds his blessing.

Information office

Piazza San Pietro

Obelisk

Colonnades

Via della Conciliazione This straight boulevard, lined with shops selling religious souvenirs, was laid out by Mussolini as a symbolic link between the new Vatican state and Italy after the signing of the Lateran Pacts in 1929.

Vatican Gardens Vatican City has its own microclimate thanks to the fountains within the Vatican Gardens. The moisture from these fountains gets trapped by the huge St Peter's, making the area more humid and misty than the rest of Rome.

Piazza San Pietro Designed by Bernini and laid out between 1656 and 1667, the Piazza San Pietro is the narrow space in front of St Peter's, which opens out into an enormous ellipse flanked by 284 marble colonnades.

Prices given are for a family of four

The Lowdown

- **Map reference** 3 B5
  Address Vatican City, 00120
- **Metro** Ottaviano San Pietro (Line A)
- **Price** Vatican Gardens: €64–128; under 6s free (tours; includes entry to the Vatican Museums)
- **Skipping the queue** Visit Piazza San Pietro before 7am and see it minus the crowds. For St Peter's, *see pp204–5*. For Vatican Museums, *see pp206–13*
- **Guided tours** Vatican Gardens: 2-hr-long guided tours (Mon, Tue & Thu–Sat) in all major European languages; suitable for older children; not recommended for those who have difficulty walking

- **Age range** 8 plus
- **Allow** Piazza San Pietro and the Vatican walls: 1 hr
- **Wheelchair access** Through most of the museums and churches
- **Shops** There is a post office on the left side of Piazza San Pietro, and souvenir and postcard shops on the roof of St Peter's
- **Toilets** Public toilets on Piazza della Città Leonina

Good family value?
Families will enjoy a visit to the smallest country in the world and kids are bound to be fascinated by the fact that they can stand in two countries at the same time.

KIDS' CORNER

Water on the ropes!
The obelisk in the centre of the Piazza San Pietro was moved to its present position on the orders of Pope Sixtus V. A great crowd watched in silence as 900 men, with 150 horses and 47 winches, set about moving the obelisk – the pope had announced that he would execute anyone who made a sound. All went well until they began to haul the obelisk upright into its new position. The ropes were stretched so taut that they seemed ready to snap. Suddenly the words "Water on the ropes!" shattered the silence. The advice was followed and the obelisk was safely set into place.

154-PIECE SUIT
The pope is protected by an army of about a hundred Swiss Guards, who can been seen dressed in their ceremonial costume at the Vatican's gates. When a new tailor was appointed to the Vatican in 2006, he discovered that there was no pattern for the Swiss Guards' uniform. He and his wife took an old uniform apart in order to see how it had been made, and found that it was made up of 154 pieces!

Millennium babies
As part of the millennium celebrations in 2000, Via della Conciliazione's streetlamps were connected to Rome's maternity units on Christmas Eve. Every time a baby was born, the lights began to pulse slowly. A plaque set into the pavement on the left as you approach St Peter's records the event.

Tree-filled Parco Adriano, at the foot of Castel Sant'Angelo

Letting off steam
Run around the **Piazza San Pietro** or go to the playground in **Parco Adriano** below the Castel Sant'Angelo *(see pp214–15)*.

Eat and drink
Picnic: under €25; Snacks: €25–40; Real meal: €40–80; Family treat: over €80 (based on a family of four)

PICNIC Alimentari *(Borgo Pio 27, 00193; open 9am–2pm & 5–7:30pm, Mon–Sat)* sells bread and deli items and will make sandwiches. Eat in Parco Adriano.
SNACKS Fa-bìo *(Via Germanico 43, 00193; 06 6452 5810; closed Sun)* is a great sandwich bar with a large selection of sandwiches, wraps and juices, all prepared with fresh, organic ingredients.
REAL MEAL Er Sor Guido *(Borgo Pio 13, 00193; 06 687 5491; closed Sun)*, a tiny eatery with indoor and outdoor seating, offers made-to-order sandwiches as well as pasta dishes and main courses.

FAMILY TREAT Hostaria da Cesare *(Via Crescenzio 13, 00193; 06 686 1227; open daily)* is a lovely old-fashioned restaurant that serves Tuscan specialities such as *ribollita* (bean and cabbage soup with bread) and Chianina steak.

Find out more
DIGITAL For more information about the Vatican, check *www. vaticanstate.it*, which includes a virtual tour of the gardens and heliport, links to Vatican Radio and allows access to the webcams on the roof of St Peter's.
FILM *We Have a Pope* (2011) is an engaging film about a newly elected pope who is too beset by panic and doubt to take office.

Take cover
The colonnades offer ample shelter from the rain or hot midday sun. If the weather takes a turn for the worse, the nearest indoor sight is the **Castel Sant'Angelo** *(see pp214–15)*.

Next stop...
PILGRIMS' PROGRESS Follow the pilgrims' route in reverse – cross the Tiber at Ponte Sant'Angelo and walk up **Via dei Coronari** *(see p121)* to **Piazza Navona** *(see pp116–17)*. To make the walk fun for kids, get them to document their pilgrimage on a camera, and reward them with an ice cream in Piazza Navona.

② St Peter's
Bulletproof statue and ice cream on the roof

The centre of the Roman Catholic faith and the largest church in the world, St Peter's draws pilgrims from all over the globe. A 4th-century church marked the site where St Peter was martyred and buried, but in the 16th century Pope Julius II commissioned Bramante to replace the old church with a grand new basilica. The church took over a hundred years to build, cost the equivalent of £460 million in today's money and involved all the great Roman Renaissance and Baroque artists and architects – not only Bramante, but also Raphael, Bernini and Michelangelo. It was finally completed in 1626.

Key Features

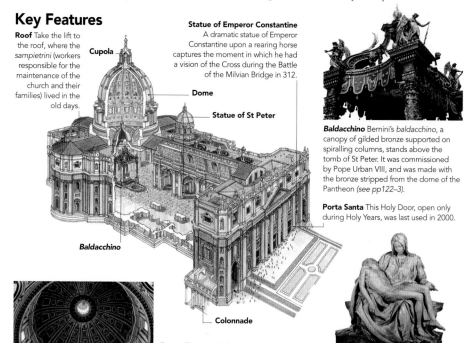

Roof Take the lift to the roof, where the *sampietrini* (workers responsible for the maintenance of the church and their families) lived in the old days.

Statue of Emperor Constantine A dramatic statue of Emperor Constantine upon a rearing horse captures the moment in which he had a vision of the Cross during the Battle of the Milvian Bridge in 312.

Cupola

Dome

Statue of St Peter

Baldacchino

Colonnade

Baldacchino Bernini's *baldacchino*, a canopy of gilded bronze supported on spiralling columns, stands above the tomb of St Peter. It was commissioned by Pope Urban VIII, and was made with the bronze stripped from the dome of the Pantheon (see pp122–3).

Porta Santa This Holy Door, open only during Holy Years, was last used in 2000.

Dome The spectacular dome was designed by Michelangelo. A broad ramp followed by a spiral staircase around the inside of the dome leads from the roof to the cupola, which offers stunning views over Rome and of Bernini's colonnade.

Pietà Michelangelo's sculpture of Mary holding the dying Christ stands in a chapel to one side of the nave. It has been protected by bulletproof glass since the 1970s, when a geologist attacked it with a pick.

The Lowdown

Map reference 3 C5
Address Piazza San Pietro, 00120; 06 6988 3145; www.vatican.va

Metro Ottaviano San Pietro (Line A). **Bus** 23, 34, 40, 62, 64, 81, 271 & 982. **Tram** 19

Open Basilica: 7am–7pm daily, till 6:30pm Oct–Mar. Dome: 8am–6pm daily, till 5:30pm Oct–Mar. Necropolis: by appointment only (06 6988 5318). Papal audiences: Wed am. Roof: 8am–5pm daily

Price Basilica, Necropolis and Grottoes: €26–52. Roof: €16–24 (lift), €12–18 (on foot); under 10s free. Treasury: €26–52 (not open to under 15s). Papal audiences and Masses: free; book in advance on the website

Skipping the queue Arrive early in the morning or at lunchtime. Those visiting for religious reasons should arrive early in the morning

Guided tours Audioguides (€5) focus more on religion than art.

Tours (€60–70; under 7s free) in Italian, English, Spanish, German and French

Age range 11 plus

Allow Roof: 1 hr; Basilica: 30 mins–1 hr

Wheelchair access Partial; to the basilica and roof

Café The café on the roof sells coffee, soft drinks and delicious ice cream

Pope Francis in St Peter's Square in Vatican City

Letting off steam

Play hide-and-seek in the shade of the colonnade on Piazza San Pietro. Then head for **Parco Adriano** *(see p215)* or go for a walk up the **Janiculum Hill** *(see pp190–91)*.

Eat and drink

Picnic: under €25; Snacks: €25–40; Real meal: €40–80; Family treat: over €80 (based on a family of four)

PICNIC Franchi Gastronomia *(Via Cola di Rienzo 200, 00193; www. franchi.it)* has a great deli counter and hot takeaway dishes. Eat at Parco Adriano.

Variety of ham and cheese on display, Franchi Gastronomia

Shops The shops in the piazza and on the roof sell souvenirs and postcards

Toilets On the roof

Good family value?
St Peter's is of far more interest to older children, although kids of all ages will enjoy going up to the roof, where they can eat ice cream and even drop off a postcard.

SNACKS Pizza Rosticceria Vecchio Borgo *(Borgo Angelico 9–13, 00193; closed Sun pm)* offers *pizza al taglio* and oven-baked pasta dishes.
REAL MEAL De' Penitenzieri *(Via dei Penitenzieri 16, 00193; 06 687 5350; closed Sun)* is ideal for lunch or an early dinner. Try the *pasta alla carbonara*, sausages or a frittata.
FAMILY TREAT Borgo Antico *(Borgo Pio 21, 00193; 06 686 5967; closed Sun)* serves *papalina* (potatoes baked with mushrooms, truffles and cheese), a favourite with Pope Benedict XVI, who used to eat here when he was a cardinal.

Shopping

Via della Conciliazione has many shops selling gawdy icons and other religious souvenirs. Follow humorous writer Bill Bryson's advice and buy a set of dinner plates stamped with a portrait of the pope.

Find out more

DIGITAL A virtual tour of the basilica is available on *www.vatican.va*. The website also offers a Vatican app for download.
FILM Certain movies featuring St Peter's, such as *Pope Joan* (1972) have not met with Vatican approval. However, the Vatican has published a list of movies it recommends at *http://en.wikipedia.org/wiki/Vatican's_list_of_films*, which includes some surprising choices, such as *2001: A Space Odyssey* (1968), *The Wizard of Oz* (1939) and *Fantasia* (1940).

Next stop...

VILLA BORGHESE If papal culture becomes too much to absorb, take the tram to Villa Borghese *(see pp168–9)*, a paradise for families.

KIDS' CORNER

Holy tour!
1 Look up inside St Peter's dome. It is 41 m (136 ft) across and 137 m (448 ft) high.
2 Look for the bronze markers in the floor showing the inferior length of other cathedrals – they are not accurate: Milan cathedral is 20 m (66 ft) longer than marked!
3 Kiss the foot of the bronze statue of St Peter to gain a 50-day indulgence (a discount on time served in purgatory, heaven's waiting room).
4 Bernini's colonnade was designed so that the wealthy could approach St Peter's in their carriages, sheltered from the weather.

St Andrew's snail
The staircase curling around the inside of the dome is known as the Lumaca di Sant'Andrea. Lumaca means "snail," and Andrea, or Andrew, was St Peter's brother.

HOLY OR UNHOLY?
Holy Years or ordinary jubilees are traditionally held every 25 or 50 years. However, the pope can announce one to mark a special event. These are known as extraordinary jubilees. The last jubilee was the "Great Jubilee" in the year 2000 – two millennia after the birth of Christ. The next Holy Year is not yet known.

Bearded queen
One of the few women to be buried inside St Peter's is Queen Christina of Sweden, who moved to Rome in 1655 after renouncing Protestantism and abdicating her throne. Her statue is very elegant, although it seems that she was not. According to an observer,

"She is exceeding fat... and she has a double chin from which sprout a number of isolated tufts of beard..."

③ Vatican Museums
Take a tour with an angel

With no fewer than 12 museums, the Vatican's complex of museums is the largest in the world and contains far more than any adult, let alone child, could absorb. The complex has two signposted routes – one takes in the most popular museums, including the Sistine Chapel and the Raphael Rooms, and the other everything else. The most enjoyable way to explore the museums is to rent a Family Audioguide, which has a series of narrator-guides ranging from a Melozzo da Forlì angel to Michelangelo. The museums also have excellent information boards in Italian and English.

Statue of Venus, Vatican Museums

Key Sights

Pinacoteca *(see p213)*

Entrance

Spiral staircase

Pio-Clementino Museum *(see p212)*

Egyptian Museum *(see p212)*

Room of the Animals
Roman mosaics decorate the walls and floors of this room, which is devoted entirely to sculptures of animals *(see p212)*.

Gallery of the Candelabra
Once an open loggia, this gallery of Greek and Roman sculpture has a fine view of the Vatican Gardens.

Cortile Ottagonale *(see p212)*

Cortile della Pigna

Gallery of the Maps

Sistine Chapel *(see pp208–210)*

Raphael Rooms *(see p211)*

Gallery of the Maps
The 16th-century maps of Italy's regions and papal territories displayed here were painted as if Rome was literally the centre of the world, with areas south of Rome such as Calabria and Sicily appearing "upside down".

Cortile della Pigna Named after a giant pine cone flanked by two bronze peacocks and dominated by the *Sphere within a Sphere* – a revolving bronze sculpture by Arnaldo Pomodoro – this beautiful courtyard is the most pleasant place to relax in between exploring the complex of museums.

Prices given are for a family of four

Spiral staircase This spectacular stairway leads down from the museum to street level. It was designed by Giuseppe Momo in 1932.

The Lowdown

🌐 **Map reference** 3 C4
Address Viale Vaticano, 00120;
06 6988 4947 (bookings);
mv.vatican.va

🚗 **Metro** Ottaviano San Pietro
(Line A). **Bus** 23, 49, 81, 492 &
990. **Tram** 19

🕐 **Open** 9am–6pm Mon–Sat (last
adm: 2 hrs before closing),
9am–12:30pm last Sun of the
month (last adm: 90 mins before
closing); visit the website for
updated information on night
opening hours

💶 **Price** €48–64; under 6s free.
Last Sunday of the month: free

👥 **Skipping the queue** Book in
advance online, and join the
separate queue on the ground
floor to pick up prebooked
tickets. There are seven booths
for buying tickets upstairs, and
queues move relatively quickly

🎫 **Guided tours** Yes; book on the
website. Audioguides (€7) available in eight languages

👫 **Age range** 8 plus

👫 **Activities** The Family Audioguide
(€5) takes visitors through a fun
treasure hunt

⏱ **Allow** 3–4 hrs

♿ **Wheelchair access** Yes

☕ **Café** In the Cortile della Pigna

🛍 **Shops** Several shops selling
books, Sistine ceiling jigsaws
and souvenirs are scattered
around the musuem

🚻 **Toilets** By the entrance hall,
café, Sistine Chapel, Raphael
Rooms & Cortile della Pigna

Good family value?
Entry is expensive, but if there is
even a flicker of interest from the
children, it is money well spent.

KIDS' CORNER

Can you find…
1 A bird pecking at
a dead rabbit?
2 Two bronze
peacocks?
3 An upside-down world?
4 The Popemobile?
5 An open mummy case
and mummy?

Answers at the bottom of
the page.

Museum stroll
If you visit every single
museum in the Vatican
Museum complex, you
will have ended up
walking over 7 km
(4 miles).

Letting off steam
Children can take a break in the
Cortile della Pigna, or in the green
area near the **Carriage Pavilion**,
although they cannot run wild here.
For that, leave the museums and
jump onto bus 23, which goes
straight to the wooded hills of the
**Monte Mario Nature Reserve and
Park** *(Via Gomenizza 81, 00195; 06
3540 5326; http://romanatura.roma.
it/i-parchi/r-n-monte-mario).*

Find out more
DIGITAL The official Vatican website,
www.vatican.va, offers a virtual tour of
the Sistine Chapel. When back home,
follow the instructions and photographs on *www.tinyurl.com/77boswp*
to make your own fresco.
FILM The *Michelangelo Code* (2005)
is a fascinating documentary by
Waldemar Januszczak on the hidden
meaning behind the frescoes on the
Sistine Chapel ceiling.

LAOCOÖNOMANIA
The *Laocoön*, on display in the
Cortile Ottagonale *(see p212),*
captured the Renaissance
imagination to such a degree
that it even became a fashion
item – Isabella d'Este, the
Marchesa of Mantua, ordered a
Laocoön logo for her hat.

Eat and drink
Picnic: under €25; Snacks: €25–40;
Real meal: €40–80; Family treat: over
€80 (based on a family of four)

PICNIC Alimentari *(see Vatican
City, p203).*
SNACKS Caffetteria Sistina *(Viale
Vaticano, 00120; same opening
hours as museums),* near the Sistine
Chapel, serves pastries, sandwiches,
soft drinks and coffee – perfect for a
quick bite.
REAL MEAL The Pizzeria in the
museum complex opens into the
garden near the Pavilion of Carriages,
and makes a good choice for an
easy lunch of pizza or salad.
FAMILY TREAT The Caffetteria, with
its terrace laid out in the Cortile della
Pigna, is a lovely place for a leisurely
lunch, afternoon tea or apéritif and
has space in the courtyard for
children to play while adults relax.

Interactive activities for kids at Explora,
Villa Borghese

Next stop…
CHILDREN'S MUSEUMS Take tram
19 to **Technotown** *(see pp178–9)* or
to **Explora** *(see p173),* the children's
museums in Villa Borghese.

Costly sphere
Arnaldo Pomodoro's
Sphere within a Sphere
was commissioned by
the Vatican in 1990 and cost €5
million. It is made of about the
same amount of solid bronze
that was used to create the orb
on the top of St Peter's. Sit down
and watch the changing
reflections of the statue's
surroundings as it rotates.

Answers: 1 On the mosaic floor of the
Egyptian Museum. **2** Flanking the
Room of the Animals. **3** In the Cortile della
Pigna. **4** In the Gallery of Maps. **5** In the
giant pine cone in the Cortile della
Pigna. **3** In the Gallery of Maps.

③ Vatican Museums continued ►

Vatican Museums continued...

Sistine Chapel Ceiling

In 1508, Pope Julius II decided that the ceiling of the Sistine Chapel needed repainting. The walls of the chapel were already covered with frescoes, but the ceiling was simply blue sprinkled with golden stars. Michelangelo spent the next four years painting 366 figures on the ceiling of the chapel, illustrating the biblical stories of the Creation of the World, the Fall of Man and the Coming of Christ. Julius was exasperated by how long Michelangelo was taking. "When will you finish?" he railed. "When I can," replied Michelangelo.

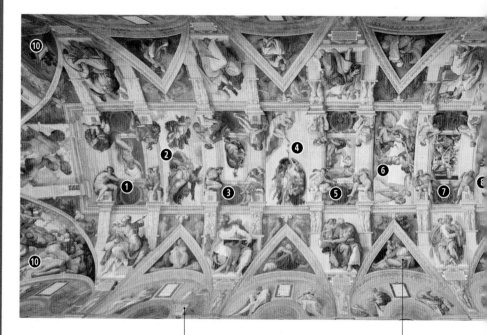

Lunettes Above each window in the chapel is an arched shape or lunette.

Spandrels The eight lunettes above the windows have triangular spandrels above them depicting various ancestors of Christ.

① **God Dividing Light from Darkness** Michelangelo represents God as a blurry figure barely emerging from the chaos – on one side of him is darkness, and on the other, light. According to Genesis, it was on the first day that God divided light from darkness.

② **God Creates the Sun and the Moon** A more defined God creates the sun with one hand and the moon with his other. A patch of green in the bottom left corner shows life beginning on earth.

③ **God Separates the Waters from the Land** God is shown pushing water away from land. According to the Bible, God created the sun and moon after he separated water from land.

Prices given are for a family of four

④ **Creation of Adam** God reaches down from a cloudy heaven to create Adam, who is shown lying on land, beside water.

⑤ **Creation of Eve** Eve is shown emerging from Adam's rib as he sleeps.

⑥ **The Fall of Man** This is a two-part story. In the first part, Eve is tempted by Satan – shown as a snake with the body of a woman – to reach for the forbidden fruit from the Tree of Knowledge. In the second half, Satan expels Adam and Eve from Paradise.

⑦ **The Sacrifice of Noah** This scene shows Noah sacrificing a sheep to God before the Great Flood. However, in the Bible, Noah's sacrifice was made after the Flood, not before. It is unclear why Michelangelo changed the order of the story.

⑧ **Flood** God, angry at human behaviour, floods the world. Michelangelo shows land occupying the same corner of the panel as it does in God Creates the Sun and the Moon and the Creation of Adam, maybe to emphasize that the world could be destroyed as well as created.

⑨ **Drunkenness of Noah** After the Flood, Noah became a farmer and planted a vineyard. In an episode whose significance remains obscure, Noah is shown getting drunk on the wine he has made.

The *Ignudi* No one knows who these athletic male nudes are.

⑩ **Old Testament Scenes of Salvation** During the Renaissance, certain Old Testament events and figures were considered to predict the Coming of Christ. In the four corners of the ceiling are Esther, Judith, David and Moses – all of whom had saved their people by killing an evil or monstrous enemy – a symbolic echo of Christ triumphing over evil.

⑪ **The Sibyls** The Sibyls, such as the Delphic Sibyl, were figures from pagan mythology, who had the power to see into the future. In the Renaissance, they were adopted by Christian artists and writers. The future these Christianized Sibyls could see was the Coming of Christ.

KIDS' CORNER

Candy-coloured fortune-tellers

Look up at the Prophets and Sibyls seated around the edge of the ceiling and imagine that their luscious shot-silk robes are really sweets and ice cream. Find out who is dressed in:

1 Strawberry and lime
2 Lemon and lime
3 Blackcurrant and orange
4 Strawberry and pistachio
5 Tangerine and apricot
6 Orange and lime

....

Answers at the bottom of the page.

Trust no one
Michelangelo decided to take no chances with his scaffolding – rather than trusting anyone else to build it, he designed it himself!

PROPHET OR PAINTER?

The despairing prophet Jeremiah is a self-portrait of Michelangelo, probably expressing the frustration he felt with the impatient and demanding Pope Julius II.

Fresh paint

Fresco means "fresh" in Italian. The fresco technique involves painting on wet plaster. Every day, a new area of fresh wet plaster was prepared. This area had to be covered in paint before it dried – Adam was painted in three days and his Creator in four. The artist left hogs' hair from his brushes and even the occasional mucky thumbprint embedded in the paint. He also took short cuts – Adam's eye is simply unpainted plaster.

....

Answers: 1 Persian Sibyl **2** Erythraean Sibyl **3** Prophet Ezekiel **4** Prophet Isaiah **5** Libyan Sibyl **6** Delphic Sibyl.

③ Vatican Museums continued ▶

Vatican Museums continued...

Michelangelo's famous The Last Judgment *on the Sistine Chapel walls*

Sistine Chapel Walls

The old and the new

The walls of the Sistine Chapel are decorated with frescoes by artists such as Botticelli, Perugino, Signorelli and Michelangelo's one-time teacher, Ghirlandaio. The Renaissance fascination with discovering parallels between the Old and New Testaments is clear from these frescoes – on one side are episodes from the life of Christ and on the other are scenes from the life of Moses. The first panels of these frescoes originally began with the Birth of Christ, and its Old Testament parallel, the Finding of Moses, but these were destroyed in 1536 to make room for *The Last Judgment*.

A key theme in the frescoes is the power of the papacy. Moses was both a spiritual and temporal leader of his people, so he was a convenient example for those who wanted to argue that the pope too should be both. The political message is further emphasized in a scene by Perugino, which shows Jesus handing over the keys of the kingdoms of both heaven and earth to St Peter.

The Last Judgment

Twenty-four years after he had finished the Sistine Chapel ceiling, Michelangelo was commissioned by Pope Paul III Farnese to create a fresco of *The Last Judgment* on the altar wall of the Sistine Chapel. It is a bleak, harrowing work, reflecting the pessimism Michelangelo himself felt at the time, showing the damned hurtling towards a putrid hell and the blessed being dragged up to heaven. Saints demand vengeance for their martyrdoms, and Christ is shown as an unusually pitiless figure, with the Virgin sitting helpless beside him. Michelangelo drew from Dante's *Inferno* – he shows the ferryman, Charon, pushing passengers off his boat with an oar into the fiery depths of hell.

The Council of Trent, responsible for deciding what was permissible in religious art, objected to the painting. One of the pope's own officers, Biagio da Cesena, thought it was disgraceful that Michelangelo had included so many nude figures, and declared that the painting was suitable not for a chapel but rather "for the public baths and taverns". Michelangelo retaliated by painting Cesena as Minos, judge of the Underworld, on the far bottom-right corner of the painting with donkey ears and in the grip of a coiled snake. Apparently, when Cesena complained to the pope, he said he could do nothing since his jurisdiction did not extend to hell. Michelangelo included a portrait of himself, too, in the fresco – his face can be seen on the flayed skin held by St Bartholomew.

The ferryman pushes damned souls into hell in The Last Judgment

Raphael Rooms
Thieves in the temple, Greeks in the bath

In 1508, Pope Julius II decided to have a suite of four rooms that had already been frescoed by artists such as Piero della Francesca, redecorated. Julius asked his favourite architect, Bramante, to recommend some new artists and, in 1509, after a long trial, Bramante suggested he call in a young artist named Raphael. The work took over 16 years and Raphael died before its completion.

Hall of Constantine
Raphael had very little to do with the paintings in this hall – most of the work was done by his pupils. As a result, they are not held in the same high regard as those in the other rooms. The theme is the triumph of Christianity over paganism, with the four main frescoes focusing on key moments in Emperor Constantine's life. These include the *Vision of the Cross* and *The Battle of the Milvian Bridge*.

Room of Heliodorus
The theme of the next room is divine intervention. *The Expulsion of Heliodorus from the Temple* shows two flying youths and a rider on a rearing horse felling Heliodorus, a thief, as he tries to escape after robbing a temple. The theme continues in the dazzlingly lit *Liberation of St Peter*, in which an angel is

shown freeing St Peter (Pope Julius) from prison. The chains depicted are now on display in the church of San Pietro in Vincoli (*see p96*), where Julius had been assigned as a Cardinal.

Room of the Segnatura
The first room to be painted was the Room of the Segnatura. The frescoes in this room effectively bring together Christian and pagan themes to celebrate a rather optimistic, and very typical, idea, drawing from the Renaissance – the ability of the intellect to discover the truth. The most famous of the frescoes is the *School of Athens*, in which the artist painted his contemporaries as Greek philosophers in a vaulted hall, somewhat like the Baths of Diocletian.

Room of *The Fire in the Borgo*
Pope Julius had passed away by the time work began on the Room of *The Fire in the Borgo*, and the theme was selected by his successor, Pope Leo X. The most famous fresco here is *The Fire in the Borgo*, which celebrates the miracle that took place in 847, when the-then pope, Leo IV, extinguished a fire in the quarters around the Vatican, by making the sign of the cross. Leo X considered the event to be a reflection of his own success in extinguishing the flames of the wars that had recently ravaged Italy. Consequently, the pope standing at the back of the painting with his hand raised was given Leo X's chubby face.

The Fire in the Borgo, *after which one of the Raphael Rooms is named*

③ Vatican Museums continued ▶

Vatican Museums continued...

Pio-Clementino Museum
Copycat sculptures

The Vatican's prize pieces of Greek and Roman sculpture form the nucleus of the 18th-century Pio-Clementino Museum. Most of these are Roman copies of famous, but lost, ancient Greek works. In the pavillions of the **Cortile Ottagonale** and surrounding rooms are sculptures considered among the greatest achievements of Western art. These include the dramatic and exciting *Laocoön*, a violently contorted Hellenistic work (3rd century BC) showing the Trojan priest, Laocoön, and his two sons struggling to escape from the writhing coils of a sea serpent. In contrast is the elegant, aloof

Laocoön, *one of the most famous sculptures in the Pio-Clementino Museum*

Prices given are for a family of four

Apollo del Belvedere, believed by Renaissance artists to be a paragon of physical perfection.

Opening straight off the courtyard is the **Room of the Animals**, which has a stone menagerie of beasts ranging from pigs and sheep to horses and lions, with an animal-themed Roman mosaic floor to match. Beyond this is the muscular *Belvedere Torso*, whose influence on Michelangelo can be seen in some of the mysterious *Ignudi* on the Sistine Chapel's ceiling. Fittingly, the collection also includes a Roman copy of the *Aphrodite of Cnidias* – considered to be the most perfect sculpture of a woman in existence.

Egyptian Museum
From the land of the Nile

As is evident from the number of obelisks in the city, all things Egyptian were extremely popular in ancient Rome. The collection in this museum consists chiefly of Egyptian antiquities brought to Rome to adorn buildings such as the Temple of Isis which once stood near the Pantheon (see pp122–3), Villa Adriana (see pp238–9) at Tivoli and the Gardens of Sallust to the southeast of the Villa Borghese park. The Canopus Serapeum, a temple from Villa Adriana, has been rebuilt here. Among the statues found in it are a bust of Isis, and a statue of Hadrian's lover, Antinous, as the god Osiris. In the

Top *Sculptures in the Room of the Animals* **Above** *Mosaic on the floor of the Room of the Animals*

hemicycle overlooking the giant pine cone of the Cortile della Pigna (which came from the Temple of Isis) are more statues of Isis, several of the lioness-goddess Sekhmet and baboon-god Bes, along with one of Caligula's sister, Drusilla, in the guise of the Egyptian Queen Arsinoe II.

More interesting are the Egyptian objects, which include gloriously painted mummy cases; a mummy with an exposed shrivelled face, hands and feet; several Canopic jars and finds from a tomb – pieces of bread, cereal grains, a pair of sandals and a nit-comb.

Transfiguration by Raphael in Room VIII at the Pinacoteca

Pinacoteca

From Fabriano to Pinturicchio

Many important works of art by Renaissance masters are on display in the 18 rooms of the Pinacoteca. The art collection in this gallery is unmatched by any other in the Vatican City, or for that matter, Rome. Exhibits include the beautiful 15th-century *Stories of St Nicholas of Bari* by Gentile da Fabriano. On display in Room II, this painting is of four episodes from the life of St Nicholas of Bari. One of these scenes shows the saint throwing golden balls through a window to three poor girls – two balls are on the bed, while the saint is shown aiming the third at a red sock that one of

the girls is removing from her father's foot – this started the tradition of hanging up stockings at Christmas.

Walk through to Room IV to see works of art by Melozzo da Forlì, including the fragments of a fresco of an orchestra of angels created by the artist around 1472. On the way, stop by Room III to see the gorgeous romantic Madonnas by the monks Filippo Lippi and Frà Angelico. Go to Room VI, devoted to the fabulous world of the Crivelli brothers – 16th-century Venetian artists who painted doll-like Madonnas, and created ornate frames carved with fruits to display them in.

Raphael has a whole room (Room VIII) dedicated to his work, the most arresting of which is *Transfiguration*, dominated by a stunning woman with lustrous red-gold hair who is thought to be La Fornarina, his love interest. The next room features a single, rare work by Leonardo Da Vinci. This is an unfinished *St Jerome*, showing an ancient, emaciated saint who went on a retreat to the desert with only a lion for company. Beyond, in Room X, is the *Vision of St Helena*, a painting by the 16th-century Venetian artist, Veronese. Veronese always set religious scenes in contemporary Venice, and Helena is no exception, dressed as a weary Venetian *contessa*, leaning heavily on the True Cross that she had discovered, according to legend, in the Holy Land. Introducing his usual note of realism, Caravaggio is represented in Room XII by the *Deposition*, in which two men heave Christ's slumped body from the cross as Magdalene weeps into a handkerchief and Mary looks on with quiet disbelief.

A portion of a fresco by Melozzo da Forli, Pinacoteca

④ Castel Sant'Angelo
Mausoleum, fortress and prison

A huge brick cylinder rising from the banks of the Tiber, Castel Sant'Angelo began life as a mausoleum for Emperor Hadrian. Since then it has played several roles: as part of a city wall, as a medieval citadel, as a prison and as a retreat for popes in times of danger. In summer, it is possible to follow the popes' Vatican escape route along a secret passageway. The most theatrical approach to the castle is from across the Ponte Sant'Angelo, a bridge adorned with marble statues of angels by Bernini.

Ponte Sant'Angelo and the castle

Key Features

The Treasury Part of the original Roman mausoleum, this circular room was used as a treasury in later centuries and then as a prison. From here a narrow staircase cut into the Roman walls leads to the roof.

Hall of Justice Giordano Bruno (see p130) was among those put on trial here. It now holds prisoners' chains and arms, including hand grenades and a collection of hollow glass and terracotta cannonballs.

Diametric Staircase Built by Pope Alexander VI, this staircase cuts right through the heart of the building.

Helicoidal Ramp This spiralling ramp (helicoid is Greek for "spiral") dates back to Roman times and was the entrance to Emperor Hadrian's Mausoleum.

Terrazza dell'Angelo

Sala Paolina

Hall of the Urns This chamber held urns containing the ashes of Hadrian, his wife and son, and was encased with precious marble.

Moat bridge

Sala Paolina This is one of a suite of rooms decorated for Pope Paul III Farnese, with illusionistic frescoes including one of a courtier entering the room through a painted door.

Historic Armoury The armoury, located on the second level, hosts a wide range of weaponry of the times, such as a 15th-century cannon, 17th-century armour and elaborate 16th-century pistols, their walnut handles inlaid with unique designs.

Terrazza dell'Angelo Peter Verschaffelt's large bronze statue of an angel, cast in 1752, rises from a base of travertine and dominates the Terrazza dell'Angelo.

The Lowdown

🌐 **Map reference** 4 E5
Address Lungomare Castello 50, 00193; 06 681 9111; www.castelsantangelo.beniculturali.it

🚇 **Metro** Lepanto (Line A). **Bus** 23, 34, 40, 46, 49, 87, 271, 280, 926, 982 & 990

🕐 **Open** 9am–7:30pm daily

💶 **Price** €20–30; EU under 18s free; under 6s free. First Sunday of the month: free. Prices vary for exhibitions. Check website for details

👜 **Skipping the queue** Visit at lunchtime, or buy a Roma Pass to enter via a special turnstile

🎧 **Guided tours** Audioguides (free) available in English, Spanish, Italian, French and German. Secret passageway: 8pm on summer evenings

👫 **Age range** 5 plus

🕐 **Allow** 90 mins

♿ **Wheelchair access** Partial; only up to the second level

☕ **Café** The café in the museum sells snacks and drinks

🛍 **Shop** The shop inside the museum sells books and souvenirs

🚻 **Toilets** By the entrance, in the café and in Parco Adriano

Good family value?
This is the only authentic castle in Rome and the prisons offer plenty of scope for adults and kids to let their imagination run free.

Prices given are for a family of four

Slide and swings in the playground at Parco Adriano

Letting off steam

There is space to play in the **Parco Adriano**, at the foot of the castle, where an ice-skating rink is set up in winter *(8 Dec–late Feb: 10am–midnight daily)*. Or skip across the pedestrianized Ponte Sant'Angelo spotting river boats on the way.

Eat and drink

Picnic: under €25; Snacks: €25–40; Real meal: €40–80; Family treat: over €80 (based on a family of four)

PICNIC Coop Tirreno *(Via Alberico II 3, 00186; closed Sun)* offers *pizza bianca, cornetti*, different types of cheese and *prosciutto*. Put together a picnic lunch and eat it in Parco Adriano.

SNACKS The Castel Sant'Angelo bar *(open during museum hours)*, with tables on the terrace, serves sandwiches and flavoured hot chocolate – try the delicious white hot chocolate, caramel hot chocolate and hazelnut hot chocolate.

REAL MEAL Antico Caffè di Marte *(Via del Banco di Santo Spirito 7, 00186; 06 6813 6546; open daily)* is a friendly bar, restaurant and pizzeria great for breakfast, or a hearty lunch of soup, pasta and beans followed by roast chicken and potatoes.

FAMILY TREAT Simposio *(Piazza Cavour 16, 00184; 06 3211 1131; closed Sun; www.pierocostantini.it)*, one of the finest places to eat in the city, boasts a very refined restaurant and a more relaxed wine bar. Gorge on the cheese, meat and sandwiches here.

Find out more

DIGITAL Go to *www.tinyurl.com/cacxve7* for links to a wonderful selection of medieval-themed and castle-defending online activities as well as a create-your-own-coat-of-arms game.

FILM Audrey Hepburn and Gregory Peck go dancing at a bar below the castle in *Roman Holiday*, and end up falling into the river as they fight off security men.

Next stop...

FROM GOD TO A GARDEN St Peter's *(see pp204–5)* and the Vatican City *(see pp202–3)* are close by. And a short walk across the river leads to the grand monument of **Ara Pacis** *(see p147)*. Alternatively, take the metro to Flaminio, or tram 19, to the Villa Borghese *(see pp168–9)*.

Visitors inside the enormous St Peter's basilica, Vatican City

Beyond the Centre

To the north and south of central Rome are interesting sights well worth exploring. Follow the atmospheric Via Appia Antica south from the Baths of Caracalla to the outskirts of the modern city and discover the evocative ruins of palaces, a circus and curious funeral monuments, half-hidden under creepers or in the shade of umbrella pines. To the north, MAXXI and the Auditorium Parco della Musica – both ground-breaking buildings – give a tantalizing taste of the Rome of the future.

Highlights

MAXXI
Take a walk through the astounding MAXXI – Rome's museum of 21st-century art – with an interactive audioguide on a Nintendo *(see pp222–3)*.

Catacombs of Priscilla
Explore the network of spooky tunnels and see the oldest known image of the Madonna and Child at the Catacombs of Priscilla *(see p225)*.

Via Appia Antica
Escape the city on foot – or hire a bike – and head out along the umbrella-pine-shaded Via Appia Antica *(see pp228–9)*.

Baths of Caracalla
Visit the extensive ruins of the beautiful Baths of Caracalla – ancient Rome's biggest baths complex *(see p230)*.

EUR
Wonder at the eerie streets of EUR, visit a giant model of 4th-century Rome in its Museo della Civiltà Romana, and stargaze in its Planetarium *(see p230)*.

Cinecittà si Mostra
Step behind the scenes at Italy's most famous film studios, where children can walk around a fake New York and ancient Rome *(see p231)*.

Above right Wildflowers among the lush greenery bordering the Via Appia Antica
Left Visitors in MAXXI, Rome's impressive contemporary art gallery

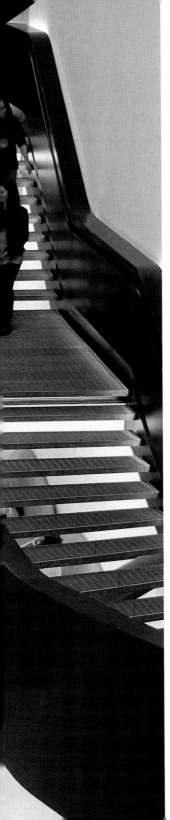

The Best of...
Beyond the Centre

Beyond Rome's centre there lies a fascinating miscellany of sights from parks, ruins and catacombs to experimental Fascist-era buildings and ground-breaking 21st-century architecture. Explore the nature reserve of Via Appia Antica, step behind the scenes at Cinecittà si Mostra and take a trip into the future at MAXXI and the Auditorium Parco della Musica, all of which are interesting as well as educational for children of all ages.

Ancient discoveries

Explore the brilliant **Baths of Caracalla** *(see p230)*, one of the most famous sights of ancient Rome – best approached by walking from the Colosseum *(see pp70–71)* and across the Celian Hill *(see p72)* to avoid traffic. Take advantage of the entrance ticket to the baths, which lasts seven days and includes entry to the **Tomb of Cecilia Metella** *(see p228)*. This, and the **Catacombs of San Callisto** *(see p228)*, the most extensive system of catacombs in Italy, are only a few of the barely excavated, atmospheric ruins along the **Via Appia Antica** *(see pp228–9)*. The **Parco della Caffarella's** *(see p229)* information office has maps plotting the monuments. In the north of Rome, the **Catacombs of Priscilla** *(see p225)* below **Villa Ada** *(see p225)* have a fresco that is thought to be the oldest representation of the Madonna and Child.

Right Relaxing in the grassy grounds of Villa Ada
Below The Tomb of Cecilia Metella, Via Appia Antica

Above Auditorium Parco Della Musica, a popular attraction for Roman families *Right* Zaha Hadid's MAXXI , a museum of contemporary art and architecture

Entertainment

MAXXI *(see pp222–3)* and the **Auditorium Parco della Musica** *(see p224)* have a rich programme of events for families throughout the year. Drop by the **Auditorium Parco della Musica** on a Sunday morning in winter for a family concert; let kids loose on the adjacent ice-skating rink after the show. Rent **MAXXI's** interactive Nintendo guide to the building and current exhibitions, likely to appeal to even the most uninterested kids. Seek out strange angles with a camera or sketchbook on the contemporary Ponte della Musica, the foot-bridge to the Mussolini-era sports complex, **Foro Italico** *(see p224)*. In summer, **Villa Ada** and the **Baths of Caracalla** are among the city's major music and dance venues.

The great outdoors

A day out along the **Via Appia Antica** on a Sunday, when cars are banned, can give the sense of getting far away from the city. The ancient road is actually part of the **Parco della Caffarella** nature reserve, which, apart from archaeological monuments offers more nature-oriented activities. Alternatively, **Villa Ada**, a vast sweep of wild wooded hills fringed with landscaped gardens, plus a playground and café, is an ideal destination when kids have had enough of sightseeing.

Visions of the future

While most people visit Rome for its ancient sites, medieval core and Baroque piazzas, fountains and churches, it can be refreshing to see how the city is still developing. Visiting Mussolini's model suburb of **EUR** is a little like walking around the set of an old-fashioned science fiction movie with sets designed by Surrealist artist Giorgio De Chirico – its rational, authoritarian buildings reduce human beings to Lilliputian proportions. Mussolini's sports arena, the **Stadio dei Marmi** *(see p224)*, on the other side of the city is a far more kitsch affair, surrounded by statues of muscled young ath-letes representing an ideal of Fascist youth. A far more egalitarian, even spiritual, vision of society permeates Rome's newest buildings – **MAXXI**, by avant-garde architect Zaha Hadid, and the **Auditorium Parco della Musica** by Renzo Piano.

MAXXI and around

Until the last decade, the area in northern Rome known as Flaminio – littered with vainglorious monuments erected by Mussolini in the late 1920s and 1930s – was something of an embarrassment to many Romans. However, in the last ten years, since the opening of the Auditorium Parco della Musica in 2002, it has become popular with both locals and visitors. The three main sights are within walking distance of each other, while to the east the residential district around Villa Ada and the Via Salaria – well off the tourist trail – is an ideal destination for days when children need to take it easy. Tram 2 makes access to the area straightforward.

View from the curved walkways, MAXXI

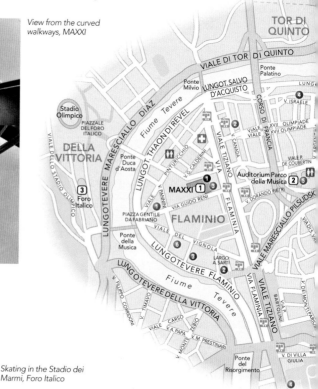

Places of Interest

SIGHTS
1. MAXXI
2. Auditorium Parco della Musica
3. Foro Italico
4. Catacombs of Priscilla

● **EAT AND DRINK**
1. Mercato Rionale Flaminio II
2. Pizzeria Salernitana
3. MAXXI21
4. Ristorante Pizzeria Popolo Caffè
5. ReD Restaurant & Design
6. Bar Due Fontane
7. Ada lo Scoiattolo
8. Locanda Filomarino

● **SHOPPING**
1. MAXXI

● **WHERE TO STAY**
1. Hotel Delle Muse
2. Hotel Astrid
3. A Casa di Lia
4. La Casa di Momi

Skating in the Stadio dei Marmi, Foro Italico

The Lowdown

🚗 **Getting there** Ottaviano San Pietro (Line A), then bus 32 to MAXXI. **Bus** 32, 63, 69, 86, 92, 186, 224, 271, 280 & 312. **Tram** 2 from Via Flaminia

🚢 **Markets** Mercato Rionale Flaminio II, Via Guido Reni, near the Ponte della Musica; daily am

🎪 **Festivals** Roma Incontra il Mondo (Jun & Jul), music festival in Villa

Ada. International Tennis Championship (mid-May), at Foro Italico. International Film Festival (late Oct–Nov), at the Auditorium Parco della Musica. Rome Jazz Festival (Nov), at the Auditorium Parco della Musica

➕ **Pharmacies** Sbarigia: Viale Pinturicchio 19/a, 00196; 06 323 1385; open 8:30am–8pm Mon–Sat. Farmacia Tagliavini:

Via di Priscilla 77, 00199; 06 8621 9999; open 4–7:30pm Mon–Sat

🎯 **Nearest play areas** Villa Ada

🚻 **Public toilets** Piazza Mancini, near MAXXI. Viale Pietro de Coubertin, near Auditorium Parco della Musica. Via di Ponte Salario, inside Villa Ada

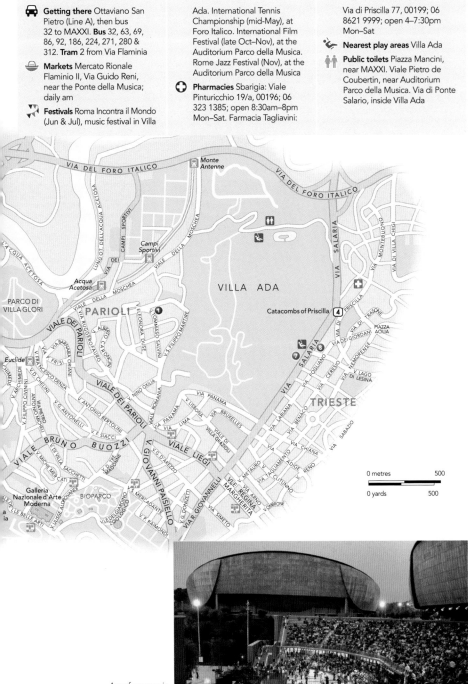

A performance in progress at the Auditorium Parco della Musica

① MAXXI

Virtual futuristic building made concrete

Built in a complex of disused barracks in the north of Rome, MAXXI was designed by the Iraqi architect Zaha Hadid. It presents a permanent collection of 20th- and 21st-century architectural drawings and models, specially commissioned photography, and contemporary art in a series of concurrent thematic exhibitions that change frequently. To make visits more stimulating for children, MAXXI has developed an interactive guide to the building and its exhibitions on a Nintendo DSi XL portable console.

The Overhang, MAXXI

Key Features

Reception desk A slanting curl of white resin, the reception desk has been likened to a distorted marrow bone, a ear and a comma. Let children look at it from the walkway above, and draw their own conclusions.

Stairways and walkways The free-standing stairways and pedestrian flyovers are illuminated, suggestive of a transport system for a futuristic city.

Glass ceiling The ceiling, together with an ingenious system of movable grilles, glass panels and concrete fins, fills the building with natural light while filtering out the fierce heat and glare of the midday sun.

The Overhang The most dramatic feature of MAXXI is a gravity-defying dramatic overhang, like a bridge that has never been completed. Windows reflect the original barracks and adjacent buildings, as if creating a virtual and symbolic link between the past and the present.

Lights Lighting in MAXXI is provided by a series of short, straight hollow red tubes of carbon fibre, suspended at abrupt angles in the atrium.

Atrium The polished cement floor in the atrium reflects the colours of the surrounding buildings. Notice how the walls slope back on themselves, and how the floors curve up to meet them, without a joint.

Video room Short art films and videos are screened for free in this small cinema on the ground floor.

Original barracks Hadid decided to retain two of the original barracks buildings in the complex – one of them houses the museum's restaurant, the other the Carlo Scarpa photography exhibition space.

The Lowdown

🌐 **Map reference** 1 C3
Address Via Guido Reni 4A, 00196; 06 320 1954; *www. fondazionemaxxi.it*

🚋 **Tram** 2 to Flaminia/Reni

🕐 **Open** 11am–7pm Tue–Fri & Sun, 11am–10pm Sat

💶 **Price** €24–48; under 14s free

👪 **Skipping the queue** Queues are most likely on Saturdays and Sundays, and in the first days of a new exhibition; book in advance via the website or call 892234

🚩 **Guided tours** Audioguides (€5) for adults and the MAXXI Pixel

Nintendo interactive audioguide (free with every adult audioguide rental; otherwise €5) are available in English and Italian. Tours are organized in several languages on various themes; check the website or call 06 3996 7350

👫 **Age range** All ages

🏃 **Activities** Book readings and art classes among others; book on 06 3996 7350 or online

⏱ **Allow** 2–3 hrs

♿ **Wheelchair access** Yes

🍽 **Café** MAXXI21 is a pleasant café with seats outside, with another branch inside the atrium

🛍 **Shop** A tempting array of books for kids and adults on contemporary art and design, along with stylish souvenirs, are available in the shop on the ground floor

🚻 **Toilets** On the ground, second and third floors

Good family value?
Stunning architecture, huge galleries, and mind-blowing display techniques in exhibitions, to say nothing of the Nintendo guides, make MAXXI one of the most family-friendly attractions in Rome.

Above *Ice-skating, Auditorium Parco della Musica* **Left** *Children cycling outside MAXXI*

with a wide selection of starters, firsts and seconds laid out for diners to help themselves.
FAMILY TREAT Ristorante Pizzeria Popolo Caffè (*Via Flaminia 9/11, 00198; 06 321 2573*) serves Roman classic and thin-crusted pizza and delicious *spaghetti alla carbonara*. It also has a good-value-for-money tourist menu.

Letting off steam

There is plenty of space outside MAXXI between the main building and the barracks housing MAXXI21. In winter, go ice-skating at the **Auditorium Parco della Musica** (*see p224*) nearby. Alternatively, go for a walk on the path along the Tiber – best accessed, while finishing touches are being added to the Ponte della Musica, from the Ponte Duca d'Aosta, a little futher upstream.

Eat and drink

Picnic: under €25; Snacks: €25–40; Real meal: €40–80; Family treat: over €80 (based on a family of four)

PICNIC Mercato Rionale Flaminio II (*Via Guido Reni, 00196; open daily*) is a lovely neighbourhood market. Buy fruit, vegetables, fresh bread, ham, salami and cheeses and eat on the benches on Piazza Gentile da Fabriano. Finish with a delicious ice cream from **Neve di Latte** (*Via Poletti 6, 00196; closed Tue*).
SNACKS Pizzeria Salernitana (*Piazza Grecia 3, 00196; 06 9970 9040; closed Sun*) is an excellent pizzeria that sells pizza by the slice, fried snacks such as *supplì* and zucchini flowers, as well as desserts.
REAL MEAL MAXXI21 (*inside MAXXI grounds*) offers seating indoors and outdoor. The best-value meal here is the buffet lunch

Find out more

DIGITAL Look at the floor plans of MAXXI at *www.tinyurl.com/8a7pmuo*. There are great photos and digital drawings of MAXXI at *www.tinyurl. com/82vnr3x*.

Next stop...

CONTEMPORARY ARCHITECTURE To see more contemporary and modern art, as well as contemporary architecture, head to **MACRO** (*see p179*).

An interior view of the contemporary MACRO arts centre

Cracking great architecture
A new and specially patented kind of concrete had to be developed for MAXXI that was especially strong and flexible, with a smooth, satiny texture – nevertheless cracks developed. Architects discovered that the solution was to pour the concrete at night in summer, so that it had time to set before it dried out in the sun.

2 Auditorium Parco della Musica
Music and more

Designed by Renzo Piano and opened in 2002, the Auditorium Parco della Musica – a subtle building complex so integrated with its surroundings that it is almost invisible from a distance – has become a favourite with Romans. Piano studied acoustics with contemporary composers such as Pierre Boulez, Luciano Berio and Luigi Nono while designing the complex. Stepping inside one of the auditoriums can feel like a voyage into the interior of a musical instrument thanks to its complex geometries and use of fine wood.

Piano's vision was not merely to create a concert venue, but a multi-purpose space, with an outdoor amphitheatre, shops and restaurants. Families flock here for the Sunday-morning children's concerts, ice-skating and free exhibitions, or to let children ride scooters or rollerblade in the amphitheatre. Take a guided tour of the fabulous concert spaces, or a casual walk around the interior, which is punctuated by neon signs beaming a selection of aphorisms in several languages that will get older children thinking.

Letting off steam
There is plenty of space outside the concert hall, but for a greener alternative the **Villa Glori** park (*Viale Maresciallo Pilsudski, 00197; open dawn to dusk daily*) is just a short walk away.

Statues in the Stadio dei Marmi, Foro Italico

3 Foro Italico
Kitsch Olympic bid

Mussolini built the Foro Italico sports complex in the hope of following in the footsteps of Hitler and snaring the Olympic Games. Its original name, Foro Mussolini, was changed after he died, but a huge obelisk inscribed with the words "Mussolini Dux" has survived. The stadium, **Stadio dei Marmi**, is surrounded by 60 colossal travertine statues of athletes, each donated by one of the 60 Italian provinces and sculpted by unknown young sculptors. The running track in the centre is open for public use – people even walk their dogs here!

Letting off steam
Kids will enjoy a run around the stadium, and could even stage a mini-Olympics.

The Lowdown

- 🌐 **Map reference** 1 D3
  Address Viale Pietro de Coubertin 30, 00196; 06 802 41281 or 06 808 2058; www.auditorium.com
- 🚋 **Tram** 2 to Piazza Apollodoro
- 🕐 **Open** 11am–8pm Mon–Sat, 10am–8pm Sun
- 🎫 **Price** Children's concerts: €52–62
- 🎫 **Skipping the queue** Book in advance on website for concerts and events
- 🎧 **Guided tours** Hourly tours (€28 for a family) of the concert spaces from 11:30am–4:30pm
- 👫 **Age range** All ages
- 🎨 **Activities** Kids' activities include

trying out musical instruments; check website for details
- ⏱ **Allow** 1–2 hrs
- ♿ **Wheelchair access** Yes
- 🍴 **Eat and drink** PICNIC *(see MAXXI, p223).* FAMILY TREAT ReD Restaurant & Design *(Viale Pietro Coubertin 12–16, 00196; 06 8069 1630; open daily)* inside the auditorium offers a children's menu on Saturdays and Sundays. On weekdays choose between small portions on plates priced as per their colour
- 🛍 **Shop** There is a bookshop on the ground floor
- 🚻 **Toilets** On the ground floor

The Lowdown

- 🌐 **Map reference** 1 A4
  Address Piazza Lauro de Bosis, 15, 00135; 06 36851
- 🚌 **Bus** 32, 69, 186, 224, 271 & 280
- 👫 **Age range** All ages
- ⏱ **Allow** 30 mins
- ♿ **Wheelchair access** Yes
- 🍴 **Eat and drink** PICNIC Mercato Rionale Flaminio II *(see MAXXI, p223).* SNACKS Bar Due Fontane *(Piazza Perin del Vaga 13, 00196; closed Sun)* is a café serving delicious light lunches, including many vegan options. Try one of their fresh fruit juices, soups and falafel sandwiches
- 🚻 **Toilets** No

Outdoor concert amphitheatre, Auditorium Parco della Musica

④ Catacombs of Priscilla

Queen of catacombs

The 1st-century AD Catacombs of Priscilla extend for 15 km (9 miles) in tunnels on three different levels below the country estate of an aristocratic Roman woman, Priscilla. Rarely visited, the catacombs are run by Benedictine Sisters and hold the tombs of around 40,000 Christians.

Take a guided tour to see several frescoed tombs belonging to wealthy families, contrasting with the simple burial places of the poor, which are simply sealed with a slab of stone or terracotta. The guide will point out *lucernari* – light shafts, which also allowed workers to climb in and take excavated soil and stone out – and little niches in which perfumed oil was burned to mask the smell of decaying corpses. These catacombs contain the oldest known image of the Madonna and Child, a fresco thought to date back to the late 1st or early 2nd century AD. Although the tombs were heavily plundered after their rediscovery in the 16th century, they are known as the "queen of catacombs" for the number of early Christian martyrs that were buried here.

Letting off steam

Villa Ada *(Via Salaria 265, 00199; 060608; www.060608.it)* is one of Rome's loveliest parks, with a pleasant playground with endless wooded hills to explore in the centre and picnic tables near the entrance on Via Salaria, and another in the valley by the lake.

Above *The beautiful lake Como, Villa Ada* **Below** *Early Christian fresco, Catacombs of Priscilla*

The Lowdown

🌐 **Map reference** 2 H1
Address Via Salaria 430, 00199; 06 8620 6272; www.catacombepriscilla.com

🚌 **Bus** 63 from Piazza Venezia; 86, 92 & 310 from Stazione Termini to Piazza Acilia

🕑 **Open** 9am–noon & 2–5pm Tue–Sun

💶 **Price** €26–32; under 6s free

🎫 **Guided tours** Visits by guided tours only; tours in Italian, English, German, French, Spanish and Japanese

👫 **Age range** 8 plus

⏱ **Allow** 45 mins

🍽 **Eat and drink** SNACKS Ada Lo Scoiattolo *(Via Salaria 273, 00199; 7:30am onwards daily)* in Villa Ada offers sandwiches, salads, ice creams and simple pasta dishes. FAMILY TREAT Locanda Filomarino *(Via di Filomarino 7, 00199; 06 8621 1815; closed Mon)* serves spaghetti with prawns and courgette, risotto with courgette flowers, saffron and prawns, or tagliatelle with octopus, wild chicory and pecorino

🛍 **Shop** Postcards are available at the shop near the entrance

🚻 **Toilets** Near the ticket office

Picnic under €25; **Snacks** €25–40; **Real meal** €40–80; **Family treat** over €80 (based on a family of four)

Via Appia Antica and around

Although it is not far from the Baths of Caracalla to the start of the Via Appia Antica at Domine Quo Vadis, the absence of pavements along traffic-heavy roads makes for an unpleasant walk, apart from on Sundays, when traffic is banned. On other days it is best to catch bus 118 as far as Domine Quo Vadis and the Parco della Caffarella office and then walk through the grounds of the San Callisto catacombs until the road gets more peaceful near the Tomb of Cecilia Metella. Cinecittà and EUR are both effortlessly reachable by metro from the centre. Since most of the sights in this area are not close to any good food shops, it is better to pick up picnic supplies before leaving the centre.

Beyond the Centre

MAXXI
p222

Central Rome

Via Appia Antica

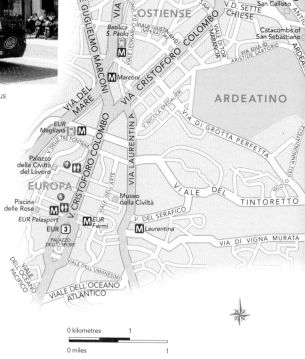

Passengers onboard a City Sightseeing tourist bus

Places of Interest

SIGHTS
1. Via Appia Antica
2. Baths of Caracalla
3. EUR
4. Cinecittà si Mostra

EAT AND DRINK
1. Alimentari
2. Il Giardino di Giulia e Fratelli
3. Qui Nun Se More Mai
4. L'Archeologia
5. Da Priscilla
6. Simply Market SMA
7. Caffè Palombini
8. Illy Caffè
See also Cinecittà si Mostra (p231)

SHOPPING
See Cinecittà si Mostra (p231)

0 kilometres   1

0 miles   1

Above Porta San Sebastiano, at the start of Via Appia Antica
Below Façade of the Museo della Civiltà Romana in EUR

The Lowdown

🚗 **Metro** Cinecittà (Line A), EUR Fermi & Circo Massimo (Line B). **Bus** 118, 218 & 660 from Via Appia Antica

ℹ️ **Visitor information** Park Office, Via Appia Antica 58, 00179

🧺 **Supermarkets** TuoDí, Via Annia 18, 00184. Emmepiù, Viale Aventino 88, 00153
Markets Street market, Via dei SS Quattro, Celian Hill; weekdays am

➕ **Pharmacy** Farmacia Santa Sabina: Viale Aventino 78, 00153; 06 574 3623; open 8am–7:30pm Mon–Fri, 8:30am–1pm Sat

🧗 **Nearest play areas** Parco degli Scipioni, Via di Porta Latina, 00179. Parco della Caffarella (see p229)

🚻 **Public toilets** Piazza Zama; Piazzale dell'Agricoltura; Piazzale Nervi

The picturesque Via Appia Antica

① Via Appia Antica
An ancient Roman motorway

Begun in 312 BC, the 560-km (300-mile) long Via Appia connected the Circus Maximus to the southern port of Brindisi on the Adriatic coast. Rome's first major road, its main purpose was to transport the soliders and military supplies needed to conquer southern Italy, but it also found another use: burials were forbidden within the city walls and it was soon lined with tombs, funeral monuments and catacombs. The best day to walk or cycle along the Via Appia Antica is Sunday, when cars are banned.

Detail on a sarcophagus

Key Sights

① Tomb of Geta This tomb was probably made for Emperor Septimius Severus's son Geta, who was killed by his brother Caracalla in AD 212. The tower above it was built in the 16th century.

② Domine Quo Vadis Inside this little church is a slab of marble with what are said to be the footprints made by St Peter when he was fleeing Rome to avoid crucifixion.

③ Catacombs of San Callisto Over half a million people were buried in these catacombs. The most famous tomb is that of Santa Cecilia, marked with a replica of the sculpture made by Stefano Maderno after the saint's intact body was found here in 1599 *(see p189)*.

④ The Palace and Circus of Emperor Maxentius The red-brick ruins of a palace and circus are visible from the road. The circus had room for 10,000 spectators.

⑤ Catacombs of Domitilla St Peter's fictional daughter, Petronilla, was buried in this catacomb. Next to it is a small burial chamber with a fresco showing Petronilla and a rich Roman woman, Veneranda, entering paradise together.

⑥ Catacombs of San Sebastiano At the entrance to these catacombs is a *triclinium*, where mourners were served refreshments after funerals. Its walls are covered with graffiti praising SS Peter and Paul.

⑦ Tomb of Romulus Located in the Circus of Maxentius, this was probably where Valerius Romulus, Maxentius's son, was buried.

⑧ Tomb of Cecilia Metella Carved with bulls' heads and fruit, this tomb was converted into a fortress by the Caetani family, who used it to demand a toll from travellers.

⑨ Capo di Bove Beyond Cecilia Metella, the road is quiet, shaded by pines and cypresses and lined by monuments, and retains much of its original paving.

The Lowdown

🌐 **Address** Catacombs of San Callisto: Via Appia Antica 126, 00179; 06 5130 1580; www.catacombe.roma.it. Catacombs of Domitilla: Via delle Sette Chiese 282, 00147; 06 511 0342; www.domitilla.info. Catacombs of San Sebastiano: Via Appia Antica 136, 00179; 06 785 0350; www.catacombe.org. Tomb of Cecilia Metella: Via Appia Antica 161, 00179; 06 3996 7700 or 060608; www.archeoroma.beniculturali.it. Parco della Caffarella office: Largo Tacchi Venturi, 00179; www.caffarella.it

🚌 **Bus** Catacombs of San Callisto: 118 & 218. Catacombs of Domitilla: 218 & 716. San Sebastiano: 118 & 218. Cecilia Metella: 660

🕐 **Open** Catacombs of San Callisto: 9am–noon & 2–5pm Thu–Tue. Catacombs of Domitilla: 9am–noon & 2–5pm Wed–Mon. Catacombs of San Sebastiano: 10am–5pm Mon–Sat, closed mid-Nov–mid-Dec. Tomb of Cecilia Metella: 9am onwards daily, closing time varies. Parco della Caffarella: 9am–5:30pm Mon–Sat, till 4:30pm in winter;

all catacombs closed Christmas, 1 Jan, Easter and religious holidays

💰 **Price** Catacombs of San Callisto: €26–32; under 6s free. Catacombs of Domitilla: €26–32; under 6s free. Catacombs of San Sebastiano: €26–32; under 6s free Tomb of Cecilia Metella: €22–32 (included in the entry to Baths of Caracalla); under 18s free

🧍 **Skipping the queue** Queues are unlikely

🚩 **Guided tours** Visits by guided tours only; tours every 30 mins

Via Appia Antica and the wooded landscape of Parco della Caffarella

Letting off steam

Part of the protected **Parco Regionale dell'Appia Antica** (*Parco Regionale dell' Appia Antica, 00179; 06 513 5316; www.parcoappiaantica. it*), the **Parco della Caffarella** is more open countryside than park, with plenty of space to run around. The park office (*see opposite*) rents out bikes, including children's bikes (€3) and toddler seats (€15). On Sundays, there are often events for children, including nature trails, insect-spotting and bird-watching.

Eat and drink

Picnic: under €25; Snacks: €25–40; Real meal: €40–80; Family treat: over €80 (based on a family of four)

PICNIC Alimentari (*Via Appia Antica 210, 00178; closed Sun*), not far beyond the Tomb of Cecilia Metella, near the bus 660 stop, is the only shop selling provisions along the road. Picnic in the open spaces of Parco della Caffarella.
SNACKS Il Giardino di Giulia e Fratelli (*Via Appia Antica 176, 00179; 347 509 2772; closed Mon*) is a

grassy playground with a café. There is usually a hot dish of the day, such as lasagne, as well as toasted sandwiches, pastries and ice creams.
REAL MEAL Qui Nun Se More Mai (*Via Appia Antica 198, 00178; 06 780 3922; closed Sun pm & Mon*) is a great family-run trattoria, known for its wood-fire grilled steaks, baked potatoes and four-cheese pasta.
FAMILY TREAT L'Archeologia (*Via Appia Antica 139, 00178; 06 788 0494; open daily*) is an elegant choice for delicious, refreshingly original dishes such as fettuccine with wild fennel and fillet of grouper fish, or spaghetti with courgette, prawns, fresh tomato and basil.

Find out more

DIGITAL www.learn4good.com/games/simulation/timemanagement. htm is an online game in which kids build their own Roman road in a race against time, Caesar and Barbarians. Go to www.youtube.com/watch?v=T_cLnMwbl_8 for an intriguing video on how Roman roads were built.

Take cover

If it rains or gets too hot, take shelter in one of the many catacombs that line the road.

Next stop...

MUSEO DELLE MURA Children with a keen interest in the defences, roads and bricklaying techniques of Rome should visit the Museo delle Mura (*Via di Porta San Sebastiano 18, 00100; 060608; www.museo dellemuraroma.it*), housed inside the Porta di San Sebastiano in the Aurelian Walls, at the beginning of Via Appia Antica.

Age range All ages

Allow 4–5 hrs

Café There are vending machines at San Callisto

Shops There are shops and stalls selling souvenirs at all catacombs

Toilets At all the catacombs

Good family value?
Via Appia Antica is perfect for a family outing – carry a picnic lunch and the only expense will be the entry fee to the catacombs.

KIDS' CORNER

Treasure hunt
Pick up a map from the Parco della Caffarella office and, starting at the Tomb of Cecilia, see if you can find...
1 The Torre Capo di Bove
2 A Roman hero wearing a cape
3 The ruined temple of Jupiter
4 A tomb with five portraits
....
Answers at the bottom of the page.

Appia Express
When the Via Appia was completed in the 1st century AD, it was possible to get from Rome to Brindisi in 13 or 14 days. Today, it takes six and a half hours to drive through.

KATA KYMBAS
The word catacombs comes from the Greek *kata kymbas*, which means "near the cave".

Domine Quo Vadis?
According to Christian legend, St Peter fled Rome, hoping to escape death by crucifixtion. However, he stopped when he encountered Jesus at this spot on the Via Appia. "Domine quo vadis?" (Lord, where are you going?), he asked. "Back to Rome to be crucified for a second time," replied Jesus. St Peter, suitably shamed, turned back to Rome to die.
....
Answers: 1 The tower on the left-hand side of Via Appia Antica, just after the junction with Via Cecilia Metella. **2** The tomb of Cneo Bebio Tampilo, out along the road, on the right-hand side. **3** On the left after St Urban. **4** The tomb of Ilario Fusco, on the right, diagonally opposite the temple of Jupiter.

The ruins of the frigidarium in the Baths of Caracalla

② Baths of Caracalla

Ancient Roman leisure centre

Surrounded by grass and umbrella pines, and not very crowded, the Baths of Caracalla is one of the most enjoyable ancient sites in the city. Begun by Emperor Septimius Severus in AD 206 and completed by his son Caracalla, it had room for 1,600 people and gardens, snack bars, a library and lecture rooms as well as the usual baths and gyms.

The marked route through the baths has lively information boards in English and Italian and takes visitors first to the *apodyterium* (dressing room), which has remains of mosaic pavements, and then to the huge *frigidarium* (cold pool). The two granite bathtubs on Piazza Farnese (*see p132*) were once here, with water cascading out of them into what was an open-air Olympic-sized swimming pool or *natatio*. Beyond this is evidence that part of the baths

was originally on two levels – there is a stairway leading to nowhere, and fragments of the upper storey's mosaic pavements decorated with tritons, dolphins, cupids and marine monsters can be seen in the grass.

Letting off steam

Visit the **Horti Scipioni** (*entrances on Via di Porta San Sebastiano and Via di Porta Latina*), a lovely park with a superb playground.

③ EUR

Progress of Civilization

In 1937, Mussolini decided to mount an Esposizione Universale di Roma (EUR), devoted to the "Progress of Civilization" to demonstrate the achievements of Italian Fascism. A huge area to the south of Rome was cleared, and archictect Marcello Piacentini was given the job of creating a monument to Modernism and megalomania by 1942. However, work stopped in 1941, after Italy entered World War II. After the war,

EUR was turned into a new residential and business zone. Half-finished buildings were completed, new ones were built and amusement parks were opened.

The **Museo della Civiltà Romana** displays plaster casts of statues and monuments and models of ancient Roman war machines. The museum houses Rome's **Planetarium**, with scale models of the universe, cross-sections of planets, video footage of various astronomic phenomena and the chance to walk inside the nucleus of a replica star. Since the museum is closed for renovation, events scheduled to be held at the Planetarium will take place at Technotown in Villa Torlonia (*see p178*).

Letting off steam

There is plenty of open space around EUR's vast lake for kids to let their hair down and for families to enjoy picnics. In summer, make a beeline for the complex's open-air Olympic swimming pool, the **Piscina delle Rose** (*Viale America 20, 00144; 06 5422 0333; May–Oct; www.piscinadellerose.it*).

The Lowdown

🌐 **Address** Museo della Civiltà Romana: Piazza G Agnelli 10, 00151; 060608; *www.planetarioroma.it*

🚇 **Metro** EUR Fermi (Line B)

🕐 **Open** Museo della Civiltà Romana: Closed for renovation, check website before planning a visit

💶 **Price** Museo della Civiltà Romana, Planetarium & Museo Astronomico: €32 for one activity at Technotown

👫 **Age range** 8 plus

👫 **Activities** Check the Planetarium website for details

⏱ **Allow** 45–90 mins

♿ **Wheelchair access** Yes

☕ **Eat and drink** PICNIC Simply Market SMA (*Viale Beethoven 48, 00144; closed Sun*) has all the ingredients for a picnic on the shores of EUR's lake. REAL MEAL Caffé Palombini (*Piazzale Konrad Adenauer 12, 00144; 06 591 1700; www.palombini.com; closed Sun*) offers crisp sugared pastries, fresh sandwiches and, at lunchtime, simple pasta dishes. In the evening, it is a popular aperitivo place

🛍 **Shop** The shop on the ground floor has excellent science toys

🚻 **Toilets** In the museums

The Lowdown

🌐 **Address** Viale delle Terme di Caracalla 52, 00184; 06 3996 7700 or 060608; *archeoroma. beniculturali.it*

🚇 **Metro** Circo Massimo (Line B). **Bus** 118, 160 & 628

🕐 **Open** 9am onwards daily; closing times vary, check website for details

💶 **Price** €12–18 (inclusive of entry to Tomb of Cecilia Metella & Villa dei Quintili; valid for 7 days); under 18s free

👫 **Skipping the queue** Book tickets online

🎧 **Guided tours** Audioguides (€4) are available. Tours: 3pm Sun; Italian only

👫 **Age range** All ages

⏱ **Allow** 1 hr–90 mins

♿ **Wheelchair access** Yes

☕ **Eat and drink** PICNIC There are no food shops or cafés nearby. If coming from the Circo Massimo metro station, shop first at the excellent Alimentari Giacomini (*see p106*) or, if coming from the Colosseum, pick up a picnic lunch from Panificio Disa (*see p71*). REAL MEAL Da Priscilla (*Via Appia Antica 68, 00147; 06 513 6379; closed Sun pm*), a short bus ride away (bus 118), serves hearty dishes such as pappardelle with wild boar ragù or pasta with broccoli and sausages

🛍 **Shop** The shop sells books on archaeology in English

🚻 **Toilets** Yes

④ Cinecittà si Mostra

Show-off film studios

Rome's newest attraction, Cinecittà si Mostra, or Cinecittà Shows Off, not only offers the chance to step behind the scenes of Italy's most famous film studio, but also the chance to see films being shot at the studio.

The main lawn is dotted with impressive props, including two giant claw-footed mock-bronze braziers used in the film *Gladiator* (2000), while a nearby pavilion has replicas of several famous statues ranging from the ancient Roman Capitoline Wolf to Pauline Borghese.

The section entitled "How a Film Is Made" has more props as well as costumes, including Elizabeth Taylor's from the film *Cleopatra* (1963). A short, amusing video shows how a film is made – an entertaining sequence shows how adding music,

sound and special effects to a bland scene in a costume drama can turn it into something very scary. Also worth seeing is a film of scores of young actors taking screen tests.

Tours of the film sets take visitors through "Broadway", created for the Martin Scorsese film *Gangs of New York* (2002), and then to an ancient Rome built with polystyrene, resin and printed cement for the British-American TV series *Rome*. A longer tour takes in a mock Florence and Assisi, along with a visit to a working film studio. Families should aim to visit during weekends, when there is a packed programme of workshops for kids in the Cinebimbicittà pavilion.

Take cover

A major portion of Cinecittà si Mostra is outdoors. For shelter, head for the **Cinecittà Due** shopping centre (*Viale Palmiro Togliatti 2, 00173; 06 722 0902; www.cinecittadue.com*).

KIDS' CORNER

In the Baths of Caracalla, can you find...

1 The fragment of a mosaic of an athlete?
2 A spotted mosaic floor of red, green, yellow and white marble?
3 Evidence that there was an upper storey?
4 A mosaic of a horse; what kind of a horse is it (clue: this was a bath house)?

....

Answers at the bottom of the page.

Big Brother
Grande Fratello, *Italy's version of* Big Brother, *was filmed at Cinecittà.*

DOCTOR WHO?

In 2008, the ancient Rome set at Cinecittà was used for an episode of *Doctor Who* that was set in ancient Pompeii.

Bathtime fun

In ancient Rome, going for a daily bath was a major social event and one of the main ways of meeting people. When the first public baths opened in the 2nd century BC, there were separate baths complexes for men and women, but by the 1st century AD there was nothing to stop everyone from bathing together – except general disapproval. However, as the women-only baths had no gyms, women who wanted to work out as well as bathe had no choice.

....

Movie costumes on display at Cinecittà si Mostra

The Lowdown

🌐 **Address** Via Tuscolana 1055, 00173; 06 72 2931; *www. cinecittasimostra.it*

🚇 **Metro** Cinecittà (Line A)

🕐 **Open** 9:30am–5:30pm Wed–Mon

💲 **Price** Family ticket: €25 (exhibit); €45 for guided tour of the studios; under 5s free

🕴 **Skipping the queue** Weekends are busy; book children's workshops in advance via the website

🚩 **Guided tours** 11:30am & 3:15pm daily in English

🧍 **Age range** 5 plus

🏃 **Activities** Regular weekend schedule of film and crafts

workshops for children: 10:30am– 7:30pm (free with entrance ticket)

⏱ **Allow** 1–2 hrs

♿ **Wheelchair access** Yes

🍴 **Eat and drink** PICNIC Cinecittà Café offers seats on a terrace and serves coffees, soft drinks, sandwiches and pastries. REAL MEAL Illy Caffè (*third floor, Cinecittà Due*) serves pizza, pasta, simple main dishes, cakes, biscuits and coffee on a huge outdoor terrace

🛍 **Shop** There is a bookshop by Cinecittà Café

🚻 **Toilets** In the second pavilion

frigidarium: it is a sea horse.
changing rooms. **4** At the far end of the frigidarium to nowhere as you walk from dressing rooms. **3** Look for a staircase leading to nowhere as you walk from the frigidarium to the far end of the changing rooms. **2** In the courtyard leading to the **Answers: 1** In the first dressing room.

Day Trips

For most visitors to Rome there is more than enough to see in the city itself, but those staying for longer might be lured out of the city for a day or two. The ancient sites of Ostia Antica and Villa Adriana, verdant and scattered with ruins, make idyllic settings for picnics. Those fed up with ruins can spend a day exploring the Castelli Romani, or swimming in Lake Bracciano, both favourite getaways for modern Romans.

Highlights

Ostia Antica
Get a taste of everyday life in the ancient Roman port of Ostia, where taxi drivers had their own baths and local businesses advertized with mosaics. Spend the day relaxing and picnicking amidst its creeper-covered ruins (see pp236–7).

Villa Adriana
Explore Villa Adriana, the luxurious private retreat of Emperor Hadrian. Walk through its ruins and spend time on the island where the emperor indulged in his favourite activities – writing and painting (see pp238–9).

Parco dei Mostri
Check out the Mannerist sculptures and monstrous exhibits at the world's first theme park (see p240).

Castelli Romani
Visit the hill towns of the Castelli Romani to sample the local produce, and stop by a museum dedicated to two giant ancient boats (see pp240–41).

Lake Bracciano
Spend a lazy morning taking in the views from the majestic Castello Odescalchi and then go for a refreshing swim in Lake Bracciano (see p241).

Above right Water gushing out of the mouth of a stone lion, Villa d'Este
Left Young visitor taking pictures near the well-preserved Canopus canal, Villa Adriana

Day Trips from Rome

When Rome gets too much, it is quite easy to escape. The Villa Adriana at Tivoli is perfect for a relaxed day out, while the ancient Roman remains of Ostia are far less crowded than any of the city centre's sites; trains leave every 15 minutes for Ostia Antica and buses every 20 minutes for Tivoli. To the north is the mad monster park of Bomarzo and, to the south, the pastoral Castelli Romani. For a break from culture, head to Lake Bracciano for the simple pleasures of boating, swimming and picnicking.

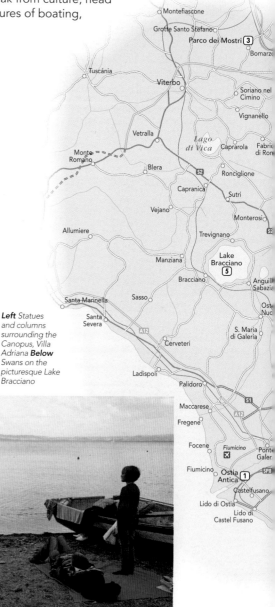

Left Statues and columns surrounding the Canopus, Villa Adriana **Below** Swans on the picturesque Lake Bracciano

Places of Interest

SIGHTS
1. Ostia Antica
2. Villa Adriana
3. Parco dei Mostri
4. Castelli Romani
5. Lake Bracciano

The ruins of the Terme di Nettuno, Ostia Antica

0 kilometres   15

0 miles   15

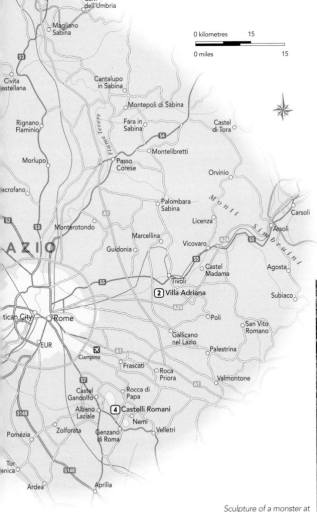

The Lowdown

🚗 **Train** Ostia Antica: trains depart every 15 mins from the Stazione di Porta San Paolo, next to metro Piramide (Line B). **Bus** Although there are trains to Tivoli, it is far easier to take the COTRAL bus, which departs every 20 mins from metro Ponte Mammolo (Line B). Local bus 4 runs from here to the site and to Tivoli town, for those wanting to visit Villa d'Este & Villa Gregoriana. Check *pp240–41* for transport to other sights.

ℹ️ **Visitor information** 060608; *www.060608.it*

🛒 **Supermarkets** Carrefour, Piazza della Stazione del Lido 19, 00122 Lido di Ostia, Ostia. PAM, Via Lago di Lesi, 00010 Tivoli, Lazio. CONAD, Via Villa Adriana 138, 00010 Tivoli, Lazio. Carrefour, Via Tomei 92, 00019 Tivoli, Lazio. **Markets** Piazza Tolosetto Farinati degli Uberti, 00122 Lido di Ostia, Ostia; Mon–Fri am. Piazza del Plebiscito, 00019 Tivoli, Lazio; Mon–Fri am

🎪 **Festivals** International festival of Villa Adriana (Jul); music, dance and arts festival

➕ **Pharmacies** Farmacia Zincone: Via Vasco De Gama 137, 00121 Lido di Ostia, Ostia; 06 567 4862. Farmacia Dr E. Pallante: Piazza del Plebiscito 17, 00019 Tivoli, Lazio; 07 7431 2183

Sculpture of a monster at the Parco dei Mostri

① Ostia Antica
Shifting sands of time

The remains of the ancient port of Ostia are among the most extensive and evocative Roman ruins in Italy. The town was originally built on the coast but, over the centuries, the Tiber shifted course further west and Ostia now lies stranded quite a distance from the sea. It is a fun site to explore with children – spend a relaxing day rambling along creeper-covered ruins that rise from the long grass, scattered with wild flowers in spring, and look out for oddities such as a taxi drivers' bath house and a toilet decorated with a crocodile.

Mosaic in one of the bath houses

Key Features

- Museum
- Shop
- Café
- Decumanus Maximus (main street)
- Entrance
- Forum

① **Terme dei Cisiarii** Since driving a *cisia* (taxi-wagon) to and from Rome was dirty work, the *cisiarii* (taxi drivers) had their own baths, which had wonderful aquatic motifs and mosaics.

② **Porticoes** A series of arched porticoes, which had shops and taverns in little rooms, once lined Ostia's main street. Some of these are now partially hidden by bushes, but it is possible to peep and even crawl inside them.

③ **Terme di Nettuno** This large bath complex has fantastic black-and-white mosaics and, in the next room, a huge mosaic of the sea god Neptune in a carriage drawn by serpent-tailed sea horses.

④ **Theatre** In the 4th century AD, the theatre – by then 200 years old – was converted so that the orchestra could be flooded for aquatic shows. When the Goths invaded in the 4th or 5th century, it was turned into a fortress.

⑤ **Piazzale delle Corporazioni** This futuristic corporation square is surrounded on three sides by the column stumps of the porticoes. These once sheltered the offices of various maritime traders, each advertising its trade on a mosaic pavement in front.

⑥ **Via dei Balconi** Along this street are several houses that had wooden balconies.

⑦ **Casa di Diana** One of Ostia's best-preserved *insulae*, this apartment block has views as far as the river from its 3rd floor. Imagine standing here in ancient times.

⑧ *Thermopolium* **of Via Diana** This well-preserved ancient Roman tavern has its vaulted roof intact, a mosaic floor, a fresco of a carrot and chickpeas and marble counters with holes where pans of ready-cooked food were set.

The Lowdown

🌐 **Address** Viale dei Romagnoli 717, 00119 Ostia; 06 5635 8003; *www.ostiaantica.beniculturali.it*

🚗 **Train** From Stazione di Porta San Paolo, next to metro Piramide (Line B), to Stazione Ostia Antica. **Distance** 26 km (16 miles) SW of Rome

🕐 **Open** 8:30am onwards Tue–Sun; closing times vary; check website

💲 **Price** €16–24; under 18s free

👥 **Skipping the queue** Avoid coming between March and June, when school groups visit

🚩 **Guided tours** Audioguides (€4) available in English, Italian, French and Spanish

👫 **Age range** All ages

⏱ **Allow** 4–5 hrs

♿ **Wheelchair access** Partial; along the main streets

☕ **Café** There is a café on site with tables on an outdoor terrace. It

serves *tavola calda* at lunchtime and snacks throughout the day

🛍 **Shop** Books for children in several languages and appealing ancient Roman souvenirs are sold at the shop near the café

🚻 **Toilets** By the café

Good family value?
With easy access and plenty of space, this site is great for a lazy picnic or for children to play Roman shop or house in the ruins.

The main road, Decumanus Maximus, in front of the Terme di Nettuno

Letting off steam

There is plenty of space around the ruins for children to run about and play games.

Eat and drink

Picnic: under €25; Snacks: €25–40; Real meal: €40–80; Family treat: over €80 (based on a family of four)

PICNIC Volpetti (Via Marmorata 47/a, 00153; 06 574 2352; closed Sun) located close to the Stazione di Porta San Paolo in Rome, stocks picnic supplies. Eat on the train or amidst the ruins.

SNACKS The Station Bar (at the train station, Stazione Ostia Antica) is a conveniently located snack joint that serves sandwiches, soft drinks, coffees and pastries.

REAL MEAL Lo Sbarco di Enea (Via dei Romagnoli 675, 00121; 06 565 0034; closed Mon lunch) is a convenient place for lunch, with a set menu and plenty of simple dishes that appeal to children, along with pizza and char-grilled meat.

FAMILY TREAT La Vecchia Pineta (Piazza dell'Aquilone 4, 00122 Lido di Ostia; 06 5647 0255; closed Sun eve in winter) offers delicious antipasti of mixed raw fish, spaghetti alle vongole and prawn tempura. The fish of the day can be cooked according to individual taste.

Find out more

DIGITAL Check out the clickable plan of the site on www.ostia-antica. org, which has photographs and interesting information in English.

FILM The TV version of Caroline Lawrence's popular children's books called Roman Mysteries (2007) is set in Ostia and available on DVD.

Entrance to the on-site museum in Ostia Antica

Take cover

If there is a brief shower, shelter in the museum, which displays ancient Roman objects. But if the heavens open up, it is probably wiser to head back to Rome and visit the **Centrale Montemartini** (see p109) or the Museo Nazionale Romano's **Palazzo Massimo** (see pp98–9).

Next stop...

LIDO DI OSTIA For a touch of sea breeze, head to the seaside resort of Lido di Ostia (get off the train at Lido Centrale), just a couple of stops from Ostia Antica. The water there has a reputation for being polluted, so it is best to limit the kids to playing on the beach and splashing.

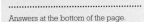

② Villa Adriana
The emperor's retreat

Shaded by pines and beautifully set in the countryside, Hadrian's Villa was built by the emperor in AD 128 as a magnificent private retreat, with bath houses, libraries, a fire station, temples and theatres as well as a palace. Hadrian had been very impressed with the buildings he had seen during his travels in Greece and Egypt and had a few of them reproduced here. Today, the villa is a wonderful place for a peaceful day out, with plenty of space to relax and enjoy picnics and games.

Wild orchid in Villa Adriana

Key Sights

① **Poikile** This arcaded court with a large basin and pool was originally used as a gymnasium. The pool has survived, and topiaried bushes imitate the shapes of the original columns.

② **Maritime Theatre** This is a round pool with an island in the middle, surrounded by columns. The island, reached by a swing bridge and with an Ionic temple-like pavilion, was probably where Hadrian retired to think, write and paint.

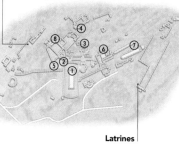

③ **Winter Palace** Hadrian's Winter Palace had a sophisticated heating system clearly visible under its pavement. In the courtyard is a water tank known as the fish pond, probably designed to fill the palace with beautiful reflections of light and water.

⑤ **Garden** Overlooked by two elegant summer dining rooms, or possibly libraries, this garden retains the traces of a *nymphaeum* and a long, but now dry, canal with octagonal pools at each end.

⑥ **Grandi Terme** The west side of this bath house was open to let in the light of the setting sun, and its underfloor heating system is still visible. The big holes in the sides were used for scaffolding during construction, while the little holes contained clamps to secure decorations.

⑧ **Hospitium** Guests slept in rooms on either side of this rectangular hall. There were three beds in each room, probably screened by curtains. Notice how the mosaics in the rooms are much plainer at the edges, where they would have been covered by the beds.

The Lowdown

🌐 **Address** Largo Marguerite Yourcenar 2, 00010 Tivoli, Lazio; 07 7438 2733; www. villaadriana.beniculturali.it

🚗 **Getting there** Ponte Mammolo (Line B), then COTRAL bus to Tivoli. **Distance** 29 km (18 miles) E of Rome

🕐 **Open** 9am onwards daily; closing times vary

💲 **Price** €16–24; under 18s free

👥 **Skipping the queue** Buy tickets in advance from www.coopculture.it

🎫 **Guided tours** Audioguides (€5) are available in Italian, English, French, German and Spanish

👫 **Age range** All ages

⏱ **Allow** 4–5 hrs

♿ **Wheelchair access** Partial

🛍 **Shop** The shop near the museum has books about ancient Rome for children

🚻 **Toilets** By the shop and ticket office, and in the room with the scale model

④ **Piazza d'Oro** Hadrian's palace had great views over the Vale of Tempe, and opened onto this fine courtyard with alternating green Egyptian granite and pale *cipollina* marble columns. The courtyard also had a pool surrounded by hedges in the centre and a *nymphaeum* at the end.

⑦ **Canopus** This exquisite canal, surrounded by delicate columns and graceful statues, was created by Hadrian in memory of his lover, Antinous, who was drowned near Canopus in Egypt in AD 130.

Good family value?
A fascinating history and extensive grounds make Villa Adriana a site with something to please every family member.

Prices given are for a family of four

Walkway in the picturesque gardens of Villa Gregoriana, Tivoli

Letting off steam

Kids can have fun on swings and slides in the playground opposite **Caffè Morelli** *(see Eat and drink)*.

Eat and drink

Picnic: under €25; Snacks: €25–40; Real meal: €40–80; Family treat: over €80 (based on a family of four)

PICNIC PAM *(Via Lago di Lesi, 00019; 0774 380 615; closed Sun)* is the ideal place to pick up provisions for a family picnic, since no refreshments are available on site.

SNACKS Caffè Morelli *(Via Casal Bellini 14, 00019; 0774 382 124; open daily)* is a simple neighbourhood bar serving pastries, coffee and soft drinks.

REAL MEAL La Tenuta di Rocca Bruna *(Strada Roccabruna 30, 00019; 07 7453 5985; closed Mon)* is set in gardens, and serves a variety of pastas and excellent meat dishes.

FAMILY TREAT Ristorante Sibilla *(Via della Sibilla 42, 00010; 07 7433 5281; closed open summer: daily; winter: Tue–Sun)* is one of Tivoli's best restaurants. Try the ricotta in crisp *kaitafi* (shredded filo dough and syrup) pastry, or the *maccheroncini alla carbonara* spiked with truffle, and the home-made desserts.

Find out more

DIGITAL Interactive maps – using photos of the 3D replica of the villa and satellite images – and information about the villa are available on *www.villa-adriana.net*.
FILM Watch *Hadrian* (2008), a BBC documentary which tells the story of Emperor Hadrian.

Take cover

The site museum, which displays archaeological finds (if open), and the room housing the replica of the villa, are the only places to shelter from the heat or rain.

Next stop...

GARDEN PARADISE Head to **Villa d'Este** *(Piazza Trento 5, 00198)*, a summer retreat where people from the arts world met and exchanged ideas in the 16th century. Although the villa is lovely, the extravagantly frivolous fountains in the gardens steal the show – looking like something Disney might have designed had he been a Renaissance prince. For something wilder, there is plenty of open space and gardens to enjoy at **Villa Gregoriana** *(Largo Sant'Angelo, 00019 Tivoli, Lazio)*. Go for a walk down the wooded paths here.

Rows of eye-catching fountains in Villa d'Este

③ Parco dei Mostri

Mannerist monster mash

One of Lazio's top attractions, the Monster Park, outside the little town of Bomarzo, is sprinkled with bars, a restaurant, a playground and even a football field for kids. Created in the late 16th century by the hunch-backed Duke of Orsini, it was the world's first theme park. At the time, a style of art known as Mannerism was at its height – full of distortions and exaggerations designed to break the strict rules of the Renaissance – and the sculptures here, far from capturing beauty, celebrate the grotesque. Most famous of all is a 6-m- (20-ft-) high screaming face – queue up to walk into its mouth and have photographs taken. Other monstrous exhibits include a life-sized elephant crushing a Roman soldier, a giant ripping a man in two, and a number of dragons, nymphs and mermaids.

Letting off steam

If driving, and in need of an antidote to Mannerist madness, head for the various *terme* (hot baths) outside the nearby town of Viterbo. These are a legacy of the area's volcanic origins – try them out at the free public pools at the **Piscine Carletti** on Strada Terme (3 km/4 miles west of Viterbo), where the temperature can reach up to 58°C (136°F), perfect for a dip on a cool day! Check *www. termediviterbo.it*.

The screaming face in the Mannerist Parco dei Mostri

The Lowdown

🌐 **Address** Località Giardino, 01020 Bomarzo, Lazio; 0761 924 029; *www.sacrobosco.it*

🚆 **Train** From Rome's Termini or Ostiense stations to Viterbo, then COTRAL bus. **Distance** 102 km (55 miles) NW of Rome

🕐 **Open** 8:30am onwards daily; closing times vary, check website

💰 **Price** €36–40; 4–8s: €8; under 4s free

👫 **Skipping the queue** The park is busiest in spring

👫 **Age range** 3 plus

⏱ **Allow** 3–4 hrs

♿ **Wheelchair access** Partial

🍽 **Eat and drink** PICNIC The park's picnic area has barbecues, and a self-service restaurant. REAL MEAL Al Vecchio Orologio *(Via Orologio Vecchio 25, 01100 Viterbo; 335 337 754; open summer: Mon–Sat; winter: Tue–Sun)* serves pizzas

🛍 **Shop** Souvenirs are sold at the shop by the ticket office

🚻 **Toilets** Near the ticket office

④ Castelli Romani

Strawberry fields forever

To the south of Rome lie 16 hill towns sprinkled over the long-since-dormant volcanoes of the Alban Hills, known as the Castelli Romani (literally, the "Roman castles"). The towns are famous for wine, strawberries, mushrooms, flowers, and several festivals celebrating all of these. They offer the perfect escape from the city for Romans, who flock

Café in one of the narrow backstreets of Castel Gandolfo, Castelli Romani

here on summer weekends to eat at the many restaurants or picnic on the shores of lakes that have filled the volcanic craters. Most of the towns are accessible by bus, but it is easiest – and most fun – to tour the lakes by car.

The Palazzo Pontificio in **Castel Gandolfo** is the summer residence of the pope. Below the town is a lido with a beach on the shores of **Lake Albano**. There is a path right around the lake from here; the entire circuit takes around 2 hours to cover by foot.

From Castel Gandolfo, take Via dei Laghi towards the little town of **Nemi** perched high above Lake Nemi, and perhaps the most attractive of the Castelli towns. It is a great destination for food and there is a steep cobbled road down to the lakeside through fields of strawberries, for which Nemi is famous.

The Lowdown

🌐 **Address** Palazzo Pontificio: Via Cardinal Merry del Val, 00040 Castel Gandolfo, Lazio. Museo delle Navi Romane: Via del Tempio di Diana 13, 00040 Nemi, Lazio; 06 939 8040; *www.museonavi romane.it*

🚆 **Metro** Laurentina (Line B), then COTRAL bus. **Bus** See bus times and connections at *www.cotralspa. it/TrovaPercorso*. **Distance** 60 km (37 miles) SE of Rome

🕐 **Open** Museo delle Navi Romane: 9am–6pm Mon–Sat, 9am–2pm Sun

💰 **Price** Museo delle Navi Romane: €12; EU under 18s free

🚩 **Guided tours** Museo delle Navi Romane: 10:30am & 11:30am Sun (in Italian only)

👫 **Age range** Any age; Museo delle Navi Romane: 9 plus

⏱ **Allow** 1 day; Museo delle Navi Romane: 30 mins–1 hr

♿ **Wheelchair access** Villages: partial; Museo delle Navi Romane: yes

🍽 **Eat and drink** PICNIC Bar delle Fragole *(Corso Vittorio Emanuele 7, 00040 Nemi; 06 936 8102; summer: daily; winter: closed Tue)* serves excellent treats, including strawberry cakes, strawberries with yogurt and strawberry crêpes, in summer. FAMILY TREAT Sirena del Lago *(Via del Plebiscito 26, 00040 Nemi; 06 936 8020; open daily)* is a good place to lunch on local hams and salamis followed by pasta, roast quail, grilled trout or roast chicken

🚻 **Toilets** At the museum

Continue to **Genzano** on the other side of the lake to visit the **Museo delle Navi Romane**, a fascinating museum dedicated to the intriguing remains and impressive replicas of two giant boats built by Emperor Caligula for the extravagant parties that he organized. The larger ship had mosaic floors, baths and a heating system.

Letting off steam

Spend time splashing around **Lake Nemi** and pick up local produce for a delicious picnic.

Flower garden leading down to Lake Nemi, Castelli Romani

⑤ Lake Bracciano

Down by the lakeside

To the northwest of Rome is Lake Bracciano, a huge expanse of water filling a volcanic crater. Head for one of its resorts – **Bracciano**, **Trevignano** or **Anguillara** – or go to one of the small lakeside restaurants to eat and swim in peace: La Valletta, in Trevignano, has space to sunbathe and pedalos to hire. The main town, Bracciano, on the western shore, is dominated by the **Castello Odescalchi**, which has frescoed vaults and fantastic views over the lake. Swim or rent a boat from the beach at Lungolago Argenti – a 10-minute walk along Via del Lago.

Take cover

Duck into the beautiful **Castello Odescalchi** fortress for lake views, ancient sculptures, ceramics, medieval furniture, armour, frescoes and paintings.

The Lowdown

- 🌐 **Address** Lake Bracciano, 00062 Lazio. Castello Odescalchi: Piazza Mazzini 14, 00062; 06 9980 4348; www.odescalchi.it
- 🚗 **Train** From Stazione Ostiense to Bracciano, then local bus or taxi. **Boat** From Bracciano to Anguillara and Trevignano. **Distance** 40 km (25 miles) NW of Rome
- 🕐 **Open** Castello Odescalchi: 10am–6pm Tue–Fri (to 5pm in winter), 10am–7pm Sat & Sun (to 6pm in winter)
- 💶 **Price** Castello Odescalchi: €17–29; 6–10s: €5; under 6s free
- 👫 **Age range** All ages
- 🤸 **Activities** Boating and pedalos on the lake
- ⏱ **Allow** 1 day
- ♿ **Wheelchair access** Castello Odescalchi: yes
- 🍴 **Eat and drink** PICNIC L'Isola dei Formaggi *(Via Settevene Palo 39, 00069; 06 998 7072; closed Thu & Sun pm; www.formaggiroma.it)* offers great artisan cheeses. Take a picnic to the beach at Lungolago Argenti. REAL MEAL L'Orso Goloso *(Viale Garibaldi 99, 00069 Trevignano Romano; 327 884 5841; closed Mon & Tue lunch)* serves creative dishes made with local ingredients, including fresh fish from the lake. The friendly service makes for a pleasant experience
- 🚻 **Toilets** In the restaurants

Colourful sailing boat on the picturesque Lake Bracciano

KIDS' CORNER

Caligula's wrecks

Local fishermen had always known there were wrecks at the bottom of Lake Nemi. In 1535, adventurer and entrepreneur Francesco De Marchi discovered marble paving stones, bronze, copper and lead decorations, and a great number of timber beams on the bed of the lake. He made walking sticks and boxes from the wood, which he sold as souvenirs. Four centuries later, the Fascist government pumped water out of the lake and brought the boats to the surface in 1932. A museum was constructed over the boats; however, the boats were burned by Nazi soldiers during World War II.

Row, row, row your boat...
Lake Albano was used for the rowing competitions in the 1960 Olympic Games.

SWEET TREATS

The Castelli Romani towns of Ariano and Genzano are famous for their bread. During World War I, when sugar and honey were scarce, Roman children were brought to the towns on special occasions to eat pizza with figs.

Here we go gathering nuts...

It is fun to collect sweet chestnuts from the forests along Via dei Laghi in autumn. To roast them, peel the prickly outer layer off and then ask an adult to score them – a cross-cut works best. Head to the Giardino di Diana picnic area on Via Tempio di Diana and roast them on one of the barbecues.

Picnic under €25; **Snacks** €25–40; **Real meal** €40–80; **Family treat** over €80 (based on a family of four)

Where to Stay in Rome

From chic boutique hotels and luxurious five-star establishments to simple B&Bs, Rome has accommodation to suit all budgets. Most have large family rooms or extra beds. While the more traditional options are located in the heart of the city, an increasing number of B&Bs have opened in areas outside the centre.

AGENCIES

Girasole Reale Rome City
www.girasolereale.com
Artist-chef couple Barbara and Marco offer several options suitable for families, rentable by the day or week.

Italian Connection
www.italian-connection.co.uk
Great range of top-quality apartments throughout the historical Roman centre.

Ancient Rome

HOTELS

Domus Aventina Map 9 A3
Via di Santa Prisca 11/b, 00153; 06 574 6135; www.hoteldomus-aventina.com; Metro: Circo Massimo
This hotel occupies a refurbished 14th-century convent. Rooms are simple and spacious, and many have balconies overlooking Santa Prisca church next door. There is also a roof terrace. Extra beds can also be added for children.
🐾 🛏 €€

Duca d'Alba Map 9 B1
Via Leonina 14, 00184; 06 484 471; www.hotelducadalba.com; Metro: Cavour
Dating back to the 1940s, this hotel has rooms with parquet floors and modern prints. Six of the 27 rooms have space for extra beds, and there are very good deals in low season. Tea is served every winter afternoon at 5pm – a service that is included in the price – making the hotel more sociable than many others.
🛏 €€

Hotel Artorius Map 5 B6
Via del Boschetto 13, 00184; 06 482 1196; www.hotelartorius.com; Metro: Cavour
Enter this mid-19th-century Monti palazzo through a door bearing a stained-glass peacock, to look into a courtyard full of plants. Rooms are smart; some have terraces, and

Luxuriously decorated room with mosaic flooring, Hotel Celio

breakfast can be enjoyed in the sunny courtyard. Children can entertain themselves by feeding grapes to the two resident parrots.
🛏 €€

Hotel Aventino Map 8 H4
Via San Domenico 10, 00153; 06 570 057; www.aventinohotels.com; Metro: Circo Massimo
A perfect choice for families, this hotel occupies a former villa set on the green, leafy Aventine Hill, and many of the rooms open straight onto a garden where breakfast is served in good weather. It has 21 rooms, of which two are triples and 19 are doubles. An independent room known as the "tower room" has a terrace that provides a panoramic view of the city. Parking, baby-sitting and bicycle rental facilities are available.
🐾 🛏 €€

Hotel Celio Map 9 C2
Via dei Santi Quattro 35/c, 00184; 06 7049 5333; www.hotelcelio.com; Metro: Colosseo
Located in a quiet neighbourhood, this hotel is run by a friendly couple. Rooms – including two for families – are elegant, featuring red and gold brocades, and motifs. A

Turkish bath in the basement is decorated with replicas of black-and-white Roman mosaics. There is also a miniature cinema in the basement. Best of all is the roof terrace, perfect for a quiet afternoon drink, and a children's paddling pool in summer.
🛏 €€

Hotel Grifo Map 5 B6
Via del Boschetto 144, 00184; 06 487 1395; www.hotelgrifo.com; Metro: Cavour
The owners of this hotel have all manner of original suggestions for things to do with children. Rooms are fairly simple, and include several triples and quads; some rooms have their own – and one, a shared – terrace. There is a new double room on the second floor of the nearby annexe building, but guests have to take the stairs as there is no lift.
🛏 €€

Hotel de Monti Map 5 B6
Via Panisperna 95, 00184; 06 481 4763; www.hoteldemonti.com; Metro: Colosseo
This centrally located, modern hotel is run by a family of hoteliers and offers seven comfortable rooms on the third floor of a 16th-century building. There is no lift, though. The

clean rooms, charming ambience and friendly service make this a favourite with frequent Rome visitors. The complimentary breakfast is delicious, made with local ingredients and served directly in the rooms. Free Wi-Fi access is also available. €€

Kolbe Hotel Rome   Map 9 A2
Via di San Teodoro 44, 00186; 06 679 8866; www.kolbehotelrome. com; Metro: Colosseo
This luxurious four-star hotel occupies a 15th-century convent. Many of the contemporary rooms retain original architectural features such as exposed stone arches. There are two family rooms – one of them on two floors – but four people can stay in the deluxe suites too. €€

Paba   Map 9 B1
Via Cavour 266, 00184; 06 4782 4902; www.hotelpaba.com; Metro: Colosseo
This tiny *pensione*, run by a lady who welcomes families with children, is housed on the second floor of an elegant building on Via Cavour. Paba is very convenient for a visit to the Roman Forum (*see pp76–9*), and for the child-friendly Monti area, with its many cafés, restaurants and boutiques. Rooms are spacious and have air conditioning, fridges, kettles and Wi-Fi. €€

Relais Fori Imperiali   Map 9 B1
Via Madonna dei Monti 96, 00184; 06 837 7113; www.relais-fori-imperiali.rometravelhotel.com; Metro: Colosseo
This luxurious and elegant boutique hotel has just four rooms and a suite in a separate medieval building,

and all are furnished with Italian antiques. The main hotel has two doubles, one twin and a family room, while the suite on the fourth floor can accommodate up to four people. There is no lift to the suite; it is best avoided if you have a pram or toddlers. €€

Sant'Anselmo   Map 8 H4
Piazza Sant'Anselmo 2, 00153; 06 570 057; www.aventinohotels.com; Metro: Piramide
An enchanting ochre- and russet-washed villa on Aventine Hill, this hotel is hidden in a garden – perfect for a lazy breakfast, or for recovering after trudging around ancient sites. However, with original, antique interiors, it is not the best place for young, lively kids (unless they are happy to keep busy in the garden). Baby-sitting services, private guided tours and bike rental facilities are available. €€

Villa San Pio   Map 8 H4
Via Santa Melania 19, 00153; 06 570 057; www.aventinohotels. com; Metro: Piramide
This is a very special hotel occupying three 19th-century villas within a delightful leafy, light-dappled garden. The rooms are steeped in elegance and are very pretty. All rooms have air conditioning and heating along with Internet access, minibars and satellite TVs. Many of the doubles have Jacuzzi baths. There is no bar, but refreshments can be ordered in the garden, and breakfast can be had in bed at no extra cost. Parents can avail of the baby-sitting service. €€

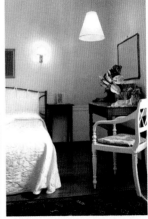

Tasteful decor in the family-friendly Lancelot hotel

Hotel Forum   Map 9 B1
Via Tor de' Conti 25, 00184; 06 679 2446; www.hotelforumrome.com; Metro: Colosseo
Staying in this charming, old-fashioned hotel is as near as it gets to living in ancient Rome – the views over the Roman Forum and Trajan's Markets (*see pp86–7*) are spectacular, and children and adults can have fun identifying monuments over breakfast, lunch or dinner in its rooftop restaurant. Housed in a former convent, the hotel has spacious rooms with 12 triples and eight communicating rooms. The lobby is suitably decorated with antiques. €€€

Lancelot   Map 9 C2
Via Capo d'Africa 47, 00184; 06 7045 0615; www.lancelothotel.com; Metro: Colosseo
A family-owned hotel, the Lancelot is located on a quiet street close to the Colosseum (*see pp70–71*). The staff is charming and helpful. There are four spacious family rooms, three with balconies, one with a terrace; another plus is that they do a good half-board deal with dinner (including wine and coffee) in their restaurant. Breakfast is served in a patio garden. €€€

Price Guide
The following price ranges are based on one night's accommodation in high season for a family of four, inclusive of service charges and any additional taxes.
€ Under €150 €€ €150–300 €€€ Over €300

Attractive exterior of Hotel Aventino, surrounded by greenery

Key to symbols *see back cover flap*

Radisson Blu
Map 6 E6
Via Filippo Turati 171, 00185;
06 444 841; www.radissonblu.com;
Metro: Vittorio Emanuele
The main attraction of this five-star
hotel is the 20-m (66-ft) rooftop
swimming pool and the children's
pool, although the contemporary
rooms with raft beds inspired by
Robinson Crusoe are lovely too.
There is a spa, a fitness centre
and free Wi-Fi throughout. Prices
vary according to availability; it is
often possible to pay less here
than in a three-star hotel in the
historic centre.

€€€

BED & BREAKFAST
BB Colosseum B
Map 9 C2
Via Capo d'Africa 59, 00184;
06 700 4623; www.bbrome.com;
Metro: Colosseo
This small B&B is in a fine location
for anyone wanting to visit the
ancient historical centre. It also
offers the chance to make a quick
escape to the solitude of the Celian
Hill *(see p72)*. Colosseum B has a
total of five rooms, including two
triples and a family room
with bunk beds.

€

I Fotografi
Map 9 C2
Via Celimontana 22, 00184;
33 9112 7629, www.bbifotografi.it;
Metro: Colosseo
Situated between the Colosseum
and the Celian Hill, this centrally
located B&B with a lovely courtyard garden is a great family
choice. There are three tastefully

decorated rooms that can
accommodate up to four people.
Breakfast is served in a bar across
the road, but bring your own
supplies to enjoy a picnic in
the garden.

€

BB Il Covo
Map 5 B6
Via del Boschetto 83, 00184; 06
481 5871; www.bbilcovo.com;
Metro: Cavour
A classic B&B, Il Covo has 20
rooms spread between several
historic houses in Monti, including
four triples and three quads.
However, some rooms are located
on the third and fourth floors and
there is no lift access. The buildings
retain original features such as
brick vaults and painted beams,
and have fridges to stock provisions.
Choose between room-only and
B&B, which includes breakfast in
a local bar.

€€

SELF-CATERING
Retrome
Map 9 C2
Via Marco Aurelio 47, 00184; 06
7049 5471; www.retrome.net;
Metro: Colosseo
Located conveniently close to the
Colosseum and all the major sights
of the historic centre, this modern
hotel is furnished in a unique
mid-century style. The quadruple
suite has its own outdoor patio and
a kitchen. The hotel organizes a
guided tour of ancient Rome and
the Vatican, an Italian food and wine
tour and a classic Fiat 500 tour.

€€

Piazza Navona &
Campo de' Fiori
HOTELS
Arenula
Map 11 D6
Via Santa Maria de' Calderari 47,
00186; 06 687 9454;
www.galahotels.com
With functional rooms and an
excellent location on a street in
the quiet Jewish Ghetto *(see
pp134–5)*, Arenula is within easy
walking distance of both the historic
centre, Campo de' Fiori *(see
pp130–31)* and Piazza Navona *(see
pp116–17)*. The hotel has plenty of
triples, but only two quads, so book
ahead if in need of four beds.
Guests can also make use of the
Wi-Fi area and an Internet station,
as well as two breakfast rooms.

€€

Hotel Campo de'
Fiori
Map 11 D5
Via del Biscione 6, 00186; 06 6880
6865; www.hotelcampodefiori.com
Classical music in the reception
area and friendly staff make this an
excellent place to arrive, and to
return to after a busy day of sightseeing. The finest feature of this
hotel is a roof terrace with 360°
views – guests can picnic here in the
evenings. Rooms are comfortable,
though not huge, but there are four
spacious apartments with kitchens
on nearby Via de' Cappellari, a great
choice for guests who plan to cook.

€€

Hotel Due Torri
Map 11 D2
Vicolo del Leonetto 23,
00186; 06 6880 6956;
www.hotelduetorriroma.com
Rooms in this old-fashioned, two-star
hotel include four mini-apartments
(two rooms and a bathroom, but
without a kitchen) close to Piazza
Navona. There is a common area
with a shelf of books and chess-
board, and a small breakfast room.

€€

Hotel Fontanella
Borghese
Map 4 G4
Largo Fontanella Borghese 84,
00186; 06 6880 9504;
www.fontanellaborghese.com
There are two triples and two quads
in this gracious five-star hotel in a
quieter part of the historic centre.
Baby-sitting is available on request.

€€

Elegantly furnished dining room, Hotel Fontanella Borghese

Room with traditional furnishings, Teatro Pace 33

Hotel Navona   Map 11 D3
Via dei Sediari 8, 00186; 06 686 4203; www.hotelnavona.com
This friendly, relaxed hotel is located just across the road from Piazza Navona and is run by a welcoming Italo-Australian family. It has plenty of rooms for three or four people. €€

Hotel Parlamento   Map 12 F1
Via del Convertite 5, 00186; 06 6992 1000; www.hotelparlamento.it
An old-fashioned place on the fourth floor of a palazzo close to Piazza Colonna and the seat of the Italian parliament, this friendly hotel has pleasant and pretty rooms. There are several triples and quads, and a room for up to five persons. There is a terrace for breakfast, and one double and adjacent single room open onto their own terrace – a great option for smaller families. €€

Hotel Portoghesi   Map 11 D2
Via del Portoghesi 1, 00186; 06 686 4231; www.hotelportoghesiroma.it
This hotel is another good *centro storico* option. Its best feature is a rooftop terrace garden where breakfast is served. The terrace can be used by guests in the evenings if there are plans for a do-it-yourself picnic dinner. There is one triple and two communicating rooms. Wi-Fi is available in the rooms. €€

Hotel Santa Chiara   Map 12 E4
Via Santa Chiara 21, 00186; 06 687 2979; www.albergosantachiara.com
With plenty of triples, along with three quads and an apartment without a kitchen for five persons with its own terrace, Santa Chiara makes for a great family choice near the Pantheon (*see pp122–3*). Although there are 100 rooms, attentive staff make the place feel intimate. Enjoy a drink at one of the tables at the hotel's open-air bar that overlooks the Piazza della Minerva (*see p124*). €€

Kame Hall   Map 12 E5
Via Paganica 9, 00186; 06 6813 5568 & 339 1122460; www. kamehall.com
Housed in a 17th-century palazzo overlooking lovely Piazza Mattei and the Fontana delle Tartarughe, this hotel has four delightful white rooms. Its location – in the quiet, romantic heart of the Jewish Ghetto, a short walk from both the ancient sites and Piazza Navona and Campo de' Fiori, is hard to beat, as is the value for money. All rooms have space for an extra bed or, if children are small, there is room for a family of four. Baby-sitting is available on request. €€

Little Queen Suite   Map 12 E5
Via Florida 20, 00186; 339 1122460; www.littlequeen.it
This hotel has five beautiful spacious white rooms, which include two triples and a family room on the fringe of the Jewish Ghetto. Little Queen Suite is located on Largo di Torre Argentina, a well-known square where Julius Caesar was killed, and is a short walk from the Pantheon, Campo de' Fiori, Piazza Navona and the historic centre. €€

Pensione Barrett   Map 12 E5
Largo Argentina 47, 00186; 06 686 8481; www.pensionebarrett.com
The Roman walls of this fascinating little hotel belonged to the Curia of Pompey, where Julius Caesar was assassinated. The friendly owners, who have a passion for antiques, have filled the place with statues. Rooms come with coffee machines, cereal, milk and jam. Fresh *cornetti* are brought every morning. Rooms are quite small, so families will need to take two rooms. All rooms are equipped with Jacuzzis. €€

Sole al Biscione   Map 11 D4
Via del Biscione 76, 00186; 06 6880 6873; www.solealbiscione.it
This happy, relaxed hotel is just off Campo de' Fiori, with 60 rooms, of which half are triples and quads. Large families, or families travelling together, have the option of taking the entire attic floor – with a double, two triples and a quad opening onto a private roof terrace. Fridges in rooms are empty for guests to fill – and there are two more large fridges for those who take picnicking seriously. €€

Teatro Pace 33   Map 11 C3
Via del Teatro Pace 33, 00186; 06 687 9075; www.hotelteatro pace.com
Located close to Piazza Navona, the most striking feature of this hotel is a huge stone spiral staircase coiling up through the hotel's four storeys (there is no lift). The furnishings in the bedrooms reflect the elegance of the late Baroque period. There are three triple rooms – one with its own terrace – and all of them have kettles. €€

Hotel Locanda Cairoli   Map 11 D5
Piazza Benedetto Cairoli 2, 00186; 06 6880 9278; www.hotelcairoliroma.com
Decorated with eclectic art, the hotel has 15 soundproofed rooms, all with tea- and coffee-making facilities. There are no family rooms, but several rooms have space for an extra bed, so the hotel is well suited for small families. Baby cots are also available. The hotel overlooks the tiny garden of Piazza Benedetto Cairoli, between the Jewish Ghetto and Campo de' Fiori, and is well served by buses. €€€

Key to symbols *see back cover flap*

Hotel Ponte Sisto
Map 11 C6

Via dei Pettinari 64, 00186; 06 686 3100; www.hotelpontesisto.it

An elegant modern hotel in a former monastic complex just off Via Giulia, Hotel Ponte Sisto is just across the Ponte Sisto bridge from Trastevere. This hotel is ideal for families keen to experience Rome's atmospheric streetlife, while having a quiet shady inner courtyard where adults can relax as kids play. There are 11 family suites, each with two connecting rooms.

€€€

Hotel Raphael
Map 11 C3

Largo Febo 2, 00186; 06 682 831; www.raphaelhotel.com

Ivy-curtained Hotel Raphael is one of the most famous hotels in Rome, its gorgeous public areas gleaming around antique statues, contemporary sculptures, paintings by Miro, De Chirico and Morandi, and ceramics by Picasso. Rooms on the top two storeys have been splendidly redesigned by architect Richard Meier *(see Ara Pacis, p147)*, while others adhere to a more classical luxury style. Suites, in both contemporary and classic styles, are the best solution for families, with several sleeping four. There is a baby-sitting service, and a children's menu as well.

€€€

Navona Palace Residence
Map 11 C3

Via della Pace 36, 00186; 06 684 1051; www.navonapalace.com

Located in the heart of the *centro storico*, a short walk from Piazza Navona, this stylish hotel has contemporary apartments; several have kitchens and spacious terraces. There is also a spa with sauna, Turkish bath and a tropical rain shower. Wi-Fi is available throughout the hotel.

€€€

BED & BREAKFAST
B&B Little Queen
Map 12 E6

Via della Reginella 21, 00186; 339 1122460; www.littlequeen.it

B&B Little Queen offers all the charms of the *centro storico* without the chaos of the areas around Piazza di Spagna *(see pp142–3)* and Piazza Navona. *Reginella* means "little queen" in Italian – hence the name of this little bed

Lobby of Hotel Raphael, decorated with antique statues and modern paintings

and breakfast. There are just three stylish rooms, each dedicated to an aspect of the Buddha, and each with a fridge and television. Unless the children are very young, families of four will probably want to take two rooms.

€€

Piazza di Spagna & Trevi Fountain
HOTELS
Hotel Panda
Map 4 H4

Via della Croce 35, 00187; 06 678 0179; www.hotelpanda.it; Metro: Spagna

Housed in a 19th-century building, this simple, inexpensive hotel is located in the heart of the pricey Piazza di Spagna area. Rooms are clean, with air conditioning and Wi-Fi access, and are available with and without bathrooms. There are six triples and five quads. There is no breakfast, but the hotel is affiliated to the bar downstairs.

€

Class House
Map 4 H4

Via del Corso 79, 00186; 06 3600 6233; www.hoteldelcorsoroma.com; Metro: Spagna

This newly opened annexe to the Hotel del Corso, with six contemporary designed rooms, is a short walk from Piazza di Spagna and the Trevi Fountain *(see pp154–5)*. Breakfast is served on site in winter; in summer, guests can choose to have breakfast on Hotel del Corso's terrace. There are three sets of communicating rooms, two triples and one quad.

Free Wi-Fi is available and guests can also rent bicycles and motorcycles.

€€

Hotel Accademia
Map 12 G2

Piazza Accademia di San Luca 74, 00187; 06 6992 2607; www.travelroma.com; Metro: Barberini

A short walk from the Trevi Fountain, this is a mid-sized hotel that has 75 soundproofed, air-conditioned rooms with LCD TVs, minibars and direct telephone lines. Decor is functional, but the hotel is comfortable with friendly staff. It has eight quads and over 23 triples. Breakfast is not served on site, but the hotel is affiliated with a nearby café and a restaurant, where guests are given discounts. Wi-Fi is available for a fee.

€€

Hotel del Corso
Map 4 H4

Via del Corso 79, 00186; 06 3600 6233; www.hoteldelcorsoroma.com; Metro: Spagna

Conveniently located between the Spanish Steps and Piazza del Popolo *(see p150)*, this is one of the best three-star hotels around town. The rooms are cosy and extremely comfortable. There is a wonderful roof terrace where a sumptuous breakfast buffet is dished out in summer. There are four rooms big enough to sleep three or four, and one set of communicating rooms. Facilities include free Wi-Fi, car and bicycle rental. Parking is available for a fee.

 €€

Hotel Elite
Map 5 A4

Via F Crispi 49, 00187; 06 678 3083; www.travelroma.com; Metro: Barberini

This small two-star hotel, with simple but perfectly functional rooms, is a short walk from Piazza di Spagna. Part of the Travelroma group of hotels, it offers the same discounts to guests as another hotel of this group, Hotel Accademia, at an affiliated café and restaurant.

 €€

Hotel Erdarelli
Map 12 G1

Via Due Macelli 28, 00187; 06 679 1265; www.erdarelliromehotel.com; Metro: Barberini

Established way back in 1935, this is a good family-run hotel halfway between the Trevi Fountain and Piazza di Spagna, and it is ideally located for sightseeing. There are 28 rooms in total, which are basic but extremely clean. Some rooms have private balconies, but air conditioning is extra. There are three family rooms.

€€

Hotel Julia
Map 12 H1

Via Rasella 29, 00187; 06 488 1637; www.hoteljulia.it; Metro: Barberini

This friendly three-star hotel, located near the Trevi Fountain, has a total of 33 rooms, including three family rooms. Two spacious apartments with cooking facilities are available next door in the Domus Julia B&B. Guests can enjoy a buffet breakfast in the lovely breakfast hall. The hotel also offers guests the possibility of booking Rome tours online at reasonable prices. Small pets are allowed and there is free Wi-Fi for guests.

€€

Hotel Mozart
Map 4 H3

Via dei Greci 23/b, 00187; 06 3600 1915; www.hotelmozart.com; Metro: Spagna

This lovely hotel is just a short walk from Piazza di Spagna and Piazza del Popolo. Rooms are classical and very comfortable, but for a real splurge book one of the fourth-floor suites with its own private terrace. In good weather, breakfast is served on the sunny roof terrace; at other times, have it in the cosy downstairs bar. The hotel also has several small luxury apartments, with and without cooking facilities.

€€

See also Hotel Parlamento, p245

Hotel Piazza di Spagna
Map 4 H4

Via Mario de' Fiori 61, 00187; 06 679 6412; www.hotelpiazzadispagna.it; Metro: Spagna

This small, family-run hotel is an excellent mid-budget choice for families who want to stay close to Piazza di Spagna. There are just 17 rooms, including four triples and three quads, a small sunny terrace on the first floor where drinks and breakfast are served, and a roof terrace for relaxing with a magazine or quiet playing.

€€

Boscolo Exedra Roma
Map 5 C5

Piazza della Repubblica 47, 00185; 06 489 381; www.exedra-roma.boscolohotels.com; Metro: Repubblica

Occupying one of the semicircular buildings that define Piazza della Repubblica, this five-star luxury

Shuttered windows above the entrance of Hotel Piazza di Spagna

hotel has central Rome's first rooftop swimming pool. Families with children are welcome, with accommodation available in suites and connecting rooms. Deluxe rooms have space for an extra cot.

€€€

Hotel dei Borgognoni
Map 12 G1

Via del Bufalo 126, 00187; 06 6994 1505; www.hotelborgognoni.com; Metro: Barberini

This efficiently run hotel has intelligently designed rooms, many with bathtubs. Four of the rooms have their own terraces shaded with orange trees. Breakfast can be served in rooms. There is also a common terrace where drinks and snacks are served. Wi-Fi is available in the lobby and there is car-parking facility next door for a fee.

€€€

Hotel Hassler Roma
Map 5 A4

Piazza della Trinità dei Monti 6, 00187; 06 699 340; www.hotelhasslerroma.com; Metro: Spagna

A splendid location above the Spanish Steps, and a roof garden with a panoramic view over the city, make the Hassler one of Rome's best five-star hotels. The rooms are spacious; service and facilities excellent; and there is a lovely garden restaurant and bar. Families are welcomed, with children's menus in the restaurant, and the possibility of booking child-oriented guided tours. There are several sets of communicating rooms.

€€€

Dining area in Hotel Hassler Roma with spectacular views of the city

Key to symbols *see back cover flap*

Hotel Locarno
Map 4 G3

Via della Penna 22, 00186; 06 361 0841; www.hotellocarno.com; Metro: Flaminio

A short walk from Piazza del Popolo, Hotel Locarno is a great option for families who want a daily break in the Pincio Gardens *(see p151)* or Villa Borghese park. In winter, there is a log fire in the charming sitting room, and in summer there is a roof garden and a flower-filled patio. Rooms are available for three or four persons and there is also a three-bedroom apartment with a kitchen – perfect for larger families. Facilities include free Wi-Fi and free bicycle rental.

€€€

Hotel Madrid
Map 12 G1

Via Mario de' Fiori 93–95, 00187; 06 699 1510; www. hotelmadridroma.com; Metro: Spagna

Located in the Piazza di Spagna area, in a prestigious 17th-century building, this elegant three-star hotel has six tastefully decorated suites that are ideal for families of four or five. There is also a fantastic roof terrace – where breakfast is served – with stunning views of the city. There is free Wi-Fi throughout the hotel.

€€€

Hotel de Russie
Map 4 H3

Via del Babuino 9, 00187; 06 328 881; www.roccofortehotels.com; Metro: Flaminio

With an enchanting terraced garden behind it, this luxury five-star hotel welcomes families with children. There are plenty of communicating rooms and the gardens host a restaurant and bar, while the hotel is home to one of the city's best spas, with hydropool, Jacuzzi, sauna and Turkish bath. Wi-Fi is available in the public areas of the hotel.

€€€

Portrait Suites
Map 4 H4

Via Bocca di Leone 23, 00187; 06 6938 0742; www.lungarno collection.com; Metro: Spagna

Not only are the spacious rooms and the panoramic terrace of this hotel stunning, service is also superb. There are 14 exclusive luxurious suites, designed and owned by the House of Salvatore Ferragamo.

€€€

Spacious suite in Casa Montani, with stylish furnishings

Villa Spalletti Trivelli
Map 5 B5

Via Piacenza 4, 00184; 06 4890 7934; www.villaspalletti.it; Metro: Barberini

Set on the fringes of the Quirinale within its own grounds, this hotel has 12 suites and an apartment, a spa with saltwater pool and a Turkish bath. Breakfast is served in the garden or in the elegant dining room. Lunch and dinner – with wines from the family's country estate – are available on request.

€€€

BED & BREAKFAST
B&B Pantheon View
Map 4 H6

Via del Seminario, 87, 00186; 06 699 0294; www.pantheonview.it; Metro: Spagna

Situated on the upper floor of an authentic Roman Palazzo, Pantheon View is centrally located and has a charming terrace with breathtaking views of the Pantheon. The rooms are furnished with luxurious drapery, Persian carpets and antique furniture. The family suite is comfortable and roomy and is equipped with air conditioning as well as Wi-Fi.

€

B&B Corso 22
Map 12 F2

Via del Corso 22, 00186; 335 141 9964; www.bbcorso22.eu; Metro: Flaminio

Located in the heart of the Tridente, in an 18th-century palazzo on Rome's main shopping street, this pleasant, tastefully furnished B&B has spacious rooms with frescoes on the ceilings, several triples, a cot for little ones, and a two-room apartment next door with cooking facilities, in which the fridge comes stocked with basic provisions.

€€

Casa Montani
Map 4 G2

Piazzale Flaminio 9, 00196; 06 3260 0421; www.casamontani.com; Metro: Flaminio

A super-chic, bijou B&B just off Piazza del Popolo, Casa Montani is perfect for families with older kids seeking an indulgent base close to Piazza di Spagna and the Villa Borghese. There are five rooms, including two suites designed for families with children, and a two-bedroom apartment with cooking facilities. Guests can use the hotel's Wi-Fi service for free.

€€€

See also Hotel Fontanella Borghese, p244 and Hotel Parlamento, p245

Comfortable lounge of Hotel de Russie

Villa Borghese & Northern Rome

HOTELS

Aldrovandi Villa Borghese
Map 2 F6

Via Ulisse Aldrovandi 15, 00197; 06 322 3993, www.aldrovandi.com; Metro: Flaminio

This luxurious hotel occupies a prime spot beside the gardens of Villa Borghese (*see pp168–9*) – ideal to stay away from the bustle of the city centre. Piazza di Spagna is a pleasant walk away across the park, or take the free shuttle bus. The splendid swimming pool is bound to attract kids, while the food, created by prize-winning chef Oliver Glowig, should keep parents happy.

€€€

Hotel Rome Garden
Map 6 E2

Via Nomentana 28, 00161; 06 4425 2049; www.romegardenhotel.com; Metro: Castro Pretorio

This small, tranquil hotel occupies a delightful early 20th-century aristocratic villa – complete with a cupola – surrounded by a garden scattered with Roman finds. Yet, it is just a couple of blocks away from Termini station. There are triples and quads, and breakfast is served on the lovely roof terrace below the cupola.

€€€

BED & BREAKFAST

Almacromondo
Map 5 D2

Via Messina 31, 00198; 34 8080 1863; www.almacromondo.it; Metro: Castro Pretorio

Close to MACRO (*see p179*) and Villa Borghese, this charming B&B has three spacious rooms – all with a double bed and a queen-sized sofa bed – with air conditioning. Breakfast is outstanding and features home-made cakes and jams – a rare thing in Rome's B&Bs.

€

Il Bacio delle Stelle
Map 6 E2

Via Alessandria 160, 00198; 06 8351 2136; www.ilbaciodellestelle.com; Metro: Castro Pretorio

There are funkily styled rooms at rock-bottom rates at this B&B in the stylish Nomentana neighbourhood, just round the corner from MACRO, and within walking distance of Villa Borghese and Villa Torlonia (*see p178*). Younger kids might like the

Swimming pool in the sumptuous Aldrovandi Villa Borghese

room with a toddler-sized photo of an elephant. The suite has an attached bathroom. Breakfast is provided at no extra cost.

€

Parioli House
Map 6 E2

Viale Regina Margherita 192, 00198; 06 855 2040; www.pariolihouse.com; Metro: Policlinico

This inexpensive B&B is in Rome's stylish Nomentana neighbourhood, a good location for families within walking distance of Villa Borghese, Villa Ada and Villa Torlonia, and very close to MACRO. Singles, doubles, triples and quads are all available – the rooms are plain, but spacious, and breakfasts are basic, but the use of kettle, coffee machine, fridge and microwave make it a convenient option for families with babies and young children. Cots, pushchairs and highchairs are also available.

€

Trastevere

HOTELS

Hotel Santa Maria
Map 8 F2

Vicolo del Piede 2, 00153; 06 589 4626; www.htlsantamaria.com

Tucked away behind Piazza di Santa Maria in a 16th-century cloister in Trastevere, this hotel is centred on a pebbled courtyard surrounded by a portico with whimsical frescoes. There is a comfortable breakfast room and lounge with plenty of board games to keep children entertained. Bicycles are available for guests. Except for two, all rooms have bathtubs, and several have let-down bunks. Santa Maria is an ideal family choice.

€€

Villa della Fonte
Map 8 F2

Villa della Fonte d'Olio 8, 00153; 06 580 3797; www.villafonte.com

A short hop from Piazza di Santa Maria in Trastevere, this tiny hotel has five rooms and space for an extra bed in many of them. Despite being in the heart of this lively neighbourhood, it is lovely and quiet, and even has its own roof garden, where breakfast is served in good weather. Small and well-trained dogs are welcome in this hotel. Rooms have classic furnishings, air conditioning and free Wi-Fi.

€€

BED & BREAKFAST

Kimama
Map 8 F3

Via E Morosini 18, 00153; 339 3858509; www.kimama.it

A stylish but relaxed B&B, Kimama is beautifully furnished with minimalist ethnic pieces and natural fabrics. It is one of the few places in this area accessible to those on a budget; it has its own large kitchen for guests to use, with three rooms, including one for a family.

€

Orsa Maggiore
Map 8 E1

Via San Francesco di Sales 1/a, 00165; 06 689 3753; www.foresteriaorsa.altervista.org

This women-only B&B is ideal for mums travelling alone with children under 12. Housed on the second floor of the International Women's Home, it has simple rooms, with terracotta-tiled floors and beamed ceilings; there is room for eight people in a group of families travelling together. Each room offers views of Janiculum Hill (*see pp190–91*). Breakfast is included in the package.

€

Key to symbols *see back cover flap*

Il Boom
Map 8 E3

Via Dandolo 51, 00153; 33 5599 8583; www.ilboom.it

Occupying the top two floors of an 18th-century apartment with a lovely roof terrace, this B&B is decorated in retro style. It is influenced by films of the 1950s, 1960s and 1970s and the three rooms are named after Anna Magnani, Sophia Loren and Monica Vitti respectively. The rooms are big and stylish, with air conditioning and space for extra beds; and breakfast is served on the terrace in good weather. Parking is available for a fee.

€€

Homely decor in a room at Maria-Rosa Guesthouse

Casa Cibella
Map 7 D3

Via Giovanni Livraghi 1, 00152; 33 8993 2900; www.acasacibella.com

Within walking distance of Villa Doria Pamphilj *(see p195)*, this B&B has two light, airy rooms with good, solid period furniture. There is a fridge and a microwave that guests can use and extra beds are available if needed. Small pets are welcome.

€€

Maria-Rosa Guesthouse
Map 8 H2

Via dei Vascellari 55, 00153; 33 8770 0067; www.maria-rosa.it

A cheerfully furnished guesthouse on the third floor of a renovated 19th-century building; there is no lift. It has just two rooms and one bathroom, making it ideal for a family who want the place to themselves. There is room for up to six people. Breakfast is not included, but there are plenty of cafés nearby.

€€

Buonanotte Garibaldi
Map 8 F2

Via Garibaldi 83, 00153; 06 5833 0733; www.buonanottegaribaldi.com

This jewel of a B&B has one room with its own terrace and another two opening onto an enchanting tree-shaded courtyard hidden behind a high stone wall. It also boasts a very comfortable living room and a delightful breakfast room. It has only double rooms with air conditioning, but extra beds can be added if needed. Free Wi-Fi is available in rooms.

€€€

Residenza Santa Maria
Map 8 G2

Via dell'Arco di San Callisto 19, 00153; 06 583 35103; www.residenzasantamaria.com

Located in a quiet Trastevere street, this small but exclusive B&B has six rooms, and a breakfast room in an ancient water cistern. All rooms are on the ground floor, and there are a couple of quads with bunk beds. Guests can also use free Wi-Fi.

€€€

The Vatican

HOTELS

Le Stanze di Federica
Map 4 E3

Via Cola di Rienzo 28, 00192; 06 8110 6641, www.lestanzedi federica.it; Metro: Lepanto

This boutique hotel is best for families with older children. The hotel lies close to Vatican City *(see pp202–3)* and the stylish shopping street of Via Cola di Rienzo. There are just six rooms, including a suite with a Jacuzzi, but several rooms can be turned into triples.

€€

BED & BREAKFAST

A Roma San Pietro
Map 3 D4

Via Crescenzio 85, 00193; 06 687 8205; www.ftraldi.it; Metro: Lepanto

There are three simply furnished rooms in this 19th-century palazzo close to the Vatican. Each room has a private bathroom and fridges. Breakfast is served in the rooms.

€

Alle Fornaci di San Pietro
Map 3 C6

Via delle Fornaci 20, 00165; 329 441 2754; www.bb-sanpietro.it

There are three stylish, colourful rooms in this B&B in one of the elegant 1920s palazzi typical of the area, within 50 m (165 ft) of Piazza San Pietro. The best room has a breathtaking view of the dome of St Peter's, but all the rooms are

Colourful tableware and furniture in Gli Artisti

spacious, with space for two extra beds. Children are welcome; under 3s are free. Facilities on offer include fridges and tea- and coffee-making machines, while breakfast is served in a nearby bar.

🚫 🛏️ €

B&B Musei Vaticani   Map 3 C3
Via Sebastiano Veniero 78, 00192; 06 6821 0776; www.bbmuseivaticani. com; Metro: Ottaviano San Pietro
A comfortable and affordable B&B, Musei Vaticani has four double rooms and two triples. It is just a few minutes from the entrance to the Vatican Museums *(see pp206–13)*. There is also a kitchen where guests can make breakfast or a snack. Facilities include air conditioning, centralized heating, Wi-Fi in the office and a private shuttle to and from the airport on request.

🚫 🛏️ €

Residenza Madri Pie   Map 3 C6
Via Alcide De Gasperi 4, 00165; 06 631 967; www.residenzamadripie.it
There are 73 simple, rather spartan rooms at this B&B, with plenty of triples and quads, equipped with an individual heating-cooling system. It is run by a religious order to support charitable works. The best feature of this B&B is the lovely garden, laid out with tables and chairs under trees where guests can relax after sightseeing.

🛎️ 🛏️ €

Ted's Vatican   Map 3 C4
Via Virgilio 3, 00192; 347 345 7117
Just a short walk from the Vatican, and off the bustling Via Cola di Rienzo, this very basic B&B is a good choice for those who want to shop as well as do some sightseeing. There are three rooms that can easily accommodate up to four people. Breakfast is not included in the price of the rooms.

🚫 🛏️ €

Vaticano 68   Map 3 B5
Viale Vaticano 68, 00165; 347 7613329; www.vaticano68.com; Metro: Ottaviano San Pietro
This light and airy B&B in an elegant apartment building close to the Vatican has two doubles – with room for an extra bed. Rooms are neat and cheerful, and breakfast is served on a delightful terrace shaded with fruit trees and plants.

There is a microwave, fridge and coffee machine that guests can use.

🚫 🛎️ 🛏️ €

Gli Artisti   Map 3 D3
Via degli Scipioni 53, 00192; 338 2078356; www.bbgliartisti.com; Metro: Ottaviano San Pietro
A short distance away from the Vatican, Gli Artisti is a good option for young families. There are two more B&Bs and a great self-catering apartment nearby. It offers 13 air-conditioned rooms and each room – some with kitsch Classical frescoes, some in French country-style and others in bright colours – can accommodate up to five persons.

🛏️ 🛄 €€

Beyond the Centre
HOTELS
Hotel Astrid   Map 1 C5
Largo A Sarti 4, 00196; 06 323 6371; www.hotelastrid.com
Part of the Best Western chain, this hotel is convenient for the Auditorium Parco della Musica *(see p224)* and MAXXI *(see pp222–3)* – ideal if you have tickets for concerts or exhibitions. Located right by the river, it offers magnificent views over the city from the terrace. Breakfast is served here, and during the day guests can help themselves to tea and coffee.

🛏️ €€

Hotel delle Muse   Map 2 G3
Via T Salvini 18, 00197; 06 808 8333; www.hoteldellemuse.it
This is a pleasant hotel with 58 rooms (including triples and quads) and a lovely garden in the smart

residential area of Parioli. It is within walking distance of Villa Ada, and has buses connecting it to the centre. There is also a restaurant with special emphasis on vegetarian dishes, and in summer meals are served in the garden.

🛎️ 🛏️ 🍽️ €€

BED & BREAKFAST
La Casa di Momi   Map 1 D2
Piazza Jan Palach 30, 00196; 339 311 3325; www.lacasadimomi.it
Located on the second floor of an elegant house, this apartment has three attractively furnished bedrooms with wood-panelled flooring and big windows. Cots can be arranged for children up to four years of age. Facilities include air conditioning, LCD TVs, Wi-Fi, car and bicycle rental upon request and home-made breakfast. The Auditorium Parco della Musica, MAXXI and Villa Glori *(see p224)* are nearby.

€

A Casa di Lia   Map 1 B4
Lungotevere Flaminio 48, Palazzo 3, Scaletta 3, A21, 00196; 33 9237 3563; www.acasadilia.net
A B&B with two rooms in a 1920s apartment complex, it is surrounded by gardens by the river, and is close to the auditorium and Maxxi. It is not only ideal for concert-going families on a budget, but is within walking distance of Villa Borghese, and has good public transport links. There is buffet breakfast and the helpful owner lives next door with her cats and dogs.

🚫 🛎️ €€

Connecting rooms in Hotel delle Muse, ideal for families

Key to symbols *see back cover flap*

Aerial view of Rome with St Peter's and Piazza San Pietro in the foreground

ROME

Maps

Rome City Maps

The map below shows the division of
the 12 pages of maps in this section, as
well as the main areas covered in the
sightseeing section of this book. The
smaller inset map shows the sights
covered in *Beyond the Centre* and
Day Trips from Rome.

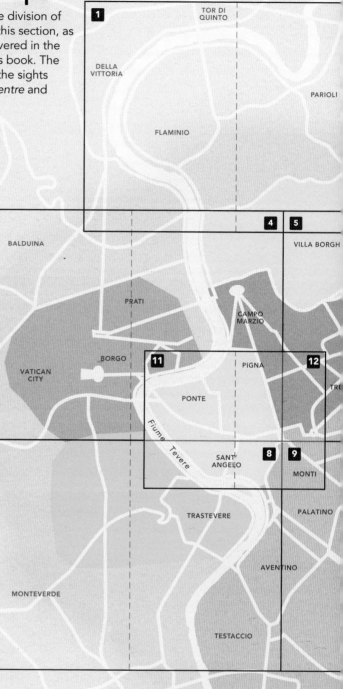

1

TOR DI
QUINTO

DELLA
VITTORIA

PARIOLI

FLAMINIO

3

BALDUINA

4 **5**

VILLA BORGH

PRATI

CAMPO
MARZIO

VATICAN
CITY

BORGO

11

PIGNA

12

TRE

PONTE

Fiume Tevere

7

SANT'
ANGELO

8 **9**

MONTI

TRASTEVERE

PALATINO

MONTEVERDE

AVENTINO

TESTACCIO

0 kilometres   1

0 miles   1

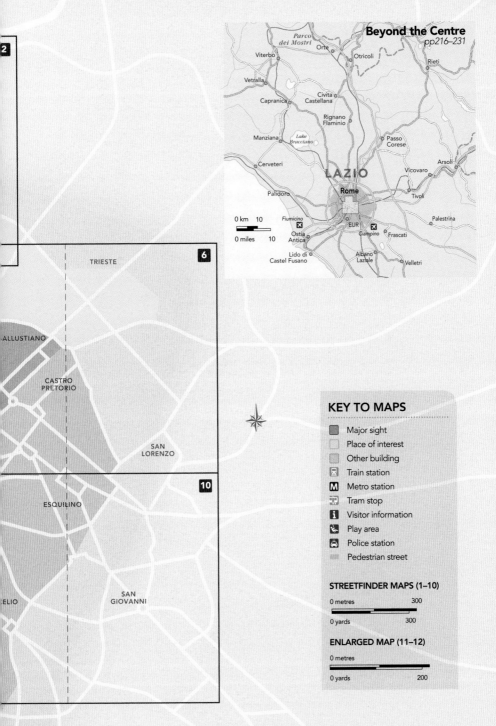

Beyond the Centre
pp216–231

Parco dei Mostri
Orte
Viterbo
Otricoli
Rieti
Vetralla
Civita Castellana
Capranica
Rignano Flaminio
Manziana
Lake Bracciano
Passo Corese
Cerveteri
Arsoli
Vicovaro
LAZIO
Palidoro
Tivoli
Rome
Palestrina
0 km   10
0 miles   10
Fiumicino
EUR
Ciampino
Frascati
Ostia Antica
Lido di Castel Fusano
Albano Laziale
Velletri

TRIESTE

6

ALLUSTIANO

CASTRO PRETORIO

SAN LORENZO

10

ESQUILINO

ELIO

SAN GIOVANNI

KEY TO MAPS

- ◼ Major sight
- ◻ Place of interest
- ◻ Other building
- Train station
- Ⓜ Metro station
- Tram stop
- ℹ Visitor information
- Play area
- Police station
- Pedestrian street

STREETFINDER MAPS (1–10)

0 metres   300
0 yards   300

ENLARGED MAP (11–12)

0 metres
0 yards   200

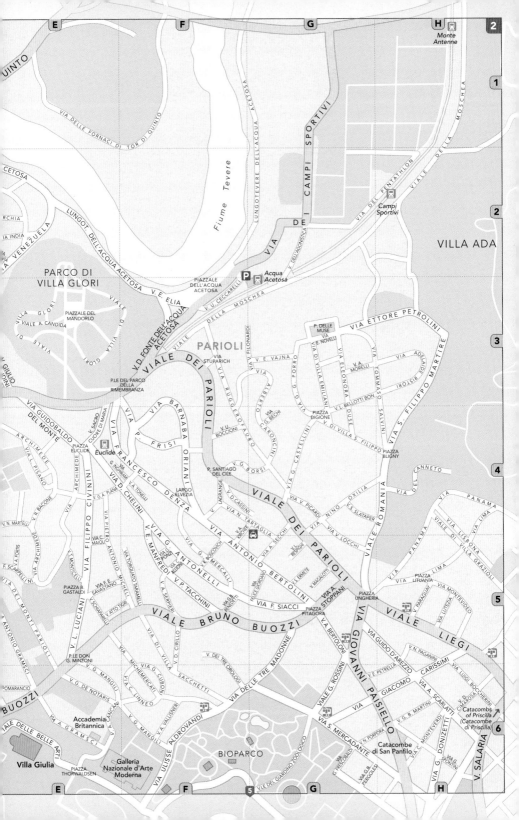

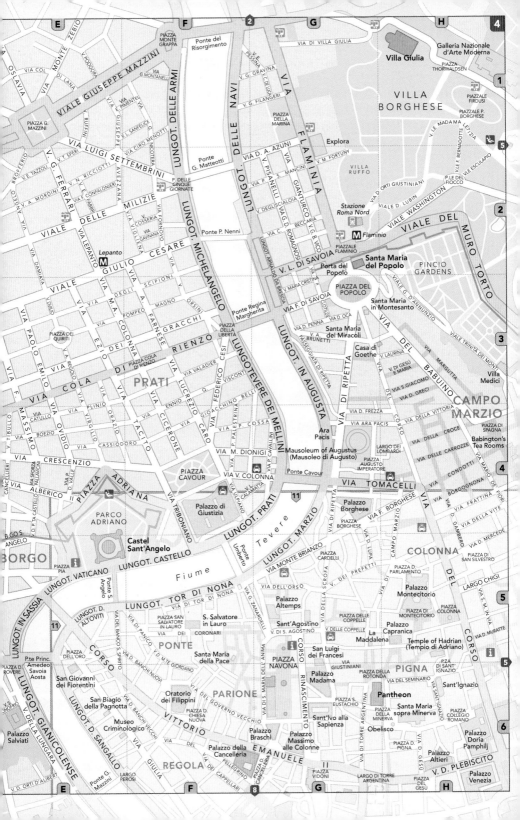

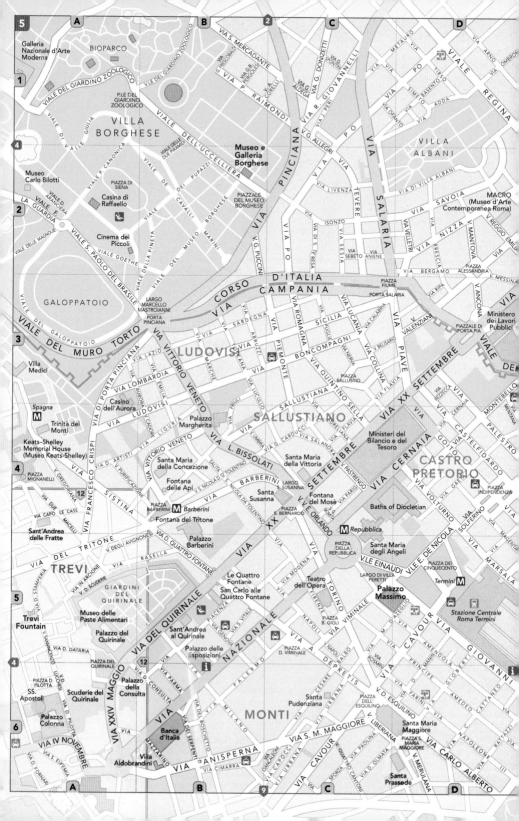

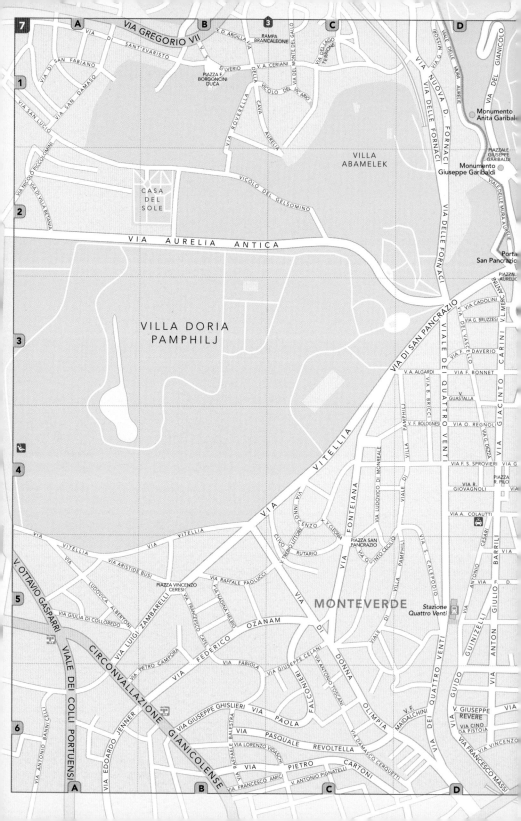

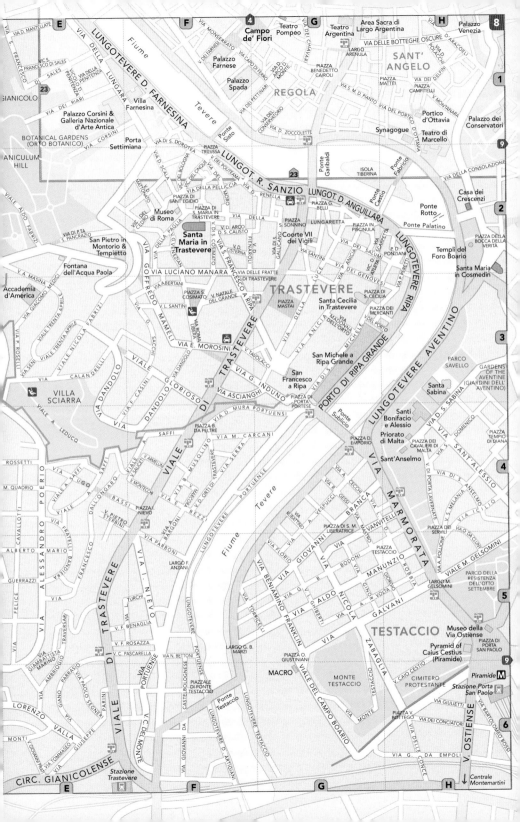

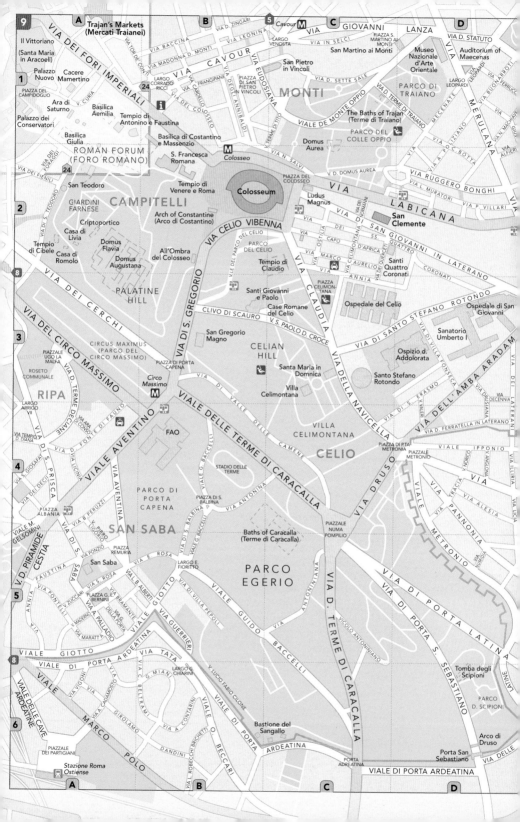

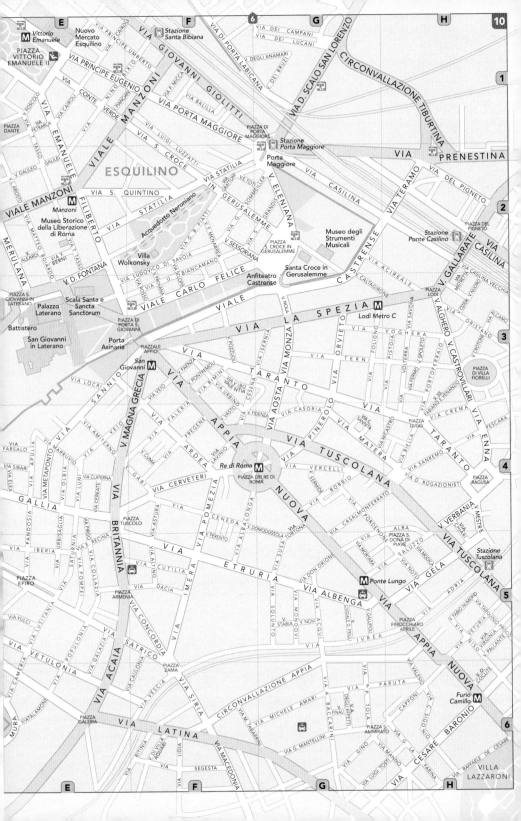

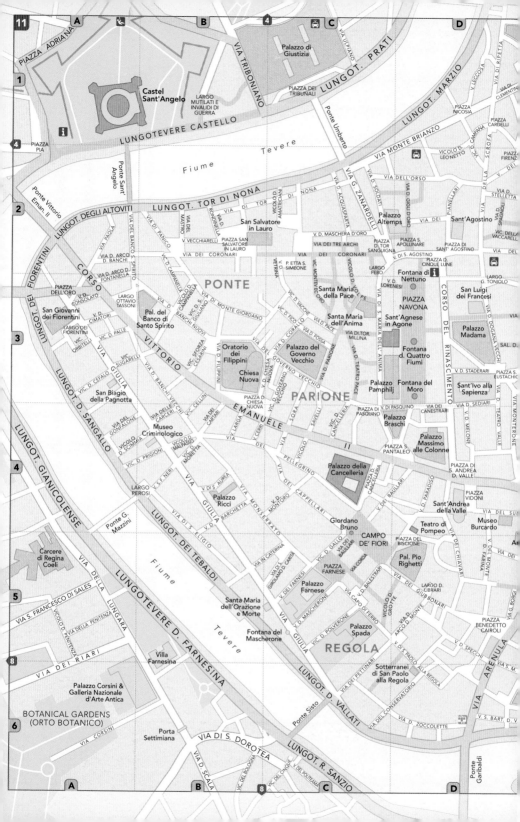

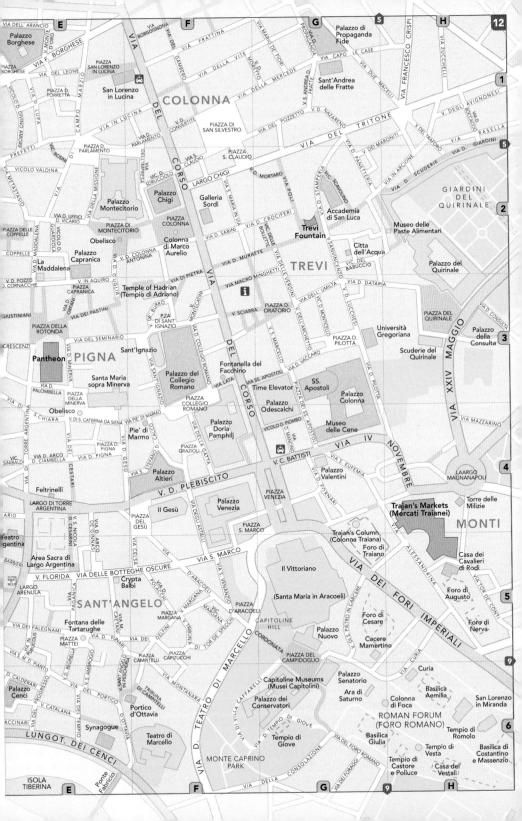

Rome Maps Index

Tola, Via
   Pasquale   **10 G6**
Tolemaide, Via   **3 C3**
Tomacelli, Via   **4 G4**
Tomassetti, Via
   Giuseppe   **6 F1**
Tommaseo, Via   **8 E6**
Tonelli, Via Alberto   **2 F4**
Tor de Conti, Via   **12 H5**
Tor di Nona,
   Lungotevere   **11 B2**
Tor di Nona,
   Via di   **11 B2**
Tor di Quinto, Via
   delle Fornaci di   **2 E1**
Tor di Quinto,
   Viale di   **1 C1**
Tor Millina, Via di   **11C3**
Torino, Via   **5 C5**
Torlonia, Via
   Alessandro   **6 F1**
Torre Argentina,
   Via di   **12 E4**
Torricelli, Via   **8 F5**
Tortolini, Via
   Barnaba   **1 D4**
Tortona, Via   **10 G5**
Toscana, Via   **5 B3**
Toscani, Via
   Antonio   **7 C6**
Tosti, Via Luigi   **10 G6**
Toti, Via Enrico   **10 F2**
Tracia, Via   **9 D4**
Traforo, Via del   **12 H1**
Trastevere, Viale di   **8 F4**
Traversari, Via
   Ambriogio   **8 E6**
Tre Archi, Via dei   **11 C2**
Tre Madonne,
   Via delle   **2 G6**
Tre Orologi,
   Via dei   **2 F6**
Trenta Aprile,
   Viale   **8 E3**
Treviso, Via   **6 G3**
Triboniano, Via   **11 B1**
Tribuna di
   Campitelli   **12 F6**
Tribuna di Tor de'
   Specchi, Via   **12 F5**
Trinità Dei Monti,
   Viale   **4 H3**
Trionfale,
   Circonvallazione   **3 B3**
Trionfale, Via   **3 B1**
Tritone, Via del   **12 G1**
Tunisi, Via   **3 C3**
Turati, Via Filippo   **6 E6**
Turchi, Via Luigi   **8 F5**
Turchia, Via   **2 E2**
Tuscolana, Via   **10 G4**

U

Uccelliera, Viale
   dell'   **5 B1**
Udine, Via   **6 G3**
Uffici del Vicario,
   Via degli   **12 E2**
Ulpiano, Via   **11 C1**
Umbria, Via   **5 B4**
Umilta, Via dell'   **12 G3**
Unione Sovietica,
   Via   **1 C3**
Università,
   Viale dell'   **6 F4**
Urbana, Via   **5 C6**
Urbinoi, Via   **10 F3**
Urbisaglia, Via   **10 E5**

V

Vaccarella, Vicolo
   della   **11 D2**
Vaccaro, Via del   **12 G3**
Vacche, Vicolo
   delle   **11C3**
Vajna, Via Eugenio   **2 G3**
Valadier, Via   **4 F3**
Valdina, Vicolo   **12 E2**
Valenziani, Via   **5 D3**
Valeri, Via   **9 D4**
Valesio, Via   **10 H6**
Valla, Via Lorenzo   **8 E6**
Vallati, Lungotevere
   dei   **12 C6**
Valle delle Camene,
   Via di   **9 B3**
Valle Giulia,
   Viale di   **5 A1**
Vallisneri, Via
   Antonio   **2 F6**
Vanvitelli, Via   **8 G5**
Varese, Via   **6 E4**
Varisco, Via
   Bernardino   **3 B2**
Varrone, Via   **3 D4**
Vascello, Via del   **7 D3**
Vasto, Via   **10 F4**
Vaticano, Viale   **3 B5**
Vecchiarelli, Via   **11 B2**
Veio, Via   **10 F3**
Velletri, Via   **5 D2**
Venezian, Via
   Giacomo   **8 F2**
Venezuela, Via   **2 E2**
Veniero, Via
   Sebastiano   **3 C4**
Venticinque, Via
   Giulio   **3 B3**
Verano, Via del   **6 H5**
Verano, Vicolo del   **6 G5**
Verbania, Via   **10 H4**
Vercelli, Via   **10 G4**

Vergini, Via delle   **12 G2**
Verona, Via   **6 G2**
Vesalio, Via Andrea   **6 E2**
Vescia, Via   **10 F6**
Vespasiano, Via   **3 D3**
Vespignani, Via
   Virginio   **1 B4**
Vespucci, Via
   Amerigo   **8 G4**
Vetrina, Via della   **11 C2**
Vetulonia, Via   **10 E5**
Veturia, Via   **10 H5**
Vibo Valentia, Via   **10 F3**
Vicario, Vicolo del   **7 C1**
Vicenza, Via   **5 D5**
Vico, Via Gian
   Battista   **4 G2**
Vidaschi, Via
   Lorenzo   **7 B6**
Vigevano, Via   **6 G3**
Vigliena, Via   **4 F2**
Vigna Filonardi, Via   **2 F3**
Vignola, Viale del   **1 B4**
Vigoni, Via   **9 A6**
Vila Massimo,
   Largo di   **6 G1**
Villa Albani, Via di   **5 D2**
Villa Alberici, Via   **3 B5**
Villa Aquari,
   Via di   **10 F6**
Villa Betania,
   Via di   **7 A2**
Villa Caffarelli,
   Via di   **12 F6**
Villa Emiliani,
   Via di   **2 G3**
Villa Fonseca,
   Via di   **9 D3**
Villa Giulia, Via di   **4 G1**
Villa Glori, Viale di   **2 E3**
Villa Grazioli,
   Viale di   **2 H5**
Villa Massimo,
   Viale di   **6 G2**
Villa Pamphili,
   Viale di   **7 C5**
Villa Patrizi, Via   **6 E3**
Villa Pepoli, Via di   **9 B5**
Villa Ricotti, Via di   **6 G1**
Villa Sacchetti,
   Via di   **2 F6**
Villa San Filippo,
   Via di   **2 G4**
Villari, Via Pasquale   **9 D2**
Villini, Via de   **6 E3**
Viminale, Via   **5 C5**
Virgilio, Via   **4 E4**
Virginia, Via   **10 H5**
Visconti, Via Ennio
   Quirino   **4 F3**
Vite, Via della   **12 F1**
Vitellia, Via   **7 A5**

Vittoria, Lungotevere
   della   **1B5**
Vittoria, Via della   **4 H4**
Vittorio Emanuele II,
   Corso   **11 B3**
Vittorio Veneto, Via   **5 B3**
Vittorio, Borgo   **3 D4**
Vodice, Via   **1 A6**
Voghera, Via   **10 G3**
Volpe, Vicolo
   della   **11 C2**
Volsci, Via dei   **6 G6**
Volta, Via
   Alessandro   **8 G5**
Volterra, Via   **10 H3**
Volturno, Via   **5 D4**
Vulci, Via   **10 E5**

W

Washington, Viale   **4 H2**

X

Ximenes, Via
   Ettore   **1 D4**
XVII Olimpiade,
   Viale   **1 C2**
XX Settembre, Via   **5 D3**
XXI Aprile, Viale   **6 H1**
XXIV Maggio, Via   **12 H3**

Z

Zabaglia, Via
   Nicola   **8 G5**
Zambarelli, Via
   Luigi   **7 B5**
Zanardelli, Via   **11 C2**
Zara, Via   **6 F1**
Zingari, Via degli   **9 B1**
Zoccolette, Via
   delle   **12 D6**
Zuccari, Via   **9 A5**
Zucchelli, Via   **12 H1**

Index

Page numbers in **bold** type refer to main entries.

Acknowledgments

Dorling Kindersley would like to thank the following people whose help and assistance contributed to the preparation of this book.

Main Contributor
Ros Belford has written and contributed to guides to Italy and Rome for many publishers including Dorling Kindersley, Rough Guides, Time Out and Cadogan. She has also written articles for magazines and newspapers ranging from *National Geographic* and *Conde Nast Traveller* to the *Independent* and the *Sunday Times*. Ros spends as much time as possible in Italy, on the island of Salina, with her two daughters.

Editorial Consultants
Susie Boulton, Scarlett O'Hara

Additional Writing
Tiffany Parks, Solveig Steinhardt

Additional Photography
Demetrio Carrasco; Kate Davis; Mike Dunning; John Heseltine; Nigel Hicks; Britta Jaschinski; Colin Keates; James McConnachie; Kim Sayer; Natascha Sturny

Design and Editorial
PUBLISHER Vivien Antwi
LIST MANAGER Christine Stroyan
SENIOR DESIGN MANAGER Mabel Chan
SENIOR CARTOGRAPHIC EDITOR Casper Morris
SENIOR EDITOR Georgina Palffy
JACKET DESIGN Shahid Mahmood, Nicole Newman, Tracy Smith
ICON DESIGN Claire-Louise Armitt
SENIOR DTP DESIGNER Jason Little
PICTURE RESEARCH Marta Bescos, Ellen Root
PRODUCTION CONTROLLER Kerry Howie
READER Anna Streiffert
FACT CHECKER Solveig Steinhardt
PROOFREADER Scarlett O'Hara
INDEXER Hilary Bird

With thanks to Douglas Amrine for his help in developing this series.

Special Assistance
Simone Di Santi at Turan Productions and Stefano at Rome Cabs.

Revisions Team
Ashwin Raju Adimari, Parnika Bagla, Mohammad Hassan, Bharti Karakoti, Sumita Khatwani, Priyanka Kumar, Rahul Kumar, Daniel Mosseri, Gabriela Di Rosa, Azeem Siddiqui, Rituraj Singh, Nikky Twyman, Ajay Verma

Photography Permissions
DORLING KINDERSLEY would like to thank MAXXI and all the museums, galleries, churches and other sights that allowed us to photograph at their establishments.

Picture Credits
a = above; b = below/bottom; c = centre; f = far; l = left; r = right; t = top

The publisher would like to thank the following individuals, companies and picture libraries for their kind permission to reproduce their photographs:
123RF.com: marcovarro 73ca
4 CORNERS: Pietro Canali 136-137; Johanna Huber 196-197; Zoltan Nagy 162-163; Maurizio Rellini 8-9.
ALAMY IMAGES: AA World Travel Library 119bl; Vito Arcomano 218cr; Carlo Bollo 117tl; Caroline Commins 71cb; Deco Images 70c; Adam Eastland 38b, 41cl, 186bl; Michele Falzone 183t; Paolo Gallo 16bl; Kevin George 31b; INTERFOTO 57bl; Norma Joseph 15bl; Marion Kaplan 198cr; Brenda Kean 145b; Raimund Kutter 57bc; Harry Lands 172tl; Jonathan Little 240tr; Elio Lombardo 130cl; Trevor Neal 29bl; North Wind Picture Archives 51tr; Platinum GPics 219cr; Prisma Archivo 56bl; Purepix 2-3; RanaPics 212t; Helene Rogers 82cl; Fabrizio Ruggeri 104bl, 190bl; Enzo Signorelli 28br; Grant Smith 48b; Gari Wyn Williams 80clb.

BAR TAVOLA CALDA LA LICATA: 87BL.
BB GLI ARTISTI: 250bl.
BUONANOTTE GARIBALDI: 28bl.
CAFFÈ PROPAGANDA: 71bl.
CASA MONTANI: David Lees 248tr.
CORBIS: Monika Bormeth 231cl; The Gallery Collection 209tl; Grand Tour/Guido Baviera 157tl,/Gabriele Croppi 12bl,/Luigi Vaccarella 180-181; Francesco Lacobelli 200cl; David Lees 210br; Massimo Listri 109tl, 192tl; Araldo de Luca 225clb, 228clb; Stapleton Collection 55bl. DORLING KINDERSLEY: Courtesy of the Museo e Galleria Borghese, Rome/John Heseltine 174cl, 174bl; Nigel Hicks 129tl; Courtesy of Roma, Musei Capitolini/Mike Dunning 82c, 82cr; Courtesy of the Vatican Museums and Galleries, Rome/John Heseltine 41tr, 51tl, 206cl, 206cr; Rough Guides/James McConnachie 155bl.
DREAMSTIME.COM: Alessandro 17br; Alessandro0770 80cra; Anaiz777 95bl; Dan Breckwoldt 70cl; Marco Caliulo 44bl; Stefano Carocci 68cl; Ron Chapple 83c; Claudiodivizia 52br; Angelo Cordeschi 205tl; Maria Feklistova 74cl; Anna Hristova 19br; Imaengine 208-209; Joyfull 25bl; Pavel Losevsky 18bl; Nicknickko 226cl; Konstantinos Papaioannou 26bl; Raysie 241cl; Reidlphoto 22br; Roza 20b; Cosmin - Constantin Sava 208br; Erica Schroeder 195tl; Ryszard Stelmachowicz 47bl; Fabrizio Troiani 66b; Tupungato 18-19bc, 20-21bc, 21b, 54br; Xi Zhang 36-37bc.
FONDAZIONE BIOPARCO DI ROMA: Massimiliano Di Giovanni 42cr, 177tl, 177bc.
FOTOLIA: 77ca.
JOHN GARCIA: 87tl.
GETTY IMAGES: AFP/Andreas Solaro 94tl; Alinari Archives 170crb; Archive Photos/ Buyenlarge 58cr; The Bridgeman Art Library/ Michelangelo Buonarroti 209bc,/Guiseppe Cesari 58clb; Paolo Cordelli 225ca; De Agostini Picture Library/DEA/G. Dagli Orti 70tr,/M. E. Smith 61clb; Franco Origlia 14bl; Robert Frerck 1c, 51bl; Getty Images Entertainment/Giorgio Cosulich 16-17bc; Hulton Archive 55bc; Marco di Lauro 14br; Lonely Planet 179tc; National Geographic/Stephen Alvarez 79c; Photographer's Choice/Slow Images 113t, Slow Images 46cc; Stringer/Andreas Solaro 17bl; Pilar Azaña Talán 64-65; Travelpix Ltd 110-111; Universal Images Group/IPS Lerner 130br.

HOTEL CELIO: Oliviero Santini 29br, 242t.
HOTEL FONTANELLA BORGHESE: 244bl.
HOTEL HASSLER ROMA: 247bl.
HOTEL LANCELOT: 243tr.
HOTEL RAPHAEL: 246tr.
HOTEL TEATRO PACE 33: 245tl.
INTERNAZIONALI BNL D'ITALIA: 15br.
FILIBERTO LANIGRO: 223tl.
LE TAMERICI: 155bl.
MARIA-ROSA GUESTHOUSE: Sylvie Ruzzin 250tr.
MARY EVANS PICTURE LIBRARY: AISA Media 56br; Edwin Mullan Collection 59tl.
PHOTOSHOT: Giovanna - Joana Kruse 13t; Cezary Wojtkowski 62–63.
MARK JOHN RICHARDS: 109bl.
ROME CABS WWW.ROMECABS.COM: Stefano 43t.
SUPERSTOCK: Marka 138b.
TURAN PRODUCTIONS: Simone di Santi 93c, 149b, 251br.

COVER IMAGES: FRONT: 4CORNERS: Pietro Canali/SIME cb; ALAMY IMAGES: Theodore Liasi tr, Joris Van Ostaeyen tc; CORBIS: Susie M Eising,/the food passionates tl; BACK: ALAMY IMAGES: mauritius images GmbH/Rene Mattes tc; AWL IMAGES: Francesco Lacobelli tl; CORBIS: Jean-Patrick di Silvestro tr; SPINE: DORLING KINDERSLEY: Mockford & Bonettit.
All other images © DORLING KINDERSLEY
For further information see www.dkimages.com

SPECIAL EDITIONS OF DK TRAVEL GUIDES

DK Travel Guides can be purchased in bulk quantities at discounted prices for use in promotions or as premiums.

We are also able to offer special editions and personalized jackets, corporate imprints, and excerpts from all of our books, tailored specifically to meet your own needs.

To find out more, please contact:
(in the US) **specialsales@dk.com**
(in the UK) **travelguides@uk.dk.com**
(in Canada) **specialmarkets@dk.com**
(in Australia) **penguincorporatesales@ penguinrandomhouse.com.au**

Phrase Book

Making Friends

Hello/goodbye	Ciao	ch-ow
Hello (formal)	Buon giorno	bwon jor-noh
How are you?	Come stai?	koh-meh sta-ehh?
Fine, thanks	Bene, grazie	beh-neh, grah-tsee-eh
What's your name?	Come ti chiami?	koh-meh tee kee-ah mee?
My name is...	Mi chiamo...	mee kee-ah-mo
How old are you?	Quanti anni hai?	kwan-tee annee a-ehh
I am ... years old	Ho ... anni	oh ... ann-ee
Do you speak English?	Parli inglese?	par-lee een-gleh -zeh?
baby	bebè	beh-beh
toddler/young child	bimbo	beem-bo
child	bambino/a	bahm-bee-no/ia
boy	ragazzo	rah-gaht-so
girl	ragazza	rah-gaht-sa

Communication Essentials

Yes	Sì	see
No	No	noh
Please	Per favore	pair fah-vor-eh
Thank you	Grazie	grah-tsee-eh
Excuse me	Mi scusi	mee skoo-zee
Goodbye	Arrivederci	ah-ree-veh-dair-chee
Good night	Buona sera	bwon-ah sair-ah
morning	la mattina	lah mah-tee-nah
afternoon	il pomeriggio	eel poh-meh-ree-joh
evening	la sera	lah sair-ah
yesterday	ieri	ee-air-ee
today	oggi	oh-jee
tomorrow	domani	doh-mah-nee
here	qui	kwee
there	là	lah
what?	Quale?	kwah-leh?
when?	Quando?	kwan-doh?
why?	Perchè?	pair-keh?
where?	Dove?	doh-veh?

In an Emergency

Help!	Aiuto!	eye-yoo-toh!
Stop!	Ferma!	fair-mah
Call...	Chiama...	kee-ah-mah oon
a doctor!	un medico!	meh-dee-koh
an ambulance	un' ambulanza!	am-boo-lan-tsa
the police!	la polizia!	lah pol-ee-tsee-ah
the fire brigade!	i pompieri!	ee pom-pee-air-ee
Where is the nearest hospital?	Dov'è l'ospedale più vicino?	loss-peh-dah-leh-pee oo vee-chee-noh?

Health

My child (son/ daughter) needs to see a doctor	Mio figlio/mia figlia deve vedere un medico	mee-oh feel-yoh/ mee-ah feel-yah de-ve-veh-deh-reh oon meh-dee-koh
asthma	asma	ah-smah
allergy	allergia	ah-ler-gee-ah
bandage	fasciatura	fah-see-ah-too-rah
cough	tosse	toss-eh
chicken pox	varicella	vah-ree-chell-ah
diarrhoea	diarrea	dee-ah-reh-ah
fever	febbre	fehb-breh
vomit	vomito	voh-mee-toh

Useful Phrases

Where is/are...?	Dov'è/Dove sono...?	dov-eh/doveh soh-noh
How do I? get to...?	Come faccio per arrivare a...?	koh-meh fah-choh pair arri-var-eh ah..?
I don't understand	Non capisco	non ka-pee-skoh
I'm sorry	Mi dispiace	mee dee-spee-ah-heh

Useful Words

big	grande	gran-deh
small	piccolo	pee-koh-loh
hot	caldo	kal-doh
cold	freddo	fred-doh
good	buono	bwoh-noh
bad	cattivo	kat-tee-voh
open	aperto	ah-pair-toh
closed	chiuso	kee-oo-zoh
left	a sinistra	ah see-nee-strah
right	a destra	ah dess-trah
near	vicino	vee-chee-noh
far	lontano	lon-tah-noh
early	presto	press-toh

late	tardi	tar-dee
entrance	l'entrata	l'en-trah-tah
exit	l'uscita	l'oo-shee-ta
toilet	il gabinetto	eel gah-bee-net-toh
beach	la spiaggia	lah spee-ah-jah
swimming pool	la piscina	lah pee-shee-nah
playground	il parco giocchi	eel par-koh joh-kee
roundabout	la giostra	lah joh-strah
slide	lo scivolo	loh shee-voh-loh
swing	l'altalena	l'al-tah-leh-nah

Shopping

How much does this cost?	Quant'è, per favore?	kwan-teh pair fah-vor-eh?
I would like...	Vorrei...	vor-ray
Do you have?	Avete...?	ah-veh-teh.. ?
Do you take credit cards?	Accettate carte di credito?	ah-chet-tah -teh kar-teh dee creh-dee-toh?
this one	questo	kweh-stoh
that one	quello	kwell-oh
expensive	caro	kar-oh
cheap	economico	ee-con-om-ee-coh
size (clothes)	la taglia	lah tah-lee-ah
size (shoes)	il numero	eel noo-mair-oh
games	i giochi	eeh joh-kee
toys	i giocattoli	eeh joh-kat-oh-lee
pencil	la matita	lah mah-tee-tah
felt-tip pen	il pennarello	eel pehn-nah-rehl-lo
crayon	il pastello	eel pah-steh-loh

Colours

white	bianco	bee-ang-koh
black	nero	neh-roh
red	rosso	ross-oh
yellow	giallo	jal-loh
green	verde	vair-deh
blue	blu	bloo
orange	arancione	ah-ran-cho-neh
purple	viola	vee-oh-lah
pink	rosa	roh-sah

Types of Shops

bakery	il forno /il panificio	eel forn-oh/eel pan-ee-fee-choh
bank	la banca	lah bang-kah
chemist	la farmacia	lah far-mah-chee-ah
delicatessen	la salumeria	lah sah-loo-meh-ree-ah
grocery	l'alimentari	lah-lee-men-tah-ree
ice-cream parlour	la gelateria	lah jel-lah-tair-ee-ah
market	il mercato	eel mair-kah-toh
post office	l'ufficio postale	loo-fee-choh pos-tah-leh
supermarket	il supermercato	eel su-pair-mair-kah-toh

Eating Out

Have you got a table?	Avete un tavolo?	ah-veh-teh oona tah-voh-loh?
breakfast	la prima colazione	lah-pree-mah koh-lah-tsee-oh-neh
lunch	il pranzo	eel-pran-tsoh
dinner	la cena	la-cheh-nah
the bill	il conto	eel kon-toh
fixed-price menu	il menù	eel meh-noo
dish of the day	il piatto del giorno	eel-pee-ah-toh dell jor-no
cover charge	il coperto	eel koh-pair-toh
highchair	il seggiolone	eel seh-joh-loh-neh
glass	il bicchiere	eel bee-kee-air-eh
bottle	la bottiglia	lah bot-teel-yah
knife	il coltello	eel kol-tell-oh
fork	la forchetta	lah for-ket-tah
spoon	il cucchiaio	eel koo-kee-eye-oh

Numbers

1	uno	oo-noh
2	due	doo-eh
3	tre	treh
4	quattro	kwat-roh
5	cinque	ching-kweh
6	sei	say-ee
7	sette	set-teh
8	otto	ot-toh
9	nove	noh-veh
10	dieci	dee-eh-cheees